CATHOLIC PACIFIST

CATHOLIC PACIFIST

THE LONG AND LONELY QUEST OF GORDON ZAHN

Benjamin T. Peters

The Catholic University of America Press
Washington, D.C.

TO MY PARENTS,

JANICE AND JOSEPH PETERS.

WITH LOVE

AND GRATITUDE.

The paper used in this publication meets the minimum requirements of American National Standards for Information Science—Permanence of Paper for Printed Library Materials, ANSI Z39.48-1992

Cataloging-in-Publication Data is available from the Library of Congress

ISBN: 978-0-8132-4009-1 | eISBN: 978-0-8132-4010-7

Book design by Burt&Burt
Text set in Meta Serif Pro with Aleo and Peccadillo MVP

Contents

Acknowledgements

As always, there are many people to thank—and while all errors are mine, any credit should be shared.

To my colleagues Mike Baxter, Kevin Callahan, Joe Fahey, Dave O'Brien, and Bill Portier for their support, encouragement, and assistance with this project—and to Bill Collinge, for his very close reading of the final draft of the manuscript. To Michael Hovey, a good friend of Gordon, for his encouragement and help with filling in some of the gaps in the story. To Fr. Charles McCarthy, another close collaborator of Gordon, for helping me to round out Gordon's life. To Andreas Schmoller at the Franz and Franziska Jägerstätter Institute in Linz, Austria, for help with sources on Jägerstätter.

Thanks also to the staffs at the archives at the University of Notre Dame and the Catholic University of America for their help and patience with my many requests. To Mary Allen at the British Jesuit Archives for her help with sources on Archbishop Thomas Roberts. To the Cushwa Center for American Catholic Studies at Notre Dame for the travel grant that enabled me to initially visit the archives at Notre Dame, where Zahn's papers are held. To Shawn Storer for generously allowing me to review Zahn's papers at the Catholic Peace Fellowship before they were donated to Notre Dame. To Greg and Carrie Doyle and Brian Baumer for their hospitality during my visits to South Bend, as well as the anonymous readers for their helpful comments and Trevor Lipscombe and the staff at CUA Press.

I also want to acknowledge and thank the late Tom Cornell for his lifelong witness to peace and the encouragement he gave me with this project before his death in 2022.

Finally, to my kids, Samuel, Ruth, Mary, and Thomas, who continually demonstrate the challenges and rewards of making peace. Mary in particular was very helpful in transcribing the documents in the appendix. And to my wife, Liza, who has been a loving and patient companion for over twenty years: thank you.

Gordon Zahn is known and beloved by many. I was able to speak with some, but certainly not everyone, who remembered him or have stories about him to share. This book is primarily an intellectual biography: much more can be said about the life of this loyal son of the church.

Illustrations

Notes on Archival Material

Gordon Zahn's papers held in the archives at the University of Notre Dame are cited as "UNDA Zahn papers."

Other material held in the archives at the Catholic University of America are cited as "ACUA Furfey papers" or "ACUA Higgins papers."

Zahn's MA thesis and PhD dissertation are also held at the Catholic University of America.

At the time of his death, some of Zahn's papers were given to the Catholic Peace Fellowship office in South Bend, Indiana, and are referenced as "CPF Zahn papers." These materials have since been donated to the University of Notre Dame archives.

Last night Gordon Zahn spoke well, on aims of the Catholic Peace movement. Less attention on 'alternative lifestyles,' more labor for peace, for prisoners of war, exiles, etc. His whole heart is in it. He spoke of Franz Jägerstätter. Then he spoke of being Catholic, faithfulness and obedience, and respect for the church. Not to call ourselves Catholics if we did not wish to abide by her disciplines. He is strong, a noble figure in the peace movement. A task for me to study his writings—call attention to them, build up esteem for him, and so imitation of his dedicated life. I was much impressed by his talk. Thank God for him.

—Dorothy Day, diary entry for June 9, 1973[1]

1 Robert Ellsberg, ed., *The Duty of Delight: The Diaries of Dorothy Day*, (Marquette University Press, 2008), 533.

CATHOLIC PACIFIST

Introduction

In his 2017 New Year's Day message, Pope Francis suggested that nonviolence could be seen as a "new style of politics for peace." With this suggestion, he highlighted a remarkable shift in emphasis that has occurred within Catholicism over the previous century. Indeed, there has been no other recent change in Catholic thinking or attitude that is more dramatic than the one that has taken place over the last century regarding issues of war and conscientious objection. And perhaps nowhere has this shift been clearer than in the United States. While he was by no means the primary reason for this change, Gordon Zahn was a key figure in helping to shepherd it along.

During World War I, Ben Salmon was one of the only four US Catholics to declare themselves conscientious objectors (COs), while during World War II, there were 135—although many more went to prison after their CO claims were denied. When a young Gordon Zahn applied for a conscientious objector exemption in 1941, a priest on his local draft board responded that a Catholic could not be a conscientious objector—a position Pope Pius XII repeated in 1956. But by 1965, the Second Vatican Council was able to include a call to protect the rights of COs, Catholics or otherwise, along with a condemnation of total war in its document on the Catholic Church and the modern world, *Gaudium et Spes*. Not long after, in 1971, the US bishops declared that the war in Vietnam no longer met the criteria of a just war—the first time an episcopal body had ever made such a declaration regarding its own nation's ongoing war effort. Then, in 1983, the US bishops' peace pastoral *The Challenge of Peace* declared that two "traditions" existed within church teaching on war: just war and pacifism. And by 2016, at an international conference led by US Catholics and held at the Vatican (where they were welcomed by Pope Francis), participants went so far as to call upon the church to cease teaching the just-war theory all together. Indeed, a lot has changed.

As this book highlights, Gordon Zahn's biography maps neatly onto the (relatively very short) history of this shift in thinking on war and conscientious objection within the Catholic Church. Zahn was born in 1918 just as the United States had entered World War I and was one of those 135 US Catholic COs in World War II. After the war, he went onto get his PhD in sociology at the Catholic University of America, where he studied with Paul Hanly Furfey—one of the handful of US clerics who had publicly supported Catholic COs during the war and was later credited with helping to initiate the US Catholic peace movement. In the 1960s, as a professor at Loyola University in Chicago, Zahn "discovered" an Austrian Catholic named Franz Jägerstätter, who had been executed by the Nazis for refusing to fight in Hitler's military. Zahn's 1964 book on Jägerstätter, *In Solitary Witness*, not only had a profound influence on many of the bishops gathered at Vatican II but also became a guidepost of sorts for the growing number of Catholic COs to the US war in Vietnam.

By the early 1970s, Zahn was widely recognized as something of the "dean" of the US Catholic peace movement, writing important works on Catholic pacifism, a notion that he spent his life articulating, defending, and justifying to critics. Zahn was also one of the original sponsors of the Catholic Peace Fellowship and a cofounder of the US chapter of Pax and later Pax Christi USA. In the early 1980s, Zahn was asked to testify before the committee drafting *The Challenge of Peace*, and he was still alive when Jägerstätter was beatified by Pope Benedict XVI in October 2007—Zahn died that December. In short, Zahn's life and work constitutes a subplot in the broader history of Catholic attitudes on war and peace in the United States, particularly the greater acceptance of conscientious objection and pacifism within the church.

This book demonstrates that Gordon Zahn made one of the most intellectually developed cases for Catholic pacifism—terms that both Catholics and pacifists often regarded as contradictory.[1] The following chapters show that Zahn initially made the case for Catholic pacifism in a letter he wrote in 1942 to Milwaukee Archbishop Moses Kiley looking for support for his CO application. When he first read about Franz Jägerstätter in 1957, it was Zahn's Catholic

1 This is not to say that Zahn invented the term. As Mark and Louise Zwick have reported, "In 1933, Dorothy announced in the paper that delegates of the Catholic Worker movement would attend the United States. Congress against War, and that they would represent 'Catholic Pacifism.' One might say that with this announcement, Catholic pacifism existed in the United States for the first time." Mark and Louise Zwick, *The Catholic Worker Movement: Intellectual and Spiritual Origins* (Paulist Press, 2005), 256.

pacifism that enabled him to recognize the Austrian martyr's significance, and Zahn would champion Jägerstätter's cause for the rest of his life. Out of this sense of Catholic pacifism, Zahn maintained his firm conviction that the Catholic peace movement must remain Catholic: a faithful witness *in* and *to* the Catholic Church. As we will see, in the years prior to the US war in Vietnam, Zahn's emphasis was largely on defending the notion that Catholics could be pacifist, but during and after the war, his emphasis shifted to the notion that pacifists could be Catholic. This was all very lonely work, and Zahn usually found himself the only person in the room (or contributor to the volume) making the argument. Most Catholics, at the time, thought that a Catholic could not be a pacifist, while most pacifists had given up on the Catholic Church.

Not surprisingly, then, Zahn's longstanding defense of Catholic pacifism placed him outside the US Catholic mainstream. Critics labeled him as "irresponsible" or a "sectarian." This was a Catholic mainstream working out of the belief that America was good for Catholicism and that Catholics were good for (and could even save) America. Thus, Zahn's Catholic pacifism made him much more critical of US political institutions than most of his fellow Catholics. Ultimately, Zahn came to see the Catholic Church as the only institution able to resist (and support others who resisted) the modern nation-state. Indeed, it was this view of the church that drove his assertion that Catholics could be pacifist, and it was also at the root of his argument that the church needed to serve as a "source of dissent" for Catholics—especially during wartime. Although the church at large often marginalized him, Zahn did find common cause with other US Catholics who similarly took a more critical view of the United States, including Dorothy Day, Daniel Berrigan, Eileen Egan, and Tom Cornell.

Building on this, my book presents Gordon Zahn's story as an encapsulation of the broader story of the US Catholic peace movement and the dramatic developments in Catholic attitudes on war and conscientious objection that took place within the twentieth century. Indeed, much has changed since Zahn first applied to be a CO in World War II, believing he was the only Catholic to do so. As the historian David O'Brien has noted, "it can be said that nonviolence is now the central Catholic teaching and just war the exception."[2] The fact that only six decades after Zahn was told a Catholic could not be a CO, Benedict XVI could beatify Franz Jägerstätter—a Catholic conscientious objector—is a

2 David O'Brien, "Gordon C. Zahn," *American Catholic Studies* 126, no. 3 (2015): 111.

vivid indicator of this development. And given that he was so instrumental to the legacy of Jägerstätter, Zahn's story is certainly worth knowing.

I unfold Zahn's story in thirteen chapters. Chapter 1 begins by looking at Zahn's early years growing up in Milwaukee, when his pacifism developed initially as an emotional revulsion to war, while chapter 2 explores Zahn's time at Camp Simon, the alternative service camp for COs run by the Catholic Worker in rural New Hampshire. It was at Camp Simon that Zahn not only met other Catholic COs, as well as Dorothy Day, but also began to develop a much more critical view of the United States—seeing it not as a protector of freedom but more as an institution that locked up dissidents in prisons or remote work camps.

Chapter 3 then describes the years after the war, when Zahn emerged from his experience at Camp Simon fortified in his Catholic pacifism. After finishing his undergraduate degree at the College of St. Thomas in Minnesota, Zahn went onto graduate studies in sociology at the Catholic University of America, where he was introduced to Furfey's "supernatural sociology" as a counter to the two-tiered (neo-scholastic) social theory that prevailed in Catholic sociology at the time—and which mirrored the "value-free" sociology dominant in the broader (secular) discipline. As we will see, Furfey's sociology of the supernatural would not only influence Zahn's own "sociotheological" approach but also profoundly shape his career as an activist academic—employing his sociological training in his work to resist war.

In the fourth chapter, the focus turns to the year Zahn spent in Germany on a Fulbright scholarship (1956–1957). This was a pivotal experience for Zahn, for it provided him with the foundation for his subsequent research on German Catholicism during World War II—research that would catapult him into international notoriety and controversy. Throughout his life, Zahn would continue to return to the example of German Catholics during the war as the basis for his assertion that Catholic moral theology had become irrelevant in the face of the realities of both modern war and the modern state. Perhaps even more significantly, though, it was during this year that Zahn first learned about Franz Jägerstätter, whose story and legacy would become inextricably linked with that of Zahn.

Chapter 5 looks at the controversy that quickly followed in the wake of Zahn's early critique of German Catholicism under the Third Reich. This controversy formed within the very heated context of Cold War Catholicism, when any criticism of the church was read as aiding communists. Zahn's account offered one of the earliest challenges to the Catholic postwar narratives that had been written about German Catholicism—narratives that uniformly emphasized Catholic resistance to the Nazis while skirting any notion of Catholic collaboration. The controversy surrounding Zahn's work was wide-ranging, involving Jesuit higher-ups (Zahn was still at Loyola Chicago), as well as members of the German hierarchy and even Vatican officials. In the midst of this, Zahn traveled to Austria in the summer of 1961 to do more research in Jägerstätter's home village of St. Radegund. The sixth chapter chronicles that research, the interviews he conducted, the documents he came across, and the story of Jägerstätter that Zahn ultimately began to put together—a story, it will be noted, that had striking parallels to Zahn's own story.

German Catholics and Hitler's Wars, the fruit of Zahn's Fulbright research, was published in 1962. Outside of his work on Jägerstätter, Zahn's research on German Catholics under Hitler is certainly that for which he is most noted. Chapter 7 will demonstrate that it was out of this research that Zahn began to craft his broader argument that Catholic moral teaching was inadequate in preparing Catholics for modern war. Facing similar circumstances, Zahn argued, US Catholics would have behaved in much the same manner as their German counterparts. For Zahn, sociological insights on contemporary human social behavior were necessary to develop the "new ethic of war" that was urgently needed within Catholic moral theology. Zahn described this kind of convergence of sociology and theology as "sociotheological."

In 1964, *In Solitary Witness: the Life and Death of Franz Jägerstätter* was published. This is the work for which Zahn is best remembered, and chapter 8 will offer a close reading of this book. Key to Zahn's account of Jägerstätter was his insistence that the Austrian Catholic's refusal to cooperate with the German military had been total and therefore he should be regarded as something of a Catholic pacifist. As subsequent chapters will reveal, however, decades later this claim would become controversial for both Jägerstätter and Zahn.

Chapter 9 examines how Zahn joined forces with Eileen Egan, James Douglass, and Dorothy Day during the third and fourth sessions of Vatican II, lobbying the bishops in their "reassessment" of war and conscientious objection. This lobbying took place in various venues throughout Rome, as well as on the pages of periodicals such as *The Catholic Worker*. Zahn's efforts brought him into contact with several sympathetic bishops from around the world, including Archbishop Thomas Roberts of Bombay, whose intervention on Jägerstätter Zahn would help to write. At the same time, as we will see, this lobbying also placed Zahn in direct confrontation with many members of the US hierarchy as well as the Catholic Association for International Peace (CAIP).

In chapter 10, the focus is on the period following Vatican II, when the church's attitudes toward war and conscientious objection really started to change. This was a high-water mark in Zahn's career, during which he published a collection of his earlier essays, was elected president of the American Catholic Sociological Society, accepted a new (and better) faculty position at the University of Massachusetts, Boston, and took on a more visible and prominent role in the US Catholic peace movement. This was a period, though, when the ground under the Catholic peace movement was also beginning to shift—first with the death of Roger LaPorte in 1965 and then with the Catonsville Nine draft board raids in 1968. While Zahn was initially supportive of this shift (and even compared LaPorte with Jägerstätter), there soon emerged within him very real misgivings about where the movement was headed.

In this context, chapter 11 presents Zahn's response to the Catholic "ultraresistance" that arose in the wake of the Catonsville Nine. Zahn not only justified his World War II generation's "Catholic peace radicalism" in the face of charges that it was lukewarm but also argued that leaders of the contemporary Catholic peace movement needed to remain Catholic and thereby abide by the teaching and morality of the church. As part of his argument, Zahn began making what he referred to as an "absolutized" defense of human life, one that opposed both abortion and war—including so-called "wars of liberation." With these sorts of arguments, Zahn once again found himself more and more on the margins of both the peace movement and the church. Along these lines, chapter 12 examines Zahn's work in the 1980s, particularly his contribution to (and criticism of) *The Challenge of Peace*. While in many ways a highpoint for the US Catholic peace movement, it was also a time when Zahn's Catholic critics began to marginalize his pacifism as "sectarian."

The book concludes with a final chapter on Zahn's legacy. The early 1990s found Zahn defending his account of Jägerstätter—particularly his claim that Jägerstätter's refusal to participate in the German military had been total—in the wake of newly unearthed evidence that suggested otherwise. Zahn also pushed back against rumors that his depiction of Jägerstätter's pacifism had become an impediment to the Austrian Catholic's possible canonization. All of this then leads to a broader discussion of why Zahn still matters today. As many Catholics today struggle with issues of drone-warfare, "forever wars," and the ever-present horror of nuclear holocaust, we could certainly use some of the wisdom of Gordon Zahn and his long, lonely quest toward Catholic pacifism.

1

THE FORMATION OF A CATHOLIC PACIFIST

I am a pacifist.
Someday, I pray, I'll hear the bells ring out
Tidings of peace—of Man and Immortality,
Hands joined, united in a common effort
To free the world of war's inhuman strife and hate;
Man and man's Maker united in battle with the forces of War and its patron, Hell;
For then shall Love and Love's King rule the world.

—*"Creed" by Gordon Zahn (1934)*[1]

THE EARLY YEARS

Just as the Great War in Europe was coming to a conclusion, Gordon Zahn was born Gordon Charles Roach on August 7, 1918, in Milwaukee. Growing up, he was told that his father, Charles Roach, had died in the war. Zahn later guessed that this story (coupled with the fact that he remembered always getting choked up by Memorial Day ceremonies in school) may have provided "some seeds" for his rejection of war even at a young age.[2]

1 Poem is contained in Zahn's FBI file dated May 18, 1942, CPF Zahn papers.

2 In 1994, Zahn wrote a one-hundred-page memoir of sorts that was never published. Many of the biographical details here have been taken from that memoir, which will be cited as "Zahn,

When Zahn was five, his mother, Dorothy Sporer, married Fred Zahn, and Zahn's half-brother Frederick was born a year later. Though he was never legally adopted, Zahn remembered that at school he was always listed as Gordon Zahn. It was not until 1956, when he was applying for the Fulbright scholarship, that he legally changed his name.[3] Zahn never thought much of Fred, and when the latter lost his job during the Depression, Zahn recalled that it was his mother who supported the family by working long hours at a local bakery.

Zahn attended Milwaukee public schools—a fact he later credited with not only teaching him workable German but also with allowing him to avoid being indoctrinated in the scholastic justifications for war taught in the Catholic schools. "Had I been exposed to parochial school training and education," he wrote years later, "chances are good that I would have gone off to war like most of their other products."[4] It was also his public-school education (or perhaps the lack of a Catholic schooling) that Zahn credited with opening his eyes to the church's involvement in war throughout history. Despite this, Zahn remembered that he always insisted upon his Catholic identity and defended the church.

In looking back at his childhood decades later, Zahn wrote that he was initially drawn to pacifism largely out of an "emotional revulsion" to violence and war that he felt at a young age.[5] This insistence would never leave him. When he was twelve years old, for instance, Zahn wrote a letter to the editor of *The Milwaukee Journal* protesting the paper's upbeat reporting on what looked to be that year's "bountiful" duck-hunting season.[6] "Pity and revulsion, these are essential," Zahn later wrote, yet "we Catholics are so used to playing down emotional elements of everything that we tend to undervalue them."[7] For any real commitment, though, the emotional element is fundamental to "the

---

1994," UNDA Zahn papers (9/11827). In 1988, he had written a much shorter version, here referred to as "Zahn, 1988," UNDA Zahn papers (9/11220).

3 Zahn, 1988, 2.

4 Zahn, *Another Part of the War: The Camp Simon Story* (University of Massachusetts Press, 1979), 5.

5 Zahn wrote that his pacifist leanings had some roots in both his "voracious reading" and his "sentimental aversion" to causing injury other creatures. One of Zahn's earliest memories was the "shock, even horror" he experienced in his best friend's delight over receiving a B.B. gun with which he hoped to shoot squirrels (Zahn, *Another Part*, 5).

6 Zahn remembered that for more than a week, there were angry replies from hunters (Zahn, 1994, 16).

7 Bruce Cook, "It Takes a Worried Man," *US Catholic* 23, no. 7 (November 1966): 9.

foundation on which the rest is built," he explained. This initial revulsion to violence then led to an "intellectual examination" of his feelings, an attempt to make sense of them and to rationally consider possible alternatives to war. This, in turn, led him to consider the theological implications of war and violence. According to Zahn, this kind of progressive development was essential, and he warned that those whose pacifism proceeded directly from theological premises lacked "a certain strength [and] a lasting power in their commitment."[8]

Likewise, Zahn also remembered the effect that "sentimental" antiwar films such as *Four Sons* and *Only Yesterday* had on him, though books had a profound influence, as well. "Perhaps the books," Zahn recalled,

> that impressed me most and contributed most directly to my pacifist values was a series of books about the Civil War written by a journalist named [Joseph] Altsheler with a single volume devoted to each of the major battles. The striking feature was that each volume had two young protagonists: one a Yankee, the other a Johnny Reb. Identifying with both gave me a sense of the utter and tragic futility of war.[9]

And by the time he had "graduated" to books such as Jules Romains's *Verdun*, John Steinbeck's *In Dubious Battle*, and John Dos Passos's *U.S.A.* trilogy, Zahn had already formed a "fixed commitment to social justice, nonviolence and—most definite of all—the absolute rejection of the inhumanity of war."[10]

Raised in what he described as a "religiously mixed (and religiously inactive)" home, Zahn's mother Dorothy apparently baptized her infant son herself, possibly because of the Spanish Flu epidemic raging at the time.[11] Any religious underpinnings of his pacifism, therefore, came from his own independent reading. Zahn claimed to have read the entire King James Bible and recalled that he found his pacifist commitment "validated" by the account of the Crucifixion as well as the examples of heroism in the *Acts of the Apostles*.

8 Cook, "It Takes a Worried Man," 10.

9 Zahn also remembered the impact of seeing a picture of ship sinking during a battle: "Which war it was or on which side the victims served apparently meant nothing to me. Even then, to me they were just people, doomed to perish" (Zahn, 1994, 17–18).

10 Zahn, 1994, 16.

11 Zahn, 1994, 2.

When he was in high school, a neighbor prevailed upon Zahn's mother to have him take catechism classes at the local parish to prepare for a "conditional" baptism—just in case his less than orthodox baptism had not taken. At the age of sixteen, he was baptized at the local parish, meaning, as he later recalled, that Zahn officially entered the Catholic Church already a "committed pacifist."[12] In fact, he was a pacifist before he was entirely aware of all that being a Catholic meant or required. "I knew, of course, that the Church was not pacifist and did not approve of pacifism in its members," Zahn wrote, and that pacifism was seen as "unorthodox, if not clearly heretical.[13]

Zahn remembered that while critical of the church's support for "war, ultra-patriotism, and the like," he described himself as an "obedient critic"—although he also stated that he would have maintained his pacifist commitment "regardless of what bishops and popes had to say."[14] As an adolescent, Zahn dreamt about heroically making a dramatic refusal to take part in a war and being the only Catholic to make such a stand. In those early years, Zahn came to believe that he was bound to act according to two basic "truths"—Catholicism and pacifism—which he regarded as fundamentally linked, "even if the rest of the Church was not yet aware of that fact."[15] The rest of Zahn's life can be seen as a stubborn and persistent attempt to hold these two truths together.

WORLD WAR II

Zahn graduated from high school in 1934 and went to work for an auto financing company to help support his family. His pacifist leanings did not recede, though, and they soon led him to Winnie Woodmansee, the socialite chairwoman of Milwaukee's "Women's International League of Peace and Freedom" (WILPF).[16] It was Woodmansee and the WILPF who helped Zahn come to a firmer intellectual understanding of his "pacifism."[17] Woodmansee

12 Zahn, 1988, 10–11.

13 Zahn, 1988, 10.

14 Zahn, 1988, 11.

15 Zahn, 1988, 11

16 The WILPF emerged in the wake of World War I in 1919, evolving out of the Women's Peace Party, a pacifist organization founded by Jane Addams and others who attended the International Congress of Women at The Hague in April 1915.

17 Émile Arnaud (1864–1921), who founded the "International League of Peace and Freedom" (*Ligue Internationale de la Paix et de la Liberté*) in 1861, is credited with having coined the term "pacifism."

hosted several "peace talks" in her downtown apartment, where the young Gordon Zahn met prominent left-wing political figures such as Maynard Kruger and Burton K. Wheeler.[18] In fact, it was at one such event that Zahn recalled first meeting Ammon Hennacy, the anarchist and World War I conscientious objector who would later go on to be a driving force of antiwar activism within the Catholic Worker movement in the years following World War II.[19]

Also through Woodmansee, Zahn became an active member in the local chapter of the America First Committee—an isolationist and anti-British group whose members were dedicated for various reasons to keeping the United States out of World War II.[20] Zahn described the group as a "hodge-podge" of people, everything from American Nazis (German-American Bundists) to radical socialists. While certainly uncomfortable with the more nationalistic aspects of the group, Zahn saw America First as the only political organization offering any real opposition to prowar "interventionist" organizations such as the "Committee to Aid the Allies" and the "Union Now With Britain."[21] Historian Patricia McNeal shed some light on Zahn's predicament when she explained that US Catholicism's "quest for peace" during the war could be divided into three options: pacifism, internationalism, and isolationism. These divisions also represented the "ideological diversity" among both US Catholics and Americans more broadly in the 1930s—the difference being that the former

in 1901 to describe the ideology of the "friends of peace": "Our great party needs a name; we have no name and this deficiency impedes our progress considerably. We are not passive types; we are not only peace makers; we are not just pacifiers. We are all those but also something more—we are pacifists ... and our ideology is pacifism." By World War I, the term "pacifist" was largely being applied to those who opposed all war, including defensive combat. See Sandi E. Cooper, *Patriotic Pacifism: Waging War on War in Europe, 1815–1914* (Oxford University Press, 1991), 60.

18 Kruger was a University of Chicago economics professor who was best remembered for being the 1940 vice-presidential nominee of the Socialist Party of America, sharing the ticket with Norman Thomas. Wheeler was a Democratic senator from Montana who ran for vice president in 1924 on the Progressive Party ticket with Robert La Follette, Sr.

19 Zahn recalled that on that evening, though, Hennacy appeared "in conservative dress, not at all his later Catholic Worker persona," and replied to a comment Zahn made regarding "the masses" by declaring that "the masses are asses." Years later, when Zahn saw him at the Catholic Worker, he recalled having "a measure of revenge" in reminding Hennacy of the bourgeois impression he left at that first meeting (Zahn, 1988, 12). In his recent biography of Hennacy, William Marling depicts Milwaukee at the time as an activist hotbed. See William Marling, *Christian Anarchist: Ammon Hennacy: a Life on the Catholic Left* (NYU Press, 2022).

20 Zahn, 1988, 12

21 Zahn, 1994, 21.

"reinforced these positions with a Catholic theological rationale."[22] In the end, however, as Zahn's experience reflected, the pre-war debate was essentially between interventionists (internationalism) and anti-interventionists (isolationism and pacifism).[23]

That said, Zahn portrayed his involvement in the group as "purely tactical." While the America First Committee was certainly not a pacifist organization, many of its Milwaukee chapter members were, but they could not find any pacifist group to join. Indeed, the day after the Japanese attack on Pearl Harbor, as his local chapter met for the last time, Zahn remembered that all but one of the eleven members admitted to being pacifist and intending to apply for conscientious objector status.[24] When he was granted CO status in 1942, Zahn recalled that it was Woodmansee who mentioned to him that there was a camp for Catholic COs in New Hampshire run by a group of Catholic pacifists from New York City, "thereby giving me my first introduction to its official sponsor, *The Catholic Worker*!"[25]

THE DRAFT

Even before Pearl Harbor, as the United States became less neutral toward the war in Europe, Zahn became more vocal in his pacifism.[26] In the summer of 1940, when Congress was debating conscription legislation, Zahn wrote a letter to the editor at *The Milwaukee Journal* stating his opposition to any draft and arguing that every major democracy that had adopted compulsory military service was "now a military dictatorship."[27] Despite Zahn's opposition, the Selective Training and Service Act of 1940 (also known as the "Burke-Wadsworth

22 Patricia McNeal, *Harder Than* War: *Catholic Peacemaking in Twentieth-Century America* (Rutgers University Press1992), 28.

23 This reality was also evident in Dorothy Day's use of Archbishop John T. McNicholas's famous call for a "mighty league of conscientious non-combatants" to the war, even though she acknowledged that McNicholas was motivated by his opposition to the Soviet Union rather than to the war itself. Dorothy Day, *The Long Loneliness* (Harper & Brothers, 1952), 218.

24 Cook, "It Takes a Worried Man," 10.

25 Zahn, 1988, 12; Zahn, 1994, 22

26 In March 1939, he began writing letters to the editor of the *Milwaukee Journal* encouraging the United States to stay out of war and abide by the Neutrality Act.

27 In a second letter, written in reply to an angry response to his initial letter, Zahn argued that if the conscription bill was passed, it would "put all groups under the actual or threatened domination of one powerful group—the military." See the letter dated March 13, 1939, contained in Zahn's FBI file (CPF Zahn papers).

Act") was signed into law on September 16, 1940. Within a month, Zahn submitted a "Selective Service Questionnaire," which included the line: "I claim the exemption provided by the Selective Training and Service Act of 1940 for conscientious objectors because I am conscientiously opposed, by reason of my religious training and belief, to the type or types of service checked below." The types of service offered were "combatant military service" and "non-combatant military service." Zahn checked both.[28]

Zahn was then sent a "Special Form for Conscientious Objectors," which asked for more personal information, as well as answers to various questions about his conscientious objection claim. On July 18, 1941, he submitted this form, and his answers provide a helpful snapshot of his thinking on both pacifism and Catholicism at a moment when he still believed that he was the only Catholic pacifist. In describing the nature of the beliefs that formed the basis of his claim, Zahn declared that he believed that "no one had the right to take 'or assist in taking' the life of another person; and that it was wrong for a nation to order its people to kill."[29] He explained that his belief could be summed up by the commandment "Thou shalt not kill," which he saw as being without limitation or qualification. In explaining "how, when, and from whom or what source" he had acquired this belief, Zahn wrote, "I have always been taught that it is wrong to harm, injure, or kill any creature," and he guessed that such beliefs originated from his mother, as well as his "reading the terms of the New Testament; studying the lessons of history; realizing the laws of civilized living."

To the question of whether he believed that there were any circumstances in which force could be used, Zahn replied,

> I do not believe the use of force is right at any time. The use of force is an admission that right has failed. Perhaps at times of extreme need when an individual is personally threatened, he may use force; but a nation had no right to force its citizens to kill or use force. Such action must be taken only when the person involved is convinced his action is right.

Describing his "religious sect or organization" and its "creed or official statements" with regard to participation in war, Zahn noted that the position of

28 That said, Zahn believed "that at less than 120 lbs. with poor eyesight—I had worn bi-focals for a time in high school!—I was a fairly sure bet for a 4F classification" (Zahn, 1988, 5).

29 These details are contained in Zahn's FBI file, which he obtained in 1976.

the Catholic Church regarding war was "to cooperate with the government of each nation in which it is established," but he went onto explain that "each member is guilty of sin if he does not act in accordance with what his conscience dictates, based on his religious beliefs." While the Catholic Church did not condemn participation in war, Zahn pointed out that individual Catholics were certainly allowed to do so. Zahn reported that he had never belonged to any "pacifist" organizations, since many were "backed subversively and therefore are not sincerely concerned with the advancement of peace." He did acknowledge that he was a member of the America First Committee, which he called a "truly American organization."

On December 30, 1941, Zahn appeared before his local draft board, which included the Catholic priest who quickly told Zahn in no uncertain terms that a Catholic could not be a conscientious objector to all war.[30] No doubt this declaration led to Zahn receiving a letter in February 1942 stating that his CO claim had been denied and that he had been classified as 1-A: "available for full service." In his appeal letter, Zahn wrote—in what would be one of his last appeals to liberal democratic ideals—that he had long viewed conscription as being contrary to "the principles of democracy" since it unjustly placed "in the hands of certain men the powers of limiting the liberties of other men who might fall under their jurisdiction."[31] Zahn pointed out that, in spite of his opposition to the draft, he had been fully cooperative in the conscription process, but that his local board had failed in its obligation to impartially judge his claim.

But it was the board's dismissal of his statement of convictions that bothered Zahn the most. These were convictions that as an American he believed he was privileged to have and more importantly that as a Christian he was obligated to hold. He pointed to one board member who stated (in reference to Zahn) that the military needed "some kind of a camp where we can put

30 An example of Catholic thinking on conscientious objection at the time can be seen in a booklet (to which Zahn often referred) published by the Catholic Association for International Peace (CAIP), which stated: "If the necessary conditions are verified and the war is in every way a just war, if I fall within the military age, and if my country actually needs my service, and, especially if I am conscripted for military service, I am *forbidden* to be a conscientious objector. My refusal to give my services, far from being more perfect—'the better part'—would undoubtedly be a direct violation of the natural law and, hence, positively sinful. Naturally, under these conditions, there can be *no question of either right or duty* to object conscientiously." See Cyprian Emmanuel, OFM, *The Morality of Conscientious Objection to War* (The Catholic Association for International Peace, 1941), 26–27.

31 Zahn, 1988, 22.

fellows like this." As unjust as he believed the draft to be, Zahn argued that it still did not give the government the power to simply "punish or segregate a person for his belief." Still holding onto his faith in US political institutions (a faith that his time at Camp Simon would soon stamp out), Zahn argued that to employ the provision for "alternative service" in the draft legislation as a way of "interning" COs would make a mockery of the democratic norms that the US military claimed to be protecting.

In his appeal to the board's decision, Zahn also included a four-page letter he had sent to Milwaukee Archbishop Moses Kiley. In that letter, he made an argument against Catholic participation in the war that was surprisingly sophisticated for someone with little formal theological education.[32] Zahn wrote that as a Catholic he was "obligated to follow the dictates of my conscience" and that his conscience instructed him that war was an "extreme expression of evil" that he did not support.[33] He stated that he could not accept the notion that Christians all over the world should take up arms against other Christians: "It cannot be right for spiritual brothers to kill each other, regardless of by whom such an act is commanded." And if it is wrong for a Christian to kill another Christian, he asked, how much more unjustifiable was it for a Catholic to kill another Catholic. "Where can it be right," he asked Kiley, "for an American Catholic to believe he is blessed in fighting Germany, when the German Catholic he is trying to kill is also a Catholic blessed in defending his nation?" Noting that bishops from all the nations fighting in the war had exhorted their Catholic soldiers to kill their fellow "enemy" Catholics, Zahn asked, "Are we not restricting the international, the universal, the catholic aspect of the true church when we place the man-made limits of nationality above its teachings of world-wide brotherhood?"

For Zahn, the true enemy was "greed, selfish intolerance, and hatred," and since these vices were the real causes of every war, they could never be defeated by war. Zahn reminded the archbishop that Jesus was crucified for his teachings and beliefs, and that on every battlefield in history, Jesus

32 He also included a letter he sent President Roosevelt, which stated: "I am a pacifist. . . . I may not kill—I may not help another to kill. Even in a war of defense, I do not recognize a right or obligation to kill; for the things being defended are temporal and the crime I would be committing would be a violation of Divine law"—no government, he stated, had the right to veto or suspend "the laws of Christianity" (FBI File, CPF Zahn papers).

33 Zahn also wrote, "I believe it is wrong to kill another man for any reason whatsoever." See Zahn to Kiley in a letter dated February 10, 1942 (FBI file, CPF Zahn papers).

was being crucified again by those who abandon his teachings. "We did that before," Zahn declared (borrowing from a popular prowar slogan), "and until those who believe in Him combine behind His Church and refuse to support war, we will do it again."[34] Perhaps not surprisingly, Kiley never acknowledged Zahn's letter. Like his answers on the draft questionnaire, though, this letter reveals something about Zahn's reasoning at the time and highlights the fact that even before encountering any other Catholic COs or pacifists, the twenty three-year-old had already developed a fairly solid theological foundation for his pacifism.

In April 1941, during his appeals, Zahn's mother, Dorothy, died of cancer. With Fred largely out of the picture, Zahn and his brother Freddie moved into an apartment together. The following summer, Freddie, who had always been sickly, also died. That fall, Zahn received word that his appeal had been granted and that he had been reclassified as a conscientious objector (IV-E). He was sent an "Order to Report for Work of National Importance" in the Civilian Public Service (CPS) program. Despite the sadness of losing both his mother and brother, Zahn recalled that in a very real sense these losses made it easier for him to carry through as a conscientious objector.[35] Zahn began his time as a CO very much alone, therefore, not only without any family support, but also without much of any support from the church.

CATHOLIC AMERICANISM

In many ways, Zahn was alone. Indeed, he went off to the CPS program at Camp Simon not knowing that the weight of an entire tradition loomed over him and was about to fall on him. This tradition, following Michael Baxter's suggestion, can be labeled the "Americanist Tradition" within US Catholicism. It is rooted in a particular belief that America is essentially good for Catholicism and that Catholics are good for (and perhaps could even save) America.[36] Dating back at least to the writings of Orestes Brownson and Isaac Hecker in the nineteenth century, this belief was clearly articulated by the US bishops gathered at the Third Plenary Council of Baltimore in 1884 when they declared

34 Zahn, 1994, 20.

35 Zahn, 1988, 3.

36 Michael Baxter, "Notes on Catholic Americanism and Catholic Radicalism: Toward a Counter-Tradition of Catholic Social Ethics," in *American Catholic Traditions: Resources for Renewal*, ed. Sandra Yocum-Mize and William Portier (Orbis Books, 1996), 53–71.

that America—"this home of freedoms"—was divinely established and that its founders were God's instruments "building better than they knew."[37] For Catholics living in a largely Protestant nation, no freedom was more sacred than the one that allowed them to practice their faith. If the United States, the protector of such freedom, were ever threatened, the bishops promised that Catholics would stand together and defend her.

Theologically, this Americanism was enabled by a neoscholastic separation of nature from the supernatural that prevailed within Catholicism at the time. As I will later explain, this separation allowed for Americanist Catholics to regard the nation-state (and politics) as "natural" and separated from the supernatural standards of the Sermon on the Mount. The actions of the state could thereby be judged according to natural law standards, which in the case of war were articulated in the just-war theory. This also allowed for the separation of sociology from theology—which, as we will see, was something Zahn clearly opposed.

In the wake of the so-called "Americanist controversy" at the end of the nineteenth century, Pope Leo XIII listed a series of errors under the heading of "Americanism" in his 1899 encyclical *Testem Benevolentiae*. The pope was careful, though, to distinguish the theological meaning of "Americanism" from its more cultural or political meaning, and he only condemned the former.[38] This distinction proved to be extremely helpful to Cardinal James Gibbons (the recipient of the encyclical), as it allowed him to assure the pope that nothing like the "Americanism" condemned in the encyclical existed in the US Church. However, as Baxter noted, this distinction also allowed "Americanism" in the cultural and political sense to continue to develop unimpeded, thus forming a Catholic Americanist tradition.[39]And as later chapters will reveal, this tradition

37 The Archbishops and Bishops of the United States, "Pastoral Letter of the Third Plenary Council, 1884," in *The National Pastorals of the American Hierarchy*, ed. Peter Guilday (Newman Press, 1954).

38 Leo accused advocates of "Americanism" of harboring a desire to create "a church in America different from that which is in the rest of the world." See Pope Leo XIII, *Testem Benevolentiae*, in *American Catholic History: A Documentary Reader*, ed. Mark Massa (NYU Press, 2008), 67.

39 While significant differences existed among the thinkers within this tradition, Baxter suggested that a central idea ran through them all: "the idea that reality is divided into two basic spheres, the spiritual and the temporal; the idea that the integrity of the spiritual sphere is best preserved by a government that protects religious freedom; the idea that when they established this political order, the Catholic leaders in Maryland were drawing on the political wisdom of the Catholic Church; the idea that the Church's wisdom was the inspiration behind the U.S. Revolution in general as well; the idea that the work of Catholic medieval and scholastic political theorists, in particular, Aquinas, Suarez, and Bellarmine, was transmitted through the English Whigs to the Founding

passed seamlessly into the twentieth century with the National Catholic War Council (precursor to the US Catholic Conference of Bishops), the Catholic Association for International Peace, the pivotal mid-century contributions of John Courtney Murray, SJ, and even the US bishops' 1983 peace pastoral *The Challenge of Peace*—all justifying US war-making and marginalizing Catholic critics like Zahn.

All this is to say that Zahn's belief that he was the only Catholic CO was not unjustified, at least from the radical perspective that he was formulating in his mind. Catholic support for the US war effort in World War II was strong. In fact, a month after Zahn reported to the Civilian Public Service, the National Catholic Welfare Conference—successor to the National Catholic War Council—issued a statement in the *New York Times* titled "Victory and Peace," which proclaimed:

> We ask our people to be united and prepared to make every sacrifice which our government deems necessary for a just and enduring peace through the victory of our armed forces. We are confident that they will perform their wartime duties gladly because they know that our country has been the defender, not the destroyer, of liberties."[40]

Not long after, in 1943, the moral theologian John Connor, SJ, summed up the prevailing US Catholic attitudes toward the war in an article offering advice to clergy on what to do if they were asked by a young Catholic conscientious objector (such as Zahn) to sign a military questionnaire attesting to the sincerity of his belief. Connor noted that while there had been little support for US Catholic COs during World War I, the horrors of the Great War led a number of Catholics to question whether such a war met the traditional criteria of a just war.[41] These discussions came to an abrupt end, however, with the entrance

Fathers upon whom it had a shaping impact as they hammered out the First Amendment of the U.S. Constitution; the idea that the commitment to religious freedom embodied in the Constitution provides the surest source of political stability and the only true foundations for Christian society in the modern world." See Michael Baxter, "The Unsettling of Americanism: A Response to William Portier," *Communio* 27 (Spring 2000): 165.

40 The letter, which appeared in the November 15, 1942, issue, was signed by ten bishops. For the full text, see "Victory and Peace," in *Our Bishops Speak*, ed. Raphael Huber, OFM Conv. (Bruce Publishing, 1952), 110–15.

41 Connor did highlight the case of Ben Salmon, one of the four US Catholic COs in World War I noting that Salmon was sentenced to twenty-five years in federal prison in 1917 after he was told that his Catholic religion did not forbid him from participating since the Catholic hierarchy was

of the US into World War II following the attack on Pearl Harbor and the US Catholic hierarchy's quick endorsement of the war effort. Almost overnight, Connor explained, any argument in support of Catholic COs became "lost by default" and unacceptable. In the end, Connor concluded that he doubted a Catholic could be a conscientious objector.

Of course, this kind of US Catholic hyperpatriotism during wartime was nothing new; indeed, it has been described as the "hallmark of the American Catholic community" even before the United States existed.[42] However, as historian William Halsey pointed out, the First World War marked a significant turning point for US Catholics—a moment when they finally felt "secure enough to claim America."[43] Indeed, two weeks after Woodrow Wilson broke his campaign promise and asked Congress on April 6, 1917, for "a war to end war," Cardinal Gibbons, Archbishop of Baltimore and *de facto* head of the US Catholic Church, sent a letter to Wilson declaring unconditional Catholic support for the US war effort.[44] And as proof of this support, Gibbons set up the National Catholic War Council to coordinate Catholic support for the war. By the outbreak of the Second World War, therefore, the US Catholic Church was, to say the least, unwelcoming to Catholic COs.[45] As one US priest publicly declared in 1941: "If a conscientious objector is found among our Catholics, it is not because of the moral teachings of our Church but because he is afraid for his hide—he is a coward."[46] This was the theological and historical context into which Zahn made his conscientious objection.

---

actively supporting the war. See John Connor, SJ, "Can a Catholic be a Conscientious Objector?" *The Ecclesiastical Review* 58 (February 1943): 127.

42 Harry J. Browne, "Catholicism in the United States," *The Shaping of American Religion*, ed. James Ward Smith and A. Leland Jamison (Princeton University Press, 1961), 77.

43 Halsey asserted that just as non-Catholics were becoming disillusioned with "American innocence," Catholics, "latecomers to the promises of America," were just beginning to "taste its material benefits" and so were opposed to anyone who appeared to undermine these promises. See William Halsey, *The Survival of American Innocence: Catholicism in the Era of Disillusionment: 1920–1940* (University of Notre Dame Press, 1980), 3.

44 The letter (dated April 18, 1917) was quoted in full in the *Sign of Peace: Journal of the Catholic Peace Fellowship* 6, no. 1 (Spring 2007): 17.

45 "If it is too much to describe the Catholic conscientious objector as a religious outcast," Zahn would later explain, "this is only because the general Catholic population took no notice of him" (Zahn, *Another Part*, ix).

46 Richard Klaver, OSC, in *Crozier Missionary* (July 1941), quoted in Zahn, *Another Part*, 25.

CONCLUSION

As Zahn himself suggested, his commitment to pacifism predated his Catholicism and was initially rooted in an emotional, not theological, rejection of war. Zahn, therefore, was always well aware that the church was not comfortable with pacifism and that he would be holding a minority position within the church. But he also realized that the horrors of modern war were fundamentally in conflict with the Gospel message of peace, love, and forgiveness. He clearly saw that war and the modern nation-states that waged them were tearing apart the Mystical Body of Christ—pitting Catholic against Catholic. Recognizing this provided Zahn with the confidence and fortitude necessary not only to object to war but also to begin to build his argument that Catholics could (and should) embrace pacifism, conscientious objection, and Gospel nonviolence. And as we will see in the following chapters, this lonely work brought Zahn into direct conflict with a tradition of Catholic Americanism that Zahn would resist the rest of his life.

2

CAMP SIMON

> *Internment in the Civilian Public Service camps or in federal prisons was a formative experience for a new generation of pacifist leaders, providing them the equivalent of a postgraduate education. . . . Many hundreds of conscientious objectors became, in effect, full-time pacifist revolutionaries.*
>
> —*Maurice Isserman*[1]

In October 1942, Zahn was inducted into the Civilian Public Service (CPS) and ordered to report to Camp Simon in Warner, New Hampshire.[2] The CPS program had only recently come into existence that February through an executive order responding to a need brought about by the Selective Training and Service Act of 1940. Of the over thirty-four million men who began to register for the draft in September 1940, some 72,000—including Zahn—stated on their questionnaire that they could not fight in the war for reasons of conscience. Of these, around 25,000 accepted noncombatant service in the US military (classified as I-A-O), while another 27,000 simply failed the military's basic physical exam and were discharged.[3] Another 6,000 or so of these men went to prison for refusing to

1 Maurice Isserman, *If I Had a Hammer: The Death of the Old Left and the Birth of the New Left* (Basic Books, 1987), 132–33.

2 Zahn, *Another Part of the War*, 5–6.

3 These numbers are from Albert Kiem, *The CPS Story: An Illustrated History of Civilian Public Service* (Good Books, 1990), 8.

participate in any form of military service, including registering for the draft itself.[4] The remaining men (around 12,000) were granted IV-E classification, indicating that they had convinced authorities that they were sincere in their conscientious objection to the war.[5] Zahn was classified IV-E.

For COs of previous generations, the 1940 draft law seemed to offer clear improvements to earlier draft laws by at least recognizing the rights of conscientious objectors.[6] Important for Catholic COs, it also expanded the CO exemption beyond members of traditional "peace churches" to include anyone whose objection was rooted in their "religious training and belief," thereby opening the CO exemption to Catholics, Jews, and mainline Protestants. In addition, the appeal process, which Zahn went through after being initially denied CO status, was moved from the Department of War to the Department of Justice—a shift that allowed for CO cases to be tried in civilian courts rather than by a military court-martial.[7] Furthermore, the 1940 act recognized COs whose objection was not simply to killing *per se*, but to participating in any aspect of war-making—including noncombatant service. The 1940 law was a generous improvement, but within limits.

Significantly, the 1940 law went a long way toward defining what it meant to be a conscientious objector in the United States. On the Selective Service form that Zahn and other COs filled out, the applicant agreed to the statement: "I claim the exemption provided by the Selective Training and Service Act of 1940 for conscientious objectors, because I am conscientiously opposed by reason of my religious training and belief to participation in war in any form and to participation in any service which is under the direction of military authorities." In other words, a CO was defined as someone who would not participate in any war in any form—a stance also sometimes referred to as

4 The bulk of whom (4,441) were Jehovah's Witnesses.

5 The 1940 Act stated: "Nothing contained in this Act shall be construed to require any person to be subject to combatant training and service in the land and naval forces of the United States who, by reason of religious training and belief, is conscientiously opposed to participation in war in any form. Any such person claiming such exemption from combatant training and service because of such conscientious objections whose claim is sustained by the local draft board shall, if he is inducted into the land or naval forces under this Act, be assigned to noncombatant service as defined by the President, or shall, if he is found to be conscientiously opposed to participation in such noncombatant service, in lieu of such induction, be assigned to work of national importance under civilian direction" (Quoted in Kiem, 24).

6 Kiem, *The CPS Story*, 24.

7 In World War I, Ben Salmon was tried by a military court martial.

an "absolute" or "total" pacifist. It was in this sense of the term that Zahn had been told that a Catholic could not be a conscientious objector. Excluded from this definition, of course, were any Catholics who opposed participating in particular wars or particular kinds of wars or particular actions in a war because they did not or could not meet the criteria of the church's just-war teaching—a stance that would later come to be called "selective conscientious objection."[8]

CIVILIAN PUBLIC SERVICE

In lieu of military service, the Selective Training and Service Act of 1940 required that those granted CO status perform "work of national importance under civilian direction." This alternative service work would be performed in 150 or so camps and "special units" operated by the Civilian Public Service.[9] The CPS was a unique partnership between the US military and the National Service Board of Religious Objectors (NSBRO)—an umbrella group for historic peace churches that had been formed the year before in response to the draft law.[10] In this arrangement, NSBRO agreed to assume full financial and (at least in theory) administrative responsibility for the operation of CPS camps. NSBRO saw this concession as a necessity, since it seemed unrealistic that Congress on a war-footing would provide any funds for conscientious objectors. This partnership, however, was always precarious. In his history of the CPS, Albert Kiem reported a conversation Tom Jones, president of Fisk University and first director of Friends CPS, had with an army colonel who was an official of the Selective Service Administration. As Jones was enthusiastically describing his hopes for the CPS camps, the colonel cut him off and said, "Who do you think you are? Don't you know that I'm in charge of these camps under Selective Service?" When Jones replied that NSBRO was supposed to have autonomy in running the camps, the colonel stated, "My dear man, the draft is under United States government operation. Conscientious objectors are draftees just

8 Catholic Peace Fellowship staff, "Selective Conscientious Objection," *The Sign of Peace* 4, no. 2 (Spring 2005): 16–21.

9 Kiem, *The CPS Story*, 33.

10 Such peace churches usually included Quakers, Mennonites, and the Church of the Brethren.

as soldiers are. Their activities are responsible to the government. The Peace Churches are only camp managers."[11]

The CPS program opened its first work camp in Patapsco State Park near Baltimore on May 15, 1941—seven months before the Japanese attack on Pearl Harbor. By the time the program ended in March 1947, some 12,000 men had served in the CPS.[12] The "work of national importance" performed by COs initially consisted in a continuation of the work done by the Civilian Conservation Corps during the Depression. Soon, though, two general hospital units were also opened where COs worked as orderlies, one of which was a unit for Catholics at the Alexian Brothers' Hospital in Chicago. As the war progressed and needs arose, several more "special units" opened in various state mental hospitals and schools, such as the one at Rosewood State Training School where Zahn was sent after the Warner camp closed. Zahn would later estimate that in total, COs in the CPS program collectively performed over eight million days of labor, work with a monetary value of $24 million.[13]

Around 13,500 men were assigned to the CPS program (though some 1,600 never reported), and of these, 149 were listed as Catholic in NSBRO's *Directory of Civilian Public Service*.[14] Zahn would later point out that fourteen of these men neither considered themselves members of the Catholic Church nor based their stands in Catholic teaching.[15] This left, he argued, 135 Catholic COs.[16] A small number, though it should be remembered that of the 16,000 "delinquents" convicted and imprisoned for violations of the draft law, over 6,000 had claimed to be conscientious objectors—some of whom would have been Catholic. Zahn would describe these imprisoned COs as "some of the

11 Kiem, *The CPS Story*, 32.

12 Kiem, *The CPS Story*, 33.

13 Zahn, *Another Part of the War*, 37.

14 Another twenty-five thousand men were granted I-A-O classification and assigned to noncombatant duty during the war. Zahn described draft boards as attempting to "sell" the I-A-O classification to all draftees who requested CO status. See Zahn, *A Study of the Social Backgrounds of Catholic Conscientious Objectors in Civilian Public Service During World War II* (MA thesis, The Catholic University of America), 12.

15 Zahn, *Catholic Conscientious Objectors*, 42.

16 In World War I, of course, there had only been four: John Dunn, Francis X. Hennessy, and Christian Lellig, along with Salmon. Ammon Hennacy was a CO during WWI who later converted to Catholicism (McNeal, *Harder than War*, 269n18).

most sincere objectors" to the war.[17] According to NSBRO records, sixty-one Catholic COs were imprisoned during the war, the largest number (eighteen) were held in the Federal Prison in Danbury, Connecticut.[18] The Association of Catholic Conscientious Objectors lobbied on behalf of these imprisoned Catholics, and all but two of those at Danbury had at least one-third of their sentence commuted and were assigned to work in nearby hospitals. All of this led Patricia McNeal to suggest that imprisoned COs may have actually "fared better" than their counterparts in the CPS camps.[19] In fact, Zahn remembered debates taking place during his time in the CPS on whether "perhaps jail is better."[20]

ASSOCIATION OF CATHOLIC CONSCIENTIOUS OBJECTORS

The idea of a CPS camp specifically for Catholics originated with the Association of Catholic Conscientious Objectors. The ACCO was an off-shoot of the Catholic Worker that was formed "to promote Catholic opposition to war and conscription and to serve as a central organizing and clearing house for Catholics who intended to reject participation in the looming war."[21] Arthur Sheehan, a New York Catholic Worker, took charge of the ACCO in 1940. Sheehan, as the self-appointed Catholic representative on NSBRO, applied for permission from the Selective Service Administration to operate a CPS camp for Catholics. In 1941, he was granted a forestry camp in Stoddard, New Hampshire, to give Catholic COs an opportunity to work in an atmosphere

17 Zahn also pointed out that some minor shifting occurred from one group to another as COs in prison were paroled into the CPS or those in the CPS "went I-A-O" and joined the military, or simply walked out of the camp and were subsequently caught and sent to prison. Zahn speculated as to whether some of the Catholics charged with desertion or insubordination were actually motivated by a "latent conscientious objection" to the war and practices. This, he explained, would be the course of action required by "the traditional moralist of any Catholic who was called upon to do something he sincerely believed to be an immoral act of war" (Zahn, *Catholic Conscientious Objectors*, 14n4).

18 J. F. Powers, the winner of the 1963 National Book Award, was one of these imprisoned Catholic COs.

19 McNeal, *Harder than War*, 64.

20 Zahn, *Another Part of the Wat*, 52.

21 The ACCO was unveiled with a full-page article in the September 1941 issue of *The Catholic Worker* (Zahn, *Another Part of the War*, 33).

"oriented to Catholic principles and religious practices."[22] All told, the ACCO operated four CPS camps or work units during the war.[23] As we will see, the ACCO was not only one of the first groups to join in the CPS program but also the first to withdraw from it.

Throughout its brief history, the ACCO was always in the minority. It was an organization, after all, for objectors to what was perhaps the most popular total war effort in US history. It was a minority, as well, within the Catholic Church—evidenced, Zahn wrote, by the fact that the "great mass of Catholics," laity and clergy alike, were either unaware of or unsympathetic toward their stand.[24] Indeed, Bishop John Peterson of Manchester, the diocese where both the Stoddard and Warner camps were located, was not an enthusiastic supporter. Years later, while doing graduate research on the camps, Zahn found a letter (dated January 23, 1943) written by the New Hampshire Selective Service Director, which stated:

> This camp has been the object of considerable annoyance to the Roman Catholic Bishop of New Hampshire who has taken the position that, inasmuch as that Church does not recognize among its adherents conscientious objection to fighting for one's country, there cannot be such an establishment as a Catholic conscientious objector's camp. His official opinion is that a person could not be a Roman Catholic and a conscientious objector at one and the same time.[25]

22 Zahn, *Another Part of the War*, 38.

23 The camp in Stoddard; a second camp in Warner, New Hampshire, when the Stoddard camp closed in 1942; a unit at the Alexian Brothers Hospital in Chicago; and another unit at the Rosewood State Training School near Baltimore (Zahn, *Another Part of the War*, 38).

24 Zahn, *Catholic Conscientious Objectors*, 24. Zahn noted that a few bishops—such as John T. McNicholas in Cincinnati, who famously called for a "mighty league" of Catholic conscientious objectors—were supportive of Catholic COs before the US entrance into the war, but quickly cooled in their support once the US war effort began.

25 Zahn also found a second letter (dated February 24, 1943) that Peterson wrote to the Selective Service headquarters in Washington, DC, stating that he did not seek to "suppress" the camp. He explained that although the camp had elicited some criticism that placed the church "in a false light" (since the church had declared that participation in this war was "an essential duty"), he did admire the "manly character" and sacrifices of the objectors (Zahn, *Catholic Conscientious Objectors*, 25).

Such alienation within the church was captured perfectly by Zahn when he described Catholic COs as having been "orphaned by that spiritual mother in whose name they had taken their unpopular stand."[26]

Without any real support from their bishops, the ACCO was almost entirely dependent upon donations, chiefly from the Catholic Worker, itself a hand-to-mouth operation. This meant that there was a tendency by camp administrators to regard the ACCO camp along the same lines as a Catholic Worker house of hospitality, and so there was an expectation for COs to gladly sacrifice creature comforts and happily volunteer extra work hours. Indeed, in *Loaves and Fishes*, Dorothy Day wrote that Catholic COs at the camp "wanted to make a demonstration of 'going the second mile' with the government and offered civilian service instead of war service."[27] And Zahn remembered that Catholic Worker "agrarian idealism" served as the model of the ACCO camp, as a "decentralized and communitarian way of life."[28]

In reality, life could be hard at the camp. Day wrote that the COs were not paid and, in fact, they were expected to pay for their keep: "No pay, no honor, and—for the first year—not enough food."[29] At one point, COs at other CPS camps even voluntarily skipped meals so that the money saved could be sent to the Catholic camp, a situation Zahn remembered as yet another indignity:

> Not only did they need regular support and gifts from those friends and family with whom they remained in good standing, they were also competing with the homeless derelicts of the Bowery for the meagre funds contributed by the readers of the Worker. Now, to top it all off, these members of the largest and wealthiest religious community in the world found themselves obliged to accept the self-sacrificial offerings from other religious groups.[30]

26 Zahn, *Another Part of the War*, xi. Zahn remembered that his first contact with Germans occurred while in the ACCO unit at Rosewood. "There was a prisoner of war camp nearby, and those in the camp seemed no different from anyone else to us. We did not frankly feel the great hatred for them that seemed to prevail in the area. I remember that we suggested to the local pastor that he sponsor a Christmas party for the POWs. He simply ignored us" (Cook, "It Takes a Worried Man," 12).

27 Dorothy Day, *Loaves and Fishes* (Harper & Row, 1963), 67–68.

28 Zahn, *Another Part of the War*, 155.

29 Day, *Loaves and Fishes*, 67–68.

30 Zahn, *Another Part of the War*, 157.

As Zahn noted, the ACCO's financial dependence placed the Catholic COs in competition with the others looking for help from the Catholic Worker. In a 1942 appeal letter for the camp, Day wrote: "It is 27-below zero . . . they need socks, sweaters, mufflers at the camp," but she also reminded her readers that "the men on the breadlines need them too."[31] Zahn even recounted needing a winter coat while at the camp and finding one in the grab bag of donations sent from the Catholic Worker. "I was fortunate enough to find a fleece lined woman's coat left behind by a 'pleasantly buxom' (Miss Day's description) young lady," he remembered, "Serviceable despite its quaintness, wearing it made me the object of much camp humor as 'the ghost of Polly.'"[32] All this inevitably led to tensions between the COs who resented being forced to endure "Catholic Worker standards and life style" and camp administrators—all Catholic Workers—who were inclined to interpret the constant complaints by COs as "shocking evidence of selfishness, possibly even insincerity."[33]

Adding to all this was the reality that the Catholic Worker movement was not of a single mind when it came to the ACCO. Taking Dorothy Day's lead, some in the movement made no effort to hide the fact that they did not really approve of the stand taken by the Catholic COs. They regarded the entire CPS program as collaboration with the conscription system and the broader US war effort. Zahn wrote that Day had had little sympathy for the CPS from its inception, favored the "non-registrant's position," and was opposed to any degree of cooperation with the Selective Service in its operation of the conscription program.[34] Day was clear, as Zahn put it, that "a truly authentic witness against the war and conscription called for total noncooperation, beginning with a refusal to register for the draft."[35] However, she did not publicly oppose the efforts of the ACCO.

Dorothy Day was certainly not the only one who felt this way. As the historian Leilah Danielson has noted, many COs at the time viewed the CPS program as a compromise with the draft and an increasingly authoritarian state; as one CO put it, "he who accepts [conscription] is molded by it in its own

31 Zahn, *Another Part of the War*, 50.

32 Zahn, *Another Part of the War*, 72.

33 Zahn, *Another Part of the War*, 156.

34 Zahn, *Catholic Conscientious Objectors*, 23.

35 Zahn, *Another Part of the War*, 36.

image."[36] And indeed, COs had good reason to be skeptical, as many in the US military regarded the CPS as a solution to an annoying wartime problem. In fact, when legislation was introduced in 1943 to eliminate the CO exemption from the conscription law, the director of the Selective Service Administration himself opposed it, arguing that it was far better to simply send COs to out-of-the-way work camps than to have to deal with them in the military. "The CO, by my theory," he declared, "is best handled if no one hears of him."[37]

Beyond their alienation from the church and society (and even the Catholic Worker), the ACCO was also a minority within the CPS. Catholics COs found themselves patronized by some of their CPS counterparts who shared in the belief that a Catholic could not really be a conscientious objector. Zahn recalled that this kind of alienation within the CPS "carried the heaviest load of resentment."[38] Catholic COs were more educated that many of the other COs in the CPS program, and Zahn guessed that this may have been a major reason why they were a "disruptive and dissident element" in the CPS almost from the start.[39] Catholics COs became increasingly disillusioned with the original CPS "bargain" with the military, and their opposition to it took the form of continual rumblings of resentment toward NSBRO. Not surprisingly, ACCO camps were seldom visited by NSBRO leadership. Decades later, Zahn came across an internal NSBRO memo from 1945 titled "the Catholic dope," which reported that the total cost of the Catholic CPS camps was around $45,000, while the total contributions received for their support was just over $3,700. For Zahn, such a large deficit served as "the most fitting summary of the Catholic CPS experience."[40]

CAMP SIMON

With little support from just about anybody, the first ACCO camp opened on August 15, 1941, when sixteen Catholic COs arrived in Stoddard, New

36 Leilah, Danielson, *American Gandhi: A.J. Muste and the History of Radicalism in the Twentieth Century* (University of Pennsylvania Press, 2014), 237.

37 Kiem, *The CPS Story*, 32.

38 Zahn, *Another Part of the War*, xi.

39 Catholic COs were also considerably better educated than men in the US military as well as comparably aged men in the general US population. Zahn did note, however, that Quaker COs were generally the most educated (Zahn, *Catholic Conscientious Objectors*, 87).

40 Zahn, *Another Part of the War*, 44.

Hampshire. The campers quickly christened it "Camp Simon" after Simon the Cyrene who, so they reasoned, had been conscripted to carry Jesus's cross.[41] Zahn arrived to Camp Simon in October 1942, just after the camp had been relocated to Warner.[42] When the camp was shut down in March 1943, Zahn was transferred to the ACCO unit at Rosewood State Training School, where he stayed until he was released from the CPS program in 1946.[43]

While the work was tedious and the food insufficient, Zahn remembered that not all was bad there. There were weekends in Boston, parties and late-night drinking sessions, endless political and theological debates, and even a visit from Smith College students. The COs were also able to sporadically publish a newsletter called *The Catholic C.O.*, which Zahn coedited with Robert Ludlow, who would later become the long-time editor of *The Catholic Worker*.[44] But ultimately, as Zahn would later concede, it became clear almost from the beginning that Camp Simon was doomed to failure. In his memoir on life in the camp, Zahn listed several features of the CPS that frustrated many of the Catholic COs and would eventually lead to the ACCO withdrawal from the CPS program. One, which Day had noted, was that the men were not paid for their work. Zahn recalled that what many of the ACCO leaders saw as "going the second mile" was, in fact, a severe hardship for the COs, especially those with families.[45] The fact that the CPS had originally planned to charge COs a monthly fee of $35 (though it never did) only added to the charges of "slavery" and "injustice" that Zahn remembered hearing—and voicing—at Camp Simon.

There was also an ever-growing concern over the fact that the real authority in the camps was not civilian, as the 1940 draft law had specifically stipulated. As a result, the CPS camps were regarded as simply "isolation camps" designed by the US military to keep COs out of public view. Many of the Catholic COs felt abandoned by NSBRO, who they believed to be largely

41 Zahn noted that the irony that the task Simon was conscripted to perform was that of "sharing Christ's burden on the way to Calvary" was not lost (Zahn, *Another Part of the War*, 23).

42 He described his journey from Milwaukee to Boston in a sleeper-car as the "last luxury I was to enjoy through the courtesy of the U.S. Government and its Selective Service System" (Zahn, *Another Part of the War*, vii).

43 Zahn, "Social Thought of the Catholic Conscientious Objector," in *War, Conscience, and Dissent* (Hawthorn Books, 1967), 163.

44 Ludlow is depicted by Zahn (who used pseudonyms for the various campers) in *Another Part of the War* as the character Lowell Bartlett.

45 Thirteen of the Catholic COs were married, and three had children (Zahn, *Catholic Conscientious Objectors*, 47).

moving toward an all-out collaboration with the military "in a desperate attempt to save some vestige of the alternative service program regardless of the cost."[46] And as time went on and the number of COs assigned to perform alternative service increased, these tensions only increased. The result was that many of the Catholic COs came to regard the ACCO as "stooges" for the government, and some began to engage in work stoppages, while others simply walked out, preferring imprisonment.

As already noted, there were also tensions with the Catholic Worker. Chief among these was the resentment of many COs to what they saw as an unwarranted imposition of Catholic Worker ideals under the duress of conscription.[47] Underlying much of this was the suspicion on the part of camp leadership that the Catholic character of the camp was being threatened, while many of the COs worried that "perfectionist Catholic Worker" values (voluntary poverty and detachment from creature comforts) were being imposed on them. Zahn quoted one camper, a former Catholic Worker in New York City, who recalled that the diet at Camp Simon was worse than "even the usual Catholic Worker standards."[48] Zahn remembered that these grievances eventually led to an almost total collapse of morale at the camp.

This controversy also led to a visit by Dorothy Day—the first time Zahn met her.[49] Zahn explained that for many of the COs, Day's visit provided them with an opportunity to air their grievances to the person they regarded as the "real authority behind the camp" and hear her response. Day met with all the camp and listened to their complaints. Regarding the COs' criticism of the CPS program, Day agreed that the camps were designed to hide them away where they could do no harm and that the work they were doing was indeed useless and stupid—she even described it as approaching the sort of "moral torture"

46 Zahn recalled that it did not help that the chain of command in the camp ran from the ACCO through the NSBRO to the Selective Service Administration (Zahn, *Catholic Conscientious Objectors*, 21).

47 Zahn, *Another Part of the War*, 47. For instance, Zahn recalled that the more personalist form of camp governance, in which campers self-governed and would be ready and willing to do what was needed, shifted due to campers' concerns to a more representative governance structure in which camp procedures and rules were determined by the majority. But when campers voted to empower themselves to mete out their own discipline and elect a new director and assistant director (both of whom had been Catholic Workers selected by Dorothy Day), the camp director resisted and declared that the camp would instead operate under "a sort of functional authoritarianism" (Zahn, *Another Part of the War*, 146).

48 Zahn, *Another Part of the War*, 158.

49 Zahn, *Another Part of the War*, 185.

depicted by Dostoevsky in *The House of the Dead.* When asked if work without pay was slavery, Day simply replied that "all conscription means slavery," and she went onto state her belief that the CPS and the CO classification itself was a compromise with the war effort. Only total noncooperation with the draft, in her mind, offered a true and consistent witness against war and militarism. Day told the campers that she had not been in favor of the Catholic Worker taking responsibility for Camp Simon and had only agreed after others had persuaded her that it would be important to have Catholic representation in the program. Despite these reservations, Day told the men that she respected their decision and believed that they were making a more effective witness than those who had chosen noncombatant duty in the military. Isolated and frustrated as they were, she told them that they could at least enjoy the satisfaction of knowing that they were causing problems for the military, if only in the fact that their very existence challenged the illusion that the whole nation was united in support of the war.

Day also noted the hostility toward the Catholic Worker that she sensed within the camp, which she guessed was the result of the peculiar mix of Catholic and non-Catholic COs, along a suspicion that "Catholic Worker ideas" were being imposed upon them. She told the campers that it was probably a good thing that not all them were Catholic, and that living with these tensions in the camp was preferable to the life in the military, where "there is no thought, no responsibility, no protesting, and people are no longer alive."[50]

While Day assured the men that Catholic Worker ideas should not be imposed upon them—and that ideas should never be imposed on anyone—the financial situation of the Catholic Worker (and therefore that of the camp) did put very real constraints on them. She told the COs that while the Catholic Worker and ACCO were not willing to appeal to outside peace groups for financial support, individual COs were certainly free to do so. She pointed out that the New York Catholic Worker community had a $4,500 debt at that moment (certainly not an unusual situation), and therefore the camp was also in debt. And to that extent, she admitted, the Catholic Worker was imposing its philosophy on them—the camp, like the Catholic Worker, would continue on as it always had by "trusting in God."[51]

50 Zahn, *Another Part of the War*, 187.

51 Day reminded them that sufficient funds could also be harmful, bringing too much ease and satisfaction (Zahn, *Another Part of the War*, 187).

Day's visit did seem to have an impact. Zahn remembered that by the end of the evening, though not all the COs were in complete agreement, Day appeared to have won their admiration. Zahn recalled that Day's critics that evening were at a distinct disadvantage addressing their complaints about their material hardships at the camp to "this plainly garbed practitioner of voluntary poverty."[52] And she had clearly defined the situation at the camp. While the Catholic Worker was not trying to impose anything on anyone, by necessity the ideas and values of voluntary poverty and mutual aid, along with a general willingness to suffer lack of privacy, sufficient food, and other comforts would continue to govern ACCO operations. Campers did not have to share these values, but given the financial situation, they would have to either endure their effects or transfer to a different camp.[53]

ACCO LEAVES CPS

Although Day's visit helped ease tensions between the COs and camp administrators, it did not end the fundamental criticism many of the COs had with the CPS program itself—if anything, Day only threw more fuel onto the fire. When Camp Simon closed in March 1943 and the Catholic COs were sent to other ACCO "special units," they took these criticisms with them. Eventually, this led Sheehan to announce, in the January-March 1946 issue of *The Catholic C.O.*, that the members of the ACCO had voted to withdraw from the NSBRO and cease any further participation in the CPS program.[54] Sheehan explained that the CPS program had "degenerated into a system of punishing a minority under the guise of a democratically given opportunity to fulfill alternative service."[55] While the COs "would rather rot in concentration camps than bear arms in an unjust war," he declared that, "if slavery is the price they must

52 Zahn, *Another Part of the War*, 186.

53 She advised the men that when issues developed between them and the camp administration (she made clear that the ACCO was separate from the Catholic Worker), their best strategy would be to "take up the issues again and again, fight them out, and wear him down until you do change his mind and reach some sort of agreement." Day noted that while the campers complained about the authoritarianism of the camp leadership, others in the CPS had criticized Camp Simon as being too chaotic and even anarchistic (Zahn, *Another Part of the War*, 189).

54 Arthur Sheehan, "CPS 'Collaboration' Repudiated by ACCO," *The Catholic C.O.* (January-March 1946): 1–2.

55 In so doing, he warned that they had established a precedent whereby other minorities could be likewise punished through "enforced and unpaid labor" under the direction of "those most interested in silencing their voices."

pay for conscience's sake, let us not disguise that fact!" Sheehan went onto accuse NSBRO of working to ensure the program's success by "cushioning and absorbing" any protest within the camps.

Writing in the same issue, Zahn pointed out that the move to withdraw from the CPS had originated with the COs at Rosewood, where he was serving as the ACCO liaison.[56] He declared (borrowing a phrase from Day), the men of the ACCO had "gone on record" stating:

1) We believe that CPS is basically unjust and undeserving of the support of any pacifist group;
2) we regret that our organization ever cooperated in the institution of this unjust program, and we are ashamed that we permitted it to continue in the program until so late a date;
3) because it is basically unjust, we shall oppose all efforts to ever again establish such a program.

Zahn then challenged other camps to follow the ACCO and withdraw from the CPS.

The issue ended with an unsigned editorial pleading for support to build an organization that would actively spread the "philosophy" of the Catholic conscientious objectors, to continue to publish *The Catholic C.O.*, and to promote other educational efforts that would bring "our stand" to the attention of those who have never bothered to consider their support of the nation-state in light of the standards of Catholic morality. The editorial concluded:

> Those of us who have carried the ball for the ACCO through the last few years are now throwing it back. Many of us are willing and anxious to continue in 'the cause'; it is for those who were not called upon to take the stand themselves to help make this possible. Years of labor without pay have drained our material resources making it impossible for us to carry on by ourselves; years of effort without response from those we believed were with us makes it seem hardly worthwhile to make an attempt to do so. Now it's up to you!

56 The Rosewood COs' recommendation was passed to Sheehan, who favored the move but felt that all men in ACCO should have a say in the matter. COs in the four ACCO units (Glendora, Alexian, Mancos, and Rosewood) were contacted and, with a decisive 3–1 majority (three of the units voted unanimously), voted for withdrawal. See Zahn, "An Open Challenge," *The Catholic C.O.* (January-March 1946): 3.

As Zahn would learn, such a postwar Catholic peace organization would not soon emerge. Indeed, in a reply to Zahn's request for support for such an effort, Archbishop Michael Curley of Baltimore and Washington declared:

> I see no real purpose in trying to build up a postwar organization of the A.C.C.O.s in view of the fact that we have supplied more Catholics than might be expected out of the total population to the war and, therefore there is very little left to emphasize in the matter of the A.C.C.O. In a population of over twenty-five million, the group would be small and the Catholic men coming home from the fields of Europe and from the land and sea of the South Pacific would not be in any humor to accept the philosophy of the Conscientious Objectors.[57]

Decades later, Zahn would hold up this letter as evidence of the degree to which the church's attitudes on war and conscientious objection had dramatically changed in the intervening years.

CONCLUSION

For Zahn, the experience at Camp Simon was influential. It opened his eyes to the reality that he was not the only Catholic pacifist. He not only met other pacifists but also realized that Catholic pacifism was possible (though not popular). The period marked a crystallization of the argument to which Zahn would be dedicated for the remainder of his life: that a Catholic can be a pacifist. While he had certainly been thinking about these issues before arriving in New Hampshire in 1943, Zahn's time in the ACCO—particularly the endless discussions with other COs—clearly went a long way in helping him clarify and solidify his thinking. This experience also left Zahn much more radicalized in his view of the United States. No longer optimistic about the United States as a defender of liberty and freedom, Zahn's writings at the camp manifested a much more critical view of US political institutions. Rather than defenders of religious freedom, Zahn began to regard them as nationalist and militaristic institutions that worked to silence dissent.

At Camp Simon, not coincidentally, Zahn met and developed life-long friendships with other Catholics who also embraced this more radical view of

57 Curley to Zahn in a letter dated February 6, 1945, (CPF Zahn papers).

the United States, such as Robert Ludlow and Robert Hovda.[58] Zahn was also introduced to the Catholic Worker movement (at the time the lone source of Catholic pacifist thought in the country), its paper, and its Catholic pacifist writers, including Paul Hanly Furfey, John Hugo, and Franz Stratmann, OP. And it was at Camp Simon that Zahn first met Dorothy Day. These were the figures and ideas that would continue to shape Zahn's life and work.

58 Hovda was one of only a handful of Protestants at Camp Simon, but he would convert to Catholicism and was ordained a priest in Fargo, North Dakota. Later, Hovda became known as one of the foremost liturgists in the United States, and his column "Amen Corner" appeared regularly in *Orates Frates* (now *Worship*). Zahn wrote an obituary for his long-time friend in *The Catholic Worker* (June 15, 1992). In *Another Part of the War*, Hovda is depicted as Robert Langner.

3

SUPERNATURAL SOCIOLOGY

> *It seemed a wonderful thing to me that priests and laity could still become excited about points of doctrine, about nature and the supernatural, nature and grace, about forces, spiritual capacities far more powerful than the atomic bomb.*
>
> *—Dorothy Day*[1]

In *If I Had a Hammer: The Death of the Old Left and the Birth of the New Left*, Maurice Isserman described conscientious objectors being gradually released from CPS camps or prison after the end of World War II,

> There were no brass bands or ticker tape parades for them, no GI Bill providing jobless benefits or scholarships. The newly released conscientious objectors huddled together for companionship, and some began to apply the lessons they had learned in prison to the outside world.[2]

This was certainly true of Zahn. He remembered his release from the CPS in 1946 as an important crossroads in his life. He faced the choice of either returning to his former life in Milwaukee or taking an uncharted course toward something new. At Camp Simon, Zahn had engaged with various "radicals"

1 Dorothy Day, *The Long Loneliness* (Sheed & Ward, 1952), 258.

2 Isserman, *If I Had a Hammer*, 134.

whose critiques of US society and culture went far beyond anything he had heard before. This experience provided him with new insights and strengthened his "dedication to peace action and objectives."[3] The thought of going back to his old life seemed less attractive.

Zahn had also been a part of what he later termed the "intellectual clique" at Camp Simon, and he was impressed by the several college graduates (including two PhDs) in this group. This led Zahn, along with another fellow camper named Richard Leonard, to forgo returning to Milwaukee and instead apply to college.[4] Robert Hovda, yet another former camper, suggested that Zahn and Leonard apply to St. John's University in Minnesota, where financial aid was being given to COs at the same rate as returning GIs: full tuition scholarships and work study jobs.[5] They were both accepted, and Zahn took a job at the Benedictine liturgical magazine *Orate Fratres*.

Arriving on campus after their experience in the ACCO, Zahn and Leonard felt no need to keep their pacifism a secret. This put the two COs in tension with many of their fellow students who had served in the war, as well as with the former military chaplains on faculty.[6] For instance, Zahn continued to edit *The Catholic C.O.* at St. John's, and when a new issue came out that fall, one of his Benedictine professors, who was also a former military chaplain, held it up to his philosophy class (with Zahn sitting there), derided it an example of "tabloid thinking," and scolded Zahn for the issue's "anticlerical" contents.[7] Zahn also recalled that his professor, in a course called "Moral Guidance," had declared during a lecture that "a Catholic could not have been a conscientious objector in the last war"—a statement that also appeared as a true-false question on a course exam.[8] Zahn later learned that this same Benedictine had accused him

3 Zahn, 1994, 31.

4 Leonard also went onto to become a sociology professor and is depicted in *Another Part of the War* as William O'Flaherty.

5 Zahn, 1994, 32.

6 Zahn reported that a Benedictine faculty member who had served as an US Army chaplain during the war had stated in his lectures that he found "no evidence of direct persecution of the Catholic church under the Nazi regime." See Mark Ruff, *The Battle for the Catholic Past in Germany 1945–1980* (Cambridge University Press, 2017), 126n33.

7 Zahn, 1994, 33.

8 Zahn, *Catholic Conscientious Objectors*, 8.

and Leonard as being "disruptive elements" on campus and blamed them for inviting Dorothy Day to speak at St. John's that semester.[9]

Day's visit to St. John's in the fall of 1946 had, in fact, caused enough of a stir to instigate a campus-wide discussion on the church's teaching on pacifism and conscientious objection. As a result, the February 1947 issue of the *St. John's Quarterly* included an essay by Zahn in defense of "Catholic Pacifism."[10] Zahn opened by explaining that he was focused on those situations in which a Catholic was called upon to participate in an unjust war and therefore to commit an immoral act—situations in which "a Catholic *must be* a conscientious objector."[11]

Zahn then made it clear that he regarded the US effort in World War II as having violated the just-war criteria. In fact, he argued that the techniques of modern warfare (including the saturation bombings, starvation blockades, and controlled information and propaganda) meant that no modern war could be reconciled with the Catholic just-war teaching, and thus he declared that all Catholics should be conscientious objectors to all modern wars. As evidence, he pointed to the US attempts to provoke Japanese aggression through "economic strangulation" as a violation of the criteria that a just war must be a response only to unprovoked aggression. He asked if the starvation and sufferings in postwar Europe (not to mention the threat of Soviet totalitarianism that took the place of the Nazi fascism) outweighed whatever good the war produced: "is it possible that all this evil fruit has come forth from a good tree, the good tree of the theoretical just war?"[12]

Zahn also challenged the teaching in Catholic moral theology that Catholics must submit to their nation's legitimate authority and grant it a "presumption of justice" in times of war. This long-standing imperative had been summed up in a booklet published by the Catholic Association for International Peace before the war:

9 Zahn suggested that Day was already "a much revered and long-time friend of the St. John's and many of its monks and the lay faculty" (Zahn, 1994, 33).

10 Gordon Zahn, "Catholic Pacifism," *St. John's Quarterly* (February 1947).

11 He highlighted two main stands taken by Catholic COs during the war: those who subscribed to the "traditional" just-war theory and those who made their objection "under the acceptance of the Gospel counsels of perfection" (Zahn, "Catholic Pacifism," 20, 37–38).

12 Zahn, "Catholic Pacifism," 38.

> It is primarily the duty of the powers of government to see to it that the requisite justifying conditions be fulfilled before war is entered upon. But the conscience of the individual soldier is not, in consequence, entirely exonerated. If the soldiers are conscripted or have voluntarily enlisted prior to the outbreak of the war, they are ordinarily not obliged to inquire into the justice of the war. They may presume that their country is in the right unless it is evidently in the wrong, and in doubt they must obey the commands of their lawful superiors. But if the war is clearly unjust, the only course that is open to the individual soldier, provided he cannot evade military service, is to refrain from inflicting injury on the enemy; otherwise, as is evident, he becomes a co-operator in injustice. It will seldom happen, however, that the private soldier will be in a position to declare the war undoubtedly unjust, because of his ignorance of many facts and considerations known frequently only to the country's highest officials.[13]

Zahn maintained that this teaching failed to recognize the realities of the modern nation-state. The "days of the Christian prince" no longer applied, he asserted, for no modern secular state—"certainly not our own"—regards itself as being guided by principles of Catholic moral theology.

More importantly, though, this teaching also ignored the reality that Catholics on both sides of a conflict were taught to submit to their respective nation's legitimate authority. "Can we say (as our opponents must)," Zahn asked, "that because a German brother had no valid factual reason whatsoever to doubt the cause proclaimed 'just' by his rulers, he was following his Christian obligation in supporting the Nazi war effort?"[14] If so, Zahn lamented that it was "a strange distortion of the beautiful doctrine of the Mystical Body" to teach "that fellow-members in Christ become obliged by His law to war against each other." These arguments were not welcomed by many at St. John's.

Not surprisingly, at the end of their first year, Zahn and Leonard were informed by the dean that they had upset many of the Catholic veterans on

13 Cyprian Emanuel, OFM, *The Ethics of War* (The Catholic Association for International Peace, 1932), 54. In the CAIP booklet he wrote on conscientious objection (cited above), Emanuel also wrote, "May we not, nay more, *must* we not, presume our country to be in the right unless it is evidently in the wrong, and in doubt are we not obliged to obey the commands of our legitimate superiors? . . . To these and to all questions of a similar nature, there can be but one answer—an emphatic affirmative" (Emanuel, *The Morality of Conscientious Objection*, 33).

14 Zahn, "Catholic Pacifism," 38.

campus—including fourteen Benedictines on the faculty. On behalf of the abbot, the dean asked that the two COs not return the following semester in order to let things cool down.[15] When Zahn and Leonard returned in the fall anyway and offered to pay their own tuition, the matter was referred to the full Benedictine community. While the Benedictines at St. John's were deliberating their fate, Zahn and Leonard spent two nights sleeping in a school bus since they had been banned from the residence halls.[16] In the end, their supporters (including the liturgist Godfrey Diekmann, OSB, and his brother Conrad) capitulated for the sake of the community. Zahn and Leonard were told they could not return to St. John's.[17] Looking back decades later, Zahn wrote that even with such an ending, he had always considered that single year at St. John's to be something of a "commitment year" during which (for better and worse) he came to experience "Catholicism in its fullest sense."[18] The two COs quickly transferred to the College of St. Thomas in nearby St. Paul, Minnesota, where Eugene McCarthy, the future Senator and antiwar candidate during the 1968 Democratic presidential primary, had recently become chair of the sociology department after himself leaving St. John's. Zahn and Leonard graduated from St. Thomas "with honors" (and without incident) in 1949.

THE CATHOLIC UNIVERSITY OF AMERICA

After graduation, Zahn and Leonard moved to Washington, DC, to begin graduate studies in sociology at the Catholic University of America (CUA). "By this time," Zahn later wrote, "I had decided that to really do an effective job of promoting Catholic pacifism, I would need a Ph.D. and a college professorship as a 'prestige' asset."[19] The chair of the sociology department at CUA at the time

15 Some of the Benedictines also objected to the two COs' "spiritual pride" and hypercritical attitude toward religion and the priesthood (Ruff, *The Battle for the Catholic Past in Germany*, 127n37).

16 Michael Gallagher, *Laws of Heaven: Catholic Activists Today* (New York: Ticknor & Fields, 1992), 248.

17 Zahn reported that the noted historian Emerson Hynes, on faculty at the time, was also one of their supporters (Zahn, 1994, 33).

18 In 1982, Zahn received the Pax Christi Award from St. John's University with a citation that read in part: "You have witnessed and reminded us again and again that Christianity is a spiritual way. The signals you send have helped invite the Benedictines back to their roots, and forward in our common search for peace" (Zahn, 1994, 33).

19 Zahn, 1988, 6.

was Paul Hanly Furfey. Zahn had first been introduced to Furfey by Robert Ludlow and Paul Mundy, another Camp Simon CO who would later become Zahn's colleague at Loyola.[20] Furfey arranged for Zahn and Leonard to receive fellowships to cover tuition, and an "activist nun" arranged for them to board with a local family who were part of Washington's "black aristocracy."[21] Zahn remembered seeing the racism their hosts encountered daily.[22] Zahn also got a part-time job at recently elected Eugene McCarthy's congressional office in DC. McCarthy and Zahn remained friends, and Zahn would later be the godfather of one of McCarthy's children.[23]

Beyond the fact that it brought him under the influence of Furfey, it was significant that Zahn came to the university when he did. The Catholic University of America had been the first Catholic institution of higher education to establish a sociology department in 1895. Early Catholic sociologists such as William J. Kerby (1870–1936), who helped start the department at CUA, approached the academic study of social problems from the point of view of social reform—what at the time was cutting edge Catholic sociology. In his entry for "Sociology" in the 1912 *Catholic Encyclopedia*, for example, Kerby wrote, "Sociology can scarcely avoid interpretation and direction of human conduct and hence it can hardly be expected to avoid taking very definite attitudes towards the Christian outlook on life."[24] As C. Joseph Nuesse (a former sociology professor and provost at CUA) pointed out, Kerby described this as "concrete sociology" and he built the department at CUA for the preparation of professionals to work in Catholic charities and other social reform organizations.[25] When Furfey became chair in 1934, interest among Catholics in

20 Zahn, 1994, 32. In *Another Part of the War*, Mundy is portrayed as William Grandman.

21 Zahn was awarded a Sellew Fellowship for 1949–50, as he worked on his MA, and Knights of Columbus Fellowships for 1950–51 and 1951–52 as he completed his PhD.

22 As Zahn recalled, "Both Dick and I had rejected racial injustice and discrimination long before we met in camp; now we found full confirmation of our position and strengthened our commitment in our Washington experience" (Zahn, 1994, 36).

23 McCarthy was elected to Congress in 1948. For more on McCarthy and his connections to the Catholic Worker, see William Collinge, "'You Say You Want a Green Revolution?' Eugene and Abigail McCarthy and Catholic Agrarianism," in *You Say You Want a Revolution?": 1968–2018 in Theological Perspective*, ed. Susie Paulik Babka, Elena Procario-Foley, and Sandra Yocum (Orbis Books, 2019), 120–34.

24 William J. Kerby, "Sociology," in *The Catholic Encyclopedia*, vol. XIII (Robert Appleton Co., 1912), 117.

25 C. Joseph Nuesse, "'Catholic Sociology': Memoir of a Mid-Century Controversy," *US Catholic Historian* 16, no. 3 (Summer 1998): 100.

sociological research and theory had begun to dramatically increase as the so-called "Social Question" inspired the promulgation of papal "social encyclicals," which captured the Catholic imagination. By the time Zahn arrived at CUA in 1949, the connection between sociology and social reform had been well-established—sociology was clearly regarded as a tool for building a better society. This was the approach to sociology that formed Zahn.

ZAHN'S THESIS

In 1950, Zahn defended his master's thesis, titled *A Study of the Social Backgrounds of Catholic Conscientious Objectors in Civilian Public Service During World War II.*[26] In justifying his topic, Zahn explained that US Catholics were largely unaware that a Catholic could even be a conscientious objector, let alone that there were Catholic COs in World War II.[27] While his research presented a "descriptive analysis" of the backgrounds of his fellow Catholic COs, he hoped that it would also establish the fact that there had been such opposition to the war by US Catholics and that such opposition was based upon sound principles in Catholic moral theology.[28] He further hoped that his research would call attention to "an unusual but significant" part of US Catholic history.[29] Although 135 Catholic COs might appear insignificant within the context of the overwhelming support that US Catholics had shown for the war effort, Zahn explained that numbers could be misleading. He pointed out that Christian history clearly illustrated what the work of a small inspired group (even as few as twelve, he noted) could do in "converting and overcoming a pagan world." The Catholic COs in World War II, Zahn wrote, believed they

26 Thomas Harte, CSsR, was his "major professor" and Furfey his "reader." Harte (1914–1974) was a Redemptorist priest and member of the CUA sociology department from 1947–1974. He was also the president of the American Catholic Sociological Society in 1951. Much of his published research dealt with Catholic parish life.

27 Zahn noted that like his own experience before the draft board, Catholic COs were met with opposition, particularly from Catholic board members. He quoted the minutes of one draft board meeting during which a priest on the board told a young CO: "There is no choice, and our lives and freedom are at stake; if you have been reading the Scriptures, you must have been mis-interpreting them" (Zahn, *Catholic Conscientious Objectors*, 8).

28 Zahn, *Catholic Conscientious Objectors*, 9.

29 Zahn, *Catholic Conscientious Objectors*, 6.

were "renewing and continuing that work" and were an example to inspire future generations of Catholics.[30]

For the bulk of his research, Zahn combed through the personnel folders of his fellow Catholic COs who had been assigned to CPS program during the war. The folders contained personal information that each CO had submitted to the Selective Service Administration, along with their completed questionnaire—the same questionnaire that Zahn completed when he submitted his application in 1942. Zahn also used the records of the ACCO, which he described as a "few scattered letters and reports" sent to him by the Catholic Worker, as well articles sporadically published between 1943 and 1948 in *The Catholic C.O.*

Zahn described the Catholic COs he studied as having taken a clear "religious stand," and therefore, they should be regarded as "a religious phenomenon." This was in contrast to the overwhelming majority of Catholics who supported the US war effort for nationalistic or other nonreligious reasons.[31] That said, Zahn emphasized that each CO was essentially "a minority of one against the world"—lacking any official blessing from their church, let alone any of the formation in the kind of "non-conformist culture" that COs from more traditional "peace churches" had received. Each Catholic CO, therefore (and this was certainly the case with Zahn), necessarily arrived at his position by his own "personal route" and so very much "stood alone" in his objection to the war.[32]

Even within this small group, though, Zahn identified four "types" of Catholic COs: "perfectionists," "traditionalists," "pacifists," and "integralists." The perfectionists (a group that numbered about sixteen) based their objection to the war on a particular reading of what were referred to as "counsels of perfection" found in the Gospels and the application of these counsels in their daily lives.[33] Accordingly, these COs believed that Catholics were called

30 Zahn, *Catholic Conscientious Objectors*, 16.

31 Zahn, *Catholic Conscientious Objectors*, 45, 91.

32 Zahn pointed out that while some supportive groups such as the Catholic Worker existed, according to their draft statements, each individual Catholic considered his stand to be the result of independent decision and action (Zahn, *Catholic Conscientious Objectors*, 28).

33 He quoted one such CO as having stated: "I believe it is my duty to follow the counsels of perfection as outlined by our Lord in His Sermon on the Mount." Zahn explained that he used the term "perfectionist" because it had become the term generally used most often in materials written by and about Catholic COs, but he also noted that there was a tendency to employ the term to dismiss or marginalize a group or action as unrealistic or impractical (Zahn, *Catholic Conscientious Objectors*, 31n2).

to go beyond the justifications of the just-war theory and instead follow a "supernatural ethic" of love toward one's enemies, nonviolence, and even a martyr's death. Zahn pointed out that this position was particularly prevalent among COs associated with the Catholic Worker.[34]

Another nineteen or so COs based their objection on the church's traditional just-war teaching, and Zahn labeled them "traditionalists."[35] Many of these COs pointed to specific conditions of a just war that they believed had been violated by the United States in World War II.[36] Zahn noted that while many in this group did not reject the "perfectionist" argument, they regarded the "traditionalist" stand as more orthodox in its theology and so better able to attract a greater acceptance among Catholics.[37] This can be seen as a primary reason Zahn never fully dismissed the church's just-war tradition (or those who took it seriously) despite the grave reservations he had with it. Zahn also pointed to a subgroup of the traditionalists that he called simply "pacifists," who had expanded their objection to regard all modern wars as unjust.[38]

The largest type of COs at the camp (around fifty-six) were labeled as "integralists"—a group Zahn acknowledged to have been the most difficult to define.[39] These COs did not base their objection on any notions of Christian perfection, nor did they make any formal appeals to just-war theory or natural law. Rather, Zahn explained that the recurrent theme that ran throughout their statements was their unshakable belief that war was "just not right" and that

34 "Perfectionists" was a term often used to describe figures such as John Hugo, Pacifique Roy, SSJ, and Onesimus Lacouture, SJ, priests who preached "the retreat" that Day memorialized in *The Long Loneliness*. See Benjamin Peters, *Called to be Saints: John Hugo, the Catholic Worker, and a Theology of Radical Christianity* (Marquette University Press, 2016). For the connection of Eugene McCarthy, JF Powers, and others to this current in US Catholicism, see Garry Wills, "Relicts of a Catholic Renaissance," *New York Review of Books*, October 10, 2013, 37–38.

35 Zahn, *Catholic Conscientious Objectors*, 31.

36 Zahn again pointed to the CAIP booklet, *The Morality of Conscientious Objection to War*, as a source for this position.

37 Though he was careful to say that this position was not any more "Catholic" than any other (Zahn, *Catholic Conscientious Objectors*, 70).

38 As one such CO wrote with regard to the just-war tenets: "it is not possible that any modern war could be fought wherein one side would fulfill all these conditions" (Zahn, *Catholic Conscientious Objectors*, 34).

39 Zahn quoted one such CO: "Until the Catholic Church condemns war with the same finality and absolutism as it condemns birth control, divorce, etc., I am afraid Catholics will go on slaughtering each other as they have been doing for a long time now" (Zahn, *Catholic Conscientious Objectors*, 74).

the "spirit of war" was directly antithetical to the "spirit of Christianity."[40] Zahn saw it as unfortunate that these COs were not as inclined as others to participate in camp discussions, since there was therefore very little written evidence to explain their position. As a result, the integralist stance had often been dismissed by other COs as insufficiently Catholic.[41] Though he did not indicate this explicitly, Zahn's position clearly fell into this integralist category when he arrived at Camp Simon.

The term "integralists" was in reference the "integrating force" and "unifying effect" of the Mystical Body of Christ, which was the underlying principle for these COs' objection—an insistence that war was tearing apart of the Mystical Body.[42] As the theologian Timothy Gabrielli has noted, this notion of the Mystical Body of Christ was very much in the Catholic imagination at the time. In the United States, its chief promulgator was the Benedictine (and regular contributor to *The Catholic Worker*) Virgil Michel.[43]

Zahn recalled that there had been a distinct tendency among the Catholic COs during their time in the CPS to gravitate either toward the "perfectionist" or the "pacifist" types.[44] While the immorality of the modern means of war was mentioned by only a few COs, he remembered from his own experience that the "ever-increasing intensity of the war and its techniques of destruction" had led more and more of the COs to the position that all modern war ("and great stress was placed on the adjective") was "intrinsically evil" by virtue of the means employed. As he later wrote, "One did not need to be a finished

40 Despite these differences, Zahn highlighted the fact that there was a "deep emotional strain" among all the Catholic COs: "Reason was present and operating, but the basis upon which it operated was a distinct refusal to participate in the destruction of human life" (Zahn, *Catholic Conscientious Objectors*, 65).

41 Zahn, *Catholic Conscientious Objectors*, 73.

42 This sort of integralism was very different than the type that had been employed by Charles Maurras and other earlier twentieth-century European advocates of a greater connection between altar and throne. John Milbank refers to this latter group as "integrists." See John Milbank, *Theology and Social Theory: Beyond Secular Reason* (Blackwell, 1990), 206.

43 Timothy R. Gabrielli, *One in Christ: Virgil Michel, Louis-Marie Chauvet, and Mystical Body Theology* (Liturgical Press, 2017).

44 Zahn also reported that another thirty COs fell into a "humanitarian" type that stressed the antihumanitarian aspects of war and its rejection of the universality of humanity, though without the "integralist" emphasis on the Mystical Body. And the rest of the COs fell into one of six "individual" positions, including those who made their objection on political or economic reasons such as the followers of Charles Coughlin ("Coughlinites" and "Christian Fronters") and others opposed to the United States being an ally of the Soviet Union, as well as those who objected based upon personal revelations (such as, that President Roosevelt was the anti-Christ).

product of Scholastic philosophy to see evil in civilian saturation bombings, starvation blockades, or even in hate-inspiring propaganda and untruths."

This kind of shifting of positions also displayed the degree to which Catholics COs in the ACCO had learned from each other about nuances in Catholic teaching on war—many, like Zahn, for the very first time. It also revealed the crystallization of conscience that had occurred for many during their time in the camp. Zahn described an atmosphere of constant discussion around Catholic teachings on war and conscientious objection that prevailed throughout his wartime experience as naturally leading to a refinement of positions.[45] He quoted one Catholic CO's description of his time in the ACCO as "a hellish heaven or a heavenish hell," with members continuously preoccupied with theology and spending all their time off duty—and considerable time while on duty—discussing papal encyclicals and other theological issues. As was certainly the case with Zahn, time in the ACCO was very formative for these young Catholics.

In his thesis, Zahn made it clear that despite their differences, all the Catholic COs were united on one central point: their rejection of modern war.[46] He also highlighted the fact that their opposition to the very popular US military campaign in World War II was just one part of a broader social philosophy for this collection of "non-conforming Catholics," and that their "radicalism" could also be seen in other areas of social and moral concern.[47] He pointed to various topics covered in pages of *The Catholic C.O.*: Gandhian thought, Catholic Action, anticlericalism, anarchy, racism, anti-Semitism, labor relations (including an exposé on the exploitation of employees at Maryland's mental health institutions, where many of the COs worked during the war), as well as Personalist philosophy. For Zahn, these were examples of social engagement that went far beyond merely refusing to support the nation's war effort. Indeed, he argued that for most of these Catholic COs, their objection to

45 Zahn pointed out that the April-June 1944 issue of *The Catholic C.O.* had also attempted to place Catholic COs into different categories. One was called "The Natural Law" position, which Zahn argued corresponded with his "traditionalist" type; another, "Church Doctrine," mirrored his "pacifist" type; while "The Counsels" corresponded to his "perfectionist" type. Zahn suggested that the fact that *The Catholic C.O.* left out the largest group, his "integralists," pointed to this kind of crystallization.

46 Zahn defined "modern war" in Zahn, *Catholic Conscientious Objectors*, 61.

47 Zahn, *Catholic Conscientious Objectors*, 92.

war was only one manifestation of their entire moral commitment.[48] This was certainly what would have made the integralist position attractive to Zahn.

As we can see, Zahn's scholarship clearly revealed a strong activist bent. By recognizing these Catholic COs, Zahn was not only holding them up as examples for future generations but also presenting them as Catholics whose critique of the United States went far beyond war. And Zahn would continue to return to these World War II-era COs as models for how Catholics could more critically engage with the US society and culture.

HIS DISSERTATION

The idea of employing sociology to improve society was further displayed in Zahn's PhD dissertation, titled *A Descriptive Study of the Social Backgrounds of Conscientious Objectors in Civilian Public Service During World War II*.[49] Zahn opened with some historical context on the COs he studied. While support for the US campaign in World War II appeared overwhelming, it was certainly not total. In fact, Zahn explained that prior to the Japanese attack on Pearl Harbor in December 1941, there existed a variety of strong movements opposing US involvement in the war. The most powerful of these were anti-interventionist (or "isolationist") elements, the largest and best organized of which was the America First Committee. Zahn noted that the anti-interventionist position was supported by the majority of Americans prior to Pearl Harbor.[50] He highlighted the fact that the US entry into the war was also opposed by an antiwar movement that had emerged in the United States after World War I. Disheartened by the failure of antiwar groups in Europe, the US antiwar movement remained determined to resist and oppose US involvement in the war and militarism more broadly. Perhaps to acknowledge his own involvement within the America

48 Zahn quoted the head of the ACCO in 1946: "In the last six years, in the steady stream of letters that have poured in to the ACCO, we have noted one phenomenon, namely that the objectors to war of every political and religious hue were agreed that something must be done to reform the social order and that that something must start with themselves—even if, as they often were, the only persons in their home town who dared to be different" (Zahn, *Catholic Conscientious Objectors*, 96).

49 Gordon Zahn, *A Descriptive Study of the Social Backgrounds of Conscientious Objectors in Civilian Public Service During World War II* (PhD diss., The Catholic University of America, 1953). Harte was again listed as his "major professor," while Furfey and Mary Elizabeth Walsh served as his readers.

50 Zahn, *A Descriptive Study*, 6. The fact that the war did not have the overwhelming support from the so called "Greatest Generation" as popular depictions of the "Good War" have often portrayed, has been more recently advanced by scholars such as Elizabeth Samet, *Looking for the Good War: American Amnesia and the Violent Pursuit of Happiness* (Farrer, Straus & Giroux, 2021).

First Committee, Zahn suggested that as the "Great Debate" raged in the United States between the interventionists and the anti-interventionists, those in the antiwar camp were "virtually forced" to join the anti-interventionist side since it had at least shared the same minimum goal of continued peace, albeit for very different reasons.

The attacks on Pearl Harbor essentially "destroyed" any organized opposition to the war.[51] Almost immediately afterward, Zahn observed, most Americans, whether interventionists or anti-interventionists, came together and found agreement on what became an "irreducible core of the consensus" in support of the US war effort and its conscription program: "war had come and victory had to be its outcome."[52] The upshot was that after Pearl Harbor, only the antiwar element remained in opposition. Even that group was greatly diminished, Zahn explained, as "peacetime pacifists" quickly decided supporting the fight against the Axis powers was more attractive than resisting war.[53] And so, in the end only the "wartime pacifists" remained standing in opposition.

"ENCOURAGED" AND "RESISTER"

In his dissertation, Zahn defined pacifism as "any opposition to war that is based on some higher principle or principles than mere personal expediency."[54] Unlike the more restrictive definition in the 1940 US draft law, he argued that his definition was broad enough to include "many degrees of pacifism," ranging from particular opposition to World War II to broader opposition to all modern war, as well as "the extreme position" of opposing all war in

51 Zahn, *A Descriptive Study*, 4.

52 Zahn, *A Descriptive Study*, 5.

53 Zahn placed most US Catholics into this "peacetime pacifist" group. He pointed to a 1939 poll of Catholic college students in *America*, in which 35 percent reported that they would be COs and 56 percent of all readers stated that they would be COs. These pre-Pearl Harbor results, Zahn noted, contrasted with the fact that there were only 135 Catholic COs in the CPS program during World War II (Zahn, *A Descriptive Study*, 9).

54 He did acknowledge that his definition differed from the one common among COs in the CPS, which restricted "pacifist" to those men who opposed all war (and all forms of violence), and he used the term "conscientious objector" for those who opposed particular wars or programs of violence. "Thus, all pacifists would be conscientious objectors, but the reverse would not be true" (Zahn, *A Descriptive Study*, 11).

general.[55] Accordingly, he defined "conscientious objectors" as pacifists who were "obliged to take a more active stand in opposition" to war by gaining recognition from the government or by refusing to comply with its orders if such recognition were denied."[56] This definition included those who accepted noncombatant duty (I-A-O) as well as those who were sent to prison—Zahn called these COs "social deviants *par excellence*."[57] But it was on those COs who were assigned "work of national importance under civilian direction" (IV-E)—his group—that Zahn focused his dissertation research.[58] This research entailed looking though a sample of 980 draft board files included in the Selective Service's records held at the National Archives in Washington, DC.

As with his master's thesis, Zahn categorized these COs into four groups: "peace church," "other religious affiliation," "independent," and "Jehovah's Witness."[59] While he employed these categories throughout his dissertation, Zahn suggested that ultimately the COs he studied could simply be divided into two broader categories: "encouraged" and "resister." The "encouraged" were those who took their stand against the war with encouragement from their religious community, or perhaps even in response to pressures from that community.[60] This category included a continuum of COs, from those whose actions were prescribed by an established religious creed to those whose actions were at least tolerated by their church. In contrast, the "resisters" included COs who made their objection without any encouragement or support from any religious body, any formal religious tenet, or even any vague religious

55 While this definition was also open to a variety of criticisms, Zahn noted that the Selective Training and Service Act of 1940 limited CO status (and thus the definition of pacifism) to those who opposed "all war" based only on "religious training and belief." He noted that this excluded Jehovah's Witnesses who would fight in a divinely-mandated war (Zahn, *A Descriptive Study*, 10–11, 20).

56 Conscientious objectors therefore included pacifists who "(a) refused to register or to cooperate with the conscription program in any respect, (b) registered and requested and received one of the classifications established for men claiming conscientious objection to either combatant or noncombatant military service, or (c) registered and requested but were denied such classification and refused to comply with the subsequent orders to perform some acts leading to induction into military service" (Zahn, *A Descriptive Study*, 13–14).

57 Zahn, *A Descriptive Study*, 23–24. Zahn pointed out that the military referred to the I-A-O group as "conscientious cooperators" (Zahn, *A Descriptive Study*, 14, 20).

58 Zahn pointed out that he had been "conscripted participant" in the CPS from October 1942 to April 1946 (Zahn, *A Descriptive Study*, 53).

59 Zahn, *A Descriptive Study*, 80.

60 Zahn, *A Descriptive Study*, 69.

principles. This group also included a continuum of COs, from those who faced (either directly or indirectly) "displeasure" from their religious community to those whose objection appeared to violate the recognized moral norms of their church.[61]

Zahn argued that these encouraged and resister categories were perhaps most helpful for recognizing the degree of "deviance" that many of the COs exhibited. For instance, while all the COs deviated from the broader wartime consensus in US society, encouraged COs conformed to their religious community, while resisters conformed neither to US society nor their religious community. He suggested that these categories could also be used to understand many of the objections to the Civilian Public Service program from COs like himself. For the CPS—established by "peace church" conscientious objectors in NSBRO—had been clearly designed for encouraged COs, and therefore it was inherently problematic for resisters.[62] What this meant was that an encouraged CO from a peace church appreciated that the CPS allowed him to meet his religious duty while at the same time not violate any of his nation's laws. In contrast, the resister CO viewed the entire conscription system as an essential component to the evils of war and so saw the CPS as enabling "willing collaboration" with that system.[63] Looking ahead, Zahn guessed that the numbers of encouraged COs to future wars would inevitably grow smaller while the number of resisters would grow larger. In light of that, he recommended (perhaps too optimistically) that any future CPS program address the resisters' concerns and assign COs to civilian agencies, free from any military oversight, which would allow them to do actual "work of national importance."

For Zahn, these categories were also helpful for understanding Catholic COs, in particular. He saw them as clearly falling into the resister category—since they faced both the pressure of the broader US wartime consensus *and* the "generally unsympathetic, and often overtly hostile, attitudes" of their church.[64] While opposition to Catholic COs never translated into any official

61 Zahn, *A Descriptive Study*, 284.

62 Zahn, *A Descriptive Study*, 295.

63 Zahn, *A Descriptive Study*, 295–96.

64 He again pointed out that there was an abundance of evidence to show that during the war, Catholics, both laity and clergy, were unfamiliar with the fact that there was such a thing as a Catholic pacifist opposition to the war or that a Catholic even had a right to be a CO—let alone that any Catholic who believed the war to be unjust was obligated to refuse to participate in it. (Zahn, *A Descriptive Study*, 171n3).

actions by the church, it would have been very clear to any CO that he was acting contrary to what the majority of his fellow Catholics regarded as his duty to the nation.[65] In making their conscientious objector claims, Zahn wrote that Catholic COs not only had to spell out their objection to participating in the war but also had to demonstrate how their position was supported by church teachings—this, "in spite of the disturbing fact that the majority of the official interpreters of those teachings either opposed the pacifist stand or ignored it."[66]

Although he "stood completely alone against the stream," Zahn suggested that a Catholic CO could still have conceived of himself as conforming to what he believed was a correct form of Catholic life, since he based his stand on what he considered the correct interpretation and application of the church's traditional teachings on war.[67] All of this, Zahn explained, pointed to the fact that a Catholic CO was not necessarily a "minority of one" but rather could be understood as having drawn upon "something of a 'supra-social' support" in order to see himself as a bearer of values and ideals that transcended both his historical and geographical context.[68]

For Zahn, the significance of these Catholic COs for the church was that they both resisted the wartime consensus in the United States and offered a "reversal of values" from those that emerged from that consensus.[69] Though almost insignificant in number, Zahn suggested that further study of these COs would help explain why they, and not others in the same situation, took the stand they did. This was a question that Zahn would continue to ponder as he worked to build up "sources of dissent" within Catholicism against future wartime consensus. Perhaps more importantly, though, he hoped that his research might point to some "sources of immunity" against the various social controls employed by a nation-state to produce such a consensus. Highlighting these sorts of well-springs of resistance within the church would become a central component to Zahn's work.

65 The reality that most of the church therefore rejected their position meant that Catholic COs were "double deviants": resisting pressures from both the US society and the church (Zahn, *A Descriptive Study*, 171).

66 Zahn, *A Descriptive Study*, 173.

67 Zahn, *A Descriptive Study*, 287.

68 Zahn, *A Descriptive Study*, 284.

69 For instance, the purchase of war bonds or building of war planes should be avoided, while news of the annihilation of an enemy city would not be a cause for joy but an occasion of shame and penance (Zahn, *A Descriptive Study*, 38–41).

THE MYTH OF "VALUE-FREE SOCIOLOGY"

While Zahn's research certainly fit well with the notion of using sociology to build a better world (a notion that was still very much present at CUA at the time), such a view of sociology was becoming increasingly seen by many in the field as outdated. Zahn saw this as a real problem. Indeed, when Zahn began his studies in 1949, the discipline of sociology was in the middle of an internal debate—a debate from which CUA's sociology department was not isolated. As Zahn later recalled, in the first half of the twentieth century, many sociologists, "burdened with something akin to a professional inferiority complex," looked to establish sociology as more scientific, more like the "hard sciences."[70] As a result, many began to insist that sociological research needed to become exclusively empirical and cease to make any normative or value-based conclusions about what should or should not happen in society. Rather, sociology must limit itself to simply stating empirically "what is" happening. Critics, such as Alvin Gouldner, would describe this as the rise of the "myth of value-free sociology."[71]

But for many Catholic sociologists at CUA and elsewhere, "value-free sociology" was not value-free at all; in fact it was rooted in what they regarded as "naturalistic assumptions" often hostile to Catholicism.[72] Believing they were being denied a fair hearing in professional academic organizations such as the American Sociological Society, a group of Catholic sociologists founded the American Catholic Sociological Society (ACSS) in 1938 to provide a forum for a kind of "Catholic sociology."[73]

70 Gordon Zahn, "Tribute to a Mentor: Paul Hanly Furfey (1896–1992)," *New Oxford Review* (September 1992): 8–10.

71 Gouldner argued that by the early twentieth century, "all the powers of sociology, from Parsons to Lundberg, have entered into a tacit alliance to bind to the dogma that 'Thou shalt not commit a value judgement.'" See Alvin Gouldner, "Anti-Minotaur," *Social Problems* 9, no. 3 (Winter 1962): 206.

72 Even in 1907, Kerby wrote that sociology already showed "a marked tendency towards Agnosticism, Materialism, and Determinism," and thus "even descriptive sociology tends to become directive or to offer interpretations, and in so doing it often takes on a tone with which the Christian cannot agree" (Kerby, "Sociology," 116).

73 Nuesse recalled once hearing Ralph Gallagher, SJ, declare that "Catholics had not left the American Sociological Society but had been 'thrown out.'" He also remembered J. W. R. Maguire, a Viatorian priest who taught sociology at St. Viator's College in Illinois, quipping at the time that he did not think "that there is a Catholic sociology any more than there is a Catholic algebra" (Nuesse, "Catholic Sociology," 105).

In looking at Catholic sociology, though, it is important to again recall, as historian Philip Gleason has pointed out, that up until the mid-1960s, much of Catholic scholarship in general was governed (both theoretically and institutionally) by a broad neoscholasticism.[74] This was a worldview that placed a separation between a person's natural and supernatural ends which corresponded to two distinct planes of human activity: nature and the supernatural. While each was seen as related by analogy, within Catholic sociology, this meant that notions of "society" and "person" were regarded as falling into the natural realm. Catholic sociology, therefore, remained largely in the realm of Catholic natural law notions of society and the human person. While this was certainly in contrast to "value-free" sociology, this Catholic sociology had essentially freed itself of any theological claims regarding society as such claims had been nicely tucked away in the supernatural sphere. For Zahn, this also was a problem.

Both Catholic sociology and its value-free counterpart, therefore, can be seen as having made a similar conceptual split between theology and society. In the case of the former, by dividing nature from the supernatural (society from the church), while the latter regarded "society" as the realm of objective "facts" separated from "religion," which was placed in the realm of subjective "values." This allowed for a further antinomy between "politics" and "religion"—itself rooted in the invention of "religion" and "secular" that had occurred with the rise of the modern nation-state in the seventeenth century.[75] Here politics functioned as what Max Weber called an "ethic of responsibility" for the real world of objective facts and technical manipulation of means. Religion, in contrast, was seen as furnishing an ideal vision that formed an "ethic of ultimate ends."[76] In short, the lofty idealism of religion's ultimate ends was kept separate from the responsible (and often dirty) means necessary for the real world politics—and as Weber made clear, "the decisive means for politics is violence."[77] And without such a separation, Weber contended, one ran the

74 Philip Gleason, *Contending with Modernity: Catholic Higher Education in the Twentieth Century* (Oxford University Press, 1995), 105–24.

75 Timothy Fitzgerald, *The Ideology of Religious Studies* (Oxford University Press, 2000).

76 Max Weber, "Politics as a Vocation," in *From Max Weber: Essays in Sociology*, ed. and trans. H. H. Gerth and C. Wright Mills (Oxford University Press, 1946), 120–23.

77 Weber, "Politics as a Vocation," 121.

risk of "irresponsibly" putting impossible ideals such as those embodied in the Sermon on the Mount into political practice.[78]

EXCURSUS ON FURFEY'S "SUPERNATURAL SOCIOLOGY"

Zahn, therefore, offered challenges going in two different directions: against the value-free sociology in the secular academy and against the two-tiered Catholic sociology. But he was not alone in this work, and he turned to his teacher Paul Hanly Furfey—whose impact on Zahn cannot be overstated—for guidance. Indeed, since the 1930s, Furfey had been proposing what he termed a "supernatural sociology" as a way of incorporating theology with social theory. Born in Boston in 1896, Furfey was educated by the Jesuits at Boston College High School and then Boston College. Indeed, in his definitive biography of Furfey, Nicholas Rademacher has noted that the Ignatian desire to attain heaven no matter the cost seemed to be the "organizing principle" in Furfey's life.[79] He was ordained a priest in the Archdiocese of Baltimore in 1922, and after completing his PhD in sociology at CUA under Kerby in 1926, Furfey joined the department.[80] As he would later recall, a sabbatical year (1931–1932) in Germany left Furfey "disillusioned with the purely scientific-empirical effort to understanding human behavior," and he soon realized that there were "other roads" to understanding human behavior, "roads that do not lead through the psychological or the statistical laboratory."[81]

For Furfey, empirical (or what he called "naturalistic") perceptions of society were woefully limited, and thus sociology had to expand its sources

78 Weber, "Politics as a Vocation," 124. Elsewhere, Weber asserted that "while the Sermon on the Mount says 'resist no evil' . . . the state asserts: You shall help right to triumph by the use of force, otherwise you too may be responsible for injustice." See Max Weber, "Religious Rejections of the World and Their Directions," in *From Max Weber: Essays in Sociology*, ed. and trans. H. H. Gerth and C. Wright Mills (Oxford University Press, 1946), 334.

79 Nicholas Rademacher, *Paul Hanly Furfey: Priest, Scientist, Social Reformer* (Fordham University Press, 2017).

80 When Furfey arrived, it was the only department at a Catholic university anywhere to offer doctoral studies in sociology. See C. Joseph Nuesse, "William Joseph Kerby (1870–1936): The Approach to His Field of the First American Catholic Sociologist," *American Catholic Studies* 111, no. 1/4 (2000): 82.

81 Paul Hanly Furfey, preface, in *Love and the Urban Ghetto* (Orbis Books, 1978).

to incorporate both philosophical and theological categories in order to fully understand human society. As he explained:

> Sociology is the study of human society, of human group life. To learn about this subject, the sociologist naturally wants to use all available means. There are three such means, namely, the scientific, philosophical, and theological methods. All these can contribute their quota to the understanding of society. To neglect any one is to leave our sociological knowledge partial and incomplete.[82]

Nuesse described this as "the distinctive Catholic social theory" in which sociology was understood as "broader" in its scope, as opposed to the "narrower" sense in the value-free sociology.[83] According to Furfey, the Mystical Body of Christ, for instance, was a socially significant fact, "just as actual, just as real, just as concrete, as the infant mortality rate of Minnesota in 1939."[84] The task of Catholic sociologists was to point out the social implications of these facts.[85]

As Furfey saw it, the very word "sociology" had become something of a "consecrated term" in the contemporary discipline that was used to describe "the purely naturalistic study of society."[86] And he pointed to a certain kind of "positivism" at work—the belief that only empirical data could be accepted as fact, while all theological or metaphysical doctrines that sought "any deeper reality beneath these facts" were rejected.[87] And as a result, contemporary "materialistic sociologists" were forced to overlook any standards of right and

82 Paul Hanly Furfey, "Why a Supernatural Sociology?" *American Catholic Sociological Review* 1 (1940): 167. Elsewhere, he wrote: "Everyone admits that sociology may borrow from economics or anthropology when the nature of the case demands it. What reason is there why sociology should not also borrow from philosophy and theology whenever such borrowing would be helpful? There is no reason really, except the narrow-mined prejudices of positivists who refuse to recognize the claims of philosophy and revealed religion." See Paul Hanly Furfey, *The Mystery of Iniquity* (Bruce Publishing, 1944), 79.

83 Nuesse, "Catholic Sociology," 104.

84 Furfey, "Why a Supernatural," 167.

85 Some critics have cautioned that Furfey's epistemology here may have been too "simplistic" in its view of "theological and philosophical truths as identical to empirical "facts."" See Bruce Lescher, "The Spiritual Life and Social Action in American Catholic Spirituality: William J. Kerby and Paul Hanly Furfey" (PhD diss., Graduate Theological Union, 1991), 128.

86 Furfey, "Why a Supernatural," 168.

87 Furfey, *Scope and Method*, 55–57. Furfey was careful to distinguish empirical methods in sociology, which he saw as a necessary though limited aspect of sociology, from "positivism," which outright rejected the validity of philosophy and theology within sociology.

wrong in their quest to be value-free.[88] This left these sociologists to calibrate their norms for society upon the already existing standards. For instance, "if the current slogan is 'My country right or wrong,'" Furfey explained, then the sociologist adopted this thoroughly immoral principle, "because he has no absolute standard of right and wrong by which to refute it."[89] And this went far beyond the academy, for in professing to be entirely objective and unprejudiced in their investigation, Furfey asserted that the "dogmatic materialism" of many sociologists seeped out into society at large. "Writers of fiction weave it into their plots. It colors the editorials of the daily press," he wrote, and so gradually and almost unconsciously, "it becomes a philosophy of life (*Weltanschauung*) for large groups of people."[90]

In contrast, Furfey's supernatural sociology was resolutely theological. He rebelled against any tendency to conceive of "society" or "the social" separate from the supernatural or theology—and likewise of a politics separated from religious belief. Instead, Furfey's sociology affirmed the necessity of understanding human society (as well as political, economic, and cultural institutions) in light of its final, transcendent, and ultimate end. For while the empirical and quantitative sociological methods certainly had a great deal to contribute to understanding society, they were limited.[91] A "supernatural sociology" (or what he also referred to as a "sociology of the supernatural") recognized these limits and incorporated philosophy and theology in its quest to more fully understand and ultimately improve society. For Furfey, a sociologist could and should identify social problems, trace them to their sources, and offer possible solutions. But unless the supernatural standards of Jesus and the saints—including the Sermon on the Mount—were taken into account, social ills such as racism, poverty, and war would not be adequately addressed or even identified.

88 Furfey, *Scope and Method*, 13–14.

89 Furfey, *The Mystery*, 16.

90 Furfey, *The Mystery*, 26.

91 "Science can tell us nothing about the essential nature of man and the purpose of his existence in the universe, yet we cannot understand society without knowing these things," Furfey wrote, in fact, sociology would not live up to its definition if it did not provide some explanation regarding the "basic purpose of society's existence" (Furfey, "Why a Supernatural," 167).

Furfey's supernatural sociology was clearly on display in his book *Fire on the Earth*, published in 1936.[92] Zahn would later call it Furfey's "most inspirational and important work."[93] Particularly influential on Zahn was Furfey's discussion of a "technique of non-participation"—which he made clear was not some kind of a wholesale rejection of the world but rather the renunciation of the "desire to use it to the full."[94] According to Furfey, this kind of nonparticipation went far beyond simply avoiding those aspects of American life that were seen as sinful by also renouncing anything that was regarded as an obstacle or distraction to one's "heavenly concerns" or "supernatural purpose."[95] Furfey described this nonparticipation as a "striking form of witness-bearing"—incarnated in this world while at the same time anticipating a life beyond it.[96] This kind of eschatologically focused "witness-bearing" would become evident in Zahn's telling of Jägerstätter's story as well as in his overall defense of Catholic pacifism.

Important for Zahn as well was Furfey's discussion of "exaggerated nationalism," which Furfey described as the tendency to "look to the State rather than the Church for judgements on right and wrong."[97] Catholics' love of their nation must be limited by the infinitely more important love of God, as Furfey declared, "we are Catholics first and Americans afterwards, and very proud to own it."[98] This critique of nationalism was very much akin to Furfey's critique of US war-making.

Along these lines, in *The Mystery of Iniquity*, published in 1944 while World War II was still raging, Furfey had criticized the US bombing of Japanese and German cities and the Allied demand for unconditional surrender, as well as what he saw as the US Catholic bishops' support of these clearly unjust

92 Paul Hanly Furfey, *Fire on the Earth* (New York: Macmillan, 1936). The opening chapter was titled: "Supernatural Sociology."

93 Zahn, "Furfey: Sociology of Commitment," 173.

94 Furfey likened it to Emmanuel Mounier's "*action de rupture*. (Furfey, *Fire*, 117).

95 Furfey mentioned voluntary poverty and not voting as examples (Furfey, *Fire*, 129–34).

96 Furfey, *Fire*, 122.

97 Furfey, *The Mystery*, 167.

98 Furfey added, "Suppose we should talk like that. The smiles on our neighbors' faces would soon turn to scowls. We would be the butt of insults. We would be ostracized. This much at least—and perhaps more. Perhaps mob violence, burned churches, murdered priests. But we would be right" (Furfey, *Mystery*, 167).

actions.[99] Indeed, Zahn remembered that Furfey was one of only a handful of clergy to publicly oppose the US effort during World War II.[100] Furfey had been a close collaborator of Dorothy Day and frequent contributor to *The Catholic Worker*, particularly on issues of war. In fact, years later, it was suggested that Furfey's 1935 *Catholic Worker* essay "Christ and the Patriot" marked the birth of the US Catholic peace movement itself.[101]

KINDRED SPIRITS

It is important to read Furfey's style of sociology and opposition to the war within the context of the broader midcentury efforts to overcome the neo-scholastic dualism in Catholic thinking. As theologian Justin Menno has noted, Furfey was interested in the work of Luigi Sturzo, an Italian priest and sociologist who had been exiled to the United States for his opposition to Mussolini.[102] Indeed, Furfey helped get Sturzo's book, *The True Life: Sociology of the Supernatural*, published in the United States. What interested Furfey most was Sturzo's notion of an "integral sociology," which saw theology and philosophy as necessary to keep social theory from falling into "abstractionism." "In studying society in its complete wholeness, in the concrete," Sturzo explained, "it is found to exist within the atmosphere of the supernatural, and to act and react to it according to the sociological laws which are at its natural basis."[103] When *The True Life* was published in 1943, Sturzo wrote that Furfey was the only sociologist he knew who also presumed society's "real synthesis with the supernatural."[104]

Such affinities have not gone unnoticed. The theologian John Milbank, for instance, has suggested that Sturzo's sociology also shared much in common with the "Catholic philosophy" proposed a generation earlier by

99 Furfey, *The Mystery*, 164–166. That same year, John C. Ford, SJ, also published a critique of the Allied bombing of cities. See John C. Ford, SJ, "The Morality of Obliteration Bombing" *Theological Studies* 5, no. 3 (1944): 261–309.

100 This group also included John Hugo and Barry O'Toole (Zahn, *Another Part of the War*, 32).

101 James Forest, "No Longer Alone: The Catholic Peace Movement," in *American Catholics and Vietnam*, edited by Thomas Quigley (Eerdmans, 1968), 144.

102 Justin Menno, "Sociology and Sanctity: Paul Hanly Furfey, Franz Mueller, and Luigi Sturzo on 'Supernatural Sociology,' a Trans-Atlantic Debate, 1928–1946" (PhD diss., University of Dayton, 2017), 239.

103 Luigi Sturzo, *The True Life: Sociology of the Supernatural* (St. Anthony's Guild Press, 1943), 17–18.

104 Menno, "Sociology and Sanctity," 239.

the French philosopher Maurice Blondel.[105] And the Jesuit theologian Peter Bernardi has pointed out the kinship between Furfey's work and that of Blondel. Acknowledgment of these similarities with Blondel are noteworthy, for the French philosopher had a profound influence on the so-called *nouvelle théologie* theologians such as Henri de Lubac, SJ. In the 1940s and 1950s, de Lubac and others were arguing that the neoscholastic separation of nature and the supernatural was a break with the traditional Catholic understanding of nature as distinct but not separate from the supernatural.[106] This argument would have a profound effect on Catholicism in the second half of the twentieth century.[107] Recognizing this kind of synchronicity is important for understanding the significance of not only what Furfey and later Zahn were doing but also the theological and historical forces they were confronting.

CONCLUSION

By the time Zahn left CUA, value-free sociology was becoming more and more entrenched in the field. However, Furfey's notion of relating sociology and theology (nature and the supernatural) would be taken up by Zahn in what he called his "sociotheological" method. With this method, Zahn employed the insights of social science for understanding contemporary human society, while at the same time taking seriously theological claims regarding ultimate ends. This enabled him to maintain his work as an activist-academic—seeking to build a better society by ending war. And while Furfey would employ his sociological method to research a variety of topics, Zahn would come to focus almost exclusively on the problem of war. But really, at this point, Zahn was explaining his own life, his own striving to ultimate ends, as well as those others at Camp Simon—and those others he would discover in the years to come.

105 Milbank, *Theology and Social Theory*, 224–25.

106 Henri de Lubac, *Surnaturel: études historiques* (Desclée de Brouwer, 1946).

107 For an excellent account of de Lubac and his theological and historical context, see Joseph A. Komonchak, "Theology and Culture at Mid-Century: the example of Henri de Lubac," *Theological Studies* 51, no. 4 (1990): 579–602. De Lubac's arguments were echoed in "the retreat" embraced by Dorothy Day. See Peters, *Called to be Saints*.

4

FINDING FRANZ

For someone's life to be formally recognized as saintly by the church, there must first be at least one person who takes special note of that life, recognizes its importance, gathers the available details, and makes it his or her business to bring that life to the attention of others. In the case of Franz Jägerstätter, Gordon Zahn was that person.

—Jim Forest[1]

Upon finishing at Catholic University, Zahn was awarded a postdoctoral fellowship by the Social Science Research Council and spent the 1952–1953 academic year at Harvard doing research on Protestant attitudes toward Catholics. This mainly entailed reading through hundreds of letters sent to the Boston publisher of Paul Blanshard's widely read 1949 book, *American Freedom and Catholic Power.*[2] Cold War tensions, however, quickly turned Zahn's focus back to the problems of war and militarism.[3]

1 Jim Forest, Introduction, *Franz Jägerstätter: Letters and Writings from Prison*, ed. Erna Putz, trans. Robert Krieg (Orbis Books, 2009), xxvii.

2 Zahn ended up publishing two articles based on this research: "The Content of Protestant Tensions: Personal Experiences and 'Known Facts,'" *American Catholic Sociological Review* 16, no.1 (1955): 12–22; and "The Content of Protestant Tensions: Fears of Catholic Aims and Methods," *American Catholic Sociological Review* 18, no. 3 (1957): 205–12.

3 In 1953, Zahn also wrote an unpublished article, "McCarthyism: A Catholic Issue," in which he declared that both McCarthyism and communism were distortions of the truth (UNDA Zahn papers (3/03703)).

On November 1, 1952 (All Saints Day), the United States detonated the first thermonuclear bomb on Enewetak Atoll in the Marshall Islands.[4] The blast was reported as being seven hundred times as powerful as the bomb the United States dropped on Hiroshima.[5] The test had vaporized the islet of Elugelab. The following spring, Zahn published an article in *The Catholic World* titled "Vision of the Future: An Island Disappears," in which he began by pointing out that in the year 1139, the Second Lateran Council, under Pope Innocent II, had prohibited the use of the crossbow in war because of its deadliness.[6] With such a declaration, Zahn wrote, the Catholic hierarchy had fulfilled its "principal obligation" by making it clear to Catholics that those who persisted in the use of these condemned weapons were acting in direct violation to the moral teaching of the church.[7] Zahn contrasted this kind of moral clarity with the silence of the US bishops in the 1950s following the development of the hydrogen bomb and other such "the instruments of hell" recently tested in the South Pacific. It seemed incredible, Zahn noted, with the US military in possession of a destructive power "beyond rational calculation," that US Catholics should remain "silently unconcerned, or at best, vaguely and confusedly concerned."[8]

For Zahn, responsibility for this silence did not lie with the pope in Rome but rather with Catholics in the United States. For while recent criticism of modern war and its weapons and techniques by the Vatican may not have been as specific as that of the Second Lateran Council, Zahn wrote that US Catholics had never given Rome any reason to believe that they would support or listen to any such denunciation even if it were made. "After all, it was our own nation that developed and perfected an air force that was able to obliterate cities and civilian populations *en masse* even before the advent of atomic weapons," Zahn pointed out, while US Catholics largely remained

4 The term "nuclear" can be used to describe both atomic bombs, which employ nuclear fission, and hydrogen or thermonuclear bombs, which use nuclear fusion. See Richard Rhodes, *Dark Sun: the Making of the Hydrogen Bomb* (Simon and Shuster, 1995).

5 For an excellent account of the legacy of the nuclear weapons program in (and on) the United States, see Robert Jay Lifton and Greg Mitchell, *Hiroshima in America: Fifty Years of Denial* (GP Putnam's Sons, 1995).

6 Zahn, "Vision of the Future: An Island Disappears," *The Catholic World* (May 1953). Zahn later republished the article in *War, Conscience and Dissent* (Hawthorn Books, 1967), 66–74.

7 Zahn, "Vision," 67.

8 Zahn, "Vision," 67.

silent or even approved.[9] While some prominent US Catholics had even gone so far as to "translate" Catholic moral theology into geopolitical terms in order to justify both the development and use of such weapons, Zahn pointed out that most church leaders admitted in private the immorality of using these weapons but continued to argue in public that it would be improper for the church to label them as immoral.[10] Zahn stated that US Catholics had split with the Vatican on issues of war, highlighting the fact that the "mind of the Church," at least as it was read in US Catholics' silent acquiescence of, if not actual cooperation with, "mass-destruction murder," was completely contrary to the "mind of the Church" displayed in the heartbroken appeals regularly issued from Rome to end war and reliance on force.[11]

Instead of being a "leaven" within society, Zahn argued that US Catholics had generally become aligned with "the forces of nationalism and the adherents of power politics."[12] He explained that US Catholics had been blinded by "ethnocentric" rationalizations and beliefs regarding the United States and its place in the world—rationalizations that enabled Catholics to believe that such "instruments of hell" could be safely entrusted to the US military, but not that of the Soviets.[13] Zahn called this "the sheerest of self-deceptions," since the United States was the first and only nation to have resorted to use of atomic weapons, and "the guilt of Hiroshima and Nagasaki has not yet been purged from our national conscience by any open, public, and nationwide act of contrition."[14] For Zahn, all of this placed Catholics in the United States in a unique situation with regard to nuclear weapons.

To "encourage" US Catholics to confront this situation, Zahn suggested that the Vatican assemble an advisory committee of theologians from "neutral nations" to evaluate the morality of modern weapons, as well as their intended use. Such a committee, he argued, would go a long way in recentering the

9 Zahn, "Vision," 68.

10 He noted that the Catholic Association for International Peace (CAIP) had recently awarded its first peace medal to Brien McMahon, the Catholic senator from Connecticut and a major figure in the establishment of the US Atomic Energy Commission, where the US nuclear weapons program was housed (Zahn, "Vision," 68).

11 Zahn, "Vision,"68–69.

12 Zahn suggested that this could be the result of anticommunism or of being seen as "un-American" or fear of suffering personal loss or discomfort in the event of a national defeat (Zahn, "Vision," 70).

13 Zahn, "Vision," 73.

14 Zahn, "Vision," 71.

moral focus to "the necessary degree of personal responsibility" on any US Catholic who may be called upon to either develop or use these weapons.[15] Zahn suggested that the Second Lateran Council serve as a precedent for such a committee.

A CHRISTIAN DILEMMA

Not all of Zahn's research and writing was focused on issues of war, however. When he arrived at Loyola in the fall of 1953, Zahn quickly joined the Chicago Catholic Interracial Council. In 1956, he published an article titled "Racism: A Christian Dilemma" in *Apostolate*, a journal sponsored by the Christian Family Movement (CFM).[16] In it, he sought to provide principles to guide CFM groups as they undertook a series of "Inquires on Integration" that year. He opened by pointing to Gunnar Myrdal's influential 1944 study on race relations in the US titled *The American Dilemma: The Negro Problem and Modern Democracy*, which described the disparity between the so-called "American Creed," with its professed democratic beliefs, and the actual behavior of most white Americans that seemed to contradict those beliefs.[17]

Along similar lines, Zahn argued that a "Christian Dilemma" existed between the Christian creed and the actual behavior of most white Catholics when it came to race relations in the United States.[18] And while the American dilemma could be resolved by Americans either conforming to their professed values or finding new ones, Zahn argued that the Christian dilemma could not be so easily resolved. For if there was even "the slightest disparity between the Christian creed and the behavior of Christians," he concluded, only one option was available: "correcting our behavior so that it may fully conform with

15 This committee could also develop a formula that would serve as a "standard of action" for individual Catholics faced with a call to participate in their nation's war effort without placing upon them the burden of determining all by themselves the morality of each order given. He noted that this, of course, was based upon the "hopeful assumption" that US Catholics would follow such recommendations. To assume otherwise, Zahn wrote, "would be to convict American Catholics of a willingness to subvert the demands of their faith to the interests of national loyalties" (Zahn, "Vision,"72).

16 Zahn, "Racism: A Christian Dilemma," *Apostolate* 13, no. 4 (1956): 30–39.

17 Gunnar Myrdal, *The American Dilemma: The Negro Problem and Modern Democracy* (Harper & Row, 1944).

18 For Zahn, the fundamental aspects of the Christian Creed that should influence Catholic behavior toward minority communities included: justice, charity, and the Mystical Body of Christ—which he described as "the full exposition of Catholic sociology and social philosophy" (Zahn, "Racism," 39).

the teachings of Christ and His Church."[19] This notion of disparity or tension between the demands of Catholic moral teaching and the actual behavior of Catholics was one that would appear throughout Zahn's writing, with some critics even suggesting that Zahn expected too much from Catholics—especially with regard to following church teaching on war.

ZAHN'S FULBRIGHT YEAR

As these articles in *The Catholic World* and *Apostolate* suggest, Zahn's academic career at this time was almost completely bound to the world of US Catholicism. As the historian Mark Ruff has noted, Zahn would have likely remained relatively unknown outside that world had it not been for a Fulbright scholarship he was awarded for the 1956–1957 academic year at Julius Maximilians Universität in Würzburg in Germany.[20] The experience radically altered the course of his career.

Zahn's initial plan for the year was to study the fate of the *Friedensbund Deutscher Katholiken* (FDK), the German Catholic peace group begun in the wake of World War I. The FDK had been founded by Max Josef Metzger, a German priest who was executed by the Nazis in 1944. The group also included the Dominican theologian Franziskus Stratmann, whose book *The Church and War* had had a profound effect on Dorothy Day and others in the US Catholic peace movement.[21] At its height, FDK boasted a membership of over 40,000, but in 1933, its offices were raided by the Gestapo, its leaders were arrested, and its members (along with the movement itself) all but vanished. Zahn was interested in learning how FDK's seemingly dedicated opposition to war could have been so completely silenced to the point that its leaders were unable to report any instances of members openly refusing to serve in Hitler's military.[22] But upon his arrival in West Germany in the summer of 1956, it quickly became apparent to Zahn that this project would be nearly impossible to pursue. All FDK's membership records had been destroyed during the war. While he was

19 Zahn, "Racism," 39.

20 Ruff, *The Battle for the Catholic Past in Germany*, 128–29.

21 In *The Long Loneliness*, Dorothy Day mentioned Stratmann's book, *The Church and War: a Catholic Study* (PJ Kennedy and Sons, 1928), as having helped set forth the Catholic Worker stand toward war (Day, *The Long Loneliness*, 264).

22 Gordon Zahn, *German Catholics and Hitler's War: A Study in Social Control* (Sheed & Ward, 1962), 5.

able to track down a few former members, Zahn soon abandoned this line of research as fruitless.[23]

Zahn instead decided to broaden the scope of his research to consider the behavior of German Catholics more generally, looking at both the ways that their conformity to the Nazi war effort highlighted the effective "operating system of social controls" placed on them, as well as how that conformity revealed German Catholics' apparent "selection" of Nazi values over the values of their faith.[24] To do this, Zahn turned to a small group of mostly former FDK members for help—a group Ruff described as a "who's who of left-wing Catholicism."[25]

GERMANY IN 1956

To understand this group, some background is necessary. In the Cold War atmosphere of the summer of 1956, Zahn described East and West Germany as a "contested battleground," with West Germany a stronghold of support for the United States and of opposition to communism.[26] Noteworthy here is the fact that the political influence of Catholics in West Germany had shifted dramatically since the end of the war. In 1936, Catholics made up only around 36 percent of the German population, but after the war, they comprised over 45 percent of the population in the newly formed Federal Republic of Germany (West Germany). With this new demographic status, Catholics found new political power.[27] According to Zahn, during the early postwar years, the Catholic Church in West Germany was "a political force to be reckoned with"

23 Zahn, *German Catholics*, 5.

24 Zahn, *German Catholics*, 5–6.

25 Ruff suggested that these German Catholics did not easily fit into what had become a very fractured confessional and political landscape in West Germany at the time. In this context, this group of left-wing Catholics often found themselves on the losing side of battles over West German rearmament and the rights of Catholic COs—and they often found themselves in opposition to the German Catholic hierarchy, as well, over these issues. By interviewing these left-wing Catholics, Zahn "strode into a raucous climate that was a mixture of idealistic fervor, pent-up frustration and a grim determination to settle the score with figures in the hierarchy who had by their account inflicted grave wrongs on peace enthusiasts" (Ruff, *The Battle for the Catholic Past in Germany*, 96, 130–32).

26 Zahn, *German Catholics*, viii.

27 For instance, Konrad Adenauer, the West German chancellor from 1949 to 1963, was Catholic, and his ruling Christian Democratic Union (CDU) was largely made up of former members of the Center Party, the largest Catholic political party in Germany before it was dismantled by the Nazis in 1933 (Ruff, *The Battle for the Catholic Past in Germany*, 5).

and was "totally committed to the new Bonn government."[28] As a result, he pointed out that anything that threatened to diminish the church's influence was likely to be regarded as providing "aid and comfort to its enemies"—with communism serving as the primary enemy of both the West German state and Catholic Church.[29]

Indeed, it was the threat of communism that led many to support calls for West German rearmament after the war. By the late 1950s, Zahn recalled that the idea of rearmament "was in full swing," with not only the support of the US government but also that of the West German Catholic hierarchy.[30] And while many of the more left-leaning Catholics he had spoken with were pressing for an extension of rights for Catholic COs in any rearmament legislation, Zahn recalled that most West German bishops opposed such rights. This was not only out of political considerations but also because such a provision was regarded as a dangerous deviation from church teaching at a time when the idea of Catholics being conscientious objectors was still very much suspect within the church. In June 1956, for instance, a prominent German Jesuit theologian, Johannes Hirschmann, testified before the parliament that a Catholic could not, in fact, be a pacifist or conscientious objector.[31] Such debates even "stirred echoes in Rome" when Pope Pius XII, reportedly under the influence of a close German advisor, included what many read as a condemnation of Catholic conscientious objection to war in his 1956 Christmas address.[32]

But other layers of previous tension were also emerging. Zahn's arrival in West Germany in 1956 coincided with one of the most complex cases to come before the newly created West German Constitutional Court.[33] The case surrounded a 1954 Lower Saxony law that sought to dismantle "denominational schools"—publicly funded schools that were officially billed as either "Catholic" or "Protestant"—and convert them to "interconfessional" schools.[34] The government of Konrad Adenauer, the Catholic chancellor of West Germany, appealed to the court to strike down the law, asserting that it was in violation

28 Zahn, *German Catholics*, viii.

29 Zahn, *German Catholics*, x–xi.

30 Zahn, *German Catholics*, ix.

31 Ruff, *The Battle for the Catholic Past in Germany*, 130.

32 Zahn, *German Catholics*, x.

33 Ruff, *The Battle for the Catholic Past in Germany*, 48.

34 Ruff, *The Battle for the Catholic Past in Germany*, 48.

of the 1933 Concordat between the Vatican and Hitler that had given specific protection to Catholic schools.[35] The government of Lower Saxony rejected this claim, arguing that with the defeat of the Third Reich, the Concordat was no longer binding.

In essence, West Germany's highest court was asked to decide if the Vatican's Concordat with Hitler still held.[36] As Ruff has pointed out, the argument made by the Catholic supporters of denominational schools was a "confessional Pandora's box" that quickly turned a spotlight on the history of not only the Concordat but also on the German Catholic Church's record under Nazi rule.[37] All of which, he noted, "unwittingly helped to demythologize the narratives of [Catholic] resistance so carefully crafted between 1945 and 1949"—narratives that had begun to emerge almost immediately after the war ended.[38] The upshot here was that the German Catholic Church was not only facing blame for its past wartime complicity but also criticism that it was being complicit once again.

POSTWAR NARRATIVES

This controversy in the mid-1950s was exacerbated by the Vatican's attempts after the war to stifle any criticism of the church during the war. Less than a month after the fall of the Nazi regime in May 1945, Pope Pius XII addressed the College of Cardinals and quickly sought to quash any sense of collective German guilt by denouncing the Nazis as a "satanic ghost" that had possessed the German nation.[39] The pope then went on to list numerous examples of the courage and sacrifice made by German Catholics who suffered and died for the faith in Nazi concentration camps. Pius's speech had a profound influence in shaping how German bishops thought about their own experience under Hitler. For in the weeks immediately following the German surrender, as reports of concentration camp horrors began to emerge in Allied media broadcasts, some Catholic bishops began to question whether they should have been more

35 Ruff, *The Battle for the Catholic Past in Germany*, 49.

36 Ruff, *The Battle for the Catholic Past in Germany*, 51.

37 Ruff noted that the so-called "linkage theory" had also emerged around this time (and is still used by historians today). It asserted that the Catholic Center Party delegates had enabled Hitler's rise to power in exchange for the Concordat (Ruff, *The Battle for the Catholic Past in Germany*, 50–53, 84).

38 Ruff, *The Battle for the Catholic Past in Germany*, 84–85.

39 Ruff, *The Battle for the Catholic Past in Germany*, 16.

publicly outspoken in their opposition to Nazi crimes. Ruff reported that eleven German bishops, not yet aware of Pius's address, had even drafted a statement to the Vatican attempting to explain their relative "silence" during the war and admitting that they bore at least some responsibility for Nazi atrocities because of their reluctance to speak out.[40]

By their annual meeting in August 1945, though, the tide had shifted. All the German bishops had read Pius's address and had adjusted their tone accordingly. The bishops no longer dwelled on what they might have done differently but instead—following the pope's lead—took up the task of documenting German Catholic resistance to Hitler.[41] As many as sixteen histories of the Catholic Church's struggle in Nazi Germany appeared between 1945 and 1949.[42] Particularly noteworthy for our discussion here was the history written by an Austrian priest named Jakob Fried, which attempted to justify the behavior of the Catholic Church in Austria during the war.[43] As Zahn would later point out, one of the German Catholic Church's "most cherished assets" in the years following World War II was its record of opposition to the Nazis.[44] It was directly at that record that Zahn took aim.

THE FLEISCHERS

One of the first people Zahn interviewed when he got to West Germany was Josef Fleischer, who was a Catholic pacifist from Baden who had been imprisoned in Berlin-Tegel in May 1940 for refusing to swear an oath of allegiance to Hitler. While in prison, Fleischer claimed that he had been visited by a high-ranking Catholic military chaplain wearing a uniform adorned with swastikas who tried to persuade him to take the oath, give his unconditional obedience to Hitler, and wholeheartedly participate in the Nazi wars. When Fleischer refused, the chaplain became enraged and shouted that Fleischer

40 Ruff, *The Battle for the Catholic Past in Germany*, 16.

41 Ruff, *The Battle for the Catholic Past in Germany*, 17.

42 Twenty-five were written about German Protestants during that same period.

43 Zahn interviewed Fried, who told Zahn that he had been asked to write the history by the pope himself. Fried's history included a brief account of Franz Jägerstätter, who he described as a "typical example" of Austrian Catholic resistance to the Nazis, "albeit of a special kind." He offered no other examples, however. See Jakob Fried, *Nationalsozialismus und katholische Kirche in Österreich* (Wiener Dom-Verlag, 1947), 82.

44 Zahn, *German Catholics*, ix.

should be "exterminated" and even "shortened by a head."[45] Fortunately, his Nazi captors did not heed the chaplain's advice. Instead, he was declared clinically insane and sent to a mental hospital, where he later escaped. Zahn described Fleischer as "the only German Catholic 'conscientious objector' to Hitler's wars to live to tell the tale."[46]

After the war, Fleischer's brother Johannes—another "left wing Catholic"—began to promote Josef's story as part of his critique of the Catholic hierarchy for their support of West German rearmament. In February 1956, in the context of the rearmament debate, the West German parliament began discussing plans for a Catholic chaplaincy in the new West German military, an idea enthusiastically supported by the bishops. In the hopes of scuttling such plans, the Fleischer brothers sent a letter to the West German Defense Ministry that identified a priest named Georg August Werthmann as the chaplain who had berated Josef in prison. At the time, Werthmann was the prominent leader of the Catholic military bishop's office in Berlin and was in position to become the head of any West German Catholic military chaplaincy.[47] The Fleischers' accusation was quickly picked up by the West German newspapers, as well as by critics of the German hierarchy's role in the war. Werthmann denied ever having met Josef Fleischer or of ever even being in the Berlin-Tegel prison, setting off a series of very public charges and countercharges throughout the summer.

While the Fleischers did not offer Zahn much by way of new information, Werthmann (with whom Zahn also met) did provide material that would form the foundation for much of Zahn's research going forward. Werthmann suggested that it was his former boss Bishop Franz Justus Rarkowski—the German Catholic Military bishop notorious for his unwavering support of the Nazis during the war—who was most likely the cleric who threatened Fleischer. Werthmann (no doubt desperate to clear his name) gave Zahn copies of Rarkowski's papers, issues of various German Catholic chaplain periodicals, and other incriminating evidence from the war years. This material would become the basis for Zahn's 1962 book *German Catholics and Hitler's Wars*.[48]

45 Zahn, *German Catholics*, 147.

46 Zahn, *German Catholics*, 147.

47 Ruff, *The Battle for the Catholic Past in Germany*, 133.

48 Before receiving these materials, Zahn only had "snippets from the Catholic diocesan press from nine bishoprics that he could obtain via interlibrary loan" (Ruff, *The Battle for the Catholic Past in Germany*, 135).

Even more importantly, though, Werthmann set up a meeting between Zahn and Heinrich Kreuzberg, a former chaplain at Berlin-Tegel prison. During this meeting, Kreuzberg gave Zahn a biography he had written of an Austrian priest named Franz Reinisch, who had been executed in 1942 for refusing to take the oath of obedience to Hitler.[49] While certainly impressed by Reinisch's story, he was equally impressed, in fact more so, by the story contained in a four-page appendix to the biography. The appendix was titled "Franz II," and it told the story of Franz Jägerstätter. As Zahn later explained:

> What made this case exceptionally interesting, I felt, was the fact that Franz Jägerstätter came from a social background that one would ordinarily not associate with such an overtly rebellious act. He was a relatively untutored man from a remote and isolated rural village. Even more important, he, unlike the priest who preceded him to the executioner's block, was a married man with a wife and children for whom he was responsible and whose future welfare he was morally bound to consider.[50]

Kreuzberg's account briefly summarized Jagerstatter's life: his religious devotion, his opposition to the Nazis, his refusal to serve in the army, and his imprisonment and eventual execution.[51] It is worth noting here that, although unmentioned by Kreuzberg or Zahn, also imprisoned in Berlin-Tegel at this same time was Dietrich Bonhoeffer, the German Lutheran theologian who was also executed by the Nazis.[52] And while there is no record that they ever met, the fact that two of the most significant Christian martyrs in Nazi Germany were imprisoned together is certainly serendipitous—if not the workings of grace.

Kreuzberg told Zahn that he met Jägerstätter twice while at Berlin-Tegel. It was during his second visit that he remembered telling Jägerstätter about Reinisch, and the chaplain described the joy and relief that Jägerstätter showed when hearing that someone else—a priest, no less—had also traveled down the same path:

49 Heinrich Kreuzberg, *Franz Reinisch. Ein Martyrer unserer Zeit* (Lahn-Verlag, 1953).

50 Gordon Zahn, *In Solitary Witness: The Life and Death of Franz Jägerstätter* (Holt, Rinehart and Winston, 1964), 4.

51 Zahn offered a two-page description of "Franz II" in *In Solitary*, 268–69.

52 Dietrich Bonhoeffer, *Letters and Papers from Prison*, ed. Eberhard Bethge (Macmillan, 1972).

> Even while I was telling him this, his eyes lit up and, after a deep sigh as if a heavy burden had fallen from his soul he joyously declared, 'But this is what I have always told myself, that I cannot be following a false path. If a priest made such a decision and went to his death, then I may do so too.'[53]

Kreuzberg also asked Jägerstätter to write a full "prison statement" explaining his stand, and Zahn later described this as Kreuzberg's most significant contribution to the development of the Jägerstätter story.

Kreuzberg reported that Jägerstätter was executed on August 9, 1943, and noted that it was the feast of day of St. John Vianney—the nineteenth-century French saint who had refused to fight in Napoleon's army.[54] He also drew parallels to the life and death of St. Thomas More. Kreuzberg's account concluded with a note that Jägerstätter's ashes had been initially buried in the Brandenburg cemetery but were later returned to his parish in St. Radegund and given a Catholic burial. In addition, Kreuzberg also wrote a couple of articles on Jägerstätter prior to the Reinisch biography, suggesting, Zahn noted, that "Franz II" had not simply been an afterthought.[55] After reading Kreuzberg's account, Zahn wrote to Jägerstätter's widow, Franziska, and his former pastor, Josef Karobath. Karobath wrote back and invited Zahn to visit St. Radegund.

ST. RADEGUND

On July 27, 1957, Zahn traveled to St. Radegund, a municipality in the district of Braunau am Inn in Upper Austria, close to the border with German Bavaria.[56] There he met with Franziska and her daughters at their home, along with Karobath, who showed Zahn Jägerstätter's grave behind the parish church.[57]

53 Zahn, *In Solitary*, 268.

54 In 1969, Vianney's feast day was moved to August 4. Today, St. Teresa Benedicta of the Cross (Edith Stein), who was killed at Auschwitz on August 9, 1942, is honored on August 9. The United States dropped an atomic bomb on Nagasaki on August 9, 1945.

55 Zahn, *In Solitary*, 269.

56 Villagers told Zahn that St. Radegund dated back to the Roman Empire and that the present Church of St. Radegund was built by Cistercian monks in the fifteenth century. St. Radegund was a sixth-century Frankish queen and the patron saint of Jesus College at Cambridge University—whose full name is The College of the Blessed Virgin Mary, Saint John the Evangelist and the glorious Virgin Saint Radegund (https://www.jesus.cam.ac.uk/st-radegund).

57 Zahn had hoped to meet with Franziska alone, but when he arrived in the village and asked where the Jägerstätter farm was, no one could give him directions. After visiting Karobath at the

In his journal entry for that day, Zahn highlighted the "remoteness" of the village (two train transfers followed by a five-kilometer walk) and described the Jägerstätter house as a "simple Bavarian *hof*." Over the course of the visit, Karobath did most of the talking. He told Zahn that he had been close to Franz and that they had often discussed political matters quite openly—including the 1938 plebiscite on whether Austria should join the Third Reich.[58] While he had known Jägerstätter for years, Karobath explained that he had not been in St. Radegund during the time leading up to Franz's arrest and execution since he had been arrested himself for giving homilies critical of the Nazis while Jägerstätter was away at military training in 1941. The pastor mentioned that he had also written a few articles on Jägerstätter but that they had been rejected by the diocesan newspaper because of the "probable adverse reaction" they would have elicited from Catholic veterans.[59]

Karobath told Zahn that he did not believe that Jägerstätter had been an "out-and-out pacifist," though he did (half-jokingly) refer to Jägerstätter as a possible "patron of pacifists."[60] Nevertheless, Karobath made it clear that his former parishioner definitely would have served in a "just war against aggression" in defense of Austria and that he refused to serve in Hitler's war because he saw it as "clearly unjust and aggressive in nature."[61] He also told Zahn that Jägerstätter had rejected any idea of accepting noncombatant duty in the military (such as serving in the medical corps) because he saw this work as an essential part of military operations, and if he accepted such duty it would only send someone else into combat. This would become an important point decades later when evidence was unearthed in the 1990s that

parish to get directions, the pastor insisted on joining him on the visit and subsequently did most of the talking. Zahn kept a detailed journal of this trip, referred to here as Zahn, "Journal #1," UNDA Zahn papers (10/13233).

58 Karobath told Zahn that he had voted "Yes," while Jägerstätter had intentionally voided his ballot. Jägerstätter had initially intended to vote "No," but Karobath had suggested two reasons to Jägerstätter to not vote that way: an absolute vote in favor would clearly reveal to foreign observers that the plebiscite itself was a farce, and a vote against would simply make it easier the Nazis to find their opponents. The vote meant nothing, Karobath remembered telling Jägerstätter, and so one could vote "Yes" in good conscience (with mental reservations) knowing that it was meaningless either way. See Zahn, "Journal #1," UNDA Zahn papers (10/13233).

59 Zahn, "Journal #1," UNDA Zahn papers (10/13233).

60 Zahn, "Journal #1," UNDA Zahn papers (10/13233).

61 To confirm Franz's "non-pacifist base," the pastor pointed out that he had served two periods of military training, though when it came to "actual service," Jägerstätter refused it. See Zahn, "Journal #1," UNDA Zahn papers (10/13233).

seemed to suggest that Jägerstätter would have been willing to serve in such a capacity in the Nazi army.

Zahn remembered that while Karobath was speaking about her husband's possible pacifism, Franziska, who had been quiet for much of the visit, appeared a bit hesitant, leading Zahn to surmise that she thought her husband had perhaps been "more pacifistic that the pastor thought." In the end, though, Franziska agreed with her pastor.[62] When Zahn asked if she had been at all prepared for Franz's act of refusal, Franziska recounted that her husband had often discussed his intentions with her and added that there had not been any trouble from her neighbors and relatives following her husband's execution.[63] Franziska had a copy of Kreuzberg's book and gave Zahn a postcard picture of Franz as a memento, a larger framed copy of which hung on the wall.

That evening, after returning to Würzburg, Zahn wrote in his journal that he was resolved to return to St. Radegund to make a more complete investigation of "this act of heroism."[64] He also drafted a letter to Bob Hovda, his friend from Camp Simon. In the letter, Zahn briefly recounted the details of his visit and (for what would be the first of many times) told Jägerstätter's story.[65] Zahn acknowledged that the Austrian Catholic was "not an all-out 'pacifist' in our sense" but that "he had decided that Hitler's war was an unjust war and could not be supported by a Christian."[66] That said, Zahn clearly recognized the significance of Jägerstätter and told his fellow Catholic CO that "if we pacifists are looking for a patron, we might begin here."

"HE WOULD NOT SERVE"

When Zahn returned to the United States later that summer of 1957, he quickly began composing an article on Jägerstätter, and it was published the following

62 Zahn, "Journal #1," UNDA Zahn papers (10/13233).

63 In his journal, Zahn wrote: "As far as the children were concerned, they had not suffered any 'realities' . . . though a slight remark did indicate that a teacher was not at all sympathetic to F.J. and made this attitude quite clear." See Zahn, "Journal #1," UNDA Zahn papers (10/13233).

64 Zahn, "Journal #1," UNDA Zahn papers (10/13233).

65 Zahn asked Hovda, who had been ordained by then, to say a Mass for Jägerstätter and to write Franziska when he did: "Identify yourself as a priest who was a CO and she will be completely thrilled." See Zahn to Hovda, letter was dated July 27, 1957, UNDA Zahn papers (3/03375).

66 He also noted that while by all accounts Jägerstätter had been an intensely spiritual person, it was not in "the holy, holy way."

year.[67] Zahn opened the piece by pointing out that St. Radegund is only a short distance from Hitler's birthplace in Braunau am Inn—a remarkable coincidence, he noted, as each took on the principal roles in what could be seen as simply the latest version of the ongoing the struggle between "the spiritual power of Christ and the temporal power of Caesar."[68] Zahn explained that what little was known about Jägerstätter came from Kreuzberg's appendix and Fried's history. He pointed out that these accounts had been published in the immediate aftermath of the war, at a time when evidence of Catholic resistance to Hitler's regime was "eagerly being publicized."[69] But only a short decade later, "history had come full circle," and the change was once again in lock-step with the workings of war. Indeed, in the atmosphere of the late-1950s Cold War, even as resistance to the Nazis was still being honored, greater honor was being given to obedience to civil authority, "in particular to the willing acceptance of military duty in the face of the Communist threat."[70]

While the account of Jägerstätter found in Fried's 1947 history of Austrian Catholicism during the war (which also mentioned Karobath as one of its sources) largely followed that of Kreuzberg, Zahn later explained that the former was "more complete and apparently more accurate."[71] For example, Fried had written that Jägerstätter regarded Hitler's war as unjust and that whenever family or friends or clergy would suggest he change his stand, Jägerstätter would respond: "I may not co-operate in an unjust war. God will certainly take care of my wife and children."[72] Jägerstätter was also described as having recognized "the essential godlessness" of the Nazi movement from the start, and that over time his prayers, penance, and fasting "grew longer

67 Gordon Zahn, "He Would Not Serve," *America*, July 5, 1958, 388–90.

68 Zahn, "He Would Not," 388.

69 Zahn called Fried's description of Jägerstätter (as a "typical example, albeit of a special kind" of Austrian Catholic resistance to Hitler) as clearly an understatement (Zahn, "He Would Not," 388).

70 Zahn noted that even by the late 1940s, the story of Jägerstätter was being met with criticism. He quoted one German Catholic veteran: "Like millions of others, Jägerstätter was called to the defense of his fatherland," and he should have remembered that "some other German soldier on the Russian front was waiting to be relieved after putting in two years of service there—waiting for Jägerstätter." The veteran stated that Jägerstätter was more a "deserter" than a martyr, and that his sacrifice revealed a disregard for his duty to his family (Zahn, "He Would Not," 390).

71 Zahn, *In Solitary*, 270.

72 Quoted in Zahn, "He Would Not," 389.

and more intense."[73] It was after his second round of military training in 1941 that Jägerstätter arrived at the conviction that he could not participate in Hitler's army—the decision that was to eventually cost him his life. When the order to report for military duty arrived in February 1943, Jägerstätter went to see his bishop for advice. Fried wrote that when attempts to convince him to change his mind failed, the bishop could see that Jägerstätter "thirsted after martyrdom." He then told Jägerstätter that he could follow this path only if he was certain that he was not called to it by his own private decision, but by "some exceptional inspiration from above."[74] Fried reported that this was all the encouragement Jägerstätter needed, and he left the bishop confirmed in his belief.

After this meeting, events quickly followed what Fried called their "inevitable course." In order to avoid any unpleasantness at home, Jägerstätter traveled to the induction center in Enns, albeit six days late. When further efforts to change his mind failed, he was placed under arrest and taken to a prison in Berlin where he was court-martialed. On June 6, 1943, Jägerstätter was found guilty of "undermining the military power" and sentenced to death. While in prison, new attempts were made to save his life, but Zahn noted that Jägerstätter "refused to consider even noncombatant service."[75] When his wife and new pastor visited him in Berlin, they reported that Jägerstätter left them with the assurance that his refusal had not weakened and he was confident he could continue to the end. Zahn also included Kreuzberg's description of Jägerstätter as "one of the happiest prisoners" he had ever seen upon hearing about the story of Reinisch.

In "He Would Not Serve," Zahn went on to suggest that Jagerstatter's story had been largely forgotten even in St. Radegund, where, if it was remembered at all, it was "suppressed as an embarrassment rather than hailed as an inspiration."[76] He pointed out that Karobath's articles on Jägerstätter had been rejected by the Linz diocesan paper so as not to "disturb" any Catholic veterans.[77] Zahn also mentioned that Franziska had faced some difficulties

73 Fried also noted that Jägerstätter had been determined to vote against the 1938 *Anschluss*, despite the endorsement of the Austrian Cardinal Theodor Innitzer (Zahn, "He Would Not," 388).

74 Zahn, "He World Not," 389.

75 Zahn, "He World Not," 389.

76 Zahn, "He Would Not," 389.

77 Zahn also pointed to some postwar criticism of Jägerstätter, which argued that he had "compromised" his stand by participating in the Nazi food-production program, as well as by reporting

getting any kind of financial assistance from the government to help support her family, even after the fall of the Third Reich. He quoted from a letter Franziska wrote to Kreuzberg in 1949: "Since my husband died so holy a death, I am sure he will continue to pray and provide for me and his children so that I can succeed without the help of the state. . . . Since his sacrifice was so great, I must not lose my spirit, even though my sorrow is often too great to contain."[78] Echoing these sentiments, Zahn wrote that while Jägerstätter's story could be read as a tragedy; for the believer it was an "accent of victory." Hinting at the need for a sociotheological interpretation, Zahn wrote that "the grace of faith" was needed to see the issue as Jägerstätter had seen it. He then quoted from Jägerstätter's final letter to his wife: "Just as the wholly secular man will do everything to make this life easier and more pleasant, so must we who still believe in the eternal kingdom do everything so that we may someday find a great reward there."[79]

In what would become an ongoing attempt to hold up Jägerstätter as a "new model" for Catholic engagement with the modern nation-state, Zahn explained that in the church's long history, saints had always emerged suited to the needs of their particular time. And in this age of "the conformist, 'other-directed' man," indeed, saints were needed who would assert the right and duty of the individual Christian to judge "the demands of Leviathan" and to "refuse to render unto Caesar that which is not Caesar's," even if such refusal would lead to martyrdom.[80] Zahn stated that Jägerstätter was such a saint.[81] And although St. Radegund was a village too small to have its own post office and too remote to be reached directly by train, Zahn declared that in the tiny graveyard of the village's centuries-old church lay the ashes of a simple farmer who defied a tyrant who had brought all of Europe to its knees.

---

twice to military training 1940 and 1941. In response, both Kreuzberg and Fried argued that there was no essential break in Jägerstätter's opposition to the Nazi rule: he had refused all voluntary contributions to causes that could benefit the Nazi state, though he did generously assist the poor with donations of food, he had also refused to claim any Nazi food bonus for which he and his family had qualified.

78 Zahn, "He Would Not," 390.

79 Zahn, "He Would Not," 389.

80 The "other-directed man" was a notion made popular in David Riesman's *The Lonely Crowd: A Study of the Changing American Character* (Yale University Press, 1961).

81 Zahn wrote that, "We cannot 'canonize' him. But we can tell his story and point to the lesson it teaches" (Zahn, "He Would Not," 390).

"It is a quiet place; one feels, a holy place," Zahn noted, "It may someday be a place of pilgrimage."[82]

CATHOLICS AND ORGANIZED PEACE

That summer, Zahn also wrote an article about the Fifth International Pax Christi Conference, which he had attended the previous summer (1957) in Austria.[83] Though it had its weaknesses (its deliberate avoidance of controversial issues and the fact that it was essentially a "bishops' organization"), Zahn pointed out that Pax Christi was the only international Catholic organization at the time dedicated to peacemaking. That being the case, he noted that he was the only Catholic from the United States to attend the meeting. This was unfortunate, he explained, since US Catholics largely claimed they wanted peace, but only two Catholic peace organizations were active in the United States. One was the Catholic Association for International Peace (CAIP), which had come to be regarded "with good reason," Zahn wrote, as an organization more dedicated to the promotion of the US defense policy than its name would suggest. The other was the Catholic Worker, which was often dismissed by critics for its radical "extremism" and "idealistic" failure to grasp the "practical realities" of the world.[84]

As a third option, Zahn suggested Pax Christi as an organization for US Catholics who wished to "work for peace" without sacrificing their "100 per cent Americanism." In this sense, Pax Christi (which, he argued, represented the "absolutely minimal level of Catholic responsibility" for peace) presented US Catholics with an opportunity either to "put up or shut up." For if they could not support at least this minimum of Catholic peace activism, Zahn declared, "we stand convicted—and rightly so—of being disinterested in world peace and insincere in our fervent protestations to the contrary."[85]

Zahn's article was written with the voice of one who was emerging as an animator and leader within the postwar Catholic peace movement (small as it was) and was becoming more and more established in it. The year before, for instance, in the wake of Pius XII's Christmas message that many

82 Zahn, "He Would Not," 390.

83 Zahn, "Catholics and Organized Action for Peace," *The Catholic World* (August 1958); republished in *War, Conscience and Dissent*, 87–97.

84 Zahn, "Catholics," 96.

85 Zahn, "Catholics," 96.

read as clearly stating that a Catholic could not be a conscientious objector, Dorothy Day had written to Zahn (still in Würzburg) asking for his thoughts. Zahn replied that contrary to many commentators, he did not think that the pope had flatly or definitively condemned Catholic pacifism or conscientious objection.[86] He also pointed to what he said were several important lessons that could be gleaned from the message. Chief among these was the fact that Pius XII was not a pacifist, and so Catholic pacifists, Zahn said, should stop hoping for him to become one or for a "quick solution" in which the Vatican would simply declare modern war immoral. No such declaration was coming any time soon. Instead, the Catholic peace movement needed to applaud the pope's denunciations of modern warfare and recognize that there were many people of good will who rejected pacifism, but with whom pacifists must still be willing to work "as far as possible" for peace. In this way, Zahn kept his pacifism measured and nuanced with the hope of building the broadest possible peace movement within the church.

It was for these reasons, Zahn told Day, that he did not support her recent protests against the civil defense drills in New York City. He explained that these well-publicized actions turned off the "average Catholic" they were hoping to persuade and so ultimately harmed "the very pacifist ideals" they were attempting to serve.[87] Zahn made clear, however, that his criticisms were in no way "anti-CW" since "the Catholic Worker is Catholic pacifism in America," and that as a Catholic CO, he had a very special debt to the Catholic Worker that could never be fully repaid. Rather, he explained his concern was that the Catholic Worker not lose or diminish the "full effectiveness" of its pacifist message. This would also require that pacifists avoid tying their pacifism with other "peripheral issues" such as vegetarianism or political anarchism.[88] "I may sound like a 'compromiser' or the better-to-be-spewed-out 'lukewarm' variety Catholic pacifist," Zahn wrote, "but I fear we have an awful long road

86 Among other reasons, Zahn highlighted the fact that Pius was speaking in response to the Soviet crackdown in Hungary in November 1956. The pope seemed to suggest that a resistance to the Soviet invasion would have qualified as a "just war." See Zahn to Day in letter dated February 13, 1957, UNDA Zahn papers (2/02939).

87 Zahn explained that he disagreed with Day regarding the premise that the civil defense drills were merely prowar propaganda. He suggested that a better antiwar argument would have been to go "all out" in support of such efforts to reduce the likely death toll—and then show how futile such efforts would actually be.

88 Zahn was clearly critiquing Ammon Hennacy's rising influence within the Catholic Worker. Hennacy, well known for his vegetarianism and political anarchism, had been an initiator of the civil defense drill protests (Marling, *Christian Anarchist*, 196).

to travel before we reach our goal, and I would like to carry as little excess baggage as possible."

That said, Zahn suggested that instead of despair, the pope's Christmas message should initiate a change in the movement's approach. No doubt thinking of his own journey, Zahn argued that pacifists had been placing too much emphasis upon appeals to reason and intellect, for instance, and not enough on emotion. He described the horror he felt after visiting the monument in the Würzburg cemetery that marked the grave containing the remains of the 3,000 men, women, and children (most of them German Catholics) who had died in a single evening of Allied bombing of the city twelve years earlier. He noted that his emotional response to this had confirmed for him that his own pacifism went much deeper than any logical argument. "That these same circumstances obtain for Cologne, for Munich, for Nuremberg—and for Coventry, for London, for Warsaw as well—strengthens, rather than weakens, their effectiveness as arguments against war," Zahn wrote. He concluded his letter to Day with a call for Catholic pacifists to develop "Christian alternatives" to war, which as we will see, he was already beginning to think through.

CONCLUSION

Zahn's year in Germany as a Fulbright scholar was clearly a pivotal experience. Without his discovery of Franz Jägerstätter, Zahn's life and legacy would have been very different. He immediately recognized the significance of Jägerstätter's witness for his own efforts to promote pacifism and conscientious objection within the Catholic Church. For Zahn, Jägerstätter was a model of his idea of Catholic pacifism.

The year also saw Zahn take on a greater prominence within the still-nascent Catholic peace movement in the United States. Even before he had published his two most influential books, *German Catholics and Hitler's Wars: a Study in Social Control* (1962) and *In Solitary Witness: the Life and Death of Franz Jägerstätter* (1964), Zahn had entered into the controversy about World War II and would carefully begin to wade into the controversies on the wars yet to come.

5

THE "LONG CONTROVERSY"

Dr. Zahn's paper is controversial. . . . This is a question of prudence and loyalty and not one of academic freedom. . . . The paper will lead to a long controversy.

—*Ralph Gallagher, SJ*[1]

While Jägerstätter would continue to be a focus for Zahn, in September 1959, Zahn presented a paper at the annual meeting of the American Catholic Sociology Society (ACSS) at Mundelein College. This paper catapulted Zahn into international notoriety and controversy. Titled, "The Catholic Press and the National Cause in Nazi Germany," it was essentially "leftover" data from his soon-to-be published book *German Catholic and Hitler's Wars*, the primary fruit of his Fulbright research years earlier.[2] Zahn opened the paper by stating that only a handful of German Catholics had refused to fight in what was clearly an unjust war and that, in fact, the German Church gave its "nearly unanimous support" to the Nazi war effort.[3] The purpose of his research, he

1 Gallagher to John Kane in letter dated July 9, 1960, UNDA Zahn papers (6/08351).

2 Zahn, "The Catholic Press and the National Cause in Nazi Germany," 1–19, UNDA Zahn papers (10/13361).

3 Zahn explained that he was working on the assumption that they were in fact unjust wars, and that that possibility "imposed a response of non-cooperation and non-support" upon all Catholics (Zahn, "The Catholic Press," 2).

explained, was to seek to learn how and why national identity could take such a priority for German Catholics that they seemed to largely ignore their church's moral teaching on war.[4]

As the title indicated, Zahn focused his paper largely on the impact of the German Catholic press and its role in rallying Catholic support for the German war effort. He argued that it did so while keeping an "absolute silence" on any and all issues or events that might have stirred doubts as to the justice of the war in the minds of Catholics.[5] Almost immediately after coming to power in 1933, the Nazis quickly shut down the vast majority of Catholic periodicals. This was evidence, Zahn suggested, that the Nazis recognized the power and influence of the Catholic Church—despite the oft-repeated claim that German bishops were powerless in the face of the Nazis. Indeed, the very existence of a Catholic periodical after 1933, Zahn asserted (in what was certainly one of his more memorable lines), could be regarded as evidence that the paper's sponsoring bishop had made the judgment that it was preferable to continue to publish even at the cost of becoming "an active auxiliary of the Goebbels propaganda ministry."[6]

The result, Zahn argued, was that any German Catholic who turned to his diocesan paper with questions regarding the war would have read answers that were unequivocal: it was "the moral duty (indeed, the holy privilege) of every Christian to serve wherever and however he could in a spirit of full dedication to and identification with the nation's cause."[7] This kind of nationalistic fervor could be seen in the "hyper-nationalistic" titles of many of the articles Zahn surveyed: "Heroic Reflections of Courage," "We Play Our Part in the War," "A Saintly Soldier," and "War, School for Sacrifice."[8] Zahn concluded that the German Catholic press had failed to fulfill its function of

4 Zahn, "The Catholic Press," 3.

5 Zahn, "The Catholic Press," 4.

6 Zahn, "Catholic Press," 10.

7 He quoted one paper: "Our fathers and brothers are at the Front and we know that they are fulfilling their difficult duty to the ultimate in a spirit of comradeship and readiness for self-sacrifice. But their heroic offering would be an accusation and a judgment upon us if we at home were not similarly willing to close ranks in a mutually supporting community of action" (Zahn, "Catholic Press," 11).

8 Zahn, "Catholic Press," 12–13.

instructing Catholics in their faith and instead joined with the secular press in the "crusade to create a total consensus in support of the national cause."[9]

As noted above, Zahn did not place blame solely on the Catholic press. He argued instead that responsibility also fell on the bishops who funded and guided their diocesan papers.[10] He referred to his yet unpublished book (*German Catholics and Hitler's Wars*) in which he contended that one of the major influences inducing German Catholic support for Hitler's wars was the German Catholic hierarchy, who both individually and collectively had called upon the Catholic faithful to "do their Christian duty" by serving "*Volk*, *Vaterland*, and *Heimat*."[11] While the bishops had been "widely and justly honored and acclaimed" for opposing some aspects of National Socialism such as forced euthanasia, Zahn contended that at the same time there was no denying the fact that their opposition never came close to any kind of repudiation of the Nazi regime.[12]

Instead, the bishops continually assured their flock that the Nazis were the legitimate authority of the German nation, who must, therefore, be given a presumption of justice by Catholics regarding the war. He also argued that the bishops called upon their flock to fuse together their Catholic and German identities by teaching that unquestionable service to the nation during war was "a moral obligation binding in conscience."[13] In fact, even before the war started, when the Nazis began to publicly make charges that Catholics were not good Germans, Zahn pointed out that the hierarchy, "now a greatly weakened voice of a beleaguered church," spent an increased portion of

9 Zahn acknowledged that the alternative option would have been to resist the Nazis and face the dire consequences. He quoted a 1933 statement from the diocesan paper in Cologne that had already recognized this difficult position and yet seemed to find a source of inspiration: "If anywhere there are still martyrs for the cause of Catholicism, they will be found in the ranks of our Catholic editors" (Zahn, "Catholic Press," 14).

10 To emphasize the link between the press and the bishops, Zahn quoted a prominent German Catholic paper which in 1935 had clearly stated: "Our Catholic religious newspapers are official publications devoted to pastoral guidance as commissioned and authorized by the hierarchy. The editors of these papers are selected by the bishops and take part in the instruction and guidance of the Christian people according to policies set forth by the bishops" (Zahn, "Catholic Press," 4).

11 Indeed, Zahn contended that the bishops had served to validate the priority Catholics had given to their national identity—"making that identity and its demands nothing less than a function of the religious identity and its associated obligations" (Zahn, "Catholic Press," 3).

12 Zahn, "Catholic Press," 15.

13 Zahn, "Catholic Press," 8.

their time documenting the loyalty of German Catholics and setting a tone of "200% patriotism."[14]

Zahn contended that if the war was unjust—and he had yet to read any argument that it had somehow met the criteria of a just war—the bishops had an obligation to present a clear-cut choice between the evil actions demanded by the Nazis and the moral obligation for Catholics not to cooperate with evil. The fact that such a clear choice had not been presented by the bishops, Zahn lamented, highlighted a crucial problem for the effectiveness—if not "the very existence"—of the church in relation to "the modern secular state."[15] Accordingly, Zahn concluded with another argument he would continue to make with regularity in the coming years, that the history of German Catholics under the Third Reich necessitated "an extensive theological re-examination" of contemporary Catholic moral theology and its teaching on the church's engagement with the modern state.

Zahn later recalled that his paper was received with a polite round of applause from the audience. Nevertheless, he was concerned enough about the reaction it might arouse (or that distorted accounts of his argument could emerge) to have the public relations office at Mundelein send out a press release with the full text of his paper attached. The next morning, several local Chicago papers published a heavily edited version of Zahn's paper under headlines that read: "Hitler Backed by Catholics, Scholar Says"; "Bishops Backed Hitler, Study Finds"; and "Catholic Clergy in Nazi Germany Draws Criticism." After reading such headlines, Richard Leonard, who was also at the conference, reportedly asked Ralph Gallagher, SJ (the ACSS president and Zahn's chair at Loyola), "Well, does Zahn still have his job?"[16] It turned out that Leonard's question was not unjustified. Indeed, years later, Zahn would remember that his 1959 paper at the ACSS "unleashed a storm of protest in Germany" and eventually a controversy that would involve even some "very high-ranking prelates at the Vatican."[17]

14 Zahn did acknowledge that the question of whether any German Catholic would have refused to support the war, had their bishops called they to do so, was "one of the imponderables of history" (Zahn, "Catholic Press," 7).

15 Zahn, "Catholic Press," 16.

16 Zahn kept an extensive journal of all this which he titled: "Journal Record of a Controversial Research Report," 1–75, UNDA Zahn papers (10/13233), at 5.

17 Zahn, *German Catholics*, vii.

CONTROVERSY

A few days after these articles appeared in the Chicago press, Zahn was told about a German émigré named Regina Kühn, who was deeply upset by what she read.[18] Zahn quickly wrote to Kühn, but she did not write back. Instead, Kühn and her husband forwarded Zahn's letter to the vicar general of the Archdiocese of Berlin, as well as to fellow German émigré Mgsr. Gerhard Fittkau, the executive director of the US branch of the St. Boniface Society.[19] Fittkau immediately recognized Zahn's research as a very real threat to his work. Articles on Zahn's paper were quickly passed onto Walter Adolph, another German priest and journalist working in West Berlin, who read Zahn's criticisms as mocking his own efforts to preserve the Catholic press from both the Nazis during the war and the Communists after the war. Adolph feared that communist propaganda would be reinforced by such critiques coming out of the West—something Dorothy Day would also caution Zahn to keep in mind.[20]

Adolph and Fittkau, along with a third German cleric named Gustav Kafka, soon became the point men in what amounted to a concerted international campaign against Zahn.[21]As Mark Ruff has explained, this campaign sought not only to survey any damage Zahn's research may have done to the image of the German Catholic Church in the United States but also to counter his arguments in newspapers and scholarly publications, and to prevent Zahn from publishing any more of his research.[22] They launched a series of attacks in Chicago and Rome to make Zahn's life at Loyola miserable.

A week after giving his paper, Zahn was surprised to read a headline in Chicago's archdiocesan newspaper, *The New World*, declaring "Support of Hitler by Catholic Bishops Is Labeled 'Untrue': Dr. Zahn's Findings Contested."[23] When the editor initially refused to publish Zahn's reply, he appealed

18 Zahn, "Journal Record," UNDA Zahn papers (10/13233), 8.

19 The St. Boniface Society was an organization that ministered to German immigrants and organized relief efforts for the church in Germany.

20 Day to Zahn, letter dated May 16, 1960, UNDA Zahn papers (1/3152).

21 Fittkau sent excerpts to Archbishop Jaeger of Paderborn, who then raised the issue at the German Bishops Conference, which in turn entrusted the matter to Adolph's superior Bishop Julius Döpfner in Berlin. Cardinal Wendel, the West German military bishop, brought the noted German historian Johannes Neuhäusler on board (Ruff, *The Battle for the Catholic Past in Germany*, 143).

22 Ruff, *The Battle for the Catholic Past in Germany*, 143.

23 Zahn "Journal Record," UNDA Zahn papers (10/13233), 9.

to Chicago Archbishop Albert Meyer, who eventually stepped in and ordered that Zahn's reply be printed—which it was, but only alongside a lengthy counterpoint written by Adolph.[24] Thinking that Meyer was protecting Zahn, Fittkau personally visited both the archbishop and James Maguire, the Jesuit president of Loyola, and told them that Zahn's "violent pacifist campaign" at the expense of the church in Germany was dangerous and would certainly be exploited by the Communists. Frustrated at what he perceived as the US clerics' weak response to his warnings, Fittkau sent a letter to the renowned German (and Jesuit) biblical scholar Augustin Cardinal Bea, who quickly joined the campaign against Zahn. Bea wrote to Bishop Julius Döpfner of Berlin that Zahn should be forbidden from any further research.[25] "It is truly not acceptable that today when we have to defend ourselves with all our forces against atheism and materialism," the Jesuit cardinal bemoaned, "our own comrades in faith stab us in the back."[26] And when the Jesuit-sponsored *America* magazine published what was read as too favorable an article on Zahn's research, Bea immediately wrote the Jesuit provincial, making it clear that the leadership of both Loyola and *America* must apologize to the German bishops. The US Jesuits quickly acquiesced to Bea's orders.[27]

In the midst of this controversy, Zahn met with Maguire, who told the young sociology professor that he could "expect little support from the university if the affair broke open in Rome." Maguire also suggested that Zahn refrain from publishing any more such material that could be read as "incendiary" to Germany Catholics. In short, the leadership made it very clear to Zahn that he

24 The following week, *The New World* published a letter supportive of Zahn's research by his Loyola colleague and fellow CO Paul Mundy. Again, a critique was printed alongside which called Zahn's research an attack on "the memory of great leaders and martyrs of the faith in Catholic Germany." See Zahn, "Journal Record," UNDA Zahn papers (10/13233), 11.

25 Fittkau also wrote to Adolph, who forwarded the letter onto Julius Döpfner just before he left for Rome, where he and Meyer were about to be elevated to cardinals. After the ceremony, Döpfner pulled Meyer and Maguire aside to tell them of the harm Zahn's research could do to the church, "especially in areas like Poland and Nicaragua" (Ruff, *The Battle for the Catholic Past in Germany*, 145).

26 Ruff, *The Battle for the Catholic Past in Germany*, 145.

27 *America* editor Thurston Davis, SJ, wrote to Döpfner: "May I, on this occasion, stress to Your Eminence (as I have already declared to His Eminence Cardinal Bea), how much *America* regrets that the allusion which this Review made to the Zahn thesis is our issue of September 26, 1959, however short and indirect, not only lent itself to the unfortunate misinterpretations but also incurred the very real danger of exploitation by the Communists in the East zone to the detriment of the Church in Germany" (Ruff, *The Battle for the Catholic Past in Germany*, 145).

was *persona non grata* on campus.[28] It is worth remembering, however, that such an attitude was not embraced by all at Loyola. Indeed, despite the fact that it had been understood that no mention of Zahn's work was to appear on campus, Peter Steinfels, the editor of the Loyola student paper at the time (and later editor at *Commonweal* and a *New York Times* columnist), asked the historian Raymond Schmandt to review *German Catholics and Hitler's Wars* on the front page of the student paper. Noting the controversy surrounding Zahn's research, Schmandt wrote, "where better than in a Catholic university should that concern be manifested and discussed without fear of censorship."[29]

REINHOLD AND SHUSTER

At this point, his old teacher, Paul Hanly Furfey, wrote to Zahn to assure him "that I am on your side and that I am very proud of you."[30] Zahn also wrote to H. A. Reinhold, the exiled German priest and prominent figure in the Catholic liturgical movement, who was living in the United States at the time. In his reply, Reinhold wrote that Zahn's research was correct, but that it was "only the end of a long sad tale."[31] The German hierarchy, he explained, "under the shameless agitation of the late Bishops Groeber and Berning and of Papen and his ilk" had brought about the situation that surrounded the 1933 Enabling Act, which had put the Nazis in power and placed the church on "an incline." Once that had been accomplished, nothing could stop the church from sliding into the predicament it found itself in when Hitler invaded Poland in 1939. Reinhold remembered that Bishop Bares of Berlin had complained to him that some bishops, such as Clemens Augustus Graf von Galen, were particularly "hyperpatriotic" and had even formed groups of bishops who "pushed the others around." Reinhold also told Zahn a story that when "someone high up called on Pius XII to bail the German Catholics out just before the *Anschluss*," the pope told the prelate: "Do you think that after you initiated the 1933 surrender your clergy and laity would follow you into persecution and torture by the Nazis?" The priest reportedly replied with a shrug of the shoulder, and Pius

28 Zahn, "Journal Record," UNDA Zahn papers (10/13233), 26–27.

29 Ruff, *The Battle for the Catholic Past in Germany*, 152.

30 Furfey to Zahn in letter dated October 16, 1959, ACUA Furfey papers.

31 Reinhold to Zahn in letter dated March 4, 1960, UNDA Zahn papers (6/08331).

sent him away asking him to remedy the situation at home. And, as Reinhold explained, "that was the end of it."[32]

Before receiving Bea's denunciation of Zahn, the editors at *America* had invited George N. Shuster to participate in a "State of the Question" section dealing with Zahn's paper. Shuster was a heavy hitter: former Notre Dame professor, managing editor of *Commonweal* (1928–1937), governor of Bavaria during the US occupation of Germany (1950–51), and now president of Hunter College. Shuster summed up what he read as Zahn's main point: "that Catholics are forbidden to support an unjust war, and that therefore it was the duty of the German bishops and the diocesan press under their control to proclaim clearly that the conflict unleashed by the Nazis was morally indefensible," and that as Zahn saw it, "they failed to do so."[33] In response, Shuster wrote that he would not comment on the implications of Zahn's thesis "except to say that up to the present time it has played no part in the history of war."[34] Pointing instead to Zahn's suggestion that German Catholics had failed by not embracing the possibility of martyrdom, Shuster quipped, "Expecting Saint Michaels to spring up by the dozens is to take a pretty benign view of human nature."[35]

In his reply to Shuster, Zahn wrote that even though he believed that the bishops had had a duty to "proclaim clearly" the unjust character of Hitler's war, an acceptable alternative policy of silence would also have been reasonable given the severe circumstances they faced. Neither of these options was taken; instead, the bishops seemed to only offer "open and authoritative" support for the war effort.[36] Any honest review of this support would reveal the truth about the German church during the war, in sharp contrast to the carefully constructed postwar "myth of total and unremitting opposition to Hitler and his regime." Zahn concluded that German Catholics certainly ought to be judged by the heroism they displayed under the Reich, but they should also be judged by "the expedient (sometimes inglorious!) compromises they made."

32 Reinhold to Zahn in letter dated March 4, 1960, UNDA Zahn papers (6/08331).

33 Shuster response, UNDA Zahn papers (6/08364).

34 Zahn repeated Shuster's quote here in the 1989 preface to the second edition of *German Catholics and Hitler's Wars*, xi.

35 Shuster response, UNDA Zahn papers (6/08364).

36 Zahn to Shuster in letter dated March 3, 1960, UNDA Zahn papers (6/0865).

This was not the end of the controversy, however, nor of the roadblocks Zahn faced in his research. In 1960, when he submitted his ACSS paper to be published in the *American Catholic Sociological Review* (ACSR), Ralph Gallagher, SJ—the founding editor of the journal and still Zahn's chair at Loyola—intervened. In a letter to the current *ACSR* editor, Gallagher wrote,

> The ACSS must not get involved because of opinions and research of one of its members. This is a question of prudence and loyalty and not one of academic freedom. The ACSS stands approved by the Social Action Department of the NCWC [the National Catholic Welfare Conference]. Because of conditions in Germany at present the representatives of the Holy See and the hierarchy do not think this is the opportune time to publish the article.[37]

Hearing that his article had been delayed indefinitely, Zahn brought the issue up at the executive council meeting at the ACSS convention that year.[38] In the debate that ensued, Gallagher insisted that the *ACSR* not publish any article critical of the bishops: "we are authorized by the NCWC—and as such must avoid criticizing our sponsors."[39] At one point, another member of the executive council even declared: "Does not respect for the successors of the Apostles require that a Catholic organization refrain from broadcasting their shortcomings?"[40] By the time the council eventually agreed to allow the article to be published, Zahn had given up and published it in the Fall 1960 issue of *Cross Currents*.[41]

37 Gallagher letter to John Kane dated July 9, 1960, UNDA Zahn papers (6/08351).

38 Paul Mundy, the outgoing editor of the ACSR, indicated to Zahn that he had indeed been asked by Gallagher to delay the publication "since a lot of heat was being put on Loyola by the St. Boniface Society." See Mundy to Gordon Zahn in letter dated August 23, 1960, UNDA Zahn papers (6/08366).

39 Sylvester Sieber SVD, the new editor of the *ACSR*, stated that he had received a great deal of mail protesting the article, as well as several angry phone calls from bishops. Both Sieber and Gallagher threatened to resign if Zahn's article was published. See Loretta Morris, "Defining Prudence," presented at the Society for the Scientific Study of Religion Annual Meeting (November 4–6, 1994), 12–14.

40 Morris, "Defining Prudence," 12.

41 Zahn, "The German Press and Hitler's Wars," *Cross Currents* 10, no. 4 (1960): 337–52.

THEOLOGY AND SOCIAL THEORY

One of the fruits of this controversy was that Zahn was forced to clarify his ideas on being both a sociologist and a Catholic, as well as on the deeper relationship between sociology and theology. In short, the controversy compelled Zahn to further clarify his "sociotheological" method. Just before he presented his paper to the ACSS, for instance, Zahn had edited a volume intended for introductory sociology courses at Catholic colleges, in which he included essays by Furfey, Christopher Dawson, Pius XII, Dorothy Day, and even Peter Maurin.[42] Zahn opened by asserting that for a Catholic, "sociology cannot be a 'value-free' science" if that meant "an absolute divorce" of moral considerations from the observation and analysis of social behavior.[43] And while sociology was distinct from social reform, it was certainly not separate. For it would be "unworthy of a sociologist" to discover some new insight into a social problem and simply be content only to report the findings in "the somewhat confined precincts of the scholarly world."[44]

Instead, Zahn wrote that a "Catholic sociologist" would be compelled to "convert his research into suggestions or recommendations of specific programs of social action" designed to "help to treat or cure a social problem." Society could certainly be measured and described with "the latest empirical techniques and sociological methodology," but if that analysis did not take into account a theological anthropology (that is, the human person as "a spiritual being, a creature of intellect and—of utmost importance in the social sciences!—free will"), any study would be incomplete at best and utterly distorted at worst.[45] Far from limiting their scholarship, Zahn saw all this as allowing Catholic sociologists to more fully understand human society.

A more developed defense of this kind of sociotheological approach appeared in Zahn's 1960 essay "Social Science and the Theology of War."[46]

42 Gordon Zahn, ed., *Readings in Sociology* (Newman Press, 1958).

43 Zahn, *Readings*, x.

44 Zahn, *Readings*, 3.

45 For example, Zahn explained that a "Catholic sociologist" who works out of a value system in which divorce is regarded as a "social problem" would use the same sources and methods in analyzing and describing the social phenomenon of divorce as would a different sociologist working out of a different value system who might view a high divorce rate as healthy. The latter would not be any more "value-free" than one who sees divorce as a moral problem (Zahn, *Readings*, x).

46 It was part of a volume on the "state of the question" regarding Catholics and war published by the Catholic Association for International Peace (CAIP). See Gordon Zahn, "Social Science and the Theology of War," in *Morality and Modern Warfare*, ed. William Nagle (Helicon Press, 1960), 104–25.

Building on Furfey's notion of supernatural sociology, Zahn argued that the two world wars had illustrated the fact that there was a clear need for "a truly relevant" Catholic moral theology to replace the "sterile formulas and distinctions" that had become virtually meaningless, particularly on the question of war.[47] While certainly not calling for any kind of revision of "basic moral truths," Zahn saw the necessity for a "reinterpretation and reapplication" of Catholic theological claims to an ever changing social reality—a process within which theology and sociology could and should "come together." The result would be a "truly relevant" moral theology that, on the one hand, could overcome the "sterile superficiality" of contemporary value-free sociologists who feared that the slightest intrusion of moral considerations would destroy their scientific objectivity (what Zahn called "exaggerated positivism"). On the other hand, it could also overcome the notion that theology held exclusive domain over "all references to the moral dimensions of observable social behavior."[48] Instead, Zahn pointed to an "area of overlap" where the disciplines could and should operate interdependently and thus "serve each other."

The fact that this sort of interaction no longer existed meant that both disciplines suffered.[49] Without theology, sociology would only be able to offer "incomplete or otherwise inadequate" descriptions and analyses of society. Without sociology, theology's loss would be reflected in the sinful behavior of Catholics denied the relevant moral guidance and clarification they needed to address contemporary issues. This had certainly been the case for German Catholics in World War II, and Zahn argued that it also held true for Catholic theology's approach to all modern wars, where the majority of Catholic moral theologians avoided or ignored the issue. And if they did address it, they only offered conclusions and interpretations "almost totally irrelevant" to the actual phenomenon of modern war.[50]

In short, incorporating social science and Catholic moral theology would help to make the Church's teaching on war more relevant. For instance, Zahn pointed to the fact that contemporary psychology had revealed the "utter

47 Zahn, "Social Science," 108.

48 Zahn, "Social Science," 109.

49 For, Zahn explained, in its blind commitment to the "myth of the 'value-free social science,'" sociology had shut itself off from the "valuable insights and theoretical frameworks" of theology. Likewise, theologians missed the opportunity to employ sociological organization and analysis of social facts to better understand the "full empirical dimensions of responsible human behavior" (Zahn, "Social Science," 109).

50 Zahn, "Social Science," 110.

nonsense" of the principle of double-effect—a backbone of Catholic theology's teaching on war—by showing that human beings, moral theologians, or people in the pews never weighed good and evil effects in a state of emotional detachment or "aura of pure objectivity." Rather, "nationalistic prides and assumptions" along with "war-induced hatreds and fears" always tipped the scales of any wartime deliberation.[51] Likewise, sociology highlighted the reality that modern military training was in fact a set of "social controls" designed to subject the soldier to a process of "systematic depersonalization," leaving the soldier no longer able to see himself as a morally responsible person but rather as an "agent of destructive force" and unquestioningly obedient to his superiors.[52] At the same time, such training depersonalized human beings into abstract categories such as the "enemy."

Furthermore, Zahn suggested that sociology could be used in thinking about Catholic engagement with the modern nation-state, where it would help Catholic moral theology recognize that it still held onto "anachronistic" formulations. Here, sociologists could point to the fact that there had been a new realignment of society and the state since the days when much of the Catholic just-war tradition had been formulated. This realignment included the shattering of Christian religious unity following the Protestant Reformation but especially the "sweeping rise of an aggressively jealous nationalism." All of which had led to a new understanding of society (or "social complex") that was essentially "un-Christian," if not "anti-Christian." The upshot, Zahn argued, was that there was no longer—if ever there was—any justifiable basis for assuming that the demands or intentions of the modern secular state would meet "even the minimal standards of Christian morality."[53]

Recognizing this historical and sociological reality, Zahn contended, would force Catholic moral theologians to recognize that just-war formulations that granted secular authority a presumption of justice should no longer be assumed.[54] Rather, this new "total social complex" required a more reality-based theological approach that would need to start from what Zahn

51 Zahn, "Social Science," 111.

52 Zahn, "Social Science," 112.

53 Zahn, "Social Science," 116.

54 Zahn wrote that the "bitter proof of our theological inability to meet the challenge of the new paganism is the scandal that found Catholics of Nazi Germany granting 'the presumption of justice' to Adolph Hitler and his infamous regime!" (Zahn, "Social Science," 116).

called a general "presumption of *injustice*" toward any actual or impending war proposed by the state.[55] While not abandoning any fundamental principles in Catholic moral theology, this sort of acknowledgement of the contemporary situation (which social sciences could help expose) would require reassessment or reinterpretation of these principles and their application by theologians. The notion that Christians must be subject to the "powers and principalities" would (once again) stress that such obedience has limits. It would necessitate that the burden of proof shifts to the state, or as Zahn put it, "that Caesar first prove the legitimacy of his claim to the Christian's service."[56]

For Zahn, contemporary Catholics were not being educated about their moral responsibilities nor guided in how to make the difficult decisions and sacrifices that those responsibilities demanded.[57] This was particularly evidenced in the unwillingness of Catholic leaders to denounce any war while it was being fought—let alone a war that was still only being contemplated. While some bishops had argued that it would not be prudent to make any judgment on a war without having access to all the facts, Zahn argued that it would be even less prudent to act contrary to the Gospel admonition to love one's enemies without also having access to all the facts.[58] To the suggestion that if the hierarchy were to declare a particular war unjust it would lead not only to the persecution of the church by the state but also an "impossible conflict of conscience" for Catholics, Zahn responded that such fears assumed that Catholic moral theology taught "patterns of nonconformity that could force Christianity back into the catacombs." In reality, Zahn pointed out, most contemporary Catholics would no doubt choose participating in unjust wars over the prospect of any sort of persecution or retreat to the catacombs. He suggested that this was the result of the fact that Christians had become "spiritually soft."[59]

55 Zahn, "Social Science," 117.

56 Zahn, "Social Science," 116.

57 Zahn, "Social Science," 121.

58 Zahn noted that while this may sound like a rash judgement, it was far less so than the alternative of continuing to obligate "Catholics on both sides of every conflict to kill their fellow members of the Mystical Body on the grounds of full or partial ignorance of the facts" (Zahn, "Social Science," 119).

59 Zahn pointed to recent sociological studies that had made it clear "that values associated with personal and national survival get top priority from today's Christians 'when the chips are down'" (Zahn, "Social Science," 121–22).

To overcome all this, Zahn suggested that an "ideological restoration" was needed—an especially difficult task in a world "so openly alien and even antagonistic" toward Christian values.[60] To this end, he noted that social science offered the notion of a "hero-image" to help personify the sort of Christian values required. While within the Christian tradition, one obvious hero-image would be "the much neglected ideal" of the martyr, Zahn argued that in recent times, martyrs had become associated with "extremists" and "religious fanatics," and thereby dismissed as an acceptable model for "ordinary" Christians. Zahn called it a "modern heresy" that Catholics had come to gladly accept that the church would (or could) never require a course of action that would "force" large numbers to martyrdom. Echoing Furfey's "techniques of non-participation," Zahn suggested that Catholics must discover, develop, and practice new "techniques of resistance" to evil. And should such techniques prove insufficient, like Jägerstätter, a Catholic must be prepared to abandon himself "to the unfathomable will of God" and be ready to die as a martyr "rather than save himself and those dear to him by turning to means that are immoral."[61]

CONCLUSION

Again, we can clearly see that by the start of the 1960s, Zahn had already gained international notoriety (or infamy) as one of the first scholars to begin to question the carefully crafted postwar narratives of German Catholicism under the Nazis. The controversy and conspiracy that arose in response to Zahn revealed the degree to which many in the church cherished these narratives—and the comforting myth they told. In challenging these narratives, it is also important to note that Zahn did not focus only on German Catholicism. Zahn was (and would continue to be) consistent in arguing that there was nothing unique about Germans or German Catholics. Indeed, Zahn would continually employ his research on German Catholics as something of a launching point for his even more stinging critique of US Catholics for their failure to resist not only their nation's militarism and nationalism but also its racial and economic injustices.

60 Zahn, "Social Science," 122.

61 Zahn, "Social Science," 123.

Clearly, Zahn was not afraid to criticize the Catholic hierarchy, something many of his fellow Catholic academics were hesitant to do. But Zahn was always at pains to make clear (especially once criticism of bishops became much more fashionable for Catholic academics) that his criticisms were always made from within the church, which Zahn loved, even while recognizing its faults—especially its record on war. Zahn saw the church as a necessary source to not only form and support Catholics such as Jägerstätter to who resist the horrors of modern war but also as a bulwark (perhaps the last) against the dominance of the modern, "post-Christian," "un-Christian," or even "anti-Christian" state. It was as a "source of dissent" that Zahn put his hope in the Catholic Church, despite its many failures to live up to that hope. Zahn was certainly not afraid to call out such failure. He wanted the church to be faithful—a vision displayed in his two most famous books, *German Catholics and Hitler's Wars* and *In Solitary Witness*.

6

RETURN TO ST. RADEGUND

Jägerstätter . . . was one of God's special friends.

—*Sister Georgia*[1]

In 1961, with this idea of a "hero-image" very much in mind, Zahn received a grant from the American Philosophical Society to return to Austria, where he spent much of June and July in St. Radegund researching Franz Jägerstätter. This was a tense summer as the Cold War continued to escalate. Zahn arrived in Austria just a few months before the Berlin Wall was built in August. And as had been the case for some time now, Cold War Catholic anticommunism would certainly shadow Zahn's research.

Arriving first in Vienna, Zahn interviewed Stratmann and Fried, and he also stopped by the diocesan offices in Linz.[2] This visit did not garner much new information, but it did result in an article that appeared in the local paper a few weeks later that identified Zahn and his reason for being in St. Radegund.[3] Both Franziska and Karobath had suggested that Zahn keep his interest in Jägerstätter's story a secret out of concern that the villagers may

1 Quoted in Zahn, *In Solitary Witness*, 107.

2 This was when Fried told Zahn that he had written his history of wartime Austrian Catholicism at the request of Pius XII (Zahn, *In Solitary Witness*, 269).

3 "St. Radegund: Beheaded for Following His Conscience," *Linzer Volksblatt*, July 6, 1961 (Zahn, *In Solitary Witness*, 251).

not have appreciated it. To Zahn's pleasant surprise, though, the villagers did not react with any hostility to the news that he was researching Jägerstätter; rather, they seemed genuinely curious about what had happened to their fellow Radegunder. Many, for instance, were surprised to learn that Jägerstätter had been beheaded, as they had always assumed he had been executed by firing squad.

As with his previous visit, Karobath served as Zahn's primary contact in St. Radegund. The priest had been a long-time friend of Jägerstätter and had become the strongest promoter of his legacy. For Zahn, however, this connection with Karobath did pose a problem because the priest had often publicly declared that Jägerstätter was the only person in St. Radegund who had recognized and fulfilled his moral obligations during the war. Not surprisingly, this upset several of the villagers. Helpful, though, was the fact that Karobath had kept a file of materials on Jägerstätter, which proved to be immensely useful as Zahn's initial source of information. This "Jägerstätter File" included several hand-written documents: a letter Jägerstätter wrote to Karobath upon receiving his induction notice, the farewell letter he wrote just before his execution, and the "prison statement" he wrote in Berlin-Tegel prison at the urging of Kreuzberg.[4] The file also included the essay Karobath had written on Jägerstätter that had been blocked from publication in the diocesan paper by the bishop of Linz.[5]

While in Vienna, Zahn had obtained a copy of Jägerstätter's 1939 draft registration form from the military archives. On it, Jägerstätter had stated that he was born on May 20, 1907, and that his father was "Franz Bachmeier, a farmer's son," who had been killed in 1915 while fighting in World War I.[6] While in St. Radegund, Zahn was told that Jägerstätter's mother was born from a prominent local Catholic family named Huber and that one of his cousins

4 Zahn, *In Solitary Witness*, 272–74. Zahn quoted the farewell letter in "He Would Not Serve."

5 Zahn noted that Karobath's file was the source of information on Jägerstätter for at least four other publications, including Fried's history, as well an article written by a priest and friend of Karobath named Leopold Arthofer, who had also been imprisoned in Dachau for his opposition to the Nazis (Zahn, *In Solitary Witness*, 274).

6 Zahn, *In Solitary Witness*, 20. In 2007, the year Jägerstätter was beatified, an Austrian journalist and historian named Erna Putz published *Franz Jägerstätter: A Shining Example in Dark Times*, trans. Catherine Laura Danner (Buchverlag Franz Steinmassl, 2007). Putz had been researching Jägerstätter since the late 1980s, and her biography corrects some errors in Zahn's account. For instance, according to Putz, Jägerstätter's biological father did not die in the war but was a servant and so could not marry his mother because he was too poor (Putz, *Franz*, 9).

was the priest who had preached at the burial service for Jägerstätter's ashes in the St. Radegund Church cemetery in 1946. Another of his cousins became a leader in local the *Bibelforscher* community, whom many villagers believed had influenced Jägerstätter's stance during the war.[7] While Zahn could not find any reason why Jägerstätter's parents did not marry, he did learn that in 1917 his mother had married a different man named Jägerstätter, who was the proprietor of the Leherbauer farm and who adopted Franz and "gave over" the farm to him after Franz's marriage in 1936. In St. Radegund, after some confusion, Zahn realized that Jägerstätter was actually known by the name Leherbauer. In fact, when Zahn first visited the village in 1957, no one could give him directions to the "Jägerstätter" farm, which Zahn misinterpreted as meaning that no one remembered Jägerstätter.[8]

INTERVIEWS WITH LOCAL RESIDENTS

Equipped with Karobath's file, Fried's book, and Kreuzberg's appendix as the foundation of his knowledge of Jägerstätter, Zahn began interviewing anyone he could find who remembered Franz. During his summer in St. Radegund, he reported interviewing some twenty-five villagers in addition to Jägerstätter's family and Karobath. Most of the interviews took place in the villagers' homes. Zahn recalled that he rarely interviewed just one person at a time, as extended family would inevitably join the conversation.[9] While most remembered Jägerstätter in a largely positive light, almost everyone he interviewed told Zahn that nobody talked about Jägerstätter much anymore—and some questioned the wisdom of Zahn "stirring the whole business up again." Indeed, Zahn recounted that most of the young people he interviewed—including Jägerstätter's own son-in-law— did not seem aware of Jägerstätter's story or even care all that much about it. "Unless something should happen to change the present patterns of ignorance and indifference," Zahn later wrote, "there is a very good chance that the Jägerstätter history, perhaps even the memory of his name, will be lost to St. Radegund in a generation or two."[10] And this sense that many in St. Radegund (and Austria) wanted to forget about Jägerstätter was

7 "Bibelforscher" was a term used for a Jehovah's Witnesses.

8 Zahn, *In Solitary Witness*, 20.

9 Zahn, *In Solitary Witness*, 259.

10 Zahn, *In Solitary Witness*, 150.

only further confirmed when Zahn could not find any articles on Jägerstätter in the local papers following his execution in 1943. In fact, the first mention he found of Jägerstätter in print was from November 1946.[11] It would not be an exaggeration, therefore, when in the years to come Zahn described himself as having "discovered" Franz Jägerstätter.

FRANZISKA

Along with any villager who remembered him, Zahn also interviewed Jägerstätter's son-in-law (married to his youngest daughter), Franz Huber (who Zahn referred to as Jägerstätter's "godson"), Franziska's sister, and Jägerstätter's mother and daughters. Zahn also interviewed Franziska, but only once and not until the end of his time in St. Radegund so as not to open any "old wounds."[12] During this interview, Franziska showed Zahn copies of her husband's writings that Zahn had not known existed—writings he would later describe as the "most significant and certainly most unexpected" material he came across in St. Radegund.[13] While Zahn had read Jägerstätter's farewell letter and prison statement in Karobath's file, he was amazed when Franziska showed him seventeen other letters her husband had written to her from prison, along with a second farewell message, as well as a composition book full of nine essays (which Zahn labeled "commentaries") that Jägerstätter had written from the time he returned from military training in 1941 until his arrest in early 1943.[14] For Zahn, these "moving and at times frankly inspirational" documents introduced to him a whole new dimension to understanding Jägerstätter's

11 An article in the November 6, 1946, issue of *Neue Warte am Inn*, a regional newspaper out of Braunau, described a meeting of a group of former political prisoners that had recently taken place. According to the group, twenty-two people from the area were listed as having been murdered during the Nazi period, including "Jägerstätter, Franz, of St. Radegund, August 3, 1943—executed by shooting in Braunschweig." Likewise, the St. Radegund village records contained a report on villagers who died in the war that included Jägerstätter. However, this report was not submitted until seven years after his death and also contained errors in the date, location, and manner of execution (Zahn, *In Solitary Witness*, 267).

12 Franziska wrote Zahn after reading a translated copy of an article he wrote on Jägerstätter after he returned from his Fulbright year. After expressing her gratitude for the article and the joy it brought her, she wrote that "I had to cry anyway when I read it. Whenever I read my husband's letters, everything comes back to my mind as if it all took place a few months ago. But when I look at my grandchildren, I can see that many years have already gone by, for my children were then as small as these" (Zahn, *In Solitary Witness*, 263).

13 Zahn, *In Solitary Witness*, 5.

14 Franziska also showed Zahn a formal notice of his execution from 1943.

life, revealing his "subjective awareness and evaluation of the events as they developed."[15] Zahn described Jägerstätter's writings as "a graphic statement of his Christian witness."[16]

ST. RADEGUND INTERVIEWS

Over the course of his interviews, a narrative began to emerge that Franz's life was a story of "two Jägerstätters." Villagers described an "early" Jägerstätter who was an above-average student (particularly in reading and religion) but whose formal education came to an end after his fourteenth birthday.[17] They remembered the young Jägerstätter attending weekly Mass and other religious services, but they also remembered that he was "a little wild" and always "ready for a fight"—he was even part of a *Burschen*, a local gang known for fighting with gangs from other villages.[18]

Likewise, almost all the villagers told Zahn that at some point Jägerstätter became a "new man." Many thought that this change was a result of his marriage to Franziska in 1936.[19] Others said that they remembered seeing a change in Jägerstätter around the time he returned from his "exile" when he left St. Radegund for a period of time. While there was some confusion over when and why he left, the villagers seemed to agree that it was upon his return that they started to notice a change in Jägerstätter—a change marked by both an intense religiosity and an intense hatred for the Nazis.[20] While Jägerstätter had

15 Zahn, *In Solitary Witness*, 6.

16 Zahn, *In Solitary Witness*, 110.

17 Zahn, *In Solitary Witness*, 24.

18 Zahn, *In Solitary Witness*, 28.

19 Zahn later pointed to evidence in Karobath's file that this change predated Jägerstätter's marriage, and he suggested that Jägerstätter's marriage to a devout Catholic like Franziska (and their honeymoon in Rome) should be seen as a result of this change rather than the cause (Zahn, *In Solitary Witness*, 38).

20 While some villagers told Zahn that Jägerstätter had left in order to make money, Zahn pointed out that on his 1939 military registration form, Jägerstätter had reported that he was the father of three children, even though his youngest daughter was not born until 1940. Zahn reported that it was a very well-known secret in St. Radegund that Jägerstätter had fathered a child out of wedlock in 1934, and he suggested that Jägerstätter's exile may have been involuntary—an effort to get him out of town until things settled down. Some of the villagers told Zahn that he left either in 1934 or 1935, which Zahn used as confirmation of his theory (Zahn, *In Solitary Witness*, 39). However, according to Putz, Jägerstätter left St. Radegund in the fall of 1927 in order to earn money, first by working on a farm in Bavaria and then in the Styrian iron ore mills in Eisenerz. He returned to St. Radegund in 1930. She also pointed out that his daughter Hildegard was in fact born (out

always been a dutiful Catholic, villagers explained that the new Jägerstätter sang hymns while working in the fields and often stopped his work to read the Bible or pray. One villager even told Zahn that Jägerstätter once declared that mowing his fields constituted "killing God's flowers" and he had even prayed for the flowers. They also told Zahn that there had been some concern that Jägstätter's new found religious fervor had become an impediment to his obligations on the farm.

They recalled that the "new" Jägerstätter also no longer played cards or visited the local tavern—though, in her attempt to set the record straight, Franziska explained that her husband would still occasionally play cards with the pastor, and that while he did stop going to the tavern it was mainly to avoid arguments over politics.[21] Villagers also remembered that Jägerstätter started fasting before and after receiving communion (Kreuzberg told Zahn about Jägerstätter fasting and doing penance in Berlin-Tegel prison) as well as regularly performing works of charity despite his own financial struggles, struggles exacerbated by his refusal to accept government wartime relief funds. Karobath told Zahn that around this time, Jägerstätter started making regular pilgrimages to a shrine in Altötting (Fried had listed this as a sign of his conversion)—though, again, Franziska said that her husband made his first such pilgrimage with her right after they were married. Other villagers also reported that Jägerstätter had made the almost thirty-mile pilgrimage by foot just before he declared his refusal to serve.

In his interview, Ferdinand Fürthauer, the priest who had replaced Karobath as pastor from the time of Jägerstätter's return from military training in 1941 to his execution 1943, recalled that when Jägerstätter returned from training, he was a regular at daily Mass, and so he asked Jägerstätter to be the parish sexton because the previous sexton had recently died. Jägerstätter accepted and remained the sexton until he left St. Radegund for the last time.[22] Fürthauer remembered Jägerstätter as being very conscientious in his duties:

---

of wedlock) in August 1933 and that Jägerstätter maintained a relationship with Hildegard and her mother up until the time of his arrest. Putz reported that living in Eisenerz was the first time Jägerstätter had ever lived in an environment hostile to the church, and that he even stopped going to mass for a time, but that when he returned to St. Radegund he was "stronger in his faith than ever" (Putz, *Franz*, 12–15).

21 Zahn, *In Solitary Witness*, 40.

22 Franziska appears to have carried on in this role after Franz's imprisonment, and they had even discussed these duties in their letters (Zahn, *In Solitary Witness*, 46).

he would not allow any gossip in the sacristy, and he was even known to lock the church doors once Mass had begun to prevent late entries. The pastor also told Zahn that Jägerstätter had once admonished him for giving a homily at a soldier's funeral in which Fürthauer seemed to praise the virtues of military life. Jägerstätter insisted that such a life brought about many occasions of sin, particularly for young men, and he encouraged the priest to preach more on the sufferings of those in purgatory as a way to encourage his listeners to strive more for perfection.[23]

Equally intense as his religious fervor was the "new" Jägerstätter's complete opposition to the Nazis. For instance, villagers reported that Jägerstätter had been a member of the local *Bauernbund* (Austrian Peasant Association) and that he had threatened to resign if it weakened its opposition to the Nazis.[24] They also remembered that Jägerstätter started publicly saying "pfui Hitler" in response to "Heil Hitler."[25] During their interviews, villagers gave Zahn several examples of Jägerstätter refusing to support the Nazis, starting with his refusal to vote "yes" in the March 1938 plebiscite (something that seemed to be common knowledge in the village) despite a great deal of pressure to do so, including from the Austrian hierarchy.[26] Once the *Anschluss* had passed, Jägerstätter refused to donate to Nazi-sponsored welfare and patriotic organizations or accept Nazi family and farm financial assistance, the only villager to refuse these funds. His godson also told Zahn that Jägerstätter was the reason he had refused joined the Hitler Youth.

While Jägerstätter seemed to have been practicing acts of nonparticipation for some time then, Fürthauer recalled that it was upon his return from military training in 1941 that Jägerstätter became certain of his need to make what would become his ultimate refusal. It was around that time that Jägerstätter confided in the priest that he believed that the Nazi war effort was unjust. Fürthauer told Zahn that he tried to persuade Jägerstätter to join the military for the sake of his family. They had even discussed the idea of Jägerstätter hiding in the woods until the war ended. Jägerstätter rejected such an option both out

23 Zahn, *In Solitary Witness*, 44.

24 Zahn, *In Solitary Witness*, 46.

25 Zahn, *In Solitary Witness*, 46.

26 For instance, Cardinal Innitzer of Vienna had infamously called upon Austrian Catholics to support the *Anschluss*. See Robert Schwartz, "Burckel and Innitzer," in *Conquering the Past: Austrian Nazism Yesterday and Today*, ed. F. Parkinson (Wayne State University Press, 1989): 137–48.

of fear for his family and because he said that he desired to offer his life to highlight the injustice of the war as well as the Nazi persecution of church.[27]

When Jägerstätter persisted in his stand, Fürthauer advised him to talk to other priests in neighboring villages. He knew that Jägerstätter had spoken with at least two other priests.[28] One named Franz Krenn had already died, but Zahn learned that he was the priest with whom Jägerstätter stayed the night before he reported to the induction center in Enns. Zahn was able to speak to the other priest (named Taimer), who said he remembered Jägerstätter had visited him in 1941 asking questions about the morality of the war. Fearing he could be a Nazi spy, Taimer told Jägerstätter to write down his questions and place them under a statue in the church. He told Zahn that Jägerstätter had left a several page-statement explaining why the war was unjust.[29]

Fürthauer also suggested that Jägerstätter meet with the bishop of Linz, which he did. Though no official record of that meeting remained, Bishop Josef Fliesser (who had also since died) did recount his meeting with Jägerstätter in a letter to a priest written years after the war, which Zahn found in Karobath's file. "I knew Jägerstätter personally, since he spent more than an hour with me before his scheduled induction," the bishop wrote, "To no avail I spelled out for him the moral principles defining the degree of responsibility borne by citizens and private individuals for the acts of the civil authority. I reminded him of his far greater responsibility for his own state of life, in particular for his family."[30]

LEO FELDMANN

Karobath's file also contained a letter from an attorney named Friedrich Leo Feldmann, who had been assigned to defend Jägerstätter at his military tribunal in Berlin. Zahn tracked Feldmann down in Düsseldorf, and with Franziska's permission, the lawyer agreed to speak with him. Feldmann

27 Zahn heard reports that another villager had been hiding in nearby woods at the time and had been supported by the villagers—including visits from a local dentist (Zahn, *In Solitary Witness*, 61).

28 Fürthauer admitted to Zahn that he had had a very difficult time counseling Jägerstätter.

29 Zahn saw this as evidence that Jägerstätter at that point was already fully committed to his stand against the war (Zahn, *In Solitary Witness*, 58).

30 The letter was written to a priest named Leopold Arthofer explaining why the bishop would not allow an article Arthofer had written on Jägerstätter to be published in the diocesan paper (Zahn, *In Solitary Witness*, 58, 170).

began by acknowledging that representing Jägerstätter had definitely helped his postwar career in de-Nazified West Germany, and he showed Zahn a letter written by a chaplain at Berlin-Tegel prison testifying to his efforts on behalf of "an Austrian peasant who refused military service on the grounds that he could not support a regime that was attacking his Church."[31] Feldmann did not seem to remember much about Jägerstätter's religious motivations and appeared genuinely surprised when Zahn told him that Jägerstätter had discussed his refusal with his bishop. But he did remember that when he had pointed to the reality that millions of other Catholics found it possible to support the Nazi war effort, Jägerstätter had simply replied that "They have not been given the grace."[32]

In a pivotal piece of information for Zahn's portrayal of Jägerstätter (and what would later prove to be the most controversial part of Zahn's account), Feldmann gave a detailed description of Jägerstätter's July 6, 1943, trial.[33] According to the attorney, there had been a delay at the start of the trial, and so he was able to convince the presiding officers to speak directly with Jägerstätter before the hearing began in the hope of changing his client's mind. Zahn later described this meeting as a "moment of high drama" during which the simple farmer faced two high-ranking military officers who represented "the power he had chosen to reject and who were soon to pass final judgment upon him for his act of rebellion."[34] As their meeting went on, however, and Jägerstätter refused to change his mind, Feldmann recalled that a distinct shift began to take place in the tone of the officers' appeals until they were essentially begging Jägerstätter to accept some form of noncombatant service and thereby not force them to sentence him to death. The officers guaranteed Jägerstätter that he would never be called upon to bear arms.[35] However, Jägerstätter rejected their

31 Zahn, *In Solitary Witness*, 85.

32 Jägerstätter gave a similar response when he could not think of a single instance in which a bishop had called upon Catholics not to support the war (Zahn, *In Solitary Witness*, 86).

33 He assured Zahn that none of the court records survived the war, but that his memory was accurate—both these points would later be challenged.

34 Zahn clearly wanted to believe Feldmann and later described this request as the lawyer's first "unusual effort" to save Jägerstätter's life (Zahn, *In Solitary Witness*, 87).

35 Putz suggested that Feldmann had "incorrectly described" the trial to Zahn (Putz, *Franz*, 107).

pleas and declared that such a compromise would only complicate things by adding "the sin of falsehood" onto an already immoral act.[36]

After the meeting, Feldmann recalled that the trial moved fairly quickly, and Jägerstätter was given the mandatory death sentence under the section of a wartime law dealing with harm done to the war effort.[37] Immediately afterward, the lawyer wrote a letter (dated July 6, 1943) to the "Catholic Pastor of St. Radegund." He described the verdict, but explained that Jägerstätter's life could "still be saved" if he changed his mind, and he invited the pastor and Jägerstätter's wife to come to Berlin to try to do so.[38] Franziska and Fürthauer left for Berlin the day after receiving the letter.

In a letter she wrote to Karobath after this visit, Franziska described meeting her husband in prison. While it was obvious that he had suffered much, Jägerstätter told his wife that he was happy and would not change his mind. "He could not bring himself to promise us he would become a soldier," she wrote, "He still has several days to think it over, but only the dear Lord knows how much longer he has to live."[39] After about twenty minutes, the meeting ended and Franziska recalled that "with heavy hearts we had to take leave of each other." Franziska ended her letter by adding that the Nazis could easily have assigned her husband to the medical corps, but that "they were naturally too proud for that, for it might have looked like a compromise on their part." Zahn would later end up dismissing this suggestion.[40]

36 Zahn speculated that perhaps Jägerstätter's rebellion had struck a chord with the officers—one that was "not totally repugnant to them"—and that their concern was to save the life of a man whose sincerity and courage moved them deeply. He pointed to an earlier failed assassination attempt of Hitler that exposed the degree of dissatisfaction within German military circles (Zahn, *In Solitary Witness*, 88–89).

37 The regulation, in part, read: "The death penalty shall be levied against...anyone who publicly advocates or incites the refusal to perform the required service in the German army...or who otherwise openly seeks to weaken or undermine the desire of the German people . . . to maintain its military effectiveness" (Zahn, *In Solitary Witness*, 89).

38 Zahn found this letter in Karobath's file. Noting that Jägerstätter had avoided mentioning his trial or its verdict in his July 8th letter to Franziska, Zahn described Feldmann's letter as the lawyer's "second extraordinary effort" to save Jägerstätter's life (Zahn, *In Solitary Witness*, 93).

39 Zahn, *In Solitary Witness*, 94.

40 Sensing that Feldmann's account could be seen by some as "an ingenious concoction," Zahn argued that the lawyer had no real reason make up the story and that "his manner in telling the story was thoroughly persuasive." He suggested that, most likely, Jägerstätter simply did not want his wife to know that he had rejected an opportunity to save his life, and that Feldmann had not told Franziska either because he was too busy or wanted to protect his client's confidentiality (Zahn, *In Solitary Witness*, 95).

In his recollections of the meeting, Fürthauer told Zahn that (presumably on the advice of Feldmann) he had explained to Jägerstätter that all charges would be dropped if he recanted, but that Jägerstätter had replied that even if he did agree, he doubted the Nazis would keep any such promise.[41] In the end, Fürthauer said that he gave his former sexton a final blessing and assured him that if he was following the dictates of his conscience, he was not committing a sin. The pastor also recalled that Jägerstätter told him he had spoken with a prison chaplain and that their conversation had brought him a great sense of "inner peace." Zahn guessed that this was when Jägerstätter had expressed joy and relief in hearing Kreuzberg tell the story about martyred Father Reinisch's refusal to cooperate with the Nazis.[42]

Zahn was also able to track down another chaplain named Bernhard Kunza who had met with Jägerstätter in Berlin-Tegel.[43] Kunza called Jägerstätter a "*radikaler* Catholic" who had stated that he could not simply turn the responsibility for his actions over to Hitler.[44] When Kunza advised Jägerstätter to seek some kind of a pardon from the Nazis, since the church and Germany would need individuals like him after the war, Jägerstätter refused. The chaplain also remembered that Jägerstätter had justified his position by referring to a priest (Reinisch) who had taken a similar stand.

"ONE OF GOD'S SPECIAL FRIENDS"

Beyond these interviews, Zahn was contacted by two individuals with additional information on Jägerstätter who had read about his research in the July 1961 article in the Linz paper. The first was a priest named Franz Baldinger, who had served as a chaplain at the Linz prison where he said he had met Jägerstätter. Zahn was able to meet with the priest, who informed him that the most of the prisoners in Linz were there for committing serious offenses against military discipline, such as desertion. While he could not remember the details of Jägerstätter's imprisonment, he told Zahn that he knew that Jägerstätter had been an exception. He also recalled that his attempt to distinguish support

41 Zahn, *In Solitary Witness*, 95.

42 Zahn, *In Solitary Witness*, 100.

43 Kunza was the priest who had written the letter after the war attesting to Feldmann's work on behalf of Jägerstätter.

44 Zahn, *In Solitary Witness*, 105.

for the Nazis from support for the German nation had failed to persuade Jägerstätter. Baldinger reported that Jägerstätter was certain in his belief that the Nazis were evil and that the war was unjust.

Zahn also received a letter from an Austrian nun he referred to as "Sister Georgia," who had likewise read the article in the Linz paper.[45] She wrote that during the war, she had served at a Catholic hospital in Berlin, where the chaplain, a priest named Albert Jochmann, would often tell the sisters about the prisoners he had visited just before their executions. The nun remembered Jochmann talking about Jägerstätter the evening after he had been executed. Since Jägerstätter had already received the sacraments, Jochmann told the sisters that he found the prisoner in his cell and very calm. When the priest pointed out a document on the table that Jägerstätter could sign in order to save his life, he recalled that he had pushed it aside and said, "I cannot and may not take an oath in favor of a government that is fighting an unjust war."[46] Jägerstätter also declined the chaplain's offer to read from the Bible, saying, "I am completely bound in inner union with the Lord, and any reading would only interrupt my communication with my God." That evening, back at the hospital, Jochmann told the Austrian sisters, "I can only congratulate you on this countryman of yours who lived as a saint and has now died a hero. I say with certainty that this simple man is the only saint that I have ever met in my lifetime."[47]

Sister Georgia went on to explain that after the war, she had been sent to Berlin by her superior to find Jägerstätter's ashes, and with a letter from Karobath, she took them back to be buried at St. Radegund.[48] On her return trip with the ashes, the nun recounted having received "extraordinary help" in a spiritual matter through the intercession of Jägerstätter. She concluded that Jägerstätter was "one of God's special friends." All of which led Zahn to write, hinting at the theological lens needed to fully understand Jägerstätter,

45 In her account, Putz identified "Sister Georgia" as Kallista Vorhauer of the School Sisters of Vöcklabruck (Putz, *Franz*, 118).

46 Zahn, *In Solitary Witness*, 107.

47 Zahn, *In Solitary Witness*, 107.

48 Zahn noted that this task was aided by Kreuzberg's letter to Franziska (dated August 21, 1943), in which he indicated that Franz's ashes had been initially buried at the Brandenburg crematorium on August 17 (Zahn, *In Solitary*, 107).

that "there may be more to the story than we are now able to reach or even to understand."[49]

At the end of the summer, Zahn returned to Chicago and a few months later received a letter from Franziska in which she informed him about letters she had since received from two of her husband's former cellmates. In one letter, the author mentioned that Jägerstätter had given him a rosary and recounted how Jägerstätter was always praying or reading a religious pamphlet, and he told Franziska to assure her children that their father had died "in God's friendship."[50] Franziska wrote back, and this brought a second letter from another former cellmate. He told Franziska that Jägerstätter's "faith in God and justice was beyond measure" and that he belonged "without question to the heroes of our time . . . a fighter to the death for faith, peace, and justice."[51]

Learning of these new letters, Zahn immediately wrote to both men. Only one wrote back, stating that Jägerstätter was "very religious" and possessed a "fanatical love for his country, Austria." He also recalled Jägerstätter explaining that he resisted the Nazis because they were opposed to his religious convictions and that he refused to fight in a war that was "senseless and doomed in advance."[52] He wrote that Jägerstätter "loved Austria intensely" and he absolutely refused to serve the enemy of his beloved country. The former prisoner ended by explaining that Jägerstätter always knew that he would be executed, but that he preferred to die rather than to do evil: "as a Christian he preferred to do his fighting with the word of God and not with arms."[53]

CONCLUSION

Zahn's summer in St. Radegund confirmed his initial impression that Jägerstätter was a heroic example of a Catholic conscientious objector who maintained his resistance to what was clearly an unjust war (and a blatantly evil regime) essentially alone. The striking biographical similarities between the Austrian

49 Zahn, *In Solitary Witness*, 107.

50 Zahn, *In Solitary Witness*, 77.

51 He also wrote, "I can assure you that we found a good friend in Franz who, in the darkest moments, was always able to find a word of comfort and always managed to give us his last piece of bread from the meager morning and evening meals we took in the cell" (Zahn, *In Solitary Witness*, 78).

52 Zahn *In Solitary Witness*, 79.

53 Zahn, *In Solitary Witness*, 80.

Catholic and Zahn himself would have also certainly played a role in Zahn's interest in Jägerstätter, as well as in how he told his story. Both men were raised by single mothers and then "adopted" by stepfathers whose names they took. Both were Catholic and seemed to recognize the evils of their respective nation's efforts in World War II—and both seemed to be the only people they were aware of to arrive at that conclusion. Zahn was looking for a model, a "hero-image," of the kind of Catholic pacifism that he embraced and believed to be possible in the church, and he saw Jägerstätter as someone who could be such a model. The degree to which Jägerstätter had actually been a pacifist would be the subject of ongoing conversation and debate for Zahn and others interested in his story.

The Austrian Catholic martyr also offered an example of why Zahn's sociotheological method was necessary. The life and death of Franz Jägerstätter cannot be fully understood or explained without taking his religious claims and beliefs seriously—something contemporary ("value-free") social science was unable to do. Jägerstätter was indeed one of God's special friends.

7

"THE LESSON OF GERMAN CATHOLICISM"

Zahn's writing in the early sixties . . . sought to give non-violence a political significance rather than allowing it to be merely an a-political withdrawal from society into a utopian dream.

—*William Au*[1]

In 1962—the same year that the Cuban Missile Crisis brought the world to the brink of nuclear war—*German Catholics and Hitler's Wars* was finally published.[2] Addressing the controversy that had greeted his 1959 paper to the ACSS, Zahn opened the book by stating that his intention was not a "public washing of dirty laundry" but rather the hope that his research would reveal some of the causes (and consequences) of the moral failures of the German

1 William Au, *The Cross, The Flag, and The Bomb: American Catholics Debate War and Peace, 1960–1983* (Greenwood Press, 1985), 115.

2 Gordon Zahn, *German Catholics and Hitler's Wars: A Study in Social Control* (Sheed & Ward, 1962). Zahn had originally intended to publish the book with Helicon Press, a Catholic press that was based in Baltimore, but Helicon's German affiliate had been the target of pressure, with one German cardinal reportedly even threatening to end contracts with the press to publish Catholic school textbooks. Discouraged by delays, Zahn published his book with Sheed & Ward instead (Ruff, *The Battle for the Catholic Past in Germany*, 148).

Catholic Church during the Third Reich and thereby "benefit and perfect the Church as a temporal social institution charged with a divine mission and responsibility."[3] To illustrate this, he recounted that during his Fulbright year in Germany, he had stayed in a guest house operated by a Catholic couple and that every morning he would eat breakfast under a portrait of the couple's only son, who had been killed in action during World War II.[4] Zahn wrote that this image of a young Catholic soldier had reminded him of a former classmate back in Milwaukee, another young Catholic who was also killed in the war. Since both were Catholics, and thus bound by the same "theological value system" that taught that they could participate only in a just war, Zahn remembered thinking that both men could not have been correct—they both could not have been fighting a just war.[5] This dilemma, he explained, pointed to the crux of the sociotheological problem his book looked to expose: "the scandal" of fellow members of the same Mystical Body periodically killing each other, all in the belief that they were fulfilling their "Christian duty."[6] For Zahn, this scandal pointed specifically at the failure of church hierarchy in shepherding their flock. Over the course of his research, Zahn explained that he had arrived at one simple conclusion:

> The German Catholic supported Hitler's wars not only because such support was required by the Nazi rulers but also because his religious leaders formally called upon him to do so; not only because the actions and opinions of his fellow citizens made him feel obligated to share the nation's burdens and sorrows but also because, by example and open encouragement, the Catholic press and Catholic organizations gave their total commitment to the nation's cause; not only because of deep-felt fears of the terrible price nonconformity would bring or the warm surge of satisfaction accompanying nationalistic or patriotic identification with the war effort, but also because his most cherished

3 Zahn, *German Catholics*, 40.

4 Zahn, *German Catholics*, 40.

5 Zahn, *German Catholics*, 44. While it was a "logical impossibility that a war could be just for all participants," he noted that it was "entirely possible that none of the participants would be fighting a just war" (Zahn, *German Catholics*, 196). This, of course, is a much-debated point in just-war theory.

6 Zahn *German Catholics*, 56.

> religious values had been called into play to encourage him to take his post "on the field of honor" in the "defense of *Volk* and *Vaterland*."[7]

To justify such a conclusion, Zahn's book offered pages and pages of specific examples of German bishops doing just that during the Nazi regime.

THE GERMAN BISHOPS

Zahn acknowledged that the German hierarchy of the Catholic Church had often displayed heroic resistance to the Nazis. But he noted that such resistance was generally limited to issues involving assaults on church rights and property or the Nazi euthanasia programs, which the bishops saw as a clear violation of Catholic moral principles. Active participation in and support for Hitler's wars of aggression were apparently not recognized as such a violation.[8] In fact, quite a contrary view was indicated by the tenor of the hierarchy's wartime directives.[9] In 1939, for instance, the German bishops issued a joint pronouncement stating that they wished "to encourage and exhort our Catholic soldiers to do their duty in obedience to the *Führer*, ready for sacrifice and with the commitment of the whole being."[10] Such a statement, Zahn explained, clearly implied that participation in the war was regarded as permissible, if not obligatory, for German Catholics.[11] In contrast, Zahn noted that he did not find any episcopal statements that ever questioned—or even a hinted at questioning— whether or not Hitler's wars met the conditions of a just war laid out in Catholic moral theology. For Zahn, such silence was extremely telling and would have certainly left German Catholics to conclude that either the war must have been just or that the question of its justice held little or no relevance. As a result, the only standards the German bishops seemed to offer for determining a Catholic's

7 Zahn, *German Catholics*, 56.

8 Zahn explained that he saw Hitler as having engaged in three separate and somewhat distinct "wars": the war against Poland and its allies; the war against the European "neutrals" in 1940 and 1941; and the war against the Soviet Union (Zahn, *German Catholics*, 53).

9 Zahn, *German Catholics*, 78.

10 Zahn, *German Catholics*, 64.

11 Zahn quoted one bishop as declaring that serving in the German military "is for the Christian, not only a patriotic but also a religious obligation" (Zahn, *German Catholics*, 67).

obligations to the war were "unquestioning service to *Volk* and *Vaterland*" and the "protection of the *Heimat*."[12]

According to Zahn, though, the pivotal contribution made by the German hierarchy to assuring Catholic "conformity" to the Reich was their initial recognition and support of the newly empowered Nazi regime as the legitimate authority in Germany in 1933. For in doing so, they bound German Catholics to the authority of the Nazis, or at least gave them the benefit of the doubt (or "presumption of justice") with regard to war.[13] And this recognition of the Nazis by the bishops came early. Indeed, just five days after the ratification of the "Enabling Act" on March 24, 1933, which gave the Nazis power, the Cardinal-Archbishop of Cologne issued a letter calling on Catholics in his diocese "to be loyal to the legitimate authority" and to "conscientiously fulfill their civil duties," while also rejecting "on principle all illegal or revolutionary non-cooperation."[14] In various pastoral letters and statements, Zahn highlighted a clear pattern of the hierarchy similarly recognizing Hitler's regime as Germany's legitimate authority and thereby possessing a full claim upon the loyalty and obedience of all German Catholics, "not only as a civil duty but specifically as a *moral* obligation."[15]

Zahn also reported finding no evidence that German Catholics were ever led to believe that the regime was at all unworthy of their support, nor that there was ever any serious possibility that the German Catholic bishops would openly denounce the Nazis or imply that they were no longer to be considered the nation's legitimate authority. Furthermore, Nazi efforts to block the circulation of Pius XII's encyclical *Mit Brennender Sorge* in 1937 was further evidence that the Nazis were aware of the serious threat Catholic opinion could have posed to their power were it ever mobilized against them.[16] This fact, along with their efforts to shut down the Catholic press, implied that

12 Though he acknowledged the difficulty in translating these terms, Zahn likened *Vaterland* to "fatherland" and *Volk* to "people" or "nationality," while *Heimat* was a "myth-concept" that was best translated as "habitat" (Zahn, *German Catholics*, 21–23).

13 Zahn, *German Catholics*, 71.

14 Zahn, *German Catholics*, 73.

15 Zahn, *German Catholics*, 75.

16 He noted that the Vatican never took any formal steps to withdraw its recognition of Hitler's authority, even though *Mit Brennender Sorge* seemed to reveal that the pope was aware of much of what was going on in Germany under the Nazis. It would be an exaggeration, therefore, Zahn argued, to read *Mit Brennender Sorge* as "a formal condemnation of the Nazi regime which somehow released German Catholics from the moral obligation to obey Nazi authority." In fact, any claim that the bishops were helpless in the face of Hitler (or that they were simply following Pius XII's lead) was dubious. Indeed, Zahn suggested that it raised the intriguing possibility that German Catholics and their bishops were perhaps not as powerless as they often described themselves to be under the Nazis. While any concerted Catholic opposition would have certainly brought about drastic reprisals, Zahn argued that there was clear reason to question how effective those reprisals would have been "had the bishops chosen to rally the Catholic faithful to a more thoroughgoing opposition—and had they been successful in the effort."[17] All of which led Zahn to pointedly assert that the Vatican's 1933 concordat with Hitler should not be seen as a cause for the German hierarchy's support of the Nazis, but rather as a consequence of "the enthusiastic welcome" the German bishops had already given to the regime.[18]

GALEN, FAULHABER, AND GRÖBER

As if such a wholesale indictment of the German hierarchy was not enough, Zahn then turned his attention to three specific bishops who were generally considered to have been "the most renowned and respected opponents" of the Nazis.[19] Zahn called such characterizations into question. One of these, Cardinal Clement August von Galen (the so-called "Lion of Münster") had publicly opposed Nazi aggressions against the church, but Zahn noted that he was also the first bishop to swear the oath of allegiance to Hitler prescribed by the Concordat.[20] While Cardinal Michael Faulhaber of Munich, who had been associated with the FDK and had even at one point called for a "new ethic of war," quickly reversed course once the war began and even went on to publicly teach that the legitimacy of Hitler's authority could leave little room for Catholic opposition to the war.[21] Likewise, Archbishop Conrad Gröber of

he noted, it did not even terminate diplomatic relations between the Vatican and the Reich (Zahn, *German Catholics*, 76–77).

17 Zahn, *German Catholics*, 77.

18 Zahn, *German Catholics*, 71.

19 Zahn, *German Catholics*, 137.

20 Zahn noted that the German Catholic who rose to Galen's thundering challenge, "It is better to die than to sin!"—in his sermons praising the devotion to duty exhibited by the soldiers who were defending *Volk* and *Vaterland* against the evils of "godless Bolshevism"—also appeared to easily conclude that the war was a just war and that he had a moral obligation to give it every support (Zahn, *German Catholics*, 90–91).

21 Zahn, *German Catholics*, 110.

Freiburg was also associated with the FDK before the war and had even issued "a distinctly pacifist statement" in 1931. He had similarly reversed course by 1935, however, and rejected pacifism, surrendering final determination on the justice of the war to the authority of the Nazis.[22] "The Church wants no 'Hurrah Patriotism,'" Gröber publicly declared, "but neither does she want an unlimited and enfeebling pacifism."[23]

Zahn then compared these supposedly anti-Nazi bishops with Franz Josef Rarkowski, the notorious German military bishop who Georg Werthmann had identified as the cleric who threatened the German Catholic CO Josef Fleischer in a Berlin jail cell. Rarkowski had also once described the Nazis war effort as a fight for "all that is the holiest, most honorable, the dearest, and the most precious."[24] While Rarkowski was certainly an extreme example, Zahn noted that he found no evidence that any other German bishop had ever made even the slightest move to disavow him or his writings—in fact, many diocesan papers even reprinted Rarkowski's statements.[25] In the end, for all of Rarkowski's exaggerated nationalism, Zahn wrote that he found that the same basic themes had been emphasized by all the German bishops:

> the stress on the war service as a defense of *Volk*, *Vaterland*, and *Heimat*; the idealization of the fighting man as the model Christian, the self-sacrificing hero to whom wholehearted gratitude and emulation are owed; [and] the moral obligation of the individual Catholic to perform whatever service is asked of him by legitimate authority.[26]

In fact, the German bishops' consistent support for Hitler's wars, Zahn argued, constituted a social control that very clearly induced "Catholic conformity."[27] If a German Catholic in any way doubted the justice of the war and looked to

22 Zahn, *German Catholics*, 125. Gröber wrote a letter on behalf of Max Joseph Metzger during the German priest's 1943 trial for openly opposing the Nazi war effort. Zahn noted that the letter's prevailing tone was "one of prudent disapproval of the 'idealism' that had led Metzger to place his life in jeopardy." Despite this, Zahn acknowledged that Gröber's letter did represent "the strongest and perhaps the only episcopal support given any German Catholic objector to Hitler's wars" (Zahn, *German Catholics*, 136).

23 Zahn, *German Catholics*, 125.

24 Rarkowski's motto was *Deo et militi* ("for God and soldiers") (Zahn, *German Catholics*, 150).

25 Zahn, *German Catholics*, 161–62.

26 Zahn, *German Catholics*, 162.

27 Zahn, *German Catholics*, 163.

his bishops for guidance, he would have been instructed to put any doubts aside and give full support to the war effort.[28]

As he had asserted in his reply to George Shuster, Zahn contended that German bishops were not simply silent in the face of the Nazi war machine but rather had put forth "an active, concerted and continued effort" to "encourage, maintain, and intensify" Catholic contributions to the war. While the bishops clearly did call for martyrdom on the part of the German Catholics, Zahn quipped, it was martyrdom not for their faith, but only for "*Volk* and *Vaterland*."[29] To stand against this level of social control would have required both a clarity of judgement and an extraordinary degree of heroic sanctity on the part of any individual Catholic.[30]

In looking to put the Germany hierarchy's record in some kind of sociological and historical context, Zahn explained that the intensity of the *Kulturkampf* at the end of the nineteenth century had clearly left the German Catholic Church with "something of an inferiority complex." This would eventually manifest itself in a compulsive drive to prove that "Catholics *could be* good and loyal Germans, that they *were* good and loyal Germans, [and] that, in fact, their religious formation made it certain that they would be the *best* and *most loyal* Germans of all."[31] Advocates of this kind of nationalism also went on to foster the commonly heard distinction between fighting for Hitler on the one hand and fighting to defend *Volk* and *Vaterland* on the other. Zahn pointed out that neither Jägerstätter nor Hitler made such a distinction, though, as both of them clearly recognized that "German wars were Hitler's wars."[32]

Zahn warned that it would be a mistake to restrict this sort of exaggerated nationalism to the Catholics in Germany, since for Catholics on all sides, the legitimacy of the war seemed based on nothing more than the fact that their

28 Perhaps speaking from his own experience, Zahn suggested that in addition to this, a German Catholic also faced pressures from his local church; his own inner piety, which would have been "stirred by the repeated assurances that death in battle was a *Heldentod* (hero death) that ranked with the death of a martyr"; his devotion to God, which was converted into "an awareness of the moral obligations to obey the commands of the secular *Obrigkeit* (authorities)"; as well as all the patriotic fever he would encounter in Catholic periodicals (Zahn, *German Catholics*, 179).

29 Zahn, *German Catholics*, 186–7.

30 Zahn, *German Catholics*, 179.

31 Zahn, *German Catholics*, 189.

32 Zahn, *German Catholics*, 196.

respective nations were at war.[33] Pointing to a popular American wartime song, "Praise the Lord, and pass the ammunition," Zahn argued that it would not be too far-fetched to suggest that had the situation ever developed in which one or the other of these actions had to be suspended, Americans (including Catholics) "would have kept the ammunition moving."[34] Zahn was clearly directing his arguments here against Americans as well as Germans.

SOCIOTHEOLOGICAL IMPLICATIONS

Zahn ended the book by declaring that modern war signaled "a failure of Christianity," presenting a clear challenge to Catholic moral theologians and sociologists to discover what it was within Catholic teaching on war that allowed such failures to continue to occur. He concluded with a chapter titled "Sociotheological Implications."[35] According to Zahn, the Second World War and the Cold War that followed highlighted the need for a "reassessment" of the relationship the church had with the modern secular state, one that would reject the prevailing Catholic norm of almost automatic support for the legitimate authority of a nation and instead replace it with more "cautious reserve" or, in the case of war, outright "suspicion."[36] He argued that such a stance would make it much less likely that church leaders of any nationality would again be forced into a dilemma where they found themselves acting as "a recruiting agent" rallying the Catholic faithful to serve in an objectively unjust war.[37] For Zahn, this also meant that Catholics would need to be formed (or "encouraged") in preparation to reject any "excessive demands Caesar might make." And in what would become something of a mantra for Zahn in the years to come, he argued that a "new language" for the moral theology

33 He pointed to the lack of any opposition from the World War II-era US Catholic bishops to Allied demands for an unconditional surrender or "the inhuman strategic and terror bombings of civilian areas"—both "obvious violations of the conditions of the just war" (Zahn, *German Catholics*, 198). As noted above, Paul Hanly Furfey and John C. Ford, SJ, offered two of the rare critiques of these Allied actions by US Catholic clergy during the war. Of course, consistent opposition to these actions could also be found in the pages of *The Catholic Worker*.

34 Zahn, *German Catholics*, 198.

35 Zahn, *German Catholics*, 224.

36 Zahn, *German Catholics*, 211. Zahn wrote that it had become "an unchallengeable truism" that the church could accommodate itself to any regime that affirmed its property and prerogative, but "the time has come to subject this truism to more careful consideration" (Zahn, *German Catholics*, 213).

37 Zahn, *German Catholics*, 217.

of war was needed to prepare Catholics for what would be their inevitable Christian duty: the refusal to participate in war.[38]

Similarly, Zahn called for reevaluating the notion that an "ordinary" individual Catholic did not have the ability to judge the justice of a war, and therefore must give a presumption of justice to the legitimate authority of his nation.[39] For it was clear, he explained, that the limits that supposedly left an individual Catholic incapable of evaluating the morality of a war were far less serious dangers than "the Machiavellian standards of action subscribed to by the modern state in the games of international power politics."[40] Returning moral agency to the individual Catholic, Zahn declared, would not only remove the responsibility from the "area of state prerogative" but would also lead to "a rather drastic restatement of the role of episcopal authority."[41] For individual Catholics would need to be formed, educated, guided, and supported by the church and their bishops.

In contrast to the "Age of Martyrs," the twentieth-century church not only never seemed to call for martyrs but, as Zahn pointed out, "martyrs were actually unwanted."[42] All of which reflected the reality, he lamented, that the "*contempus mundi*" in traditional Catholic moral theology had turned into an approach that stressed "coming to terms" with the world rather than challenging it. It also revealed that there was nothing peculiar about Germans. Indeed, based upon the "almost total and generally unquestioning" support US Catholics had shown for their nation's war effort—in a situation where they did not face the same threats as their German brethren—Zahn declared that "had Hitler, his regime, and his wars been an American phenomena, the behavior of Germany's Catholics would have been duplicated here."[43]

38 Zahn saw his research as pointing out the need for "a contemporary reformulation" of the question of obedience to the secular authority and the limits of that obedience. He held up a 1958 statement by the West Germany bishops supporting West German rearmament as urgent evidence of this need: "No Catholic is bound in conscience, [or] on the basis of Catholic teaching," the bishops' statement declared, "to reject defensive measures that the majority of responsible politicians consider necessary to the present situation" (Zahn, *German Catholics*, 218).

39 Zahn highlighted the fact that Jägerstätter had been told by his bishop that he did not have the right to judge that the war was unjust and to therefore refuse to participate in it (Zahn, *German Catholics*, 73).

40 Zahn, *German Catholics*, 218.

41 Zahn, *German Catholics*, 218.

42 Zahn, *German Catholics*, 222.

43 Zahn, *German Catholics*, 223.

In contrast to the controversy that surrounded his earlier paper on the Catholic press in Germany, *German Catholics and Hitler's Wars* inspired little backlash. In fact, when a critical review did appear in *America*, it was lambasted in various letters to the editor, leading the editor to comment that "rarely has a critical review been so vehemently challenged as this one."[44] Perhaps more than anything else, this pointed to the reality that times were quickly changing. As Mark Ruff noted, piece by piece, the building blocks of the heroic German Catholic narratives of wartime resistance carefully sculpted in the immediate aftermath of the war were being chipped away.[45] For instance, Ernst-Wolfgang Böckenförde's 1959 article "German Catholicism in 1933" greatly undercut the myths of Catholic opposition to the Nazi's rise to power, and (following the publication of Zahn's book in 1962) Rolf Hochhuth's 1963 play *The Deputy: A Christian Tragedy* profoundly hollowed out Pius XII's moral authority, while Guenter Lewy's 1964 book *The Church and Nazi Germany* argued that Catholic resistance to the Nazis had emerged only when the church's survival and interests were at stake. With the assistance of Böckenförde, a German translation of *German Catholics and Hitler's Wars* was published in 1965—though an introduction by Stratmann was left out at the insistence of his Dominican provincial.[46]

PAUL RAMSEY AND THE "SECTARIAN" CHARGE

All of which is not to say that Zahn's research did not still have critics. In August 1963, when Julius Döpfner, now the Cardinal Archbishop of Munich, included Zahn on a list of names he submitted to the German Bishops Conference of "nonconformist Catholics"—Catholics who had "questionable ecclesiological tendencies" and whose writings were "religiously zealous but not actually pious." More significant, though, was a review of *German Catholics and Hitler's*

44 The review was written by an associate editor named Robert Graham, SJ, who had been earlier recruited by Fittkau to help block Zahn's publications (Ruff, *The Battle for the Catholic Past in Germany*, 149).

45 Ruff, *The Battle for the Catholic Past in Germany*, 120.

46 Ironically, as Ruff pointed out, had Zahn been left to his own devices his work would have appeared in a few niche Catholic publications, "where it would likely have raised a few eyebrows but never generated anything approaching a scandal"—nor the attention (Ruff, *The Battle for the Catholic Past in Germany*, 149–50).

Wars by Paul Ramsey, a Protestant ethicist teaching at Princeton (and former student of H. Richard Niebuhr at Yale), who was one of the most important contemporary articulators of the Christian just-war tradition.[47]

Ramsey began his review by stating that the "proper posture" for reviewing Zahn's book was "prostrate, or on one's knees." After noting that Zahn's research had already generated "heated controversy" among Catholics in the United States and Germany, he explained that what was ultimately at issue in the book was the just-war theory itself and "the enormous problem of how that or any other body of teachings stemming from one perfect society—the Church—is to have any effect when the chips are down in that other 'perfect' society, the nation-state."[48]

Contrary to Zahn's assertion, Ramsey argued that, in fact, Christians on *both* sides of a conflict could fight "with justified consciences."[49] He then went onto state that Zahn's demand for a "new ethic of war" would require that the Catholic Church withdraw from "the values of the secular order" so that it could pursue "the lure of a higher ideal" as a "sect."[50] He pointed to Zahn's call, in particular, for the church to prepare Catholics to "assume their most likely obligation" of refusing to participate in an unjust war as a clear example of such withdrawal. In short, Ramsey concluded, Zahn was a "sectarian." This sectarian charge was significant and would certainly continue to be a charge made against Zahn and other Catholic pacifists in the decades to come—though typically by other Catholics.

It should be noted that Ramsey's notion of a sectarian was rooted in the "church-sect" terminology of the German Protestant theologian Ernst Troeltsch.[51] According to Troeltsch, the "church-type" understood itself as a dispenser of saving grace to the world and thus "found it impossible to avoid making a compromise with the State, with the social order, and with economic conditions."[52] In contrast, the "sect-type" stood apart from and in opposition to the world, prohibiting political participation. Philip Kenneson has helpfully

47 Paul Ramsey, "The Just War Theory on Trial," *Cross Currents* 13, no. 4 (1963): 477–90.

48 Ramsey, "The Just War Theory on Trial," 478.

49 Ramsey, "The Just War Theory on Trial," 484.

50 Ramsey, "The Just War Theory on Trial," 482.

51 Ernst Troeltsch, *The Social Teaching of the Christian Churches*, 2 vols., trans. Olive Wyon (Harper Torchbooks, 1960).

52 Troeltsch, *The Social Teaching of the Christian Churches*, 1:334–35.

pointed out that moral theologians in the United States—including Catholics—have largely read Troeltsch through the lens of H. Richard Niebuhr's *Christ and Culture* (1951).[53] Kenneson suggested that the all or nothing (embrace or withdraw) view of US society and institutions implied by the term "sectarian" could be traced to Niebuhr's depiction of "culture" as a monolithic all or nothing entity. For instance, according to one widely-read source, a sectarian is someone who "is detached from the world and resistant to any involvement in the socio-political problems that exist outside the church. . . . Although sectarianism is diametrically opposed to Catholicism, a certain sectarian orientation has emerged in recent years in portions of the Catholic peace movement."[54] While much more will need to be said, it is enough to recognize at this point that to be "sectarian" was (and still is) to be seen on the fringes of Catholicism—if not, completely outside of it.

"NEW ETHIC OF WAR"

Sectarian or not, Zahn would continue his call for the church to develop a "new ethic of war," the need for which stemmed from the German Catholic experience during World War II that had laid bare: the "utter inadequacy and almost total irrelevance" of the church's teaching on war—something which had led Catholics to conclude that it was somehow their "sacred duty" to sin.[55] This was the "lesson of German Catholicism," which the German journalist Carl Amery described as the German church's "capitulation" to the milieu.[56]

For Zahn, any new ethic of war would need to emphasize three elements. The first was the role of the individual Catholic conscience. To enhance the personal responsibility of individual Catholics to follow their conscience, Zahn argued for the need to greatly reduce, if not eliminate, the emphasis

53 He described Niebuhr's book as having "shaped the contemporary debate about sectarianism within theological circles more than any other English-language text." See Philip Kenneson, *Beyond Sectarianism* (Trinity Press International, 1999), 13, 42–48.

54 *Encyclopedia of Catholicism*, ed. Richard P. McBrien (Harper Collins, 1995), s.v. "sectarianism."

55 Zahn acknowledged the "individual witness" of Reinisch, Metzger, and Jägerstätter, but he noted that they had not been appreciated or supported by their fellow Catholics or church leaders. See Gordon Zahn, "The Case for Christian Dissent," in *Breakthrough to Peace: Twelve Views on the Threat of Thermonuclear Extermination*, introduction by Thomas Merton (New Directions Books, 1962), 135.

56 Carl Amery, *Capitulation: The Lesson of German Catholicism*, trans. Edward Quinn (Herder and Herder, 1967).

in moral theology on submitting to the authority of one's national leaders.[57] Zahn argued that this teaching had led to the scandalous (though thoroughly logical) result of "sincerely devout and individually well-intentioned" German Catholics having been taught that they were obliged to give a presumption of justice to Hitler.[58] Such an emphasis, he pointed out, was in tension with (if not in contradiction with) the church's teaching on the primacy of conscience. And in a democracy, where Catholic citizens had an even greater share of moral culpability, Zahn explained that the matter was not simply about "saving our skins" but rather of "saving our souls."

Second, any new ethic would also require the church to "detach" as much as possible from the temporal interests of the state. Such detachment was needed, Zahn argued, because when demands for political change failed, Catholics needed to be ready and willing to refuse to comply with any unjust or evil institutions of the state.[59] To prepare for such "dissent and deviance," Zahn pointed to his dissertation discussion around "encouraged" resisters, which suggested that although such dissent was ultimately rooted in the individual conscience, a "value-transmitting and maintaining" community was still necessary in order to properly form and encourage that conscience.[60] To prepare individual Catholics to be ready to "go against the stream," Zahn explained, they needed the support of a broader community—in other words, "the flow of the stream itself must be changed."

For various reasons, Zahn saw families and schools as institutions no longer able to provide this type of community. However, he believed that the church was still able to offer a "different culture" and a "divergent set of values" to which Catholics could conform.[61] And so, a third element of any

57 Gordon Zahn, "The Church as a Source of Dissent," *Continuum* 1 no. 2 (1963): 160.

58 "For what purpose, then," Zahn quoted Jägerstätter, "did God endow all men with reason and free will if, in spite of this, we are obliged to render blind obedience; or if, as so many also say, the individual is not qualified to judge whether this war started by Germany is just or unjust?" (Zahn, "The Church," 161–62).

59 Zahn, "The Church," 162.

60 Zahn expanded upon this idea using insights from Peter Viereck, *The Unadjusted Man: A New Hero for Americans* (Beacon Press, 1956) and David Riesman, *The Lonely Crowd: a Study of the Changing American Character* (Yale University Press, 1961).

61 In a booklet written for the Council on Religion and International Affairs (originally the Church Peace Union), Zahn pointed to the many values the church shared with the tradition of nonviolent resistance: the belief in the limits of secular authority; a universalism that rejected "particularist nationalism or other ethnocentric attachments"; the primacy of the individual conscience; and

new ethic of war would be for the church to provide the institutional support required by those dissenting from the authority of the state.[62] It was in this sense, he suggested, that Jägerstätter did, in fact, conform to the church—albeit not the one in Germany during World War II that recommended he submit to the legitimate authority of Hitler and defend the *Volk* and *Vaterland*. Rather, Zahn argued that Jägerstätter conformed to the "Church of Martyrs"—men and women "who had taken their 'stand apart' when their secular community and it rulers made demands that could not be reconciled with the values of the religious community."[63] And while saintly figures such as Jägerstätter were often dismissed as extraordinary exceptions, Zahn noted that there had been a time when it was taken for granted that the function of the church was to "produce saints." To do so again, he argued, the church needed to detach from the state and once more become a "source of dissent and deviance."[64]

Acknowledging that the church had obviously not always lived up to what it "claimed to be" (not that it could not become what it said "it should be") Zahn suggested that the obstacles here were not fear or weakness on the part of Catholics but rather "self-imposed restraints" that undermined the influence of the Church in society.[65] For example, the hesitation of Church leaders to become involved in political questions, rooted in their tendency to "continually sharpen" the distinction between sacred and secular, resulted in the church being "virtually isolated" from discussions on issues such as war.[66] Even more of an obstacle, though, was the unwillingness on the part of church leaders to demand what some regarded as "too great a burden" on their flock. For Zahn, all of this pointed to the need for Catholics and their leaders to be "reconverted"—or at least "reawakened"—to the values and beliefs that at its moments of greatest glory had always made the church an

---

a readiness to suffer the loss of all earthly goods rather than sacrifice spiritual goods. See Gordon Zahn, *An Alternative to War* (The Council on Religion and International Affairs, 1963), 23–25.

62 Zahn wrote that while it was an individual Catholic who would dissent, "he will be more likely to do so and persist in doing so if his deviance can take the form of rational conformity to the values proposed by the religious community of which he is a part" (Zahn, "The Church," 163–64).

63 Zahn, "The Church," 164.

64 Zahn, "The Church," 164.

65 Zahn, *An Alternative*, 24.

66 As a result, he wrote, "we encounter the almost incomprehensible paradox of formal high-level church pronouncements on relatively trivial matters (sex in movies or on book covers, financial assistance in the form of school bus or lunch programs) and a crashing silence on the proposed development of the neutron bomb" (Zahn, *An Alternative*, 27).

institution whose mission was the "transformation" of society rather than an instrument of "accommodation and conformity" to the secular status quo.[67]

For Zahn, such a reawakening would mean a return to the "ascetic ideal" within Christianity. In a booklet titled *An Alternative to War* —published in 1963, when the fears of the Cuban Missile Crisis were still fresh in readers' minds—Zahn wrote that the "frantic pursuit" of security through violence had led humanity to the dead end of mutually assured destruction.[68] The clear failure of violence to provide peace and security presented a need to consider the kinds of alternatives to violence employed by advocates of nonviolent resistance, alternatives that relied on mass displays of nonparticipation in the form of civil disobedience and general strikes, as well as an acceptance of imprisonment and redemptive suffering.[69] Forming Catholics to be ready for such consequences required an asceticism that glorified nonviolent sacrifice over self-preservation though violence, and faith in the redemption of the cross.[70] For Zahn, such an ascetic ideal would mirror the ideals that currently glorified military life, duty and sacrifice for one's nation, as well as a heroic death.

Zahn recognized that (especially in the face of Soviet totalitarianism) any such nonviolent alternative implied the possibility of surrender and would almost certainly result in an initial victory for the opponent. That victory would have its limits, however. While any campaign of mass noncooperation would certainly result in the loss of life (though perhaps less than those killed in a nuclear war) Zahn believed that there would be limits to such killing, as even the most "totalitarian automaton" would have a breaking point. "Only so many trains will run over so many bodies before the trains stop running altogether, only so many hostages will be executed," he declared, "before

67 Zahn, *An Alternative*, 28. For "as clear a statement as one could ask for" of the church's potential for being a source of dissent, Zahn pointed to John XXIII's admonition in *Pacem in Terris* that if civil authorities legislated or allowed anything contrary to the will of God, "neither the laws made nor the authorizations granted can be binding on the conscience of the citizens, since God has more right to be obeyed than man" (Zahn, "The Church," 165).

68 Zahn, *An Alternative*, 8. He referenced the infamous defense of the use of a machine gun to guard one's fallout shelter by a US Catholic moral theologian named Fr. L. C. McHugh, SJ (which Merton had critiqued) as a metaphor for this kind of dead end. See L. C. McHugh, SJ, "Ethics at the Shelter Doorway," *America*, September 30, 1961. See also Thomas Merton, "The Machine Gun in the Fallout Shelter," in *Thomas Merton on Peace*, ed. Gordon Zahn (McCall Publishing, 1971), 103–6.

69 Zahn, *An Alternative*, 11.

70 Zahn, *An Alternative*, 20.

the executioners refuse to shed more innocent blood."[71] Acknowledging that Cold War critics would describe such confidence in humanity as "starry-eyed idealism," Zahn argued that to deny that such limits to the human capacity to murder and violence existed would be a denial of the very dignity of humanity that Americans claim as the hallmark of their way of life and justification for its defense.

For Zahn, the popular Cold War notion "better dead than red" reflected a "disordered theology" that implied that God is helpless in the face of the communist threat.[72] As with his call for a faith in the redemption of the cross, Zahn is clearly highlighting a more eschatological emphasis within his pacifism. As we will see, this was not the caricature of "eschatological humanism" that John Courtney Murray, SJ, portrayed as leading to a "withdrawal" from society. Rather, it was more like the animating theological strain in the work of Jesuit *nouvelle théologie*, theologians who sought to make Christianity present in the world by looking toward the eschaton. The "infinite view of the Kingdom God," Yves Montcheuil, SJ, explained, is not "a path to evasion, but rather a new dimension given to life and duty."[73] As the historian Sarah Shortall rightly highlighted, an eschatological emphasis would guide these Jesuits in their resistance to the Nazis and later the communists. For Zahn, such an eschatology meant that there was a clear difference between killing millions in a nuclear war fought in pursuit of some vague notion of "freedom" on the one hand, and millions of people ready to die for the ideals of their faith on the other.[74] This eschatological focus continued to appear throughout Zahn's writings. It would also be a focus of his critics. For as we will see, Troeltsch's "church-sect" typology (already read through the lens of Niebuhr's *Christ and Culture*) is further filtered by many US Catholic scholars through the "incarnational-eschatological" paradigm articulated by Murray.[75] The upshot is that any emphasis on the eschatological is often regarded as sectarian.

71 Zahn, *An Alternative*, 14.

72 Zahn, *An Alternative*, 13.

73 Quoted in Sarah Shortall, *Soldiers of God in a Secular World: Catholic Theology and Twentieth-Century French Politics* (Harvard University Press, 2021), 115.

74 Zahn, *An Alternative*, 15.

75 John Courtney Murray, SJ, *We Hold These Truths: Catholic Reflections on the American Proposition* (Sheed & Ward, 1960).

THE DEPUTY

As evidence of the need for this kind of reawakening in the church, Zahn pointed to the uproar that had been caused by Rolf Hochhuth's play *The Deputy*, which had not yet appeared in English translation but was already causing a stir in Germany in 1963. In two reviews he wrote of the play, Zahn sought to place it within the context of the broader challenge to the "veil of myth" that had enveloped the postwar narratives of German Catholicism—a veil which Zahn had done a great deal to pull down.[76] Zahn noted that while Hochhuth was on point in his critique of the Catholic hierarchy, his direct and "overdrawn" attack on Pope Pius XII had made it too easy to avoid the central lesson of his play: that the church has a duty to speak out against sin and must be ready to endure the penalty for speaking out: suffering and even martyrdom.[77] Such a challenge, he wrote, ought to inspire a new consideration of the place of sacrifice, even martyrdom, within Catholic theology.[78] And to reject this would mean that if similar circumstances reemerged, "the One True Church of Christ" might once again stand helplessly by as "a silent and resigned witness to the planned extermination of untold millions of our Father's children."[79]

Again, emphasizing the role of individual conscience, Zahn argued that Hochhuth had failed to highlight the fact that it was the German church, both the "'right-thinking' people of Germany and their spiritual leaders," who had an even greater responsibility than the pope in Rome to resist the Nazis.[80] This, again, was not to suggest that there was anything unique about German Catholics in this regard. Indeed, Zahn pointed to the fact that there had been no great public outcry from US Catholics over the widely seen photos of napalmed babies or 'keelhauled' Viet Cong prisoners as a clear indication that "we, too,

76 Gordon Zahn, "'The Vicar': A Controversy and a Lesson" *The Critic* (October-November, 1963)—which was reprinted as "The Record: A Church of Silence?" in Zahn, *War, Conscience, and Dissent*, 230–242—and Zahn, "Foreword: The Church and Totalitarianism," *Continuum* 2 no. 2 (1964): 153–57.

77 Zahn, "The Record," 236.

78 Zahn, "The Record," 241.

79 Zahn, "The Record," 242.

80 Zahn did note that Reinhold Niebuhr had described the play as a "work of genius" (Zahn, Foreword, 154).

would 'keep our noses clean' and look the other way if we happened to see the transports being loaded for some Auschwitz of our own."[81]

SIMON FELLOWSHIP

Not long after the publication of *German Catholics and Hitler's Wars*, Zahn was invited to lunch by Vladimar Dedijer, a Yugoslavian scholar and activist. Dedijer had been impressed with the book and asked Zahn to consider applying for the Simon Fellowship at the University of Manchester—Dedijer was himself a former Simon Fellow and offered to recommend Zahn. Zahn enthusiastically applied, seeing it both as an opportunity to travel abroad and also to escape the tension that still lingered at Loyola. His application was quickly accepted and he arrived in Manchester at the start of the 1964 academic year. Zahn brought with him to England the lessons he had learned in Germany.

In his application for the fellowship, Zahn had originally proposed researching London's "Peace News" organization, which he described as "one of the oldest and most influential forces on the international pacifist scene." When this topic became too unwieldy, though, he turned instead to looking at military chaplains and their "role in tension" caused by serving both their religious community and their nation's military at the same time. He initially planned to base his research on interviews with active and retired Royal Air Force (RAF) chaplains from three major religious groups: the Church of England, the Catholic Church, and a cluster he called "PMUB" (Presbyterian, Methodist, and United Board).

With the initial blessing and assistance of officials from the RAF military chaplaincy office, Zahn began interviewing active-duty chaplains and put together a questionnaire that he sent out to those who had retired. After completing thirty-seven of the fifty-one scheduled interviews (around a third of the 163 active-duty RAF chaplains), Zahn received a letter from the newly installed "Chaplain-in-Chief" informing him that some of the chaplains Zahn had spoken with were troubled by his questions, and he told Zahn to suspend his interviews until an official review was made. Recognizing that this was

81 Zahn reminded his readers that such failure on the part of US Catholics could also be seen regarding the various "racist atrocities" taking place in the United States at the time. He compared Father Riccardo in *The Deputy* to William Dubay, a priest from Los Angeles who that summer had publicly called for the pope to remove Cardinal McIntyre for his failure to speak out against segregation in his archdiocese (Zahn, Foreword, 156–57).

essentially the end his interviews, Zahn mailed the remaining active-duty chaplains the questionnaire. To his surprise, all fourteen replied. Of the eighty-six questionnaires he had mailed to the retired chaplains, he received twenty-two back before that, too, was shut down by the Chaplain-in-Chief.[82] In the end, this left Zahn with thirty-seven interviews as well as the thirty-six completed questionnaires (forty-four from Church of England, twenty-one from PMUB, and eight from Catholics) to base the research, which would he would eventually publish in 1969 in an important but little known book called *The Military Chaplaincy: A Study of Role Tension in the Royal Air Force*.[83]

WHAT IS SOCIETY?

Before Zahn left for his fellowship, Furfey had also asked him to write a volume as part of "The Twentieth-Century Encyclopedia of Catholicism" series edited by Henri Daniel-Rops. That volume, *What Is Society?* was published in 1964.[84] Having approached German Catholics and British military chaplains as a sociologist, it made sense for Zahn to spend time reexamining the field of sociology. Written during the still ongoing debate over Catholic sociology, this short book also offers a further glimpse into Zahn's view of sociology and how it reflected Furfey's influence. For instance, Zahn described sociology as seeking to develop valid generalizations about the "social nature" of humans manifested in human society. While that notion of social nature was very different from the one used in theology or philosophy, Zahn explained that all three conceptualizations were not incompatible, "indeed, one would hope and expect that, assuming each is correctly conceptualized, they would in fact converge."[85]

As an example of this kind of convergence, Zahn pointed to the "sometimes quite heated" debate surrounding Catholic sociology, which he described as essentially a debate over the understanding of human behavior. For a more materialistic conception of the human person (found within the "deterministic" approach of value-free sociology) was "incompatible with the acceptance of a

82 Gordon Zahn, *Military Chaplaincy: a Study of Role Tension on the Royal Air Force* (University of Manchester Press, 1969), 43.

83 It was published in the United States and Canada by the University of Toronto Press.

84 Zahn, *What is Society?* (Hawthorn Books, 1964).

85 Zahn, *What is Society?* 24.

consistent body of theological and philosophical values" found in the Catholic tradition. On the contrary, values that were found within Catholicism held that each human person was a unique creation endowed with a spiritual as well as a material nature.[86] This view of the person—one Zahn himself employed—allowed for a more "voluntaristic" approach to behavior that ascribed any irregularities to the realm of free will and took any regularities in behavior as evidence of social controls imposed by society.

With regard to the very purpose of sociology, Zahn pointed out that many of the early contributors to the development of the discipline understood its necessary connection with social reform—that sociology was "deliberately keyed towards the creation of a better, more perfect society."[87] But this focus on social reform had shifted, with a new overriding need to establish sociology's claim to be a science with all the standards and methods that entailed. A chief reason for this shift, he explained, was the almost religious acceptance by contemporary sociologists of the myth of value-free sociology.[88] But the notion that sociology and sociologists must be completely neutral, Zahn contended—echoing similar critiques made by C. Wright Mills and others—lead to the kind of indifference that would only further entrench the established social order.[89] As a result, Zahn warned that the old dictum that science sought to establish "what is and not what should be" could easily be converted into the belief that "anything that *is* must be taken as it is."[90]

What was needed, Zahn argued, was a kind of middle ground that allowed for a recognition of and commitment to values in sociology, but one that did not allow those values to dominate one's research. For such a middle ground, Zahn pointed to Furfey's "supernatural sociology," which offered a way to evaluate a sociologist's various value commitments, what Furfey referred to

86 Zahn, *What is Society?* 26.

87 Zahn, *What is Society?* 144.

88 Zahn, *What is Society?* 145.

89 Zahn noted that C. Wright Mills had protested that this more empirical shift in sociology had led to a kind of "conservative bias," which encouraged sociologists to shun research into some of the major social problems. To this, Zahn added that the "excitement" that once marked the young science had been lost and that sociology was in danger of reducing itself to "an all but sterile body of statistically significant, unquestionably objective, but unfortunately quite inconsequential fragments of knowledge" (Zahn, *What is Society?* 145). See C. Wright Mills, *The Power Elite* (Oxford University Press, 1956).

90 Zahn, *What is Society?* 146.

as "metasociological value judgements."[91] He wrote that this method would allow for "engaged" sociologists to lend their talents and devote their scholarly research to reform society without fear of being dismissed as "unscientific."[92] Indeed, he hoped that more Catholics would come to recognize the need for such sociological research and "the great promise it could hold for the betterment of human society."[93]

CONCLUSION

It was for the betterment of human society that Zahn certainly focused his research. Rooted in what he learned about the experience of the German Church—articulated in *German Catholics and Hitler's Wars*—Zahn came to see the crucial role the church could play as a source of deviance and dissent to counterbalance the state. His research also convinced him that the church was currently failing in that role, and had, instead, largely capitulated to the state. For Zahn, this was a clear social problem, and he drew on his sociotheological approach to point to a solution—a new ethic of war.

The failure of the church to be a source of resistance was in no way an exclusively German problem, though. Zahn's interviews of British military chaplains made that clear, as had his own experience during World War II. While Zahn was certainly harsh in his criticism of the German church, he was even more critical of the Catholic Church in the United States—his church. Indeed, in the years to come, Zahn would consistently compare the conformity and accommodation of US Catholics to that of German Catholics under the Reich.

As Ramsey's review showed, however, not everyone saw things as such. Zahn's vision of the Catholic Church as a source of dissent struck, and would continue to strike, many as too pessimistic (too eschatological) a view of the state and society in general, and the United States in particular—too confrontational an approach for the church to embrace. For Ramsey, a liberal Protestant, that was enough to label Zahn a "sectarian." As later chapters describe, Zahn's US Catholic critics, infusing this Troeltschian category with

91 Zahn, *What is Society?* 150.

92 While some critics charged that this looked more like theology than sociology, Zahn highlighted the various value commitments that currently guided contemporary "value-free" sociologists without such criticism (Zahn, *What is Society?* 152).

93 Zahn, *What is Society?* 159.

Catholic theological notions of the incarnational and eschatological, would further employ the sectarian charge in an attempt to marginalize and dismiss Zahn and Catholic pacifism.

FIGURE 1: Gordon Zahn.

Courtesy of University of Notre Dame Archives.

FIGURE 2: Franz Jägerstätter with his family.

Courtesy of Franz and Franziska Jägerstätter Institute, Diocese of Linz/Austria.

FIGURE 3: Franz Jägerstätter.

Courtesy of Franz and Franziska Jägerstätter Institute, Diocese of Linz/Austria.

FIGURE 4: Franz Jägerstätter's grave, St. Radegund.

Courtesy of Michael Baxter.

FIGURE 5: Gordon Zahn.

Courtesy of University of Notre Dame Archives.

FIGURE 6: Gordon Zahn at Fourth Session of Second Vatican Council, 1965.

Courtesy of University of Notre Dame Archives.

FIGURE 7: Gordon Zahn.

Courtesy of University of Notre Dame Archives.

FIGURE 8: Gordon Zahn.

Courtesy of University of Notre Dame Archives.

FIGURE 9: Gordon Zahn at Pax Christi-USA conference, Omaha, 1991.
Courtesy of University of Notre Dame Archives.

FIGURE 10: Gordon Zahn at St. Camillus Nursing Home, December 2003.
Courtesy of University of Notre Dame Archives

8

IN SOLITARY WITNESS

And yet here he stands, this Austrian peasant, showing in and through his ordinariness, his complete lack of singularity, his appeal to nothing beyond his Bible and his catechism, his utter rootedness in his peasant Catholic milieu, that in summoning the Church of prophets and martyrs to speak for him he, of all those who lived in Austria after 1938, had the best right to do so.

—*J. M. Cameron*[1]

In 1964, *In Solitary Witness: the Life and Death of Franz Jägerstätter* was published. Although his earlier research had brought him national and even international recognition, it is for his research on Jägerstätter that Zahn is certainly most remembered. His "discovery" of the Austrian Catholic martyr was the pivotal event in Zahn's career—and it is certainly it is fair to say that without Jägerstätter, Zahn would be remembered much differently. But it is also fair to say that Franz Jägerstätter and his story would not be remembered today if not for the efforts of Zahn to recover it. As the Austrian historian Andreas Maislinger noted, before the German translation of *In Solitary Witness* appeared in 1967, Jägerstätter was "completely unknown" in Austria, with references to him found only in a few Catholic publications.[2] Indeed, it was Zahn who brought

1 J. M. Cameron, "A Martyr of Conscience," *The New York Review of Books,* December 5, 1965.

2 Andreas Maislinger, "Franz Jägerstätter," in *Conquering the Past: Austrian Nazism Yesterday & Today*, ed. F. Parkinson (Wayne State University Press, 1989), 178, 183.

Jägerstätter's story to an international audience and tirelessly promoted it. This connection between Zahn and Jägerstätter went beyond Zahn's research. As noted earlier, the biographical similarities between the two men are striking. In short, then, a close reading of *In Solitary Witness* is warranted.

Zahn began the book acknowledging the different angles from which he approached Jägerstätter's story. As a sociologist, for instance, the story offered an important case study of the martyr, or rebel, as "an extreme social deviant," and his initial research began from that perspective.[3] But Zahn wrote that it quickly became clear that he was "involved" in the unfolding of Jägerstätter's narrative beyond his role as a sociologist. As a Catholic, he explained that he could not fail to be impressed by the spiritual content and theological implications of Jägerstätter's witness, especially evident in his writings. "I could not escape the suspicion," Zahn wrote, "that I might be dealing with an even more extreme form of social deviance than I had thought a martyr-*saint*." Furthermore, as a Catholic conscientious objector, Zahn saw Jägerstätter's story—in particular, the manner in which it was regarded (and continued to be regarded) by his fellow Catholics—as offering as occasion for a "careful re-examination" of the church's potential to be "a source of dissent."[4] And while these three perspectives could be seen as completely separate or even conflicting; through a sociotheological lens, Zahn suggested that by the end the book they "actually tend to converge," with each having a direct bearing upon the others.

Zahn likened his research on Jägerstätter to putting together a jig-saw puzzle: Jägerstätter's writings made up the "central pieces," while interviews and other secondary sources formed the "oddly-shaped pieces" that rounded out the image. In the end, though, he acknowledged that the "most crucial dimension" to Jägerstätter's story—the sociotheological facets of the narrative—may have been "something above and beyond mere human understanding," something more along the lines of the "workings of grace and the power of revelation."

Zahn guessed that the St. Radegund he first encountered in July 1957 probably looked much the same as it did when Jägerstätter left it for the final time in February 1943. He described it as a "totally Catholic village" in an already heavily Catholic Austria. Reportedly, the only non-Catholic resident of

3 Zahn, *In Solitary Witness*, 6.

4 Zahn, *In Solitary Witness*, 6.

St. Radegund during Jägerstätter's lifetime was his Jehovah's Witness (*Bibelforscher*) cousin. St. Radegund had been known for its annual Passion Plays. Indeed, before the Nazi takeover, Jägerstätter had played the part of a soldier in the village's final performance. In light of this, Zahn built upon his earlier observation that Jägerstätter's story was itself a latter-day Passion—"nothing less than a repetition of an old story, the ever-recurring confrontation between Christ and Caesar."[5] While in one sense, Jagerstatter's life and death was "the whole story," Zahn noted that in another (very real) sense, it was not. For what remained was to explain why Jägerstätter had made his "solitary rebellion" and what impact it had had (and continued to have) upon others.

POLITICAL OR RELIGIOUS?

While many in St. Radegund had told Zahn that they believed Jägerstätter's cousin or wife had been the primary influence on his refusal, Zahn argued that other evidence suggested that such had not been the case.[6] Instead, Zahn highlighted the two major changes that the villagers consistently told him had marked the "new" Jägerstätter: his intense religiosity and equally intense opposition to the Nazis. Zahn contended that these two changes—one religious, the other political—were not separate in Jägerstätter's mind but rather were "intimately linked," even to the point of "mutual interpenetration."[7] Here we find Zahn pushing back against any sort of Weberian separation of "religion" from "politics"—an argument that would become central in Zahn's response in the coming decades to claims that Jägerstätter should not be considered a martyr for "the faith" since his refusal was seen as largely political and not religious. "Is it 'political opposition' or is it 'religious commitment,'" Zahn asked, when Jägerstätter "reads in every act of support for the Nazis an act of personal fealty to Hitler?"[8]

To support his argument, Zahn turned to the nine "commentaries" that Franziska had shown him, which Jägerstätter had written before he left home

5 Zahn again noted that Hitler, Adolf Eichmann, and Jägerstätter all grew up in the same region, and he described Hitler as the "latter-day Caesar," Eichmann as "his willing and perhaps all-too-eager servant," and Jägerstätter as "the rebel-peasant who rejected the Fuhrer and refused his orders" (Zahn, *In Solitary Witness*, 15).

6 Zahn, *In Solitary Witness*, 109.

7 Zahn, *In Solitary Witness*, 110.

8 Zahn, *In Solitary Witness*, 113.

for the last time. In one commentary, Jägerstätter described a dream he had in 1938 about being on a train as it sped out of control down the track and hearing a voice tell him to jump off since the train was "going to hell." Jägerstätter understood this dream as a revelation from God about whether he should be a Nazi or a Catholic. He wrote that he wanted to call out to everyone else riding on the Nazi train, "Jump out before the train reaches its destination, even if it costs you your life!"[9] Zahn described this as a call to nonparticipation, even to the point of martyrdom, and stated that it epitomized "the standard of Christian political behavior" Jägerstätter sought to follow.

Furthermore, Zahn pointed out that Jägerstätter had clearly refuted the idea that it was somehow the sacred duty of German Catholics to support the Nazis in their fight against Communists, and that he had suggested that if Austrians rejected the *Anschluss* and refused to support the Nazis any further it would certainly not be a sin.[10] Again, Zahn noted that Jägerstätter clearly rejected the notion that a Catholic could somehow fight for Germany without fighting for the Nazis at the same time. The Nazis could not be separated from Germany, as Jägerstätter saw it, they were "one inseparable entity."[11]

Zahn also highlighted some of the more eschatological commentaries in which Jägerstätter acknowledged that while thousands of Catholics were fighting and dying for Hitler, he was risking his life "for a King who does not only burden us with duties, but also gives us rights; whose ultimate victory is certain, and whose Kingdom, for which we would be fighting, will last forever."[12] Similarly, Jägerstätter described the 1938 *Anschluss* as a kind of Holy Thursday for the Austrian church—the day she "let herself be taken prisoner, and ever since she has lain in chains"—and he warned that Austria's Good Friday will soon be at hand.[13] And to those Catholics who looked to simply wait out the Nazi regime, Jägerstätter cautioned that another "anti-Christian power" could follow. "We know all too well how things stand with the Christian faith in other nations on this earth: in Russia for example" Jägerstätter wrote, but "England and America are not much better."[14]

9 Zahn, *In Solitary Witness*, 113.

10 Zahn, *In Solitary Witness*, 119–20. Zahn translated these commentaries.

11 Zahn, *In Solitary Witness*, 127.

12 Zahn, *In Solitary Witness*, 116.

13 Zahn, *In Solitary Witness*, 116.

14 Zahn, *In Solitary Witness*, 116.

As Zahn saw it, the arguments in these commentaries were "foreshadowed" in a letter Jägerstätter had written to his godson in 1936, while the prison statement he wrote just before his death in 1943 was "the final seal" on his ideas. Zahn highlighted the fact that in the 1936 letter, Jägerstätter had been clear that his opposition to the Nazis did not arise from any kind of superior wisdom or courage but rather from a gratuitous gift of grace. "If God had not given me the grace and strength even to die for my faith if I have to, I too, would probably be doing the same as most other Catholics," Jägerstätter wrote.[15] Far from a political protest separate from his religious beliefs, Zahn wrote that Jägerstätter clearly understood that he was going to die for his faith and that he saw his situation as a clear choice between either Hitler or God. "I definitely prefer to relinquish my rights under the Third Reich," Jägerstätter wrote, "and thus make sure of deserving the rights granted under the Kingdom of God."[16] Again, rejecting any notion that the religious was isolated from the political in Jägerstätter's mind, Zahn wrote that the Austrian's writings revealed a position that was "clearly one of political opposition rooted in religious commitment," all of which culminated in what Jägerstätter had regarded as "a spiritual 'storming of heaven.'"[17]

It is worth noting here that in his translation of Jägerstätter's writings, Zahn did admit that while the "logical form and sequence of the argument, the imagery, and the references to Scriptures and other religious sources" were from Jägerstätter, he had slightly edited the Austrian Catholic martyr's writings (an "approximate direct translation") for clarity and style. Zahn explained that, as would be expected from someone with a limited education, Jägerstätter's writings lacked proper punctuation, paragraphing, spelling, and "other refinements of form." But such "stylistic shortcomings" were not what was relevant. For, as Zahn explained:

> The reader who is tempted to smile condescendingly at what may strike him as simple crudity of thought or overly "pietistic" illustration might do well to bear this in mind: the exact grammarians, the people who could spell faultlessly, the masters of dazzling syllogistic argument, somehow found it possible, in most cases, to come to terms with and

15 Zahn, *In Solitary Witness*, 128.

16 Zahn, *In Solitary Witness*, 128–29.

17 Zahn, *In Solitary Witness*, 60–61.

> give their support (or at least their acquiescence) to one of history's most inhuman and unjust regimes.[18]

The point was that Jägerstätter, this unlettered peasant farmer, recognized both the evil of the Nazis and his duty to resist them, even at the cost of his life. Despite this defense, however, Zahn's editorial admission would later be used to raise questions about the authenticity of Jägerstätter's witness.

BUT WAS HE A PACIFIST?

Along with his interviews of various chaplains, Zahn's account of Jägerstätter's time in prison largely came from the letters Franziska had showed him. In what would later become one of the more significant of these letters (dated March 11) Jägerstätter wrote that he had declared himself "ready to serve in the medical corps" and that maybe he could perform more "Christian charity" in such a capacity.[19] Recognizing the significance of this statement for understanding Jägerstätter's refusal, Zahn described this letter as marking the "lowest point in Jägerstätter's morale," and he quickly pointed out that this was the only place in Jägerstätter's writings where he had ever stated his willingness to serve in any capacity in Hitler's military.[20] Acknowledging that in the letter to Karobath she had written following her visit with her husband in Berlin, Franziska had also stated that Jägerstätter had been willing to serve in the medical corps, Zahn nevertheless pointed out that there were other "unquestionably reliable informants" who had reported a different account—that it was the military authorities who had asked, even begged, Jägerstätter to accept such an assignment as a way to save his life. In what decades later would become a pivotal question regarding whether Jägerstätter would have compromised his stand against the Nazi war effort, Zahn was clear:

> Taking all the available evidence together, it is best to conclude that Jägerstätter would not have accepted any form of military service, that he was sincere in his statement to his pastor and others that acceptance

18 Zahn, *In Solitary Witness*, 111.

19 Jägerstätter wrote that doing so would ease his conscience, but he also acknowledged that he "would still be punished." Zahn noted that it was not clear what kind of punishment he was referring to—whether from the Nazis or from God (Zahn, *In Solitary Witness*, 64).

20 Zahn, *In Solitary Witness*, 63.

> of limited service would only mean that he was replacing someone else who would be doing the killing for him.[21]

That he could have made such a request for noncombatant duty, Zahn concluded, was more likely "a sign of a low point in his morale bordering upon despair" than any compromise in Jägerstätter's resolve,[22] all of which leads to the question of whether Jägerstätter's refusal to serve implied some sort of "pacifist rejection" of all war as incompatible with Christian teaching and belief—a stance of "absolute pacifism." Both Franziska and Karobath had denied that this was the case, and they had even assured Zahn that Jägerstätter would have fought for an Austrian resistance to the Nazis had there been one. Acknowledging that there was certainly evidence to support their argument, Zahn stood firm on his contention that there was even more evidence to suggest that Jägerstätter had at least a "predisposition" to pacifism.[23] He pointed out, for instance, that Jägerstätter's many exhortations against the Nazis always took the form of a withdrawal of support or a refusal to contribute to the war effort—simple acts of "passive noncooperation" rather than anything that would resemble violent opposition. For Zahn, this was enough to declare (and perhaps to overstate) that the evidence was "overwhelming" that Jägerstätter did accept "the basic premises upon which the pacifist alternative—that is, the theory and practice of nonviolence—is based."[24] And while conceding that Jägerstätter had probably not been, "strictly speaking," a pacifist, Zahn insisted that if Jägerstätter had been acquainted with the writings of German Catholic pacifists such as Stratmann or Metzger, he would have certainly been "quite receptive" to their ideas. It was perhaps in making such an argument that Zahn's own story (and his own pacifism) can be most clearly seen in his telling of Jägerstätter's story. The idea that Jägerstätter had at least pacifist tendencies or predisposition—if not that he was an actual Catholic pacifist—was an important point for Zahn, and he would continue to defend it.

21 Zahn, *In Solitary Witness*, 64.

22 Zahn, *In Solitary Witness*, 64.

23 Zahn, *In Solitary Witness*, 130.

24 Zahn highlighted Jägerstätter's discussion of the use of "spiritual weapons" which he obtained through the sacraments (Zahn, *In Solitary Witness*, 130).

JÄGERSTÄTTER WANTED TO BECOME A SAINT

Likewise, in his attempt to portray Jägerstätter as a "martyr for the faith," Zahn pointed to the frequent references to scripture and other Christian sources that appeared in Jägerstätter's writings. For instance, in a letter dated April 11, Jägerstätter described the joy in reading a collection of sermons he found from St. John Chrysostom and other saints.[25] Zahn noted that the villagers had told him that Jägerstätter was always reading about the lives of the saints, and Karobath reported that Jägerstätter had even stated that he "wanted to become a saint."[26] For Zahn, this desire to be a saint was at the core of Jägerstätter's "genuine act of rebellion" against the Nazis, who he viewed to be diabolical in nature and origin. Zahn wrote that Jägerstätter saw his refusal to fight for the Nazis as "the gravest life-and-death struggle of them all," with eternal life or eternal death at stake.[27]

But not everyone saw Jägerstätter that way. While certainly warm in their recollections of Jägerstätter, most of the villagers described his refusal as "fanatical," and some even suggested to Zahn that Jägerstätter had been a little "touched in the head."[28] And certainly none of the villagers seemed to appreciate Karobath publicly declaring that Jägerstätter was a saint. The pastor told Zahn about the opposition that had erupted to his suggestion that Jägerstätter's name be included on the war memorial located behind the church. The matter was finally settled when it was decided that Jägerstätter's name would be listed, but at the bottom and with the added phrase "*seinem Gewissen folgend*" ("in obedience to his conscience"). A late addition to the list, though, had removed this qualifying phrase, and so Jägerstätter's name appears indistinguishable from the rest on the memorial.[29] That his former neighbors were not able to understand Jägerstätter's refusal, neither in the 1940s nor 1960s, did not surprise Zahn. He explained that the same elements

25 Zahn, *In Solitary Witness*, 64.

26 In his writings, Jägerstätter also referenced Blessed Anne Catherine Emmerich (stressing her peasant origins and her practice of praying in the fields) as well as a quote he attributed to St. Clare of Assisi (Zahn, *In Solitary Witness*, 133).

27 Zahn, *In Solitary Witness*, 135.

28 Zahn, *In Solitary Witness*, 141.

29 Zahn, *In Solitary Witness*, 144.

that made Jägerstätter's story so unique—that a relatively uneducated farmer from an isolated rural village could have had such profound insights into the political and spiritual implications of his time—also meant that others from the same social milieu could not fully understand or accept the path he had pointed out as being "the only path worthy of the Christian bound for salvation."[30]

Recognizing the way Jägerstätter's refusal was received during his lifetime and continued to be remembered by the Austrian church was crucial, Zahn explained, for it offered "intimations of attitudes" that could reappear "when Caesar and Christ will once again make conflicting demands upon the loyal obedience of the Christian citizen."[31] He lamented that an adequate study had not yet been made on the full measure of support given to the Nazis by the Austrian Catholic Church hierarchy: beginning with Cardinal Innitzer's infamous "Heil Hitler" greeting, extending through the Austrian bishops' efforts to assure acceptance of the *Anschluss*, and ending with the hierarchy's support of the Nazi regime, even in its final days. Zahn found no evidence that there had ever been any inclination among the Austrian hierarchy to repudiate their acceptance of Hitler's rule in 1938, nor that they had ever offered any support to Catholics like Jägerstätter who objected to the Nazis.

Though future scholars would challenge Zahn's account on this point, he argued that while there certainly had been some "sufficiently annoying" Austrian Catholic opposition to the Nazis, Austrian Catholic support for the Reich as the nation's "legitimate authority" was far stronger.[32] Zahn pointed to the fact that every single member of the clergy that Jägerstätter had turned to for guidance saw his refusal as "imprudent, foolhardy, and an unnecessary sacrifice." All had advised him that either his duties to his family and his nation took priority over his religious beliefs, or that he did not have the competence, or even the right, to judge the justice (or injustice) of the war. Zahn guessed that none of these clergy would have advised him in this manner had they themselves considered the war to be unjust.[33] Indeed, none of them ever told Jägerstätter that he was correct. In a very real sense, Zahn saw Jägerstätter's

30 Zahn, *In Solitary Witness*, 159.

31 Zahn, *In Solitary Witness*, 161.

32 Zahn, *In Solitary Witness*, 161. This was another point that Erna Putz would later (vigorously) refute by highlighting the strong opposition to the Nazis by the Austrian Catholic Church, particularly in the diocese of Linz (Putz, *Franz*, 35).

33 Zahn, *In Solitary Witness*, 161.

refusal as a stand not only against the Nazis but also against his fellow Catholics and their spiritual leaders, who were wholeheartedly committed to, or at least willing to acquiesce in, Hitler's wars.[34]

THE MARGINALIZATION OF JÄGERSTÄTTER

Zahn argued that when remembered at all within Austrian Catholicism, Jägerstätter had generally been marginalized—admired from afar, perhaps, but certainly not seen as a model for ordinary Catholics to follow. As an example of this kind of marginalization, Zahn pointed to a letter that a priest named Leopold Arthofer (a friend of Karobath) had received in 1946 from the editor of the Linz diocesan paper explaining why his article about Jägerstätter would not be published. The editor told Arthofer that his article had been turned down because the bishop, Josef Fliesser, felt that Jägerstätter's case might "create confusion and disturb consciences" since Arthofer had not made any effort to avoid presenting the "danger" that Jägerstätter's story might cause if it was "wrongly understood" or "merely sensationalized."[35] Citing the bishop's recollections of his own meeting with Jägerstätter in 1943, the editor explained that the bishop, having failed to persuade him to give up his stand, had concluded that Jägerstätter "thirsted for martyrdom and for the expiation of sin," and so he told Jägerstätter that he was permitted to make his stand only if he knew he had been called to it through "some special revelation originating from above and not in himself." Since Jägerstätter agreed that was the case, Fliesser described Jägerstätter as a "completely exceptional case . . . one more to be marveled at than copied."[36] While acknowledging that respect should certainly be given to those who, out of an "innocently erroneous conscience," had preferred to die rather than bear arms in the war, Fliesser suggested that better models could be found in the "greater heroes" who fought and died "in heroic fulfillment of duty and in the firm conviction that they were fulfilling the will of God at their post just as the Christian soldiers in the armies of the heathen emperor had done."[37]

34 Zahn, *In Solitary Witness*, 163.

35 Zahn, *In Solitary Witness*, 165.

36 Zahn, *In Solitary Witness*, 165.

37 Zahn, *In Solitary Witness*, 165.

For Zahn, the fact that the bishop had made such a statement *after* the war had ended and the Nazi threat eliminated, captured perfectly the Austrian hierarchy's continued problematic thinking on war and nationalism. While most of the early postwar narratives justified any support the bishops gave to the Nazis by stressing the overwhelming fear of reprisals that would fallen upon the church had they not done so, Fliesser wrote his letter when the Nazis were no longer a threat. Zahn noted that the bishop's comments were written in 1946, when, following Pius XII's lead, any kind of resistance or opposition to the Nazis was still being exploited to the fullest in order to disassociate the church from the Third Reich.[38] Fliesser no longer would have had to fear the Nazis, and he would have also had the hindsight to see that Hitler's wars did not meet the criteria of a just war. Yet, even from the safety of this postwar context, the bishop of Linz continued to hold up Catholics who supported the Nazi war effort as the "greater heroes." And since (if not by 1946, then certainly by the 1960s) Hitler's wars had come to be almost universally regard by Catholic moral theologians as unjust, Zahn asserted that it was, in fact, Bishop Fliesser and all the "greater heroes" who themselves had acted out of an erroneous conscience in their support for such an immoral war. While it was Jägerstätter, in contrast, who had acted correctly and in accordance with "the objective fact" that Hitler's wars were unjust wars and Catholic participation in them was sinful.[39] This all highlighted the fact that Jägerstätter was still being marginalized well after the end of World War II.

JÄGERSTÄTTER'S CRITIQUE OF CONTEMPORARY CATHOLIC MORAL THEOLOGY

For Zahn, this meant that Jägerstätter raised a serious question for Catholic moral theology regarding the extent to which a Catholic could be called to dissent or disobedience. While such dissent was generally encouraged by the church regarding issues of family or sexual morality, Zahn noted that the emphasis shifted abruptly when the topic turned to war, as the state's legitimate authority—not the individual Catholic conscience—became the focal point.

38 Zahn, *In Solitary Witness*, 171.

39 Zahn, *In Solitary Witness*, 171.

Indeed, when it came to issues of war, a Catholic suddenly seemed to lose both the competence and the right to make an independent moral judgment on what behavior would be required. In the case of any doubt on the justice of a war, Catholic moral theology taught that the presumption of justice must always be granted to the nation's leaders. All of which, Zahn argued, pointed to the fact that the church was willing to accept theological formulations that ultimately "surrender all judgement in this area to Caesar."[40]

Helpful in understanding this apparent tension within postwar Catholicism is James Chappel's recent attempt to distinguish a "paternal Catholic modernism" from a "fraternal Catholic modernism" within this period.[41] While both positions accepted the "modern" imperative of a secular liberal state (and the privatization of religious faith it required), the former emphasized the family and Catholic moral teaching on issues regarding family life. Catholics in this camp emphasized conservative family legislation and placed their faith in the modern liberal state as long as it supported and protected this notion of the family. They were also, Chappel argues, virulently anticommunist, even more than they were antifascist. Fliesser and many of the other bishops Zahn sparred with (both in Germany and the United States) clearly fell more into this camp. In contrast, fraternal Catholic modernism was concerned with protecting a robust civil society, embodied in trade unions more than the nuclear family. Chappel describes these Catholics as having strong antistatist and anticapitalist tendencies, and of also being much more wary of fascism than of communism. Zahn can certainly be seen as moving in these circles, having learned this trait from his time with Catholic Workers and Dorothy Day.

The harsh truth, as Zahn saw it, was that Jägerstätter took his stand in a time and place when the church had abandoned any pretensions of the protest and prophecy that had long ago marked its history. He argued that the church in Austria and Germany, both "shepherd and flock alike," had succumbed so thoroughly to the temptations of "conformism and accommodation" in the guise of prudence that it had lost all sense of identity and purpose.[42] Indeed, having lost its role as prophet and martyr, the church to which Jägerstätter had anchored his act of resistance proved unable or unwilling to support him. All

40 Zahn, *In Solitary Witness*, 172.

41 James Chappel, *Catholic Modernism: The Challenge of Totalitarianism and the Remaking of the Church* (Harvard University Press, 2018), 15.

42 Zahn, *In Solitary Witness*, 173.

areas of public policy had been surrendered over to the Nazis. As a result, Zahn contended, there was little effort made to even consider the possibility that the "Christian duty" they called for might actually have been a call to murder.[43]

Jägerstätter rejected all of this outright. Zahn suggested that he had been able to avoid this kind of "conformist" Catholicism by identifying not with the church around him but rather with the church he found in scripture and the lives of the saints—or as Zahn put it, Jägerstätter turned to "the community of saints," not the "Nazi Folk Community."[44] So while in one sense Jägerstätter was a solitary witness—"he knew there was nothing else for him to do"—in another sense, Zahn argued that he saw himself as part of a much broader community beyond the Austrian Catholicism of the 1930s and 1940s. For this reason, Zahn was quick to point out, as far as Jägerstätter knew, his witness would largely go unnoticed and would almost certainly fade from memory with the passing of the handful or so of people who had known him personally. Unlike other saint-martyrs, such as Thomas More, Jägerstätter would have had little confidence that anyone would notice or remember his refusal. He had "no great ambition to change the world or singlehandedly bring about the fatal weakening of Hitler's armies and the consequent collapse of the regime he recognized as evil," Zahn wrote, "nor did he give any sign that he expected (or even wanted) others to notice and follow his example."[45] Nevertheless, Jägerstätter did have a community to support and encourage him—albeit one that transcended time and place.

For Zahn, all this meant that there was a very real danger in viewing Jägerstätter's refusal (and his ability to overcome the various social controls) as the unique result of a special grace or supernatural revelation that he had been given, something even Jägerstätter had seemed to suggest. For while the workings of grace should certainly be recognized, Zahn feared that such an explanation could be (and already had been) used to marginalize Jägerstätter and make his witness irrelevant for ordinary Christians.[46] He pointed

43 Zahn, *In Solitary Witness*, 175.

44 Zahn, *In Solitary Witness*, 177.

45 Zahn, *In Solitary Witness*, 178. Zahn quoted Reinhold Schneider: "When it becomes the 'sacred duty' of a man to commit sin, the Christian no longer knows how he should live. There remains nothing else for him to do but bear individual witness—alone. And where such witness is, there is the Kingdom of God" (Zahn, *In Solitary Witness*, 179).

46 An example of this kind of marginalization is the article Baldinger had written for the Linz diocesan paper in 1963 ("He Followed His Conscience") in which he called Jägerstätter a saint

specifically to Bishop Fliesser's letter as an example of how Jägerstätter had been marginalized in this way.[47] Employing his sociotheological method, Zahn stated that it was therefore necessary for Jägerstätter's refusal to be understood not just through the theological concept of a saint but also through more sociological notions such as a "social deviant."[48]

To do this, Zahn again returned to the categories of "encouraged" and "resister" that he first used in his dissertation, but he now added the sociologist Robert K. Merton's work to suggest that social deviants often appealed (and even conformed) to some kind of "reference group" to support their nonconformity—a group that embodied the moral values either of "an earlier day which had been lost to view" or of "a time which will come to pass."[49] In this way, Merton suggested that a social deviant could be seen as attempting either to reactivate "a forgotten set of values, standards, and practices" or even to activate ones which were "not blemished by existing concessions and expedient compromises with current realities."[50]

Despite the fact that Jägerstätter received little encouragement from his religious community and so fell into the "resister" category, Zahn suggested that he was not without any encouragement, for the reference group that Jägerstätter had linked his refusal was "the Church of prophets and martyrs that had been abandoned and rejected by those who constituted the acting

but also cautioned his readers that "God seems to choose a man from whom something entirely out of the ordinary is demanded, something that is not to be generally imitated but which is to be for us at the given moment something like a pointing finger" (Zahn, *In Solitary Witness*, 164).

47 Zahn, *In Solitary Witness*, 186.

48 Zahn pointed out that the more popular category of "rebel" generally excluded the possibility of someone acting out of religious beliefs—this was certainly true of Camus's separation of what he called the "world of the sacred" and the "world of rebellion." But Zahn questioned this separation: "whether in a social order totally committed to the effective suppression or neutralization of religious values, the man who stakes his life upon this affirmation does not challenge the assumptions and authority of the world of the secular." Indeed, it was such separation of the sacred from the world that Jägerstätter had firmly rejected. For while Jägerstätter certainly "keyed" his behavior to its meaning in the world of the sacred, Zahn argued that he never lost sight of the fact that he was acting "*in history*" and that his actions were responsive to the imperatives of history almost as much as to the imperatives of his faith. Furthermore, Zahn continued, Jägerstätter was a rebel in the eyes of his own religious community—indeed, many of the clergy who spoke with Jägerstätter about his decision seemed to take specific issue with the fact that he was making his stand for religious reasons, not patriotic or prudential ones (Zahn, *In Solitary Witness*, 187–88).

49 Robert K. Merton, *Theory and Social Structure* (The Free Press, 1957), 362–63; Zahn, *In Solitary Witness*, 190.

50 Zahn, *In Solitary Witness*, 190.

Church in Nazi Germany and Austria."[51] In this sense, Jägerstätter tried to reactivate a forgotten set of values, standards, and practices. Keeping with the eschatological focus that Zahn regarded as necessary, he described Jägerstätter as having pointed to a "future reference group" in which he framed his aspiration in terms of "enjoying eternal blessedness in the life of the hereafter." Jägerstätter's church, Zahn argued, was the church of the "'saints and heroes" who had kept alive a continuing tradition of self-sacrificing witness. In this way, Jägerstätter believed himself to be acting in full compliance with the norms and expectations of the "*real* Catholic Church."[52]

"THE JÄGERSTÄTTER FORMULA"

Zahn described this "Church of Martyrs," with which Jägerstätter identified, as unflinching when it came to asking its members to take a stand that required open dissent or civil disobedience. Borrowing Fliesser's words, Zahn wrote that this church encouraged the "vocation of martyrdom" and believed that its one overriding function and purpose was to produce saints.[53] Any church that wished to produce more Jägerstätters would likewise need to become "a source of civil dissent" with Jägerstätter as its "standard." Zahn wrote:

> Instead of rising in horrified protest when the suggestion is made that religion is (or threatens to become) a divisive force in a pluralistic society, the religious community might better recognize that there are likely to be many occasions when it must be such a divisive force, as it has been in the ages past when prophets came forth to denounce an erring or sinful social order and to inspire martyrs to refuse to conform to the demands of that social order.[54]

Such a church would need to form its members to be prepared, like Jägerstätter, to stand apart from society or culture.

Zahn recognized that all of this called into question the well-worn "church-sect" typology that Ramsey had used to critique him. By challenging

51 He noted that US Catholic COs in the Civilian Public Service also fell into this group (Zahn, *In Solitary Witness*, 191).

52 Zahn, *In Solitary Witness*, 194.

53 Zahn, *In Solitary Witness*, 194–95.

54 Zahn, *In Solitary Witness*, 196.

the church to be a source of dissent, Jägerstätter's story highlighted the fact that there were times when the church was, in fact, "'called' to act like a sect."[55] Nowhere was this more the case than in the area of public policy, particularly within democracies. When the actions of the state conflicted with the moral teachings of the church, and any Catholic "voice of dissent" failed to bring about change, Zahn argued that Catholics were called to become social deviants and refuse to comply with the state's unjust demands. And in this sense, "the Church, an *ecclesia*, would bear the responsibility of becoming a source of dissent and deviance."[56] Zahn called this the "Jägerstätter formula."

Towards the end of the book, Zahn again returned to his contention that only the church remained equipped to oppose the prevailing value system of the modern nation-state and offer a "different culture" to which Catholics could "conform."[57] And while acknowledging that the church had often instead served as a form of social control for the prevailing order (as Zahn's research on German Catholics certainly confirmed), the extent to which the church still claimed to be something apart from the world meant it could never be reduced to the status of "a mere channel of secular authority."[58] All of which pointed to the reality, Zahn wrote, that there were times and circumstances when Catholics were called to be sectarian.

While the ("Paternal") Catholic Church in the United States often already called its members to act in such sectarian ways in the face of contradictory demands from the culture regarding sex, family life, or even racial injustice, Zahn noted that it rarely did so with regard to war. Indeed, very little attention had been given to the particular problem raised by Jägerstätter: the need for Catholics to stand against the state when it ordered them to participate in murder.[59] As George Shuster had suggested, such questions may have been ignored because of their implications for martyrdom. But when the "spiritual connotations" of a Catholic became so completely separated from the "secular connotations" of their daily life, as they had in Germany, Zahn wrote that "an occasional Jägerstätter" would be needed to force "a restatement and

55 Zahn, *In Solitary Witness*, 205.

56 Zahn, *In Solitary Witness*, 203.

57 Zahn, *In Solitary Witness*, 204.

58 Zahn, *In Solitary Witness*, 204–5.

59 Zahn, *In Solitary Witness*, 206.

reconsideration" of the fundamental relationship between the secular and the spiritual (or nature and the supernatural) in the Christian life.[60]

Ending his book much as he had opened it, Zahn suggested that Jägerstätter's story could be read in a few different ways. Sociologically, his social witness could be seen as a case of "rebellion directed against a totalitarian social order." Philosophically, Jägerstätter exemplified the conflict of values between the church and state; while theologically, his story could be read either as one of a believer called to witness in fulfilling the demands of his conscience, or "on a higher level," as a renewal of the confrontation between Caesar and Christ. While each of these angles on Jägerstätter's story were true, Zahn concluded that ultimately for the believer "they will be the same."[61]

REVIEWS

Zahn's account of one man's lonely act of resistance touched a nerve in the mid-1960s. In an hour-long interview with Zahn on his popular Chicago radio show in January 1965, the writer and radio personality Studs Terkel noted that *In Solitary Witness* had been well received by "enthusiastic reviewers" such as Dwight MacDonald. Terkel called the book a "theological detective story" that was as much about the contemporary American life—"in the middle of the twentieth-century with nuclear bombs, with revolutions occurring"—as it was about Jägerstätter. "You wrote this about Jägerstätter and yet the sub-theme is really us," Terkel suggested.[62] Along similar lines, writing in the *New York Review of Books*, the British critic J. M. Cameron described *In Solitary Witness* as "brilliant and dangerous."[63] He argued that Zahn portrayed Jägerstätter as not simply a witness to conscience but "to the truth." In this sense, the Austrian Catholic presented a "terrible challenge" to church authorities, convicting them of "unfaithfulness to the truth."

Though still a graduate student, the sociologist James Kelly was asked to review *In Solitary Witness* for *Sociological Analysis* (formerly the *American Catholic Sociological Review*). While he remembered thinking it was "grossly

60 Zahn, *In Solitary Witness*, 206.

61 Zahn, *In Solitary Witness*, 206.

62 Terkel interviewed Zahn on "The Studs Terkel Program," January 15, 1965, https://studsterkel.wfmt.com/programs/gordon-zahn-discusses-his-book-solitary-witness-part-1.

63 J. M. Cameron, "A Martyr."

inappropriate" that a grad student would be asked to review such a book, Kelly later found out that many in the ACSS did not consider *In Solitary Witness* to be "real sociology."[64] In his review, Kelly placed the book within the context of Lewy's *The Catholic Church and Nazi Germany* and Hochhuth's *The Deputy*, as well as *German Catholics and Hitler's Wars*—recent works which strongly suggested that the church in Germany had "stilled her prophetic tongue in order to protect her institutional hide."[65]

In her two-part review, Dorothy Day noted that if St. Radegund ever did become a place of pilgrimage, it would be thanks to Zahn that "the story of Franz" was not forgotten.[66] Like Jägerstätter, she said that Zahn was called to perform a task, and everyone should be deeply grateful to him for also being "a witness, and in a way, a solitary witness."[67] Day wrote that she regarded both the extensive quotes from Jägerstätter's writings as well as Zahn's analysis as being of "prime importance in our day." Placing the publication of Zahn's book within its historical context, Day ended her review by stating: "Let us pray that Gordon's book . . . will reach all the young men who are questioning their stand today in the face of conscription or the war which is going on in Vietnam right now."[68]

CONCLUSION

Indeed, the same year *In Solitary Witness* was published, Lyndon Johnson persuaded Congress to pass the Gulf of Tonkin Resolution, significantly ramping up US military involvement in Vietnam. Zahn's account of an Austrian Catholic conscientious objector resonated with many US Catholics who were becoming increasingly critical of their own nation's war-making. In fact, as David O'Brien notes, Zahn's book became a kind of landmark or refuge for many Catholic COs at a time when it was still generally taught that a Catholic could not be a conscientious objector.[69]

64 James Kelly, "Seeking a Methodology for the Organic Intellectual: The Legacy of Gordon Zahn," presented at the *Society for the Scientific Study of Religion* Annual Meeting, 1994.

65 James Kelly, SJ, "Review of *In Solitary Witness*," *Sociological Analysis* 26, no.1 (1965): 55.

66 Dorothy Day, "Review of *In Solitary Witness*," *The Catholic Worker*, July-August 1965, 5, 7.

67 Dorothy Day, "Review of *In Solitary Witness*," *The Catholic Worker*, June 1965, 4.

68 Dorothy Day, "Review of *In Solitary Witness*," *The Catholic Worker*, July-August 1965, 5, 7.

69 David O'Brien, "Catholic Opposition to the Vietnam War," in *War or Peace?* ed. Thomas Shannon (Orbis Books, 1982), 137.

In Solitary Witness also appeared right in the middle of the Second Vatican Council. Zahn's telling of the Jägerstätter story had a very real impact on the council, particularly on those bishops who were in the process of reevaluating the church's teaching on war and conscientious objection. The story, and Zahn's promotion of it, posed hard questions for Catholics—including the bishops gathered in Rome. Was Jägerstätter correct in refusing to fight for Hitler? If so, what did that mean for German Catholics who did not refuse? And what did all that suggest about US Catholic COs to the Vietnam war?

9

THE PEACE LOBBY

> *Despite his quite unthreatening appearance, despite his being the most loyal of Catholics, Gordon Zahn may have done more to disturb the tranquility of smug clerics than even Dorothy Day and the Berrigans.*
>
> —*Michael Gallagher*[1]

As Dorothy Day noted in her review of *In Solitary Witness*, there was a lot going in 1964. That fall, while Zahn was still in Manchester, the Second Vatican Council convened for its third session and began debate on the so-called Schema XIII, the document that specifically discussed Catholic teaching on war, certainly a timely topic in the context of the Cold War. Indeed, in response to the Cold War and its constant threat of nuclear Armageddon—which had already brought the world to the brink of war in Berlin and Cuba—Pope John XXIII had issued his peace encyclical *Pacem in Terris* in 1963. Zahn read that encyclical as fundamental to the development of the church's thinking on war. According to the pope, the arms race between the United States and the Soviet Union was of central concern to the world community, depriving individuals and nations of the economic goods necessary for social progress. Pope John proclaimed that with the terrible destructive force of modern weapons and the fear of the frightful destruction that such weapons would cause, it was "contrary to reason to hold that war is now a suitable way to

1 Gallagher, *Laws of Heaven*, 245.

restore rights which have been violated."[2] For the pope, justice, right reason and a consideration for human dignity urgently demanded an end to the arms race, reduction of stockpiles, a ban on nuclear weapons, and ultimately a disarmament agreement. "True and solid peace of nations" John declared, "consists not in equality of arms but in mutual trust alone."[3]

Zahn would later recall that it was in "the continuing glow of John's great peace encyclical" that he and others in the Catholic peace movement welcomed the council's reassessment of church teaching on war.[4] He remembered that plans were quickly made for an all-out campaign by activists to "lobby" the bishops specifically on the evils of nuclear weapons and the rights of conscientious objectors. Zahn also recalled that they did this knowing full well that they would face stiff opposition, particularly from a US hierarchy led by Cardinal Francis Spellman of New York and Philip Hannan, auxiliary bishop of Washington, DC (later bishop of New Orleans), who saw themselves as "protectors of the American faith" in both a national and religious sense—and both certainly embodied the Catholic Americanist tradition.[5]

Despite the pope's encyclical and the Cold War swirling around them, issues of war and peace were not on the forefront in the minds of most of the bishops gathered in Rome. Zahn recalled that if anything, they regarded such issues as something of an "extra." As a result, the topic of "modern war" was included last on a long list of "problems of special urgency" that were to be discussed in the drafting of Schema XIII. Though issues such as the liturgy, role of laity, religious freedom, and the structure of the church dominated the council, Zahn and other Catholic peace activists knew that this was their opportunity to make their case and they did not intend to waste it.

THE THIRD SESSION

According to James Douglass, prior to the promulgation of *Pacem in Terris*, the most precise statement on the church's view of modern warfare was found in an address Pius XII had given to the Congress of the World Medical Association

2 *Pacem in Terris*, no. 127, in *Catholic Social Thought: A Documentary History*, ed. David O'Brien and Thomas Shannon (Orbis Books, 1992), 130. David O'Brien called this the encyclical's "celebrated statement."

3 *Pacem in Terris*, nos. 112–13.

4 Zahn, 1994, 69.

5 Zahn, 1994, 69.

in 1954.[6] In it, Pius stated that "modern all-out warfare," or so-called "ABC warfare" (atomic, chemical, and biological), could only be permitted when it was absolutely necessary as a means of justified self-defense. Moreover, the pope explained,

> should the use of this method entail such an extension of the existing evil as would render man *wholly incapable of controlling it*, its use should be rejected as immoral. In such an instance it would no longer be a question of "defense" against injustice, and of the necessary "safeguarding" of legitimate possessions, but of the pure and simple annihilation of all human life within the radius of action. Under no circumstances is this to be permitted.[7]

Controllability, then—a technical, not a moral term—became the primary criteria Catholic moral theologians began to use to judge modern nuclear weapons.[8]

The initial draft of Schema XIII was presented at the opening of the council's third session in the fall of 1964; again, a moment fraught with anxiety as the US military steadily escalated its involvement in Vietnam, China announced that it had developed nuclear weapons, and news spread of fall of Khrushchev in the Soviet Union. Following Pius's lead, the draft recognized a nation's right to self-defense, while also making clear that the use of weapons "whose effects are greater than can be imagined and therefore *cannot be reasonably regulated*" should be seen as exceeding all "just proportion" and therefore must be "judged before God and man as most wicked."[9] The draft denounced "the *uncontrollable* armaments race" as an impediment to real peace and harmony among nations that placed humanity in grave danger. The draft went on to declare that every honest effort must be made so that nuclear warfare would be proscribed by all nations as "an enormous crime" and nuclear weapons "be utterly destroyed and banned."

6 James Douglass, *The Non-Violent Cross: A Theology of Revolution and Peace* (Macmillan, 1966), 103.

7 Pius XII, "Address to Participants of the VIII Congress of the World Medical Association," http://www.vatican.va/content/pius-xii/en/speeches/1954/documents/hf_p-xii_spe_19540930_viii-assemblea-medica.html.

8 Douglass, *The Non-Violent Cross*, 103.

9 Parts of the draft were published in the July-August 1965 issue of *The Catholic Worker*.

On November 10, 1964, just after a powerful plea to condemn nuclear weapons was made by Maximos IV, the Patriarch of Antioch and Jerusalem, Bishop Hannan spoke before the council. A military chaplain in World War II, Hannan was the only US bishop to speak at the council on the issue of war. He began by declaring that the question of greatest importance before the bishops should not be on how to avoid war but how to defend liberty and freedom, and he called upon his fellow bishops to praise those who had fought in its defense.[10] Having thus duly set an Americanist tone, Hannan then declared that the draft's statement on nuclear weapons had to be revised in order to "state with precision what is prohibited in waging war to those who justly and laudably defend liberty." He called it "a grave mistake of fact" that the draft implied that the use of nuclear weapons was unjust because the effects of such weapons could not be "reasonably regulated." To the contrary, Hannan argued that, in fact, there existed nuclear weapons that had "very precise limits of destruction," the effects of which were very well calculated and could be clearly foreseen. Therefore, the bishop reasoned, the use of such "limited" nuclear weapons against military objectives met the criteria of a just war and so could not be condemned.

That evening, George Higgins, a Chicago priest and director of the Social Action Department of the National Catholic Welfare Conference at the time, spoke at a US bishops' press conference. Higgins defended Hannan, and he pushed back against other interventions that had been made by European bishops calling on the council to brand all nuclear weapons as immoral and for an all-out ban on nuclear war—exactly what the Dutch Cardinal Bernardus Alfrink had done the day before.[11] In response, Higgins explained that the aim of the bishops should be to achieve a situation where war would

10 Hannan declared, "We must have complete and actual liberty to carry on a dialogue with militant atheists. No dialogue is possible if we fall into slavery." For the full text of Hannan's statement, see *Council Daybook: Vatican II, Session 3*, ed. Floyd Anderson (National Catholic Welfare Conference, 1965), 251–52.

11 Others also spoke out along these same lines, including Bishop Alfred Ancel (Lyon, France), who objected to "internal contradiction" in the statement that seemed to affirm the lawfulness of the use of nuclear weapons defensively while condemning the use of nuclear weapons in general, and Bishop Jacques Guilhem (Laval, France), who declared that the atomic bomb was the greatest and most dangerous problem and that "no moral principle can justify its use." See *The History of Vatican II, Vol. 4: Church as Communion: Third Period and Intersession, September 1964–September 1965*, ed. Joseph Komonchak (Orbis Books, 2004), 323.

be unnecessary, "Beyond that, it is hard to see what the council could say without being demagogic."[12]

"DAVY CROCKETT AND THE BISHOP"

Though still at the University of Manchester, Zahn followed all this intently, and he responded to Hannan in an essay he titled "Davy Crockett and the Bishop," which appeared in March 1965.[13] He quipped that in his speech to the council, Hannan had "reached out his hand in loving benediction of battlefield weapons like 'Davy Crockett' and his brothers—innocent creatures all, crying for protection against the abuse set forth in Schema 13." And in doing so, Hannan had "brought cheer . . . in some Pentagon quarters as the votive of martinis were raised."[14] Zahn explained that he primarily objected to Hannan's assumption that an episcopal blessing needed to be given to any nuclear weapons at all—"now even a bishop is prepared to stand before the world to 'approve' and 'condone' a weapon which can be dropped upon unwary enemies two or three miles distant and which had the properties to consume them instantly and irradiate the whole area of impact and everything in it."[15] The bishop's defense of "limited" nuclear weapons was, Zahn wrote, an "innocent-looking loophole" that would certainly open the gates of the just-war theory wide enough "to wheel in the superbombs" as well.[16] For Zahn, even "limited" nuclear weapons clearly did not meet the two absolutely essential criteria of a just-war theory: discrimination of combatants from noncombatants and proportionality of destruction.

Zahn highlighted the fact that Hannan's intervention had largely repeated an argument set out in an earlier statement by a group of so-called "Catholic experts" that included prominent officers and "star performers" of the Catholic Association for International Peace (CAIP).[17] He argued that Hannan's

12 *Council Daybook*, 243.

13 Gordon Zahn, "Davy Crockett and the Bishop," *Ramparts*, March 1965, 62–65. "Davy Crockett" was the name given to one of the US military's so-called "limited" nuclear weapons.

14 Zahn, "Davy Crockett," 62.

15 Zahn, "Davy Crockett," 65.

16 Zahn, "Davy Crockett," 64.

17 When the authors insisted that they were not voicing "CAIP policy or State and Defense Department policy either," Zahn suggested that that was "tantamount these days to saying the same thing three ways" (Zahn, "Davy Crockett," 65).

willingness to delegate the most crucial moral decision of the day to such "experts" would only lead to the same kind of "spiritual bankruptcy" that found German Catholic bishops calling upon their flocks to support Hitler's wars—wars which had also been prosecuted by experts of "proven capacity and wisdom."[18] Zahn reminded Hannan that he and his brother bishops must decide these issues themselves *"as moral experts"* and not pass that duty on to others.[19] He concluded by asserting that the only kind of denunciation that the CAIP was willing to issue would be against any Catholic who dared to question "the propriety of a situation which finds the official spokesmen of the Church in America helping to support the nuclear umbrella." In short, the CAIP was selling out.

THE ORIGINS OF THE CAIP

In criticizing Hannan and the Catholic Association for International Peace, Zahn (once again) was taking on a formidable ecclesiastical opponent. The CAIP had emerged in the wake of the First World War, led by John Ryan, a Minneapolis priest and head of National Catholic Welfare Council (NCWC), and at the time considered the "dominant American Catholic social theorist."[20] Ryan wanted to form a group of Catholics who could lobby Congress for significant legislation on issues of war and peace.[21] He founded the CAIP in 1927 as the first such Catholic organization in US history. The fact that its offices were located in the NCWC headquarters in Washington, DC, made it nearly impossible to separate the CAIP and its statements from the NCWC—or, as Zahn later noted, from the US Catholic hierarchy in general.

In her history of the Catholic peace movement, the historian Patricia McNeal described the CAIP as "elitist" from the beginning, with leaders from business, the military, and the academy invited to join—George Shuster was an early member, as was church historian Carlton Hayes.[22] For this reason, the CAIP also eschewed any type of antiwar activity and instead focused on instructing US Catholics in the value of "internationalism" rather than the

18 Zahn, "Davy Crockett," 62.

19 Zahn, "Davy Crockett," 65.

20 McNeal, *Harder than War*, 5.

21 McNeal, *Harder than War*, 5, 9.

22 McNeal, *Harder than War*, 11.

prevention of war.[23] It therefore also firmly embraced of the church's just-war position. In fact, in 1939, after determining that the Allied effort in World War II was just, Ryan declared that all Americans were "morally obliged" to do all they reasonably could to defeat "Hitler and Hitlerism."[24] He also stated that the "extreme pacifist position"—that war was always wrong because it involved violence—did not "deserve formal discussion."[25] As McNeal pointed out, by the time the United States entered the war in 1942, the CAIP "unhesitatingly continued the Catholic tradition of patriotism in war time."[26]

It was no surprise, then, when George Higgins, who as the head of the NCWC's Social Action Department was also the *de facto* executive secretary of the CAIP, responded to Zahn's critique of Hannan in a column titled, rather ironically, "Pacifist Attack."[27] Higgins did not pull any punches. He called Zahn's article "poorly researched," "outrageously superficial," "gossipy in tone," "insufferably arrogant," and "woefully irresponsible." He declared that the trouble with Zahn was that he "so casually and so dogmatically" assumed that his position was the only one that could conceivably deserve to be called Christian. What was it about some pacifists, Higgins asked, that made them "so absolutely, so unqualifiedly, and so patronizingly sure of themselves and so infuriatingly holier-than-thou?"[28] He concluded that the council would almost certainly (and unanimously) refuse to accept "Dr. Zahn's apodictic view" that all forms of nuclear weapons must be unqualifiedly condemned.[29]

23 McNeal, *Harder than War*, 12. The CAIP's emphasis on internationalism was not surprising given that it clearly reflected Franklin Roosevelt's move (after 1937) from isolationism to "collective security." Ryan's close support of the Roosevelt Administration had earned him the nickname "The Right Reverend New Dealer" from his critics (McNeal, *Harder than War*, 17).

24 McNeal, *Harder than War*, 18.

25 McNeal, *Harder than War*, 18–19.

26 McNeal, *Harder than War*, 19. William Au noted that the CAIP "sought to oppose both pacifists and isolationists, both of which were seen as being contrary to papal teaching and to the global responsibilities and interests of the United States." Cited in Eileen Egan, "The Struggle of the Small Vehicle, Pax," in *American Catholic Pacifism: The Influence of Dorothy Day and the Catholic Worker Movement*, ed. Anne Klejment and Nancy Roberts (Praeger Publishers, 1996), 123n1.

27 George Higgins, "Pacifist Attack," in NCWC news release (February 22, 1965): 9–10.

28 Higgins, "Pacifist Attack," 9. McNeal suggested that it was especially under Higgins's direction that the CAIP became almost undistinguishable from the NCWC (McNeal, *Harder than War*, 82).

29 In a personal letter Higgins sent to Zahn along with a copy of his article, he explained that he felt forced to write the column, not because of Zahn's criticism of Hannan or the CAIP but rather because Zahn's article was not based on fact but "idle gossip," failed to show even a "minimum

In a reply to Higgins, Zahn recounted that years before, he had written to the CAIP to suggest that it add a committee on "Catholic pacifism" so that US Catholics could be better informed about Catholic pacifist organizations and activities around the world, particularly the Pax movement in Europe. In response, Zahn recalled, he had received a curt dismissal of the idea, stating that such a committee would be no more justified than a "Committee on Catholic Isolationism." Since then, Zahn noted that he had read nothing from anyone involved with the CAIP that was not in keeping with its commitment to "collective security and nuclear realism (spelled 'deterrence') as the twin foundations of international peace."[30] Despite the acrimony of this initial exchange, Zahn and Higgins—who would later become known as the "labor priest" for his support of Cesar Chavez and the United Farmworkers—continued corresponding, in yet another example of Zahn's openness to working with Catholics who did not share his pacifism.[31]

While a committee on Catholic Pacifism (or Catholic Isolationism for that matter) never materialized, perhaps the most significant committee under the umbrella of the CAIP was the International Law and Juridical Institutions Committee (ILJIC). This committee wrote several of CAIP's statements on modern war, and its members (including several employees of the Departments of Defense and State) delivered lectures and participated in numerous symposiums.[32] In 1960, William Nagle, a State Department official and member of the ILJIC, edited a volume for the CAIP titled *Morality and Modern Warfare: The State of the Question*, which included essays by such US Catholic luminaries as John Courtney Murray, SJ, John C. Ford, SJ, and William O'Brien.[33]

---

of respect" for Hannan, and "completely misses the boat." See Higgins to Zahn in letter dated February 16, 1965, UNDA Zahn papers (4/0406).

30 Zahn to Higgins in letter dated March 6, 1965, UNDA Zahn papers (4/04908).

31 In one exchange of letters from late 1966, for instance, they discussed the differences between conscientious objectors to all wars ("absolute pacifists"), a legal option for Catholics in the United States, and Catholics who only objected to participating in unjust wars, a position not allowed under the US military law. Zahn wrote: "I think one position which holds that the war in Vietnam is unjust deserves the same respect that is given to the other which would hold that all war (including the one in Vietnam) is unjust." See Zahn to Higgins in letter dated November 1, 1966, ACUA Higgins papers.

32 In 1962, CAIP and the Archdiocese of Chicago cosponsored a two-day conference on "Christian Conscience and Modern Warfare," during which Zahn presented (McNeal, *Harder than War*, 85).

33 William J. Nagle, ed., *Morality and Modern War: The State of the Question* (Helicon Press, 1960). McNeal observed that in 1962, Thomas Donahue, SJ, had explained at least seven distinct Catholic views on the morality of nuclear weapons (McNeal, *Harder than War*, 85).

In his introduction, Nagle contrasted the book with the British volume *Morals and Missiles: Catholic Essays on the Problem of War Today*, published the year before, which included essays by Archbishop Thomas Roberts, SJ, and Franz Stratmann, OP.[34] While the latter was marked by a "strongly pacifist tone," Nagle noted that only one of the contributors to the US volume would call himself a pacifist—Gordon Zahn.[35] Nagle explained that this contrast highlighted the difference between US Catholic attitudes on war and those found in Europe. An obvious reason for that difference, of course, was that Europe was still mourning and rebuilding from the massive destruction of the Second World War.[36] And Nagle suggested that the presence of only one pacifist in the CAIP collection reflected "a fair representation" of the thinking on war within US Catholicism. He did concede, however, that many more "Gordon Zahns and Dorothy Days" were welcomed on the American scene, "not for the help they will give in solving the dilemma," but rather for their efforts in "prodding our consciences and forcing the rest of us to come to terms with the problem."[37] Zahn later referred this sort of marginalization of pacifists as US Catholicism's "Niebuhr Problem."

In March 1963, Harry Flannery, the president of the CAIP, wrote a memo to its members regarding the debate surrounding nuclear weapons taking place at the Second Vatican Council, pointing to some of the concerns it had raised in governmental quarters. He noted that by the opening of the council's third session, the Kennedy administration had already expressed reservations with what it perceived as the council's disapproval of nuclear weapons.[38] Reflecting these concerns, Flannery wrote that no subject was of "more importance" than

34 Charles S. Thompson, ed., *Moral and Missiles: Catholic Essays on the Problem of War Today* (James Clarke & Co., 1959).

35 Zahn, "Social Science and the Theology of War," 104–25.

36 For a moving account of Europe at the end of the war—a situation that certainly motivated Europeans attitudes on war—see Tony Judt, *Postwar: a History of Europe Since 1945* (Penguin Press, 2005).

37 Nagle, Introduction, *Morality and Modern War*, 6–8.

38 Joseph Komonchak noted that other governments also had concerns. For instance, Franco's Spain was concerned with the direction the Council taking on religious freedom, while some Arab countries were concerned about the Council's newly articulated sympathy for Jewish people (Komonchak, *Vatican II*, 622).

the nuclear question, and that the ILJIC was preparing a statement on nuclear weapons as a way of offsetting the "European pacifist influence in Rome."[39]

In October 1964, the ILJIC released its statement, titled "Morality, Nuclear War, and the Schema on the Church in the Modern World."[40] Catholic peace activists would later refer to this as the "secret memorandum."[41] William O'Brien was the primary author and opened by noting that a recent *New York Times* article (October 12, 1964) had caused some in the US government to be concerned when it reported that the wording of the council's schema on peace and disarmament "could be interpreted as a repudiation of the official United States policy of deterrence based on the use of tactical nuclear weapons at an early stage of any aggression."[42] If the council were to adopt such a position, the statement read, it would,

> place close to fifty million American Catholics in an awesome dilemma as to whether to listen to the solemn findings of a Vatican Council or to the hitherto accepted assurances of their government that America's nuclear deterrent is the foundation for international stability and the *sine qua non* of the defense of the United States.[43]

The statement urged the council to consult "experts in the field," though they noted that no outstanding experts on the morality of nuclear war and deterrence existed at the time. It also recommended that the council not express "the unrealistic hope" of eliminating nuclear weapons, but rather emphasize "a more appropriate" series of goals involving systematic arms control measures.

39 McNeal, *Harder than War*, 97. At the bishops' press conference on November 9, 1964—following Hannan's intervention—Higgins highlighted this situation and reported that a group of lay experts from the United States who had devoted years to studying the controllability of nuclear weapons had sent a letter to the competent Council committee. He explained that the authors stated that it would be "naïve" for the Council to speak of nuclear weapons without the necessary refinements and that the schema did not take into sufficient account the actual state of nuclear weaponry (*Council Daybook*, 243).

40 In August, a copy of the ILJIC statement was sent to Bishop John J. Wright, who would be introducing the draft of the schema at the Council (McNeal, *Harder than War*, 97).

41 McNeal, *Harder than War*, 97.

42 "Morality, Nuclear War, and the Schema on the Church in the Modern World," *CAIP News*, vol. 25 (1964): 6–8.

43 "Morality, Nuclear War," 6. McNeal explained that the ILJIC statement's main concern was not the communist threat but rather "the age-old form of nationalism peculiar to American Catholics known as 'Americanism'—if Catholics did not obey their lawfully elected leaders they would be considered disloyal Americans" (McNeal, *Harder than War*, 98).

The statement then concluded by expressing hope that such efforts would encourage more thinking on these issues by Catholics in the United States, "the land of Hiroshima, but also the land of the most intensive efforts to take arms control and disarmament out of the realm of fantasy and into the realm of social, natural and normative sciences."[44]

In his "Davy Crockett" article, Zahn referred to this statement, which had been submitted to the council by a group of "Roman Catholic experts." He noted that it had made virtually no mention of the "immoral uses" to which present US nuclear stockpiles could be put. Instead, these "experts," Zahn wrote, were "transfixed with horror by the possibility that weapons designed for limited battlefield use might share the fate of the big bombs of which Mr. McNamara proudly (and so frequently) boasts."[45]

JOHN COURTNEY MURRAY, SJ

To fully understand the reasoning of the ILJIC (or the CAIP in general), Patricia McNeal argued that the influence of John Courtney Murray cannot be overlooked.[46] It was Murray who provided the theological justification for the position taken by the CAIP (and ILJIC) on nuclear weapons—the belief that a "limited" nuclear war was both possible and could meet the just-war criteria.[47] Murray provided what became the standard explanation for a justifiable nuclear war in a paper he gave to the CAIP in 1958, which he later published in *Theological Studies*.[48] To support his argument, Murray turned to the "thought of Pius XII" and explained that there was no indication that the pope had ever rejected the use of nuclear weapons in defensive wars.[49] He dismissed Pius's

44 "Morality, Nuclear War," 6.

45 Zahn added that, "Apparently, Bishop Hannan has been convinced that this is indeed a real danger" (Zahn, "Davy Crockett," 63).

46 McNeal, *Harder than War*, 81.

47 McNeal, *Harder than War*, 82.

48 Murray got a lot of mileage out of this paper. He originally presented it to the CAIP on October 24, 1958, and published it as "Remarks on the Moral Problem of War" in *Theological Studies* 20, no. 1 (1959): 40–61. An edited version then appeared as a pamphlet titled "Morality and Modern War," published by Council on Religion and International Affairs (in cooperation with CAIP) in 1959. This same essay was later published as "Theology and Modern War" in *Morality and Modern War*, 69–91. Murray published it once again as "Morality and Modern War" in *The Moral Dilemma of Nuclear Weapons*, ed. William Clancy (Council on Religion and International Affairs, 1961), 7–16.

49 Murray argued that this enabled Catholic moral theology to find a way "between the false extremes of pacifism and bellicism" (Murray, "Remarks," 47–48).

fear of uncontrollable weapons as unfounded, noting that in the early 1950s there had been "a lot of loose and uninformed talk" about weapons that would be beyond human control.[50] For Murray, it was the idea of a "limited" nuclear war that should set the "terms of public debate," while all other arguments were "fanciful and fallacious." As Murray reasoned, "Since nuclear war may be a necessity, it must be made a possibility. Its possibility must be created."[51] This became the party line of the CAIP (as well as that of Hannan and other US bishops) going forward.

Beyond his defense of nuclear war, Murray is also representative of the mid-twentieth century US Catholic context within which Zahn was working. The New York Jesuit was the central Catholic figure in the post-World War II period of prosperity and consensus in the United States, a period which the theologian William Portier has described as having quickly "flattened out" and "re-directed" much of the energies produced by the political and economic pressures of the 1930s.[52] Indeed, the end of World War II had brought about a kind of social consolidation that turned many of the more radical Catholic movements of the interwar period toward more "conventional directions."[53]

The Harvard sociologist Daniel Bell shed light on this postwar consolidation in his 1960 book, *The End of Ideology: On the Exhaustion of Political Ideas in the Fifties*, in which he announced that the war had forged "a rough consensus among intellectuals on political issues."[54] Portier pointed out that the "Good War" had not only ended Depression-era struggles between capital and labor but also melted religious and ethnic groups into a sort of "vast American *unum*."[55] The creative energies of the 1930s had by the 1950s become seen as too ideological and nonpragmatic, and so generally regarded as impediments to

50 Murray distinguished between "low-kiloton" and "high megaton" nuclear weapons: the former were not weapons of mass destruction, he suggested, while the latter world not necessarily "escape from the control of man" (Murray, "Remarks," 51n31).

51 Murray, "Remarks," 58.

52 William Portier, "Theology of Manners as Theology of Containment: John Courtney Murray and *Dignitatis Humanae* Forty Years After," *U.S. Catholic Historian* 24, no. 1 (2006): 95.

53 For example, following World War II, Charles Owen Rice's Catholic Radical Alliance, the Catholic labor activist group, began to focus less on leading strikes and critiquing economic inequality in the United States and more on fighting communism. See Kenneth J. Heineman, *Catholic New Deal: Religion and Reform in Depression Pittsburgh* (Pennsylvania State University Press, 1999), 195.

54 Daniel Bell, *The End of Ideology: On the Exhaustion of Political Ideas in the Fifties* (Harvard University Press, 1960), 373.

55 Portier, "Theology of Manners," 90.

any consensus. It was the task of proponents of the consensus, Bell's "cultural arbiters," to remove such impediments. Murray, whose book *We Hold These Truths: Catholic Reflections on the American Proposition* was also published in 1960, had made a strong but qualified embrace of Bell's argument.[56] Despite Murray's disdain for what he called "the barbarian in the Brooks Brothers suit," Bell's consensus mood and the "gray flannelled stoicism" of his cultural arbiters (Murray's *sapientes*) pervaded the Jesuit's widely read book.[57]

Catholic cultural arbiters such as Murray constructed what the historian Eugene McCarraher described as "a covenant of containment, a 'public theology' or 'civil religion,'" for the Cold War order.[58] This covenant not only "ratified the managerial authority" of Bell's cultural arbiters, the sort of "experts" that Zahn was critical of, but also "stigmatized the indecorous enthusiasms of radical politics."[59] Foremost among which were the indecorous enthusiasms of Catholic pacifists, whose thinking, Murray asserted, could not be "squared with the public doctrine of the Church."[60] For Murray, any Catholic embrace of the "end of ideology" required that voices critical of the US postwar consensus be silenced or ignored.[61]

Such a task was carried out through the use of a paradigm of "incarnational" and "eschatological" humanism that Murray gleaned from earlier European debates.[62] In the aftermath of his own debates with Paul Hanly Furfey in the 1940s over intercreedal cooperation, Murray saw what he regarded as a temptation among some midcentury Catholics to "spiritually withdraw"

56 John Courtney Murray, *We Hold These Truths: Catholic Reflections on the American Proposition* (Sheed & Ward, 1960).

57 Portier, "Theology of Manners," 90.

58 For instance, Murray had described the postwar United States as "an imperialism, like it or not" (Murray, *We Hold These*, 281).

59 Eugene McCarraher, *Christian Critics: Religion and the Impasse in Modern American Social Thought* (Cornell University Press, 2000), 91.

60 Murray, *We Hold These*, 250.

61 Portier, "Theology of Manners," 95.

62 Murray, *We Hold These*, 175–96. Shortall depicts these debates as taking place largely between Dominican and Jesuit *nouveaux théologiens* during the years surrounding World War II. Dominicans such as Yves Congar and Marie-Dominique Chenu emphasized a theology of "presence" rooted in the Incarnation, while Jesuits such as Henri de Lubac and Yves de Montcheuil developed a theology of "the mystical body" focused on eschatological hope. See Sarah Shortall, *Soldiers of God: Catholic Theology and Twentieth Century French politics* (Harvard University Press), 151–52. For more on these European debates, also see Gabriel Daly, CSB, *Transcendence and Immanence: A Study in Catholic Modernism and Integralism* (Clarendon Press, 1980).

from US political and economic institutions.[63] He argued that this desire was rooted in a view that human nature and history were corrupt, and so withdrawal was an "utter prophetic condemnation" of *res humana*, which these institutions represented.[64] Murray declared that such Catholics tended toward an "eschatological humanism," which emphasized a final transcendent end of human nature "radically discontinuous" with history—an emphasis that ultimately led to a "contempt of the world."[65] US institutions and ideals were therefore viewed as necessary evils, and, at best, participation in them was regarded as irrelevant—like the basket-weaving of the Desert Fathers.[66] Murray contrasted this "eschatological humanism" with a more "incarnational" form (which he clearly preferred) that took a more affirming approach to "all that is natural, human, [and] terrestrial."[67] As Murray saw it, "The heavens and the earth are not destined for an eternal dust-heap," and so neither was US society and culture.

While Murray's own embrace of the postwar consensus may not have accurately mirrored the European origins of the incarnational-eschatological terminology he employed, it did clearly reveal his own ideological vision of America.[68] Embrace of America was equated with an incarnational humanism, while any critique of America (such as that offered by Zahn, Furfey, and Day) was regarded as being rooted in an eschatological humanism. Murray seemed to suggest as much when he distinguished eschatological Catholics in Europe, who firmly believed that "the spiritual fortunes of the Church were wedded to the earthly fortunes of the monarchy," from those in the United States, who believed that "the fortunes of the Church—and the individual soul—are completely divorced from all manner of earthly fortunes."[69] With regard to the

63 Joseph Komonchak, "John Courtney Murray and the Redemption of History: Natural Law and Theology," in *John Courtney Murray & the Growth of Tradition*, ed. J. Leon Hooper, SJ, and Todd Whitmore (Sheed & Ward, 1996): 74. For more on these debates, see Michael Baxter, *In Service to the Nation* (PhD diss., Duke University, 1996), 435–43.

64 Murray, *We Hold*, 184.

65 Murray titled this section: "Contempt of the World" (Murray, *We Hold*, 185).

66 Murray, *We Hold*, 186.

67 Murray, *We Hold*, 190.

68 And of course, Murray was still largely working out of the neoscholastic understanding of nature and grace that all the *nouveaux théologiens* were resisting.

69 Murray, *We Hold*, 190. Murray seemed to be thinking here of "altar-throne" French royalists who were so angered by Leo XIII's policy of *ralliement*, which sought to lessen the church-state

latter, Joseph Komonchak has pointed out that Murray was clearly thinking of Furfey.[70]

THE CATHOLIC WORKER, SPECIAL EDITION

Fearing that O'Brien's "secret memorandum" might be read as the official US Catholic viewpoint on nuclear weapons, Dorothy Day put together a special issue of *The Catholic Worker* to be sent to all 2,400 bishops around the world before they reconvened for the fourth session of the council in the fall of 1965.[71] The issue included articles by James Douglass, the Jesuit scripture scholar John McKenzie, the pediatrician and activist Benjamin Spock, and Day (including the second half of her review of *In Solitary Witness*), as well as Maximos IV's intervention before the third session ("Destruction Hangs Over Humanity") and a portion (article 25) of the draft of Schema XIII titled "On Making Lasting Peace."

Zahn also wrote a piece for this issue titled "American Experts and Schema XIII." He argued that there was a very real danger that when the council reconvened to discuss the schema, the use of limited nuclear weapons as a legitimate defense would be included in a revised draft.[72] As evidence, he pointed to the O'Brien statement, which he described as significant, not only because it had obviously influenced Hannan's intervention, but also because the statement had a "definite 'aura' of official standing," which magnified its impact upon the thought and actions of other bishops. For Zahn, the CAIP's close link with the US bishops gave the impression that any CAIP statement was a formal document issued on behalf of "the most official voice of American Catholicism"—when, in reality, it was written not by the whole of the CAIP but only a very small subcommittee.[73]

---

tensions in France in the late nineteenth century and called on French Catholics to abandon their monarchist loyalties and accept the Third Republic.

70 Komonchak noted that Murray was also thinking about Francis Connell, CSSR (the eminent Catholic University moral theologian) (Komonchak, "John Courtney Murray," 76).

71 *The Catholic Worker* (July-August 1965). Eileen Egan did recall that certain members of the US hierarchy "with pro-deterrent views" were omitted from the mailing list (Egan, "The Struggle," 131).

72 Zahn, "American Experts and Schema XIII," *The Catholic Worker*, July-August 1965, 6.

73 McNeal suggested that Higgins, like his predecessor John Ryan, was mainly concerned with the problems of labor and had "very little grasp of international affairs" (McNeal, *Harder than War*, 83).

While the O'Brien statement did not bless all nuclear weapons, Zahn noted that it did open the way for professionals and experts to take over any discussion of these weapons with their "slide-rule calculations" of how much their destructive power could be controlled. Echoing his earlier criticism of value-free sociology, Zahn explained that the inevitable result would be to take what was ultimately an issue in moral theology and make it subject to the findings of military experts and scientists, as well as the interests of the government that employed them. And in doing so, the authors of the statement were endorsing US Cold War efforts to maintain a balance of power, a kind of world "security" resting upon the multilateral threat of annihilation—otherwise known as "nuclear deterrence." All of which was a far cry from the kind of mutual trust that *Pacem in Terris* had advocated for as the basis for true peace.[74]

Zahn also took issue with the memo's contention that any condemnation of nuclear weapons would place *all* US Catholics in "an awesome dilemma." While there were certainly some US Catholics for whom a condemnation of nuclear weapons by the council might require them to choose between the church and the state, Zahn pointed out that an even greater number of Catholics simply assumed the US military policy was morally indifferent or irrelevant to them—or even that they were bound to resign themselves to whatever policies the legitimate authority of the nation-state deemed prudent.

Furthermore, he pointed out that the language in the draft of the schema with its more critical appraisal of nuclear weapons would actually free Catholics like himself from a "dilemma of conscience" that presently existed with current church teaching on war. While he did not expect the council to solve the moral problem of nuclear weapons, Zahn hoped that it would "correct false assumptions" regarding these weapons and inspire US Catholics to face the very real moral dilemma such weapons presented. For if the possession and use of nuclear weapons were immoral, a dilemma for US Catholics already existed between the nuclear policy of their nation and the moral theology of the church. He suggested that it would, therefore, be in their "utmost spiritual benefit" for this dilemma to be brought to their attention by the bishops.[75] Zahn wrote that he hoped US Catholics—in the "land of Hiroshima"—would remember that tragic event and "the guilt we bear for it" and lead the church and the world to a more total commitment against the kind of "pragmatic

74 Zahn, "American Experts," 6.

75 Zahn, "American Experts," 8.

empiricism and 'rational' calculation" of the experts that made such a horror even possible.

In that same issue, *The Catholic Worker* also published anonymously an intervention by John Taylor, the American bishop of Stockholm, Sweden. Though he had sent in this intervention too late to be read during the third session, it was still submitted to the schema's drafting committee. In it, Taylor wrote that the natural moral order condemned as "*mala in se*" the methods of total war, especially the use of nuclear weapons, "which strike indiscriminately at combatants and non-combatants, soldiers and civilians."[76] This was a crucial clarification. For, as James Douglass noted, the substitution of a technical term ("controllability") for a moral term ("discrimination") was decisive in permitting the council to condemn modern war with the language of traditional Catholic moral theology in a way that could be understood as referring directly to the nuclear crisis. Taylor thus enabled his fellow bishops to speak with more confidence and authority on the morality of nuclear weapons.[77]

LOBBYING THE BISHOPS

Also that spring, Zahn (still in Manchester) was invited by Richard Carbary—an old friend and Loyola colleague—to come to Rome to speak with Archbishop Thomas Roberts about conscientious objection in preparation for the final session of the council.[78] Roberts, a British Jesuit who had been archbishop of Bombay from 1937 to 1950, was widely known at the time for his more progressive stances, including on issues of war. While sometimes dismissed as "a 'loose cannon' by his more conservative peers," Zahn wrote that Roberts was "if not the most powerful, certainly the most outspoken bishop on questions of major importance to the Catholic peace community."[79] Carbary was working as Roberts' Latinist during the council. Zahn accepted the invitation, and along with consulting with Roberts, he joined Carbary, Douglass, Eileen Egan, and

76 "Whether the Human Family Will Live or Die," *The Catholic Worker*, July-August 1965, 3. Douglass identified Taylor as the author. See Douglass, *The Non-Violent Cross*, 105.

77 Douglass had noted that prior to Taylor's intervention, it seemed possible that the Council would not be able to make any pronouncement at all against modern war (Douglass, *The Non-Violent Cross*, 105).

78 Zahn, 1994, 69.

79 Zahn, 1994, 69.

other Catholic peace activists "lobbying" the bishops.[80] Dorothy Day was also in Rome at the time with an international group of women gathered in prayer and fasting for peace.

Zahn stayed at a convent where the Canadian bishops were also staying, a circumstance that he remembered as providing a "good opportunity for 'informal' lobbying." He also recalled that Carbary had a knack for spotting US bishops—though their efforts to lobby these bishops were not very successful.[81] In addition to the bishops, Zahn also met with various journalists, liturgists, theologians, and other "Catholic peripherals" who, according to Zahn, seemed to be much more aware of what was going on in the world than the majority of bishops.

That summer, back in Great Britain, Zahn attended to conference on Schema XIII. The main presenters at the gathering were Roberts and Christopher Butler, OSB, the Abbot of Downside Abbey, who was serving as the chair of the subcommittee working on the council's discussion of war.[82] Eileen Egan had given Zahn a "pirated copy" of a draft of the schema, which called upon governments to respect the rights of conscientious objectors but also reaffirmed the church teaching that a presumption of justice should be given to a nation's legitimate authority in times of war. Pressing Butler on why this teaching remained, Zahn asked for examples of "manifestly unjust" acts in war that a Catholic would be obligated to refuse even when ordered. After Butler listed actions such as killing prisoners and the use of torture, Zahn replied that in the course of his recent interviews with Catholic RAF chaplains, several had reported that they were, in fact, willing to tolerate (or at least not interfere with nor counsel conscientious objection to) such actions in situations defined as crucial by the military.[83] These sorts of exchanges led to a correspondence between Zahn and Butler, and eventually an invitation for Zahn to speak to the British bishops.

Zahn returned to Rome that fall of 1965, just as the fourth and final session of Vatican II began.[84] This time, he stayed in a priests' residence in

80 For an almost minute-by-minute account of the efforts of Egan, Zahn, Douglass, and others in Pax to lobby the bishops at the Council, see Eileen Egan, "The Struggle," 123–52.

81 Zahn, 1994, 69.

82 Gallagher, *Laws of Heaven*, 252.

83 Zahn, 1994, 71.

84 He had received a semester extension on his fellowship.

Rome, where he helped Roberts write his intervention on conscientious objection—what Zahn later referred to as his "major contribution to the Council."[85] The intervention told Jägerstätter's story. "This is what we are talking about when we speak of conscientious objection," it read, "and it is by this standard we must measure what we finally proclaim." Roberts then argued that the proposed draft of Schema XIII failed by continuing to assert that Christians must give the presumption of justice to their nation's legitimate authority as long as the injustice of a war is not manifestly clear. This teaching ignored the "tragic fact" that the injustices of the Nazis had seemingly not been clear enough for the millions of German Catholics who had accepted military service, nor clear to their spiritual leaders who encouraged and praised their service. By maintaining this teaching, the council seemed to be implying that Jägerstätter was wrong.

Roberts's intervention also pointed out that the Schema's recommendation that governments should "reflect a positive attitude" toward conscientious objectors was "lamentably weak and insufficient" in supporting COs. While Jägerstätter always knew that his refusal would eventually lead to his death, during his last weeks in prison, he was continually troubled by the fear that he might be committing a sin by not following the advice offered by the leaders of his church. Therefore, the council needed to provide "clear testimony" that the church affirmed the right to refuse military service and to assure Catholic COs that they would always have the church's fullest support so that martyrs like Jägerstätter would never again have to feel they were taking "their stand alone."

In what Zahn later described at its "key" paragraph, Robert's intervention concluded by pleading for the bishops to consider Jägerstätter's witness in "a spirit of gratitude." It was a scandal to Christianity that for too many centuries now, "almost every national hierarchy in almost every war" had allowed itself to become the "moral arm of its own government," even in wars later recognized as palpably unjust. Roberts called on his fellow bishops to break with this tragic past by making "a clear and unambiguous affirmation of the right and the obligation of each Christian to obey the voice of his informed conscience before and during a time of war."

85 Zahn, 1994, 70.

In the end, Roberts was never able to read his intervention before the council.[86] Though he had requested time (and Carbary had secured the signatures necessary to assure that he speak), Zahn recalled that the Italian cardinal who chaired the session was considered something of an "enemy" to their efforts and had adjourned the session without recognizing Roberts. And so, while the intervention was added to the written record, Zahn explained that "its message, alas, probably never reached the bishops of the world to whom it was addressed."[87]

Nevertheless, when *Gaudium et Spes* was eventually approved by the bishops and promulgated by Pope Paul VI on December 7, 1965, it declared the need for an evaluation of war with "an entirely new attitude."[88] It went onto to state that it seemed "right that laws make humane provisions for the case of those who for reasons of conscience refuse to bear arms, provided however, that he accept some other form of service to the human community."[89] As lukewarm a declaration as this was, Zahn wrote that at least the council recognized conscientious objection "as a stand deserving respect."[90] Likewise, while it did not condemn modern war outright, nor even nuclear weapons *per se*, the document did state that any act of war "aimed indiscriminately at the destruction of entire cities or of extensive areas along with their population is a crime against God and man himself" which merited "unequivocal and unhesitating condemnation."[91]

In looking back on all this, McNeal observed that what the peace lobbyists at the Second Vatican Council had ultimately sought to do was to "shut the door on scholastic just-war doctrine as a viable ethic for modern warfare," and that they had hoped to do this with both a condemnation of nuclear weapons and an affirmation of the right of conscientious objection.[92] Though a condemnation of nuclear weapons would have to wait, they were somewhat

86 Roberts's intervention is included in Appendix I.

87 Zahn, 1994, 72.

88 *Gaudium et Spes*, no. 80, in *Catholic Social Thought*.

89 *Gaudium et Spes*, no.79.

90 Zahn, 1994, 72. Spellman, who also sought to have the Council declare military service mandatory, had earlier argued that "the responsibility for judging the necessity of drafting men for service belongs to civil authorities and individuals cannot refuse their obedience to the state" (Douglass, *The Non-Violent Cross*, 103).

91 *Gaudium et Spes*, no. 80.

92 McNeal, *Harder than War*, 103.

successful with the second goal. In a letter to the Mennonite theologian John Howard Yoder, Zahn wrote that while the statement on conscientious objection in *Gaudium et Spes* was "weak," the very fact that the council included it at all in the document represented something of a victory.[93] He also noted that Catholics in Europe were much more active in "probing into questions related to the morality of war" than those in the United States. "Frankly, I think the American bishops were unprepared for the condemnatory tone taken by the majority," Zahn observed, and "their attempt to win a last-moment reprieve was both proof of their surprise and a measure of how far behind the European Catholics American Catholic thinking on peace and war had been (and still is)."

Though short of what Zahn and others would have preferred, the council went "far too far" on war for some US bishops. In fact, Hannan and Spellman had made a last-minute call to reject the entire schema if its position on war and nuclear weapons was not changed. In a letter dated December 2, 1965, Hannan and nine other US bishops challenged the final draft, arguing that the council had ignored the fact that the possession of nuclear weapons "preserved freedom for a very large portion of the world."[94] But when Hannan tried to get all the US delegation to back this "modi," he reportedly drew a warning from another US bishop that if such a step were taken, the US bishops would invite the same kind of critique by future historians as German bishops were then receiving from Zahn and others.[95]

CONCLUSION

Zahn's experience at Vatican II was certainly a high-water mark in his career. It not only solidified his place as a leader within the Catholic peace movement but also confirmed his belief that while that movement could (and should) certainly be critical of the hierarchy, it should always do so from within the church. Despite the obstacles the "peace lobby" faced, it did score some very real victories in moving the bishops on the issues of modern war and conscientious objection. Zahn would look to this kind of peace lobbying as a model for what the Catholic peace movement could do if it remained Catholic—an

93 Zahn to Yoder in letter dated October 6, 1966, UNDA Zahn papers (2/02211).

94 Douglass, *The Non-Violent Cross*, 133n18.

95 Douglass, *The Non-Violent Cross*, 133n18.

argument Zahn would make in the next decade in response to those who had given up on the Catholic Church as a force for peace.

At the same time, Zahn's efforts during the Second Vatican Council also placed him squarely within the more radical wing of US Catholicism. Perhaps more than anything else, Zahn's kinship with European bishops—and his disagreement with US bishops—made this evident. Zahn clearly saw the United States and its nuclear arsenal not as defenders of liberty and freedom but as a threat to international peace and stability. This was certainly a coherent and compelling minority position within the US church, not to mention the broader society.

10

THE GROUND BEGINS TO SHIFT

We have to face the fact that we have traveled a long way from the real Christian center. Centuries of identification between Christian and civil life have done more to secularize Christianity than to sanctify civil life. This is not a popular idea.

—*Thomas Merton*[1]

Fresh off his heady experience at the council, Zahn returned home to Chicago and saw firsthand how much opposition to the US war effort in Vietnam had grown since he left—growth that had also energized the US Catholic peace movement. In the fall of 1964, Thomas Merton had hosted what he called "The Spiritual Roots of Protest" retreat at Gethsemani.[2] The retreat brought together Catholic peace activists such as Tom Cornell, Jim Forest, Philip and Daniel Berrigan, along with John Howard Yoder and A. J. Muste—the godfather of the US peace movement. Afterwards, Merton wrote Zahn, still in Europe at the time, to report that during the retreat "Jägerstätter came up constantly."[3]

1 Letter to Zahn dated January 1962 in *The Hidden Ground of Love: the Letters of Thomas Merton on Religious Experience and Social Concerns*, ed. William H. Shannon (Farrar, Straus and Giroux, 1985), 649.

2 See, Gordon Oyer, *Pursuing the Spiritual Roots of Protest: Merton, Berrigan, Yoder, and Muste at the Gethsemani Abbey Peacemakers Retreat* (Cascade Books, 2014).

3 Merton to Zahn in letter dated December 17, 1964, in *Hidden Ground of Love*, 654.

Soon afterward, the Catholic Peace Fellowship (CPF) was established, with Forest as national secretary and Cornell as education secretary. The Berrigans, Dorothy Day, and Zahn all signed on as sponsors. As historian Penelope Moon noted, "If Pax exhibited a 'holy maturity,' the new CPF brandished a 'holy brashness,' developing more seriously the Catholic Worker's experiments with civil disobedience and emphasizing the laity as a potential force for social change and institutional reform."[4] Counseling Catholic conscientious objectors would quickly become a core activity of the CPF.[5]

Not everything was so positive, however. In fact, the day before Bishop Hannan gave his defense of the use of nuclear weapons at Vatican II, a twenty-two-year-old named Roger LaPorte set himself on fire in front of the United Nations headquarters in New York. Before he died the next day, LaPorte stated that he was a Catholic Worker and wanted to "end the war in Vietnam."[6] LaPorte's death sent shock waves through the Catholic peace movement. By that time, some Catholic Workers had already begun burning their draft cards in public to protest the war, while angry counterprotestors yelled at them to burn themselves, not their cards.[7] From his hermitage in rural Kentucky, a concerned Thomas Merton saw a connection between LaPorte's self-immolation and the draft card burnings. For most Catholics, though, LaPorte's death was simply seen as a suicide and therefore a sin. But not everyone saw it that way. Daniel Berrigan, for instance, said a mass for LaPorte and called his death "an act of misguided heroism."[8] And Dorothy Day wrote an article in the November 1965 issue of *The Catholic Worker* titled "Suicide or Sacrifice?" in which she discussed LaPorte's death through the lens of the often-forgotten Catholic notion of "victim souls."[9]

4 Penelope Moon *"We Have Got to Lead Them in the Ways of Peace": The Catholic Peace Fellowship in the Vietnam Era* (PhD Dissertation, Arizona State University, 2001), 43–44.

5 In appreciation of their work with COs, Zahn left the CPF all the proceeds from the publication of *In Solitary Witness.*

6 When asked why he did this protest, LaPorte replied, "I'm a Catholic Worker. I'm against war, all wars." See James Forest, *At Play in the Lions' Den: a Biography and Memoir of Daniel Berrigan* (Orbis Books, 2017), 91.

7 A Catholic Worker, David Miller, had been the first person to be arrested for burning his draft card in October 1965 following the passage a federal law banning such action.

8 These comments led to Berrigan being "exiled" by his Jesuit superiors to Latin America (Forest, *At Play*, 92–94).

9 Dorothy Day, "Saint or Sacrifice," *The Catholic Worker*, November, 1965.

SPEAKING CHRISTIANITY IN A POST-CHRISTIAN WORLD

In an essay titled "Saint or Suicide," Zahn also weighed in. He held up LaPorte's death as an occasion to examine the way the church had come to view both prophets and martyrs—figures who had become something of an embarrassment to many modern Catholics.[10] Zahn lamented that there was "little or no sympathy, understanding, or even respect, for the 'extremist' or 'fanatic'" whose insistence upon a total commitment to the faith or, at least the total rejection of evil, endangered the more "realistic" image of Christianity that had become so admired within the contemporary church.[11] It was along these lines that Zahn went on to compare Roger LaPorte with Franz Jägerstätter, calling both "prophets" who had insisted upon "speaking Christianity" in a "post-Christian world" (a phrase he borrowed from Merton).

While the distinction in Catholic moral theology between "direct suicide" and "indirect suicide" certainly distinguished Jägerstätter from LaPorte, Zahn argued that it failed to recognize their similarities.[12] "The Austrian's refusal was his answer (the most appropriate answer—perhaps the only appropriate Christian answer)," Zahn wrote, "to the same dilemma of conscience that the American [LaPorte] wanted to dramatize before his nation and the world."[13] In what can now be certainly read as a misguided attempt to somehow justify LaPorte's suicide, Zahn suggested that both of these young Catholics acted in accord with what they regarded as their moral obligations as a Christian in an un-Christian world—and both paid for it with their lives. And as more and more young people engaged in acts of protest and civil disobedience in the Civil Rights and anti-Vietnam war movements, Zahn suggested that the church needed to, likewise, assume a more "heroic" stance—rooted in its obligation to reject injustices, protest against them, and even "disrupt such an unjust order." He argued that seeing this kind of dissent and disobedience—no matter

10 Gordon Zahn, "Saint or Suicide," *Pax Bulletin*, September 1966, 6–7.

11 Zahn, "Saint or Suicide," 6.

12 He pointed out that Jägerstätter was as certain as LaPorte that his actions would directly lead to his death, a thought that troubled the Austrian Catholic until the day he died. In fact, Zahn wrote, the welfare of his family had been less of a concern for Jägerstätter than the fear that his refusal might be sinful and that he might face "eternal damnation as a willful suicide" (Zahn, "Saint or Suicide," 6).

13 Zahn, "Saint or Suicide," 7.

the cost—as a "religious obligation" offered a rationale for understanding the relationship between prophecy and martyrdom that linked LaPorte with Jägerstätter.

Despite the problems of comparing La Porte with Jägerstätter, comparison of German and US Catholics was something Zahn had been elaborating on for a while. Around the time his article on LaPorte appeared, Zahn also published an article in *Commonweal* titled "Crime of Silence" in which he argued that although the US atrocities in Vietnam fell far short of Nazi war crimes, "the parallels are there, and they are growing more insistent."[14] While Zahn had suggested as much in previous publications, this article seemed to provoke a particularly strong reaction.[15] It was such a reaction that prompted a profile of Zahn to be written in *U.S. Catholic*, which offers another helpful snapshot of Zahn at a moment when he was gaining more and more prominence in US Catholic peace circles.[16] The profile opened by describing Zahn as a "one-man peace movement."[17]

Zahn was asked about the then somewhat popular belief that Germans were "especially pernicious and diabolical" and so uniquely prone to embrace fascism. This was rooted in the belief some scholars had come to refer to as the *Sonderweg* theory, which had emerged in the years following World War II with the publication of William Montgomery McGovern's *From Luther to Hitler: The History of Nazi-Fascist Philosophy* in 1946. In the United States, the *Sonderweg* thesis gained popularity with the 1960 publication of William Shirer's

14 Zahn, "Crime of Silence" *Commonweal*, June 17, 1966, 354–56.

15 For instance, when Furfey wrote a letter to editor of the *National Catholic Reporter* in April 1966 on the morality of the US war in Vietnam, he mentioned German bishops' capitulation to the Nazis, "as Gordon Zahn has brilliantly proved." This brought an angry letter to the editor denouncing Zahn's research. See *National Catholic Reporter*, May 18, 1966. In reply, Zahn wrote: "We American Catholics are repeating today the scandalous failure of the German Catholics under Hitler, and future scholars will have to assign a good share of responsibility for this to a hierarchy that is far too willing to 'go along' with a war that is (to say the very least!) of doubtful justice." See Gordon Zahn, "Zahn Defends Thesis of Book," *National Catholic Reporter*, June 1966.

16 Noting that when Zahn first began his research there were few Catholic scholars interested in the "problems of war and peace," the article stated that Zahn had personally done "a great deal to change the situation." See Bruce Cook, "It Takes a Worried Man," *U.S. Catholic*, November 1966, 11.

17 Acknowledging the implication of his pacifism, particularly during World War II, Zahn recognized that the Nazis were indeed "unbelievably bad" and that if every US Christian had followed his example, the Nazis would certainly have won the war. He explained that such an uncomfortable realization had brought about a kind of tension in his life between "practical necessity and the demands of conscience," which had forced real creativity in his thinking (Cook, "It Takes a Worried Man," 11).

The Rise and Fall of the Third Reich: A History of Nazi Germany.[18] Zahn had long rejected such a notion and argued that Nazism and the fascist mentality were not uniquely German. War, Zahn explained, was "fundamentally a totalitarian enterprise," and he pointed to the adulation shown for Green Berets in the United States as not all that different from what had been shown to the Nazi SS troopers in Germany.[19] Zahn recalled meeting German POWs at a camp in Maryland not far from where he had been doing alternative service during World War II and thinking they "seemed no different from anyone else to us."[20] Zahn also noted that the whole "psychology" of the war in Vietnam was negatively affecting Americans' self-image, as the tremendous military power of the United States, supposedly the defender of freedom and democracy, was being directed against such a small impoverished nation.[21]

Similarly, in a letter to the editor of the *New York Times* published in February 1967, Zahn noted that on the previous Sunday morning a pastoral letter had been read from the pulpit regarding the US bishops' opposition to legislation being debated at the time to legalize abortion.[22] Acknowledging that he also opposed this legislation and so welcomed the letter, Zahn mourned the fact that the bishops had not similarly spoken out in opposition to the program of "post-natal abortion" and "post-pubertal infanticide" that was being conducted by the US military in Vietnam. He compared this to the German bishops who had denounced the Nazi euthanasia programs but said nothing about the Nazis' unjust wars or extermination of the Jews. Zahn pointed out that future generations will likewise question why US bishops had so emphatically opposed legalized abortion but not "the slaughter of the innocent already born in a stupid and inhuman war." In what would become a long-running argument, Zahn wrote that opposition to abortion and war were simply two aspects of the fundamental belief that all human life was intrinsically sacred and worth defending. This so-called "absolutist" stance on life would soon bring Zahn into conflict with US Catholics across the political spectrum, including many of his fellow travelers in the peace movement.

18 William Shirer, *The Rise and Fall of the Third Reich: A History of Nazi Germany* (Simon and Shuster, 1960).

19 Cook, "It Takes a Worried Man," 12.

20 He also remembered suggesting to the local Catholic pastor that he sponsor a Christmas party for the German POWs and US COs—a suggestion that was ignored (Cook, "It Takes a Worried Man," 12).

21 Cook, "It Takes a Worried Man," 13.

22 Zahn, "Lack of Pastoral Protests Against the War, *New York Times*, February 15, 1967.

A SIGNIFICANT CHANGE

Around this time, Zahn also published a collection of his earlier essays that he had complied while in Manchester. In many ways, this volume, *War, Conscience and Dissent*, can be seen as another highpoint for Zahn and his place as an intellectual leader within the US Catholic peace movement. And as he pointed out, it also marked a shift that seemed to be taking place within Catholic thinking on war. Indeed, in his introduction, Zahn noted that "a significant change" had clearly taken place since many of his articles had first been published. For instance, while certainly still a minority position within the church, he wrote that it was no longer possible to dismiss pacifism as a theological oddity or an "aberration being propagated by a 'lunatic fringe.'"[23] While at the start of the decade pacifism had appeared to many US Catholics as dissent from church teaching, it now claimed a much greater measure of respect and even acceptance within the church more broadly. Zahn also suggested that the condemnation of total war "as a crime against God and man" in *Gaudium et Spes* had come close to "fixing the seal of official approval" on arguments that he and others had long been making.[24]

Challenging the usual polarities of the time, Zahn noted that any issue that found such vastly differing figures as the "archconservative" Cardinal Ottaviani and the "ultraliberal" Archbishop Roberts in substantial agreement—as the issue of modern war did—could not (and certainly should not) be passed over in silence by Catholics.[25] Many of the US bishops at Vatican II were simply not prepared for the direction and intensity that they encountered from their fellow bishops around the world during the debates on war. This highlighted the sad fact that no attempt had been made to keep US bishops (or US Catholics in general) in touch with the developing theological critique of modern war in the church.[26] Alas, the CAIP never took up Zahn's suggestion to create a committee on Catholic pacifism. As a result, the majority of US

23 Gordon Zahn, *War, Conscience and Dissent* (Hawthorn Books, 1967), 13.

24 Zahn pointed to his own essay, along with that of John C. Ford, SJ ("The Hydrogen Bombing of Cities"), which appeared in *Morality and Modern Warfare*, as examples (Zahn, *War, Conscience and Dissent*, 24).

25 Zahn, *War, Conscience and Dissent*, 14.

26 Zahn blamed this largely on the CAIP with its "almost compulsive dedication to the task of preserving the ecclesiastical establishment against possibly 'imprudent' or 'excessive' opposition to war and military preparedness" (Zahn, *War, Conscience and Dissent*, 15).

Catholics were still not prepared to face "the essential questions" that had to be asked about the morality of modern war.[27]

In the introduction to a section of essays titled "Conscience and the State," Zahn wrote that a similar shift could also be seen taking place around an even more fundamental question: Catholic obedience to the modern nation-state. He referred to this as the "cornerstone of the whole pacifist position." Again, in just a few short years, the idea of conscientious objection and civil disobedience to secular authority had become much more acceptable thanks in large part to the civil rights and anti-war movements.[28] Zahn pointed out that Catholics were starting to realize that they needed to determine for themselves how willing they were to tolerate racial prejudice, economic inequality, or any other social injustices, and to what extent they were obligated to "give witness" in opposition—an eschatological witness rooted in hope. Nevertheless, Zahn argued that more was certainly needed to be done, particularly for Catholics drafted into a war they believed to be immoral. For while Vatican II's call for COs to be treated "humanely" was significant, Zahn stated that Catholic COs were still largely refused any measure of support or encouragement from their fellow Catholics or church leaders in their efforts to live according to the dictates of their consciences as the church required.[29]

Recent history (and his own research) had convinced Zahn that the church could no longer simply call for protections for individual Catholics who believed that they were morally obligated to conscientious objection and civil disobedience. Rather, the church itself needed to be the one to call Catholics to such dissent. Again, recent shifts had made these sorts of ideas less novel, Zahn wrote, as there was "nothing particularly daring now about emphasizing the need to restore the prophetic image and thrust of Christianity."[30] In this sense, Zahn hoped that the "restraining shell of exaggerated prudence" in Catholic moral theology had slowly begun to fall away and that the church

27 Zahn, *War, Conscience and Dissent*, 26.

28 Zahn wrote that "one is at a disadvantage today when he speaks to college audiences which may include students and professors who have been on picket lines and known the inside of jails precisely because they could not remain silent in the face of injustices perpetrated or condoned by the secular authority" (Zahn, *War, Conscience and Dissent*, 124).

29 Zahn, *War, Conscience and Dissent*, 126.

30 Zahn pointed to examples of clergy protesting the Vietnam War, as well as priests and nuns marching alongside and sometimes even being arrested with Civil Rights activists (Zahn, *War, Conscience and Dissent*, 203).

could thereby begin to have an impact upon a generation that was coming to regard religion as largely irrelevant.[31]

Promising changes could also be seen in Catholic attitudes toward nationalism, starting with Paul VI's 1964 Christmas message in which he called nationalism an "enemy of human brotherhood."[32] This was not necessarily a new trend, as there had been a growing "emotional and spiritual revulsion" stirred by the horrors of two World Wars and an increasing recognition that modern war could not be justified. As a result of this, Zahn pointed to a "twisting and trimming" of the just-war theory's classic moral principles by those looking to justify modern war in order to suit the "national imperatives" of military experts.[33] The fact that so many "expert theologians" in Germany had similarly tried to justify Hitler's unjust wars or that almost no Catholic theologians in the United States had publicly condemned the atrocities at Hiroshima and Nagasaki (or the continued preparation for similar atrocities), was evidence to Zahn of the "almost diabolical grip" that nationalism had on Catholic moral theology.[34]

If just-war teaching was to survive, Zahn stated that a "new emphasis" needed to be placed on the teaching's "mutually reinforcing" principles of discrimination and limitation that would resist any argument that attempted to justify the "anything goes" mentality of total warfare.[35] Zahn had earlier argued that if the US war in Vietnam violated the conditions for the just-war theory, Catholics had an "obligation" to refuse to support it and do what they could to bring it to a speedy end.[36] The time had come, Zahn now declared, for Catholics who took the just-war theory seriously to either "put up or shut up."[37]

It was within the context of these shifts that Zahn suggested his research might help Catholics recognize that pacifism was not only tenable but may

31 Zahn, *War, Conscience and Dissent*, 283.

32 Zahn, *War, Conscience and Dissent*, 283.

33 Zahn, *War, Conscience and Dissent*, 284.

34 Again, it is worth remembering the wartime critiques of the Allied bombing of German cities by Furfey and Ford.

35 Zahn argued that Catholics could no longer give secular rulers a "moral blank check" (Zahn, *War, Conscience and Dissent*, 286).

36 Gordon Zahn, "The Test of the 'Just War,'" *Worldview* (December 1965): 11–13.

37 Zahn noted that, sadly, it had always been the case that those who were the "most devoted to the development and dissemination of just-war theories in the abstract" had usually been lamentably reticent about "applying their fine theories to actual wars-in-progress" (Zahn, "The Test," 11).

actually be "the most theologically consistent solution" to the dilemma of modern war. He hoped that the republication of his essays would not only lead more Catholics to become COs (or take other forms of dissent) but that when they did, they would find a deeper understanding and support from their church. The fact that many of his articles no longer seemed as controversial as they once did, he suggested, was a sign of the progress that had been made to bring about a greater recognition and acceptance of pacifism among Catholics.[38] That said, Zahn stated that pacifism still needed to offer alternatives to war that went beyond being either a helpless bystander or active participant—"it simply must never again become a choice between *permitting* an Auschwitz or *committing* a Dresden."[39]

To offer a truly effective alternative, though, the "organizational and institutional properties" of the church would have to be brought to bear. Repeating his criticism of the CAIP, Zahn pointed out that smaller organizations such as the Catholic Worker, PAX, and the Catholic Peace Fellowship bore the burden of the Catholic efforts for peace in the United States, though without official episcopal support, such organizations could never truly reach their full potential.[40] All of which led Zahn to declare again that the Catholic Church had "a mission to encourage, support, and even provoke active dissent and civil disobedience."[41] For all the other promising changes that had occurred, virtually no progress had been made in effecting the kind of separation of the church and state that would free Catholics from their traditional disposition to resolve all questions of doubt regarding the justice of war in the favor of the authority of the nation-state. Indeed, it remained "an all but unchallenged first principle" of Catholic moral thinking that "the 'public order' must be underwritten and maintained at any price."[42] In contrast, Zahn contended that the threat of social disorder was preferable to the toleration of, or collaboration with, an evil regime or the evil acts of an otherwise acceptable regime.

Zahn rejected the fear that this kind of thinking would encourage a return to an era "long since closed (and happily so)" in which popes and bishops attempted to force their will through threats of interdicts or

38 Zahn, *War, Conscience and Dissent*, 19.

39 Zahn, *War, Conscience and Dissent*, 296.

40 Zahn, *War, Conscience and Dissent*, 298.

41 Zahn, *War, Conscience and Dissent*, 301.

42 Zahn, *War, Conscience and Dissent*, 301.

excommunications—"a modern version of theocracy." He did assert, however, that the church needed to again resume the role it once held as "judge of the nations and their rulers." Church leaders needed to take up their responsibility to remind Catholics that basic moral principles must never be abandoned and to strengthen them to meet whatever sacrifices they may be called upon to make to resist evil.[43] While such as suggestion may seem "radical," it was not new within the long Christian tradition. Zahn pointed to the "Church of Prophets" and "Church of Martyrs" that had little or no power over secular rulers but who had nonetheless dared to bravely voice their opposition.[44] Catholic pacifism was certainly "visionary," but in a world where the nightmare of a nuclear holocaust had become the "rational norm" of expectations, Zahn suggested that Catholics needed to be visionary.[45]

UMASS BOSTON

Around this time, as he remembered it, while in Boston to give a lecture, Zahn had been invited to a reception at the house of some friends. Also invited was a professor at the newly formed Boston campus of the University of Massachusetts, who casually asked Zahn if he would ever be interested in teaching in Boston. After recalling his pleasant experience at Harvard, Zahn replied that he would. To Zahn's surprise, what followed was an invitation for an interview and then an offer of a tenured position (with a higher salary and lighter teaching load).[46] Despite the reality that he was still not in "good standing" with the administration at Loyola, Zahn felt obliged to discuss the offer with them, both out a sense of loyalty to his colleagues and his commitment to Catholic higher education.[47] But continuing protests over his

43 Zahn, *War, Conscience and Dissent*, 302.

44 Reclaiming the Church's role as a "source of dissent and disobedience" did not require a call to immediate and blanket rebellion against the state, Zahn explained, it could begin by simply being less enthusiastic about the honor of war and military virtues (Zahn, *War, Conscience and Dissent*, 303).

45 Zahn, *War, Conscience and Dissent*, 304.

46 Zahn, 1994, 48. According to David O'Brien, it was Francis Broderick, the founding chancellor of UMass-Boston, and Thomas Brown, a history professor at UMass-Boston, who shared credit for bringing Zahn to Boston.

47 It is worth noting that in late 1972, Furfey informed Zahn that he had nominated Zahn as a candidate for the chair of the sociology department at the Catholic University of America, but Zahn later reported that he was never contacted by the search committee. See Furfey to Zahn in letter dated December, 1972; Zahn to Furfey in letter dated January 8, 1973, ACUA Furfey papers.

research, including the significant addition of Cardinal Bea into the fray, seemed to make his departure a convenient (if not welcomed) occasion for the Loyola administration.[48]

Zahn joined the sociology department at UMass-Boston in the fall of 1967. Right away, he noticed that both the students and faculty were much more involved in social issues than at Loyola. "It could scarcely be otherwise" Zahn later recalled, "in those days of Vietnam protests and developing movements for racial justice, feminist activism, and other exciting issues that invited active participation."[49] While he continued to serve on the Catholic Interracial Council and cochair of the American Pax Society (which he and Eileen Egan had started earlier that year), as well as informally counseling COs to the Vietnam War, moving to Boston further increased Zahn's activism. For instance, he joined the Scholars Against Nuclear Arms (SANE) and the Fellowship of Reconciliation (FOR). And as Zahn remembered it, he quickly became widely known in Boston as a "prominent (notorious?) Catholic of 'dissent,'" and so was in demand "if only as a 'token' voice" on various interfaith panels. With the opening of Hochhuth's *The Deputy* in New York, for example, Zahn recalled that he seemed to be the only US Catholic willing to offer a "balanced" position on the play for national media.[50] But to his pleasant surprise, such activities did not ostracize him from the local bishop, and Zahn even accepted Boston Cardinal Humberto Medeiros's invitation to be a charter member of the Archdiocesan Commission on Justice and Peace and to serve as chair of the peace subcommittee.

All of this not only reflected some of the differences between Chicago and Boston but also the steadily changing attitudes within the church, particularly its hierarchy, on war that Zahn had been highlighting. For instance, in 1967, the US bishops issued a joint statement acknowledging that antiwar protestors represented "responsible segments of our society."[51] The following year, the bishops refrained from declaring that the US war effort in Vietnam

48 Zahn, 1994, 47.

49 He described the UMass student body as a "more mature urban and principally working-class population." While the same issues had been heating up in Chicago, "the somewhat greater affluence" of Loyola students, combined with "the more authoritarian structure" of the Loyola administration, produced an atmosphere of restraint definitely not present in Boston's "liberal/radical atmosphere and setting" (Zahn, 1994, 48).

50 Zahn, 1994, 49.

51 McNeal, *Harder than War*, 157.

was just, which they had done as recently as 1966—though neither did they declare it unjust.[52] The bishops also stated that valid moral questions could be raised concerning the war and spoke out in favor of the rights of conscientious objectors, even selective conscientious objectors, as Congress debated the reauthorization of the US draft laws.[53]

Zahn's increasing activism also reflected his reputation as a leading figure within the US Catholic peace movement. For instance, he was interviewed by James Finn for his book, *Protest: Pacifism and Politics*, which also included interviews with Day, the Berrigan brothers, Muste, Bayard Rustin, and Joan Baez. Finn described Zahn as a sociologist who "wants his work to be scholarly and methodologically sound, but he also insists that it make value judgements and have contemporary relevance."[54] Explaining the development of his "absolute religious pacifist" stance, Zahn recounted that his position during World War II could have been described as "integralist"—a "humanitarian type of Catholicism" that regarded the very nature of war as being contrary to the spirit of Christianity.[55] But after other Catholic COs told him that such a position was untenable, Zahn recalled that he had "converted" for a time to their more "traditional Catholic pacifist" position—what he termed as a "limited pacifist." Since then, though, he told Finn that he had returned to something approximating his original position, which was very much in line with the "new theology" of the day—"just trying to take the *whole meaning* of the Gospel message."[56]

As Zahn saw it, the just-war theory was essentially a "compromise" from the earlier "tone or tradition" of Christianity, which held that all war was "an essentially un-Christian type of endeavor."[57] His research into German Catholics only reinforced his belief that the entire just-war tradition was "irrelevant" for

52 In response to *Humanae Vitae*, which had been promulgated earlier that year, *Human Life in Our Day* addressed both the US war in Vietnam and birth control (McNeal, *Harder than War*, 157).

53 Peter Cajka, *Follow Your Conscience: The Catholic Church and the Spirit of the Sixties* (University of Chicago Press, 2021), 156.

54 James Finn, *Protest: Pacifism and Politics: Some Passionate Views on War and Nonviolence* (Vintage Books, 1968), 59.

55 Zahn repeated the idea that he had simply made a "largely emotional" judgment that war and Christianity were irreconcilable (Finn, *Protest*, 62).

56 Finn, *Protest*, 62.

57 Finn, *Protest*, 67.

those who actually fight in wars.[58] The fact that so few US Catholic theologians or bishops had made any kind of outright condemnation of nuclear weapons or the US war in Vietnam was evidence that they were still too beholden to the nation-state. What was needed, he asserted, was more of a separation of church and state, but "from the other side than that at which the issue is usually presented."[59] In short, the church needed to break away from grip of the state.

As far as the shift in Catholic attitudes on war, Zahn pointed out that while the vast majority of US Catholics would still disapprove of the position he had taken during World War II, there was now at least more awareness of the fact that there had been US Catholic COs during that war—role models that he and other COs of his generation did not have. He also noted that while the Vietnam-era COs were outspoken and suffered abuse for their beliefs, World War II-era COs were simply "hidden away in a convenient cubbyhole set up by the whole conscription system"—a situation he guessed the current generation would not tolerate. And looking back, Zahn surmised that it might have been better had COs in his day "been beaten up a little and gotten press coverage."[60]

AMERICAN CATHOLICS AND VIETNAM

In an edited collection of essays by various authors titled *American Catholics and Vietnam*, Zahn again pointed out the "significant shift in emphasis" that had taken place since the start of the 1960s and noted that the volume highlighted the fact that "an important corner" had been turned in Catholic thinking.[61] For Zahn, US Catholicism had once again learned to "distinguish between Caesar and Christ," and therefore it could no longer be assumed that the church would be "the automatic and unquestioning handmaiden of the war-making secular authority."[62] Likewise, Catholic pacifists were far less likely to be dismissed as "some kind of lunatic fringe," even by those who

58 Finn, *Protest*, 67. Pointing to the napalm bombing of villages in Vietnam or the fire-bombing of Dresden during World War II, Zahn asserted that such actions, which carried "even by implication the intention of destroying civilian life," were a clear violation of the just-war tenets (Finn, *Protest*, 64–65).

59 Finn, *Protest*, 69.

60 Finn, *Protest*, 70.

61 Gordon Zahn, Foreword, *American Catholics and Vietnam*, ed. Thomas Quigley (Eerdmans, 1968), 16.

62 Zahn, Foreword, 16.

disagreed with them. Zahn credited all this not only to the theological impact of Pope John XXIII and Vatican II but also to changes in modern warfare that had taken place in the twentieth century—developments that he said even further highlighted the "essential and evermore inescapable contradiction between the spirit of war and the spirit of Christianity."[63]

While *American Catholics and Vietnam* offered an illustration of this shift, Zahn noted that it was both "too little," in the sense that no member of the US hierarchy had contributed to the volume, and "too late," in that for many Catholics, arguments over these issues had already given way to action.[64] Zahn pointed to the "Boston Five" as an example of how some had recently begun to turn to "the symbol of the act" in order to express their rejection of an immoral war.[65] He admitted that he and many other Catholics were not yet ready to join or actively support these sorts of actions. Nevertheless, he asserted that all Catholics needed to be "ready and willing" to understand and respect those who had concluded that anything short of such resistance was "rendering service to the wrong master."[66]

Closer to Zahn's heart, he called for renewed support for the many young Catholic COs to the war in Vietnam. This could entail parishes providing sanctuary for those who had been denied conscientious objector status, clergy and laity speaking to local draft boards on behalf of Catholics COs, and individuals persuading the parents of these young Catholics that such a stance should not be a source of shame but rather one of pride in having a son who was willing to risk so much to follow his conscience.[67] If such efforts of encouragement were to occur, "even at the sacrifice of some of the philosophical and theological niceties to which we Catholics are so addicted," Zahn suggested that there

63 Zahn, Foreword, 17.

64 While bishops from around the world had called for their governments to support the rights of conscientious objectors, Zahn noted that US bishops refused to speak out against the religious discrimination of Catholics found in the US laws prohibiting selective conscientious objection. And like his critique of military experts during Vatican II, Zahn asserted that the conscription system enabled draft board personnel to essentially function as theological experts, with "the power to decide upon the 'correctness' of any individual's religious beliefs and applications of those beliefs" (Zahn, Foreword, 18–20).

65 The "Boston Five" were a group of five antiwar activists who, in the fall of 1967, organized a ceremony at the Arlington Street Church, Boston, where draft-age men turned in their draft cards and pledged to refuse induction and go to prison. The five activists were subsequently arrested and their trial made national news.

66 Zahn, Foreword, 21.

67 Zahn, Foreword, 22.

would be hope that some future volume on war would one day reveal that US Catholics had discovered the full implications of the Christian message of "love for all men as brothers and the promise of peace to follow."[68]

Zahn's highlighting of the Boston Five and the emergence of what would soon become known as the Catholic "ultraresistance" was prescient. In October 1967, a group of Catholics including Philip Berrigan broke into a draft office in Baltimore and destroyed files. They quickly became known as the "Baltimore Four." While his concern over these kinds of actions would soon emerge, initially Zahn was supportive and he testified at a pretrial hearing on behalf of the group.[69]

In the wake of this, in an article that appeared in *Ave Maria*, Zahn pointed to the fact that some of the ideas on war and conscientious objection promoted by early "pioneers" and "experimenters" had also seemed like "fanatic ideas" at the time, but they had since become part of the Church's teaching.[70] For instance, he suggested that the "altogether new" approach to war and conscientious objection called for in *Pacem in Terris* and *Gaudium et Spes* could be found in outline in the writings of Stratmann, Reinhold, and Metzger. Zahn even compared Metzger and the tensions he had with his bishop in Germany during World War II to Daniel Berrigan and his run-ins with his Jesuit superiors. For Zahn, "idea men" like Berrigan were pointing the way ahead for the church just as Metzger had earlier done.

These kinds of generational comparisons would become increasingly important for Zahn, especially as many of the younger members within the Catholic peace movement became increasingly critical of previous generations. While looking to justify the Vietnam-era activists by highlighting their similarities to World War II-era activists, perhaps more importantly for Zahn, this also served to remind the younger generation of those who came before them—including Zahn.

68 Zahn, Foreword, 23.

69 In a letter thanking him for his testimony, the four activists told Zahn that his writing had provided them with "truth and encouragement." See Baltimore Four to Zahn in letter dated March 29, 1968, UNDA Zahn papers (5/06054).

70 Gordon Zahn, "A Man Ahead of His Times," *Ave Maria*, May 1968, 11–15.

ACTIVIST ACADEMICS

On May 17, just after this article appeared in print, Daniel Berrigan joined his brother Phillip and seven other Catholics in a raid of the draft offices in Catonsville, Maryland.[71] As he prepared his presidential address to the 1968 annual meeting of the American Catholic Sociological Society in Boston that summer, such new forms of Catholic activism were on Zahn's mind.[72] So too was the entry for "Sociology" that had been included in the 1967 *New Catholic Encyclopedia* by Raymond Potvin, a priest and member of the sociology department at CUA. Potvin wrote that for some years Catholics had disagreed as to "the nature and scope" of sociology, with "pioneers" like William Kerby approaching the study of social problems through the lens of social reform, while others rejected such an approach. But this was no longer the case, Potvin assured readers, for the "transition from meliorism and social ethics to a more strictly defined empirical sociology" was complete.[73] Indeed, by 1967, Potvin was able to confidently declare that the entire debate surrounding Catholic sociology had ended—he dismissed it as being "mainly of historical interest"—and that the majority of Catholic sociologists were now pursuing the same kind of value-free "empirical sociology" as everyone else.

It was within this context that Zahn addressed his fellow Catholic sociologists under the meeting's theme of "Religion and Milieu." He opened by stating that any religion that desired to be "relevant" needed to hold up its values so that they could be lived by its members in such a way as to bring about "the conversion and reformation" of the social order. And Zahn suggested that it was within the particular competence of Catholic sociologists to assist religious communities in both identifying the extent to which their particular society and culture had separated from their faith's "ideal social order" and then to help develop approaches to address this marginalization of the church from the established social order.[74] In short, Zahn declared that Catholic sociologists

71 Shawn Peters, *The Catonsville Nine: A Story of Faith and Resistance in the Vietnam Era* (Oxford University Press, 2012).

72 Zahn would serve as a member of a group called the "Catonsville Nine Defense Committee" along with Day, Furfey, and Abraham Heschel.

73 Raymond Potvin, "Sociology," *New Catholic Encyclopedia*, vol. 13 (McGraw-Hill, 1967), 401.

74 As if to highlight all this marginalization, Zahn's address was published in the American Catholic Sociological Society's recently re-named journal *Sociological Analysis*. See Gordon Zahn, "Religion, Sociology and the Milieu: Formula for Activism?" *Sociological Analysis* 29, no. 3 (1968): 117.

needed to encourage the kind of activism that was necessary for the church to remain relevant and, in so doing, become activists themselves. While their training as sociologists provided them with "special competences" for such activism, Zahn explained that it was as Catholics that they shared in the task of "actualizing and promoting renewal and prophetic witness."

While such a call to activism would certainly not "destroy or weaken" their commitment to professional standards, since it would only do for the church what secular sociologists had already been doing for organization and agencies "of the secular milieu," Zahn recognized that it would certainly call up the "old and, for this Society especially, all too familiar controversy" over Catholic sociology. He argued that it was time to reassess the idea, "so prevalent among us," that there needed to exist "an unbridgeable gap" between sociologists' professional activities and their values—religious or otherwise. Indeed, he suggested that, as with the church, if sociology was to remain relevant, sociologists needed to take a "critical view of the milieu" and recognize the prophetic mission of their discipline.

Again echoing earlier critiques, Zahn pointed out that it should be a concern to the sociologists gathered that many of their students (often the most gifted) had concluded that faculty like them had not only failed to "challenge the milieu and its idols" but also had largely "capitulated" to the demands of the *status quo* and placed themselves and their work at its disposal. While sociologists had made poverty, racism, and many other injustices much more visible, Zahn declared that "the cherished myths of the 'value-free' science" had prevented them from probing further into such issues or translating their findings into more specific recommendations for "corrective social action."[75] For Zahn, the problem was that sociologists were too "hung up" on drawing a sharp line between their activism on the one hand and their professional identity and responsibilities on the other. Instead, he suggested that their activism would be enhanced and even made more effective by the very fact that they engaged in it as sociologists. Likewise, their work as sociologists would be enhanced and made more significant by their involvement in social activism.

If sociologists were to be defensive about anything, Zahn concluded, it should be regarding their failure to provide leadership where it was needed.

75 In the context of the moment, Zahn reminded his audience that Camilo Torres—killed fighting with the National Liberation Army against the Colombian military in 1966—was both a Catholic priest and sociology professor (Zahn, "Religion, Sociology," 119).

Catholic sociologists, in particular, he asserted, could not afford the luxury of maintaining an "Olympian 'professional' detachment" while society rotted. Zahn explained that he hoped to spark a "reassessment" of the discipline that would encourage sociologists to resist becoming what C. Wright Mills called "celebrators" of the American milieu.[76] Rather, they needed to become "sufficiently detached (or detachable)" from the established social order so as to become "guides and molders of a new and better milieu."

CONCLUSION

All of this highlights a telling moment in Zahn's career. As he noted, Catholic thinking on war and conscientious objection had shifted, and his positions were becoming more accepted within the Church. The strength and consistency of his arguments reflected this confidence. In many ways, as well, his move to Boston, the publication of his essays in *War, Conscience and Dissent*, and his presidency of ACSS all marked high points.

But the ground was shifting under Zahn and the Catholic peace movement, something he seemed to clearly sense. The draft board raids in Baltimore and Catonsville were posing serious questions for the Catholic peace movement, particularly for members of Zahn's generation. In response, Zahn called for more activism from his generation, while at the same time defending it from criticism that they were not radical enough. As we will see, this defense would soon become a critique of the younger generation's "ultraresistance."

76 Zahn's suggestions included: giving students academic credit for volunteering in inner city communities, including faculty social activism as criteria for promotion and tenure, and viewing the goal of a college education as the creation of "people who can contribute actively to the achievement of a humane society" (Zahn, "Religion, Sociology," 121).

11

"THE GREAT CATHOLIC UPHEAVAL"

During WWII and Vietnam, I was a very active peace activist. But when peace came, my interest in the peace movement lagged. Well, perhaps it did not really lag, but it was forced into the background of other interests. You, on the other hand, keep active, even during periods of peace. Good for you. Yours in an example worthy of imitation.

—*Paul Hanly Furfey to Gordon Zahn*[1]

Despite his calls for activism, Zahn was becoming wary of these new forms of Catholic ultraresistance.[2] With the tragedy of Roger LaPorte still in mind, Zahn wrote to Dorothy Day in early October 1968 and expressed some of his "misgivings" with burning of draft files—the most recent of which, "The Milwaukee 14," had occurred a week earlier. He guessed that it was because of his misgivings that he had not been asked to join the Milwaukee action. This, even though he was close friends with several in the group, including Jim Forest, whom Zahn knew from the Catholic Peace Fellowship, and Jim Harney, a Boston priest who had written the preface for the Beacon Press edition of *In Solitary Witness*. Zahn made it clear to Day that his concerns had

1 Furfey to Zahn in letter dated July 2, 1976, ACUA Furfey papers.

2 For a history of this current in the US Catholic peace movement, see Charles Meconis, *With Clumsy Grace: The American Catholic Left 1961–1975* (Seabury Press, 1979).

nothing to do with the point of the protests, "I agree 100% with them there," he wrote. Indeed, not only had he testified in support of the "Baltimore 4," but he, along with Day, had also joined the Catonsville Nine Defense Committee.[3]

Zahn explained that his concerns with these protests were primarily tactical. For one, he worried about the effectiveness of these actions as "symbolic communications" and pointed out that while some supporters may have been impressed by the protests, many others—in particular, the sort of Catholics the protesters were trying to convince—had more likely been turned off by what they saw. Even though the actions had brought about a tremendous amount of nationwide publicity, most of it was unfavorable. More troubling to Zahn, though, was the fact the immediate result of these protests was the imprisonment of key members of the peace movement. "We simply cannot afford to have our best leadership taken from us for six or more years, and this is what is happening," he told Day. While there certainly would be a great outpouring of support for the Catonsville Nine at their upcoming trial in Baltimore, Zahn wondered if that would be enough to compensate for the long-term removal of so many deeply committed activists from an already far-too-meager number. He asked Day about making an appeal to Catholic peace activists to look for other ways to make their point that would not carry such costs.[4]

For Zahn, though, the unease went far beyond these particular protests. He confessed to Day that he was undergoing "an honest-to goodness 'crisis of faith'" for the first time in his life. He wrote that these protests had highlighted for him the "awful failure" of the US Catholic leadership on the issue of war and had left him wondering if the church had actually become an impediment to fully living out the Christian vocation. "Up till now I have made the literary point that Jägerstätter 'was the Church' in Nazi Germany, and this would indicate that the Berrigans and their colleagues 'are the Church' in America today," he explained. But Zahn admitted that he now wondered if that was

3 Zahn to Day in letter dated October 1, 1968, UNDA Zahn papers (8/11632). The Catonsville Nine Defense Committee also included Furfey, John L. McKenzie, William Stringfellow, Benjamin Spock, and Abraham Heschel—all of whom had signed a letter (September 18, 1968) in support of the group before their trial in October 1968.

4 In a similar letter to Douglass, Zahn wrote: "I am aware that I have already become one of the more conservative voices in the peace movement and that this [appeal] would merely confirm that fact. But, conservative though I may be, I am still around to talk to groups, write for periodicals, counsel potential CO's, etc.—while those who have much more inspiration to give (25 of them now!) are being removed from our already meagre number." See Zahn to Day in letter dated October 1, 1968, UNDA Zahn papers (8/11632).

just a fabrication on his part, "a way of covering the fact that something just isn't there?"

In her reply, Day told Zahn that she had also never been invited to join any of "the burnings," probably because she, too, had some well-known misgivings with them. But that did not mean that she was opposed to the people involved. And now that they have done these protests, she told Zahn, "we must all stand by and defend them, and point to the possible good (and pray for it) their acts may do."[5] As far as Zahn's crisis of faith in the church and its leaders, Day was similarly sympathetic. In what is certainly one of her more enduring quotes, Day explained that as a convert she "never expected much of the bishops." Historically, she noted that popes, bishops, and abbots had always seemed "blind and power loving and greedy," while it was the saints who kept appearing throughout history to "keep things going." Loving one's enemies, particularly those in "our own household," was difficult, she acknowledged, but Day encouraged Zahn not to give up on the church. "Please, Gordon, struggle on, resist this temptation," she implored, "Be faithful. You don't know how we depend on you, nor how much your leadership means to us."[6]

THE BERRIGANS

Zahn did resist the temptation to leave the church and also continued to raise concerns about the direction the Catholic peace movement seemed to be taking. In an essay published in a 1971 volume dedicated to the Berrigans, Zahn noted that peace activists from his generation were growing increasingly troubled by what seemed to be the willingness of many younger activists to accept violence as a tactic. He described the numerous draft-file raids that followed Catonsville as having marked a "dramatic new turn in radical peace."[7] This was only furthered by the fact that these raids, along with the "festivals" of

5 For Day, these included the mere "shock value" of awakening of the bishops to the knowledge and admission of how far they are entangled in the state and in the economy. See Day to Zahn in letter dated October 29, 1968, in *All the Way to Heaven: the Selected Letters of Dorothy Day*, ed. Robert Ellsberg (Marquette University Press, 2010), 350.

6 Dorothy Day, *All the Way to Heaven*, 351.

7 Gordon Zahn, "The Berrigans: Radical Activism Personified," in *The Berrigans*, ed. William Van Etten Casey, SJ, and Philip Nobile (Praeger Publishers, 1971), 97.

support that surrounded their subsequent trials, were almost exclusively a "Catholic operation."[8]

While the initial excitement they caused was positive (not to mention the fact that his own writings had been cited during their trials), Zahn explained that he still had concerns. Such concerns, though, were not with the Berrigans themselves, who Zahn described as "among my most valued personal friends." In fact, he wrote that he had been shocked and offended by the amount of the criticism that the two priests had received from within the church, particularly from members of the hierarchy who appeared to have "a greater capacity for indignation over the napalming of draft files" than they had over "the napalming of Vietnamese civilians."[9] Zahn explained that the Berrigans had concluded, "in the sanctuary of their conscience," that prison was the only appropriate witness for Catholics who wished to dissociate themselves from an unjust and immoral war, and so they acted, "as, indeed, any Christian who reaches such moral convictions would be obliged to act."[10]

Where he differed with the Berrigans was over the judgment of whether all other forms of protest and opposition to the war had run their course. "If we continue to speak and march and sign petitions," Zahn argued, "this is not to be taken as a *prima facie* confession of moral cowardice"—though, he noted that "in all honesty, we cannot exclude that possibility."[11] Instead, these other forms of action should be read as "an affirmation, possibly overly optimistic," that something can still be accomplished within and through "the system" which the Berrigans appeared to have rejected.[12]

Zahn also repeated his misgivings about the message these raids were communicating. He explained that when he had raised these concerns with some of those involved, they responded that their actions should be judged only as a "personal witness." But if that were the case, Zahn countered that there would be little point in making all the elaborate arrangements for press coverage.[13] Rather, it seemed clear from the very symbols they employed—the

8 Zahn, "The Berrigans," 98.

9 Zahn, "The Berrigans," 99.

10 Zahn, "The Berrigans," 99.

11 Zahn, "The Berrigans," 100.

12 Zahn did concede that time might prove the Berrigans "absolutely correct" in their analysis (Zahn, "The Berrigans," 100).

13 Zahn, "The Berrigans," 101.

pouring of blood and the use of home-made napalm—that their "overriding intent" was to communicate a message as effectively as possible. Understood as a form of communication, then, the raids—while initially successful, with hundreds of supporters rallying at their trials, at the same time turned off tremendous numbers of people, including many within the peace movement and their supporters.[14] As a Milwaukee native with ties to that community, Zahn wrote, "I can testify to the strength of the opposition to the 'Milwaukee Fourteen' raid," even by individuals who had provided him with support and encouragement during his time as a Camp Simon.[15]

For Zahn, the "Berrigan message" that was most clearly communicated to both supporters and critics was one that advocated for a "new mood of radical dissent," which appeared to endorse the notion that a person was free to disregard and disobey any law with which they disagreed, and that this kind of dissent was an invitation to anarchy. Zahn tried to distinguish this from the dissent and disobedience to which he had been calling the church to be a source. He pointed out that the latter was the more "classic" form of civil disobedience, practiced by both Gandhi and Martin Luther King, Jr., which taught that a specific unjust law or authority must be identified as part of any act of disobedience. This principle appeared to have been abandoned by the new ultraresistance in favor of a "highly indiscriminate and individualized" rejection of all authority in the name of some "vaguely defined and romanticized revolutionary ideal."[16]

While the Berrigans themselves had not fallen into this sort of "extravagant rhetoric and self-righteous posturings," the dramatic quality of their raids, together with the sometimes "excessive emotional reactions" they provoked, had contributed to an "anything goes, anytime" mood among their younger admirers in the movement.[17] Zahn was worried that historically, such a style of activism had rarely led to victory for the activists, but rather had simply transformed "covert subtle repression into overt repression" with the

14 Here, too, Zahn acknowledged that if German priests and laity similarly "disrupted" the Nazi offices in charge of rounding up Jews, few would criticize them today for extremism, even if the majority of German Catholics at the time did not understand or were offended by such an action (Zahn, "The Berrigans," 103).

15 Zahn, "The Berrigans," 102.

16 Zahn, "The Berrigans," 103.

17 Zahn, "The Berrigans," 105.

approval, or at least silent acquiescence, of the dominant majority.[18] He feared such a transformation had already begun to take place in the United States.

According to Zahn, this highlighted another shift, this one taking place within what had been the "peace movement" but which was quickly morphing into something closer to an "antiwar movement"—a shift, Zahn suggested, clearly evidenced in the replacement of the dove and olive branch as its symbol to the clenched fist.[19] Albeit understandable given the fact that the war and its casualties continued to mount unabated, Zahn argued that "old-line pacifists" and "peace radicals of yesterday," like himself, were questioning the wisdom of actions and rhetoric that seemed to only intensify a commitment to further violence and division rather than peace and fellowship.[20] And he saw the draft raids as leading to further fragmentation within the Catholic peace movement.

In fact, Zahn suggested that even the Berrigans themselves would soon become regarded as "sometimes radicals," given that their practice of waiting

18 Zahn made a somewhat similar argument in a review of Truman Nelson's *The Right of Revolution* that appeared in the *Boston Globe* (September 7, 1968). He challenged the suggestion that only a violent revolution could end generations of brutal racism that Black people had suffered in the United States. While Zahn made it clear that he certainly supported the rights of Blacks for revolution, his concern was with the contention that such a revolution needed to be violent. Zahn described such insistence on violence as displaying a "genocidal bent" that always took the form of a willingness to destroy life wholesale as the "price" for obtaining some abstract goal or ideal: "One needs only to see the nodding heads of the 'respectables' at a [George] Wallace rally, or remember the spontaneity of the applause when President Johnson hit the 'law and order' button in his State of the Union message, to know where the bodies will lie when the kind of revolution this book celebrates in advance becomes a fact." For Zahn, it was the racism that persisted in the United States—a "situation White America has created and maintained"—that had to be eliminated if such violence was to be avoided.

19 Zahn, "The Berrigans," 106. Zahn pointed out that his generation found it more and more difficult to distinguish the motto of the New Left—"We want peace, and we will use any means to get it!"—from the hawkish call for the total destruction of the enemy (Zahn, "The Berrigans," 107).

20 He pointed to the example of Tony Mullaney, a Benedictine priest and member of the "Milwaukee Fourteen" who had spoken to one of Zahn's classes on the need for every Christian to be a "public speaker" spreading the Christian message and fighting to remove social evil and injustice. Mullaney explained to the students that he had marched and preached and written letters and signed petitions but still felt ignored by the nation's leaders. In order to be a "public speaker," therefore, he decided that he needed to "raise the ante" and join the protest in Milwaukee. While persuasive, Zahn pointed out that Mullaney's argument inevitably led to the question: What if such actions did not at least somewhat deescalate the US war, as in fact they had not? Zahn asked if the next step in raising the ante would be to bomb the draft offices themselves, first with a warning, but then maybe without warning. While he had not heard of any such ideas from anyone associated with the Berrigan-style raids, that did not mean that some in the movement were not open to such ideas. Of course, in 1972, the "Harrisburg 7" (including Philip Berrigan) would be charged with making plans to blow-up tunnels under Washington, DC and kidnap Henry Kissinger. See William O'Rourke, *The Harrisburg 7 and the New Catholic Left* (Thomas Y. Crowell, Co., 1973).

around to be arrested had become increasingly dismissed as "ego-serving, bourgeois tokenism" by the members of the "hit-and-run and be ready to hit-and-run again" crowd.[21] Certainly at play here was the ideological shift that had taken place after the Berrigans and other Catonsville activists decided to "go underground" instead of turning themselves in to authorities.[22] This seemed to be a very real departure from the Catonsville Nine's original intent, which Zahn described as centering on the "principle of Christian non-violent resistance *including* the crucial spiritual dimension of accepting the penalty *because of the continued witness the penalty itself represents*."[23]

CATHOLIC PEACE RADICAL

In light of all this, Zahn wondered about the degree to which these kinds of raids were actually a move toward a more radical position, and if so, what exactly that "radicalism" entailed. For if one measured radicalism by the "dramatic content of an act or the degree of illegality involved," the COs in Camp Simon would not qualify. But if this term, instead, described "a firm conviction based in an informed interpretation of fundamental moral principles" and "a pattern of behavior which expressed that conviction," then a Catholic conscientious objector in a CPS camp during World War II was as much a radical as any Vietnam-era draft-file burner in a federal prison. In short, for Zahn, "radicalism" was rooted in the person's commitment, not just the action, and true radicalism had to involve more than "ego-gratification through exhibitionistic extravagance."[24]

Zahn wrote that "Catholic peace radicalism" must therefore entail a "thoroughgoing commitment to the Gospel of peace and love" along with a "spirit of charity" toward others—especially those Catholics unaware of the pacifist implications of the faith.[25] In the end, it was the cross, not the clenched fist nor olive branch, that was the most radical symbol of all. As we will see, Zahn would champion this sort of "spirit of charity" in Catholic

21 Zahn, "The Berrigans," 109.

22 Daniel Berrigan had reported that their intent was to show the authorities that "they can no longer lock people up on their order, any more than they can induct people into the military service on their order."

23 Zahn, "The Berrigans," 110. Italics are Zahn's.

24 Zahn, "The Berrigans," 111.

25 Zahn, "The Berrigans," 111.

peace radicalism in coming decades. For Zahn, understanding Catholic peace radicalism in this way allowed room for the younger generation's courage and creativity without overlooking or rejecting the witness his older generation—not to mention the even earlier generations of peace radicals that included the likes of Stratmann, Furfey, and Day. "In this sense still, if in no other," Zahn concluded, "it does all go together."

THOMAS MERTON

In contrast to these more recent shifts in the movement, Zahn held up the "peacemongering" of the Trappist monk Thomas Merton, with whom he had collaborated since the early 1960s and who had died at the end of 1968.[26] In an introduction to a volume of Merton's writings on peace that Zahn edited, Zahn explained that while Merton was certainly supportive of Christians protesting, he would not have encouraged the kind of "free improvisation or open-ended resistance" that surrounded the "Berrigan-style" raids.[27] Quoting from Merton's writings, Zahn described the late Trappist's reservations as resting in part on his sense that these sorts of protests were oriented too much toward the "affirmation of the rightness" and the "determination and conviction" of the protesters, but not enough on the injustice of the conscription law itself.[28] Though Merton never directly criticized the Berrigans in writing, Zahn argued that he had left little doubt that he was increasingly troubled by what seemed to be the search for "ever more bizarre forms of civil disobedience" as a means of winning attention.[29]

Recognizing that the style of nonviolence that Merton had advocated required a maturity and discipline (lacking in many of those involved in the draft board raids), Zahn quoted Merton as saying that it was all too easy for protests to give way to the "resentment, immature rebelliousness, beatnik nonconformism" that are viewed as attractive just because they are opposed

26 The two had first come into contact in 1961, when Merton invited Zahn to contribute to *Breakthrough to Peace*, which he was editing.

27 Gordon Zahn, ed., "Original Child Monk: An Appreciation," in *Thomas Merton on Peace* (McCall Publishing, 1971), xiv. A revised edition was published in 1980 as *Thomas Merton: The Nonviolent Alternative*. Zahn later explained that he had been asked by the Merton Legacy to edit Merton's writings on peace and that "it was a contribution I was honored to make given Merton's gift of 'respectability' to the Catholic peace movement" (Zahn, 1994, 50).

28 Zahn, "Original Child Monk," xxx.

29 Zahn, "Original Child Monk," xxx.

to what is "stuffy and inert."[30] While members of the Milwaukee 14—some of whom, such as Forest, had attended Merton's "spiritual roots of protest" retreat in 1964—had suggested that Merton would have been supportive of "the Berrigan innovation," Zahn asserted that the Trappist would have agreed with him that the decision by the Berrigans and others to "go underground" was a clear violation of traditional notions of nonviolence and civil disobedience.[31] This form of nonviolence had also been embraced by Martin Luther King, Jr., and Zahn highlighted the fact that both Merton and King had the same "sensitivity to the underlying unity that made what appeared to be two separate social issues, racial justice and world peace, really one."[32] Merton stressed a form of nonviolence that emphasized truth over effectiveness, and a respect for the law and acceptance of punishment, which, Zahn wrote, distinguished the nonviolent resister from "the mere revolutionary."[33] Zahn pointed to Merton's call for the Catholic peace movement to provide "patient, constructive and pastoral work" rather than "acts of defiance," which only antagonized the average person without enlightening them.[34]

While Merton had repeatedly emphasized the fact that he was not a pacifist, Zahn highlighted places in his writings where Meton had described modern war as being "shot through and through" with evil, falsity, and sin.[35] Indeed, Zahn argued that "hints of inconsistency" could be found in Merton's writings on pacifism and just war that suggested that "his heart really did belong to the former."[36] He pointed to Merton's active sympathy and support for pacifists such as Dorothy Day, as well as to Merton's early sponsorship of Pax and the Catholic Peace Fellowship.[37] All of which led Zahn to feel safe in

30 Zahn, "Original Child Monk," xxx.

31 Zahn, "Original Child Monk," xxxviii, xxxvi.

32 Zahn, "Original Child Monk," xxxi. Recently, some US Catholic activists have made the argument that the issue of war is separate from the issue of racial justice. See Benjamin Peters, "Is the Catholic Worker Racist?" *Church Life Journal* (July 17, 2023), https://churchlifejournal.nd.edu/articles/is-the-catholic-worker-racist/.

33 Quote from Merton in Zahn, "Original Child Monk," xxxvi. Zahn pointed to the example of Nicholas Riddell, a priest and member of the Chicago 15 who also went "underground" before his trial. "In the future," Riddell had stated, "I shall continue my role in the revolution, but from a hidden and secure position."

34 Zahn, "Original Child Monk," xxxiv.

35 Zahn, "Original Child Monk," xvii.

36 Zahn, "Original Child Monk," xviii.

37 Merton and Zahn were both among the original sponsors of the Catholic Peace Fellowship.

concluding that Merton was, in fact, a pacifist, if for no other reason than he had rejected the legitimacy of modern war.[38]

As he had done with Jägerstätter, Zahn seemed here to be trying to expand the Catholic pacifist tradition to include Merton, despite some very real evidence to the contrary. Pacifist or not, however, Zahn clearly recognized that Merton attracted a wider audience for the "peacemongering element." And even though the majority of US Catholics still remained largely unaware of the pacifist implications of Catholicism, Zahn saw the fact that this peacemongering minority in the church had become as large and vocal as it had in recent years as "largely due to Merton and his writings on peace."[39]

"THE GREAT CATHOLIC UPHEAVAL"

That same year, 1971, Zahn wrote a cover story for the *Saturday Review* in which he tried to describe this peacemongering element within the context of "The Great Catholic Upheaval" taking place around the issues of war and peace.[40] With the trial of the Harrisburg 7 in the news, Zahn situated the place of Catholic ultraresistance within a new wave in Catholic thought that provided these activists with much of their inspiration, as well as with a receptive audience.[41] He also looked to again highlight the historical roots of the current moment. In short, Zahn wanted to make it clear to his more secular readers that there was nothing *sui generis* about the Harrisburg 7.

While COs at Camp Simon and tradition-minded figures such as Stratmann revealed that a Catholic peace movement existed before World War II, Zahn explained that the "Good War" had largely stifled this movement. At the same time, however, it also ensured the movement's resurgence by demonstrating "with awesome finality" the moral bankruptcy of the church's just-war teaching.

38 Zahn, "Original Child Monk," xix-xx. Zahn noted that Merton's opposition may have been more to "total, or absolute" pacifism and to the type of peace movement, which he considered "so superficial as to bring its own basic principles into disrepute" (Zahn, "Original Child Monk," xviii).

39 Zahn, "Original Child Monk," xxvii. While he was not the first US Catholic writer to take up the cause of nonviolence, Zahn suggested that Merton was more successful than others in bringing it to the attention of the wider US Catholic audience, "which had it given any thought at all to the subject, would have dismissed it as an exotic but altogether impractical notion to be associated with fakirs on their beds of nails or similar manifestations of Eastern religious mysticism" (Zahn, "Original Child Monk," xxviii).

40 Gordon Zahn, "The Great Catholic Upheaval," *Saturday Review*, September 11, 1971, 24–27, 54–56.

41 See William O'Rourke, *The Harrisburg 7 and the New Catholic Left* (Thomas Y. Crowell Co., 1972).

For Zahn, the inability of adherents of the just-war theory to prevent or even limit such horrors as Auschwitz, Dresden, and Hiroshima was evidence of this bankruptcy. Following the war, several prominent church leaders began to call for a condemnation of modern war, culminating in John XXIII's *Pacem in Terris* in 1963, which Zahn described as having almost singlehandedly reversed "if not the direction at least the emphasis" of official Catholic teaching on war and peace.[42] With this encyclical, an important corner had been turned, as the pope made it possible for Catholic pacifists to gain a hearing within the church—one they had long been denied.[43] And the directives on modern war and conscientious objection that emerged from Vatican II, along with the subsequent efforts for peace taken up by Pope Paul VI, had only confirmed and extended Pope John's teachings. Zahn explained that it was out of this history that the actions of the Catholic peace movement—including the "activist imperative" and "ideology of nonviolence" displayed in the "new pacifism" of the Harrisburg 7—must be understood.[44]

Within this context, Zahn encouraged his readers to look beyond Harrisburg and any future actions to what he called "the real conspiracy" taking place within the broader Catholic peace movement—a conspiracy whose spiritual roots of protest had taken hold and would not be easily crushed. And he pointed to Merton's 1964 "the spiritual roots of protest" retreat, which both Berrigans attended, as evidence that the movement always had more commonalities than differences.[45] Despite the continued lack of support from their bishops and an increasing number of activists in prison, Zahn pointed to the strength of the Catholic opposition to the US war in Vietnam as something "almost unique in the history of the modern church." The corner had indeed been turned, and despite setbacks, Zahn declared that this was cause for optimism and hope as "the great Catholic upheaval goes on."[46]

And, in fact, in 1971, it did appear that this upheaval had finally reached the US bishops when they issued a collective statement titled "Resolution on

42 Zahn, "The Great Catholic Upheaval," 26.

43 Zahn, "The Great Catholic Upheaval," 27.

44 Zahn called these activists "peace missionaries," whose rejection of "doing nothing" overshadowed any anxiety as to whether or not their activism was winning over their fellow Catholics (Zahn, "The Great Catholic Upheaval," 54).

45 Though he did admit that the Harrisburg 7 trial might reveal that that was no longer the case (Zahn, "The Great Catholic Upheaval," 56.

46 Zahn, "The Great Catholic Upheaval," 56.

Southeast Asia," in which they (as one commentary put it) finally "caught up with their people" and declared that the US war in Vietnam was unjust.[47] The bishops stated that it was clear that whatever good the United States had hoped to achieve through its continued involvement in the war was "now outweighed by the destruction of human life and moral values it inflicts."[48] While the bishops were still far behind many US Catholics in their attitudes toward the war, this statement was nevertheless significant.[49] For it was, Patricia McNeal pointed out, "the first time in the modern world, not only in America, that during a war a nation's Catholic hierarchy had publicly judged their government's actions unjust."[50] And it was certainly no coincidence that a year later, perhaps in an attempt to take some of the energy out of the antiwar movement, Richard Nixon suspended the draft.

ABORTION

Also in 1971, Zahn weighed-in on the abortion debate that was percolating in the United States with an article in *Commonweal* titled "A Religious Pacifist Looks at Abortion." He opened by acknowledging that as a celibate male he should probably avoid becoming embroiled in controversy with "the women's liberation crowd"—a group with which he was generally in agreement and "more than ready to give it the benefit of the doubt."[51] Nevertheless, he stated that as "a religious pacifist," he found the calls for abortion on demand "thoroughly abhorrent." He wrote that he was greatly disturbed by the willingness of so many activists who shared his political and theological views on most issues to be in support of a practice which "so clearly contradicts" the values upon which those views are based.[52] Zahn pointed out that in the past, he had been critical of Catholic ecclesiastical and theological authorities for their "hypersensitivity" to the evils of killing unborn children while at the same

47 George Gallup, Jr. and Jim Castelli, *The American Catholic People: Their Beliefs, Practices, and Values* (Doubleday, 1987), 79.

48 Quoted in McNeal, *Harder than War*, 168.

49 With the US military increasingly pulling out of Vietnam, McNeal suggested that the bishops had almost missed their opportunity to condemn the war (McNeal, *Harder than War*, 168).

50 McNeal, *Harder than War*, 168.

51 Gordon Zahn, "A Religious Pacifist Looks at Abortion," *Commonweal*, May 28, 1971, reprinted in *The Linacre Quarterly* 38, no. 4 (1971): 247–53.

52 Zahn, "A Religious Pacifist Looks at Abortion," 248.

time almost completely disregarding the evils of "post-natal abortion" in war. This argument worked both ways, though, and he argued here that "those of us who oppose war cannot not be any less concerned about the destruction of human life in the womb."[53]

For Zahn, opposition to war and opposition to abortion converged in the fact that both found their justification in the underlying commitment "to revere human life and its potential and to respect all of the rights associated with it."[54] For Zahn, this was not simply a matter of consistency; it was, in a very real sense, the choice between integrity and hypocrisy:

> No one who publicly mourns the senseless burning of a napalmed child, should be indifferent to the intentional killing of a living fetus in the womb. By the same token, the Catholic, be he bishop or layman, who somehow finds it possible to maintain an Olympian silence in the face of government policies which contemplate the destruction of human life on a massive scale, has no right to issue indignant protests when the same basic disregard for human life is given expression in government policies permitting or encouraging abortion.[55]

While acknowledging that his position here could be described by critics as "irresponsible" or "unrealistic," Zahn pointed out that these had been the standard critiques to his pacifism as well.

Of course, this inherent dignity of life position Zahn was articulating offered a direct challenge to the "proportionalism" that was becoming more and more popular within US Catholic moral theology—a popularity that was greatly encouraged in Richard McCormick, SJ,'s "Notes on Moral Theology" that regularly appeared in *Theological Studies* for almost two decades (1965–1984). From the beginning, Zahn opposed the proportionalist argument and correctly saw it as having made suspect moral absolutes of any kind. He noted that "the fashions in theological and ethical discourse" had moved from "situationalism to relativism and now to something approximating indifferentism."[56] In

53 Zahn, "A Religious Pacifist Looks at Abortion," 248.

54 As to when an unborn child acquired the right to life, Zahn wrote that the only answer "compatible with a pacifist commitment" was that such a right was present from the moment of conception (Zahn, "A Religious Pacifist Looks at Abortion," 252).

55 Zahn, "A Religious Pacifist Looks at Abortion," 253.

56 Zahn, "A Religious Pacifist Looks at Abortion," 253.

contrast, Zahn stated that he sought to "absolutize" the right-to-life "if not for what it is at any given moment (a newly fertilized ovum; a convicted criminal; the habitual sinner) at least for what it may yet, with God's grace, become."[57] These aruments would bring Zahn into key debates that later took place in Catholic moral theology during the 1980s.

FUTURE OF THE CATHOLIC PEACE MOVEMENT

In the aftermath of the Harrisburg 7 trial, as historian William Au noted, the Catholic ultraresistance largely "faded away as an identifiable movement."[58] That said, small pockets of resisters found refuge in groups such as the Community for Creative Nonviolence in Washington, DC, which carried on its spirit within the Catholic peace movement until it reemerged in the Plowshares movement in the 1980s.[59] In 1972, following the lead of their British counterparts, the American PAX Association became Pax Christi-USA (PC-USA), with Zahn and Eileen Egan as cochairs. Edward Guinan, a Paulist priest and founder of the Community for Creative Nonviolence, was made general secretary. Coming in the wake of the divisiveness within the Catholic peace movement brought on by the many raids and trials—particularly the revelations about the secret relationship between Phil Berrigan and Elizabeth McAlister that had been revealed during the Harrisburg trial—the leaders of the PC-USA seemed intent on offering something different to the movement and the church. For instance, Bishop Thomas Gumbleton (auxiliary bishop of Detroit) noted that the birth of Pax Christi-USA came at a time when the broader Catholic peace movement was "deepening its commitment from a predominantly anti-war position to one of positive Christian teaching on peace and non-violence."[60] The longtime Catholic peace activist Charles McCarthy remembered that Zahn was adamant that Pax Christi-USA not exclude non-pacifist Catholics from its

57 Zahn, "A Religious Pacifist Looks at Abortion," 253.

58 Au, *The Cross*, 153.

59 Kristen Tobey, Plowshares: *Protest, Performance, and Religious Identity in the Nuclear Age* (Pennsylvania State University Press, 2016).

60 Gumbleton to Carel Ter Maat in letter dated September 25, 1972, quoted in Gerard Vanderhaar, "Pax Christi USA: the early years 1972–78" (1989): 6. Thanks to Joseph Fahey for sending me a copy of this unpublished document.

membership, including those who advocated for the just-war position.[61] This eventually led McCarthy to resign from the leadership of PC-USA. And in a letter to Guinan, Egan (echoing Zahn's earlier sentiments) put an even finer point on it when she wrote that Pax Christi-USA had "to open many doors, to bring to the peace movement many Catholics hitherto alienated from it." For Egan, that meant "no Berrigans" should be allowed into the group as their "drama" would "drown the PC message and twist the whole message out of control."[62]

The structure and relative moderation of PC-USA reflected the changing landscape of the US Catholic peace movement and church in the immediate post-Vietnam era. Indeed, in the mid-1970s, the US Catholic Church no longer appeared to be the "rabidly nationalist organization" it had been, and the US bishops could even be described as having developed much more "progressive attitudes toward international relations and military intervention."[63] Beginning with their "Resolution on Southeast Asia" in 1971 and many similar statements that followed, historian Penelope Moon characterized the US hierarchy as becoming much more of an "outspoken advocate of peace" and an "equally outspoken critic of American imperialism, the nuclear arms race, and human rights abuses (particularly in Latin America)."[64] This new posture offered an opening for the US Catholic peace movement to closer (or at least less antagonistic) relations with their bishops. As Zahn wrote, "One cannot hope to win substantial support for a position by declaring or showing contempt for an institution respected and supported by one's prospective converts."[65] This meant that Pax Christi-USA could not "even permit itself to be, or even seem to be disrespectful of" Catholic traditions and practices.[66]

It was with all this in mind that Zahn offered an assessment of what he saw as the state of the "Catholic peace-and-resistance movement" at the end of 1973. He argued that as the US involvement in Vietnam was winding down, the movement needed, first and foremost, to "force an objective after-the-fact assessment of the war" based upon to traditional just-war conditions and

61 Interview with Charles McCarthy on October 3, 2024.

62 Egan to Guinan in letter dated September 5, 1973, quoted in Vanderhaar, "Pax Christi USA," 11.

63 Penelope Moon, *"We Have Got to Lead Them in the Ways of Peace": The Catholic Peace Fellowship in the Vietnam Era* (PhD diss., Arizona State University, 2001), 293.

64 Moon, *"We Have Got to Lead Them,"* 294.

65 Gordon Zahn, "Carrying Our Weight in the Catholic Peace Movement," *America*, September 20, 1975, 143–46.

66 Zahn, "Carrying Our Weight," 143–46.

principles, along with a more fundamental assessment of whether the just-war tradition was still valid after the Vietnam war.[67] As Zahn wrote,

> Vietnam and the excesses perpetuated on both sides of the conflict have given us a second chance, a "test case" that virtually cries out for systematic theological analysis and explicit judgement as to the justice of the war and the permissibility of active participation in its prosecution.[68]

And he argued that it should be the function of a viable Catholic peace movement to put these "pacifist hypotheses" to the test.[69]

That said, Zahn noted that there remained questions as to whether a "viable" Catholic peace movement was even possible in the post-Vietnam era. He lamented that after World War II, whatever "movement" there was, represented for the most part by a handful of Catholic COs and their even fewer supporters, fragmented and dissolved until almost nothing remained except the Catholic Worker—something that "must not be allowed to repeat itself," Zahn declared.[70] In comparison to that earlier moment in the Catholic peace movement, the early 1970s had a far greater number of members with deeper (or at least more daring) levels of commitment, as well as some very real victories to point to—particularly, the hierarchy's endorsement of conscientious objection and selective conscientious objection as legitimate moral options for Catholics.

A "RECOGNIZABLY CATHOLIC" PEACE MOVEMENT

But Zahn also saw some very real weaknesses in the current movement compared to that in the previous generations. For one, many current activists tended to be involved in various causes beyond "peace issues," perhaps too many and at too many levels. While Day, Furfey, and the *Catholic C.O.*

67 Gordon Zahn, "The Future of the Catholic Peace Movement" *Commonweal*, December 28, 1973, 337–42. Zahn did note that much still needed to be done before the US war in Vietnam could really be seen as over, including offering amnesty for draft exiles and prisoners of conscience.

68 Zahn, "The Future of the Catholic Peace Movement," 338.

69 Zahn, "The Future of the Catholic Peace Movement," 338.

70 Zahn, "The Future of the Catholic Peace Movement," 338.

certainly addressed the issues of racism and labor, Zahn pointed out that peace was always given priority.[71] More provocatively, though, Zahn asserted that the Catholic peace movement also needed to always be "recognizably Catholic." And he suggested that any Catholic identity would require that the "movement and its members, at the very least, must present themselves as loyal and committed members of the institutional Church performing an important, though sadly neglected, part of her mission."[72] He lamented that many members, even leaders, in the current movement seemed to "play down or ignore—in some cases consciously divest themselves of—a Catholic identity and behavioral limitations it might impose upon them."[73] If nothing else, as a tactical consideration, "a clearly and explicitly Catholic peace movement" was the only kind that could hope to reach its "primary target audience": the great majority of Catholics, lay and clergy, "not yet alert to the pacifist implications of their religious tradition."

For Zahn, who of course had never shied away from criticism of church hierarchy, this insistence on Catholic identity within the movement meant acknowledging and respecting the "authority structure of the Church" no matter how critical one was of the failures of that structure, or how determined one was to work toward changes in it.[74] It also meant "putting the peace mission of the Church above one's personal interest and convenience." This was particularly true, he wrote, of Catholics who assumed or accepted positions of leadership in the movement. On Zahn's mind, no doubt, were figures such as Philip Berrigan, Elizabeth McAlister, Jim Forest, and James Douglass—prominent leaders in the movement who were living in canonically "irregular" marital situations at the time.[75]

71 Such peace issues included an "end to war, elimination of the draft, disarmament, effective international organizations (involving, as most saw it, an end to divisive state sovereignty) and the promotion of non-violence as the alternative to war" (Zahn, "The Future of the Catholic Peace Movement," 340).

72 Zahn, "The Future of the Catholic Peace Movement," 340.

73 Zahn, "The Future of the Catholic Peace Movement," 340.

74 Zahn, "The Future of the Catholic Peace Movement," 340.

75 In a letter to Charles Meconis, Zahn wrote about the relationship between Berrigan and McAlister, which had been very publicly revealed during the Harrisburg 7 trial: "I know that I was shocked and disappointed, viewing the whole affair as something which could bring the whole Catholic peace movement (of which the 'actors' formed only a part) into discredit. As individuals I felt for them and would never have 'shunned' association with them, but as two people who had put themselves into the position of 'recognized spokespeople,' I felt they had betrayed us all to some extent" (Quoted in Meconis, *With Clumsy Grace*, 93).

Zahn again tried to place all this within the context of a generational divide. He explained that his generation of activists, for instance, was bound to "the 'Caesar's wife syndrome" that required them to govern their personal lives, and their religious behavior in particular, in such a way as to avoid bringing discredit upon the movement—"We failed often enough, of course, but we recognized those failures as failures."[76] He acknowledged that World War II-era activists certainly were also frustrated with the unresponsiveness of the hierarchy, dull liturgies, bad sermons, but these were not seen as reason enough to "drop out and shop around" until something more congenial was found.[77] Instead, they considered the church important enough to work within its "institutional structure" and rules.

This was in stark contrast to the current generation of the Catholic peace movement. For Zahn, the problem was that their idea of spiritually "doing one's own thing" frequently translated into a kind of "elitism," with "liberated" Catholics all too ready to disregard the fact that they were "giving scandal" to the majority of Catholics who they considered as theologically lagging behind.[78] If the Catholic peace movement was to get anywhere, Zahn wrote, it must recognize that the broader Catholic community was "the target audience" it must reach and win over. Rather than suggesting any kind of a "purge" of the movement, Zahn argued that he was simply asking that individuals in positions of prominence recognize that their position may require "special obligations of self-discipline."[79] He also asserted that it was essential that a specifically Catholic peace movement exist, if only because the church remained an international body of considerable moral influence. US Catholics could play a significant role in moving the church toward embracing pacifism, but they needed to be made aware of their "opportunity and obligation" to do so. This, Zahn declared, was the primary task of the US Catholic peace movement in the post-Vietnam era.

Needless to say, Zahn's assessment generated a vocal reaction from within the movement. In one letter to the editor of *Commonweal*, for instance, Mike

76 "We saw to it that we met our Mass obligations, observed the fasts, either lived celibate lives or entered into and kept faithful to sacramental marriages" (Zahn, "The Future of the Catholic Peace Movement," 341).

77 Zahn, "The Future of the Catholic Peace Movement," 341

78 Zahn, "The Future of the Catholic Peace Movement," 341.

79 Zahn, "The Future of the Catholic Peace Movement," 341.

True, a Catholic Worker and peace activist in Worcester, argued that his old comrade Gordon Zahn appeared to want it both ways: both to build a viable Catholic peace movement and to set up guidelines as to who qualified as a legitimate "Catholic" peace activist.[80] He acknowledged that Dorothy Day was "another person who wouldn't agree with a word I've said," and that even some of the "younger" members in the movement, such as Tom Cornell, also supported the notion that activists present themselves as "loyal and committed members of the institutional Church."[81]

For True, the problem centered around being loyal to a church that was "frequently and blatantly sexist, monarchial, and capitalist in policy." Instead of such loyalty, he suggested that the Catholic peace movement needed to be more "catholic" than the church and thereby become more sensitive to an even larger constituency than Zahn recognized. True also questioned Zahn's use of the post-World War II era as an historical basis for what the Catholic peace movement needed after Vietnam. He wrote that the situation in the church and society had changed so much since the end of World War II ("in part because of the successes of the last decade") that looking to the past was of "little value as a guide to the future."[82] True concluded that unless "Bishop Zahn" instituted some kind of "excommunication of undesirable elements," he would have to accept a wider range of possibilities with regard the movement's membership and leadership.[83]

In reply to True, his friend and fellow Catholic pacifist, Zahn conceded that he was indeed "traditionalist enough" to actually believe that the structured ("institutionalized") Catholic Church was "the vehicle of salvation" it claimed to be.[84] While the church certainly had failings, many of which he had spent his career highlighting, Zahn explained that any corrections must come principally from Catholics who had enough love and respect for the church to abide by "onerous rules and practices" even as they worked for change. He pointed out that many of the changes that had already taken place within the church, including the very hesitant search for "an entirely new attitude" toward war, would never have occurred if loyal Catholics such

80 Mike True, "Letters to the Editor," *Commonweal*, March 8, 1974, 14.

81 True, "Letters to the Editor," 15.

82 True, "Letters to the Editor," 15.

83 True, "Letters to the Editor," 15.

84 Gordon Zahn, "Letters to the Editor," *Commonweal*, March 8, 1974, 15.

as H. A. Reinhold, Paul Hanly Furfey, John LaFarge, Thomas Merton, and Dorothy Day had cut themselves loose from "the institutional Church" and "its oppressive and confining authoritarianism," and instead chose to make their own rules and live according to their own private standards of "'proper' Catholic behavior."

If the designation "Catholic peace movement" was to be at all meaningful, Zahn argued that it needed to distinguish itself from the more generalized "Christian peace movement" and even more so from the broader "peace movement." For Zahn, this would require

> a profound identification with a particular spiritual and sociological entity, its history, and its values; the acceptance of a personal obligation to perfect its witness so that it may become a suitable vehicle for the truth it claims to possess (in our special case, to make it an effective vehicle for the pacifist message contained in the Gospel teachings); and to recognize a direct and prior obligation to "convert" that target audience I mentioned, our fellow Catholic Christians who are not yet ready to accept our interpretation of what "the Church" should be and should be doing.[85]

All that he hoped, Zahn wrote, was to encourage his fellow Catholic peace activists that such considerations deserved more weight than True and others seemed willing to allow.

This largely internal debate within the movement came to a head when Edward Guinan invited the long-time Catholic peace activist James Douglass to speak at the Pax Christi-USA assembly in 1974. Though Douglass had worked with Zahn and Egan lobbying bishops during Vatican II, after hearing about the invitation, Egan raised concerns over the fact that it had recently become known that Douglass had divorced and then remarried outside the Catholic Church.[86] Egan was not the only one holding such a line. In a letter to Douglass, Dorothy Day wrote that as much as she admired both him and Forest (who also remarried outside the church), "I really can't consider either of you 'Catholic.' You see I'm really 'rigid,' [with] my old Communist, radical background."[87] Added to this, there was also concern, shared by Zahn as well,

85 Zahn, "Letters to the Editor," 15.

86 Egan to Guinan in letter dated September 18, 1974, UNDA Zahn papers (6/08591).

87 Day to Douglass in letter dated September 23, 1974, in *All the Way to Heaven*, 414.

that Douglass would very likely be arrested by the FBI at the assembly for his antiwar activities. "This would in a sense have locked the fledgling Pax Christi movement into what Douglass had done," Zahn later recalled, "the activist opposition to the war which we felt was more active than we thought Pax Christi would be ready for."[88]

While initially (and reluctantly) agreeing to disinvite Douglass, Guinan—who was still an active member in the Community for Creative Nonviolence—soon wrote Egan and Zahn to say that he had reconsidered the entire affair and threatened to resign if Douglass's invitation was rescinded. "The problem," he wrote, "is not with Jim Douglass, but with reactionary attitudes within Pax Christi."[89] In reply, Zahn wrote that while he would be sad to see Guinan leave, "I simply do not feel you can expect to mold the organization to a more activist stance than it is prepared to accept."[90] Not too long after, Guinan resigned as general secretary.

In the controversy that soon erupted, Jim Forest and Daniel Berrigan also threatened to disassociate themselves from PC-USA.[91] Both also signed "An Open Letter to Pax Christi" that declared that the organization "dishonors its Lord and itself" by refusing to welcome a "heroic Christian and light of the Church." In the end, the 1974 assembly was cancelled, and Pax Christi leaders announced the beginning of a "period of reflection and decision-making" regarding the direction of the group.[92] More than anything, all of this highlights the fact that the tensions within the US Catholic peace movement, which Zahn had been identifying for years, were still very real.

88 Quoted in Vanderhaar, "Pax Christi USA," 17.

89 Guinan to Egan and Zahn in letter dated August 7, 1974, quoted in Vanderhaar, "Pax Christi USA," 18.

90 Zahn to Guinan in letter dated August 10, 1974, UNDA Zahn papers (6/08590).

91 In a letter to his brother Daniel, Phillip Berrigan wrote, "As for the Pax Christi thing—going would be a concession to Dorothy and Guinan—the remaining luminaries are hacks for my money. Though ole Gordon Zahn has made a difference with his scholarship." See letter undated, in *The Berrigan Letters*, ed. Daniel Cosacchi and Eric Martin (Orbis Books, 2016), 106.

92 It is worth noting that a news story about the 1975 Pax Christi-USA annual meeting the following year opened with the headline, "Nothing Radical about Peace Movement, Conferees Agree." See *National Catholic News Service* (November 26, 1975).

ABSOLUTE REVERENCE FOR LIFE

In January 1973, the US Supreme Court issued its decision in *Roe v Wade*. The following year, in the midst the controversy surrounding Douglass and Pax Christi, Zahn helped draft the Catholic Peace Fellowship's (CPF) "Statement on Abortion."[93] The statement insisted that abortion was not a "Catholic issue," nor was the CPF trying to impose its own morality on others any more than it had always encouraged others in their "conscientious resistance" to the war or the draft. Indeed, the statement explained that CPF's opposition to abortion reflected its pacifist values rooted a "reverence for life" and the consequent obligation to oppose any policy or practice that gives "one human being the right to determine whether or not another shall be permitted to live." Anticipating what would later come to be known as the "seamless garment" ethic of life, the statement called upon US bishops to continue their fight against abortion, while at the same time remembering "the inter-relatedness of the life issues"—war, capital punishment, abortion, euthanasia, and economic exploitation—and work to establish a social order in which "all may find it easier to be fully human." Penelope Moon noted that this statement went a long way in bringing about the eventual split between the CPF and the Fellowship of Reconciliation.[94]

Abortion was not the only issue with which Zahn's "absolutized" defense of human life placed him in conflict with others in the peace movement. In 1977, with talk of "revolutionary violence" in the air, Zahn wrote an article concerning the use of violence by the various national liberation movements that had sprung up throughout Africa, Asia, and Latin America.[95] He found very troubling the recent embrace of these movements, and a "theology of liberation" that was often associated with them, by many in the Catholic peace movement. This was particularly true regarding the acceptance of violence and

93 Tom Cornell told Dorothy Day that Zahn was the "chief architect" of the statement in a letter dated May 20, 1974, quoted in Moon, *We Have*, 291.

94 Moon, *We Have*, 291.

95 Zahn did recognize that since the end of the US war in Vietnam, many in the peace movement had left, and donations to the more traditional peace organizations were drying up, and so he admitted that he was hesitant to cause any disunity in such a "time of weakness." Gordon Zahn, "The Bondage of Liberation: A Pacifist Reflection," *Worldview* (March 1977), 20–24.

nationalism within these movements, both of which Zahn argued conflicted with the "basic, core values of pacifism."[96]

As Zahn saw it, "liberation theology"—or at least as it was "popularly interpreted and applied"—had restored respectability to a just-war theory that had largely been discredited following the excesses of World War II and Vietnam. Worse still, by essentially reducing the traditional just-war criteria—*just cause* and *right intention* ("both generously interpreted")—it had opened up the way for virtually uncritical support by Catholics not only for wars of national liberation but also for a full range of guerrilla tactics including "indiscriminate acts of terrorism."[97] And as a result, Zahn argued that violence promoted by these "popular interpretations of liberation theology" went beyond any war limits and had taken on something closer to a total war perspective.

Although proponents of these conflicts argued that the cause and intention was to restore the dignity of dehumanized peoples, Zahn questioned whether such goals should be, or even could be, achieved through violence. He pointed out that the efforts of these "would-be liberators" often ended up bringing only further oppression in response—to say nothing of the fact that the liberators' own "guerilla actions" often violently forced the compliance of those they sought to liberate. In short, Zahn wrote, "the cause of justice is as likely to be betrayed as served by the violence employed."[98]

"Revolutionary conscientization" should certainly be raised, Zahn contended, but the objective must be the conscientization of both victim and oppressor alike, so that both would come to recognize and respect the humanity of the other. What made such recognition difficult, though, was the nationalism that presented a distinct threat to any just and enduring peace. What was most urgently needed, Zahn explained, was less nationalism, not more. Indeed, even beyond war, Zahn asserted that nationalism was a divisive impediment to addressing major threats to human survival—pollution, famine, disease, economic inequality, and the threat posed by multinational corporations. "It should be eminently clear to anyone committed to the cause of world peace," he declared, "that a further fractioning of the globe and its inhabitants is an invitation to disaster."[99]

96 Zahn, "The Bondage of Liberation," 20.

97 Zahn, "The Bondage of Liberation," 21.

98 Zahn, "The Bondage of Liberation," 22.

99 Zahn, "The Bondage of Liberation," 23.

While such a global vision could be dismissed as "impractical" or "too idealistic," Zahn once again reminded his readers that the peace movement had long been marginalized with such terms. He pointed to the fact that the supposedly more "realistic" crusade to liberate Europe from fascist domination in World War II ended with half of Europe under communist rule and with the liberators essentially "converted to Hitler's infamous doctrine of total war."[100] In light of this recent history, Zahn suggested that nonviolence would serve the cause of liberation much better than any use of "pragmatic violence."[101] In a clear statement of Zahn's radicalism, he wrote that if "revolution be the objective, it might as well be the total revolution that could really change the world by rejecting *both* the vehicle of oppression, the all-powerful national state, and its ultimate claim to power, violence."[102]

ANOTHER PART OF THE WAR

In 1976, Zahn was asked to give the annual Paul Hanly Furfey Lecture at Catholic University, an occasion that gave him an opportunity to look at both the state of the discipline of sociology and the place of his own work within it. Zahn opened by declaring that Furfey had been ahead of his time in his critique of "value-free" sociology. During his days at CUA, Zahn explained that such opposition often marginalized the department and even "lessened the attractiveness of the CU degree as far as non-Catholic academic circles were concerned."[103] That situation had changed, however, and he noted that a "newer breed" of sociologists had emerged who had come to recognize value-free sociology as a myth which had put the discipline in a "theoretical and methodological strait-jacket." Suddenly, Zahn observed, it seemed that "the virtually sacrosanct distinction between the 'sociologist as scientist' and

100 Zahn, "The Bondage of Liberation," 24.

101 Zahn, "The Bondage of Liberation," 24.

102 Zahn, "The Bondage of Liberation," 24. Joe Holland from the Center for Concern was asked to reply to Zahn's article in *Fellowship*, a journal of the Fellowship of Reconciliation. Holland did not hold back. He opened by stating that Zahn represented a "paranoid reaction" to the creative theological searching coming from Latin America and revealed a "neo-conservative beach head" within the US pacifist community. He dismissed Zahn's pacifism as being outside the "mainstream"—like voluntary poverty or celibacy, "an important, but minority strand in the Christian tradition"—and argued that if nonviolent resistance were to establish a significant pacifist base within the "new Latin American theology of praxis," it would take the form of "an exploratory socialist-pacifism," not Zahn's "reactionary pacifism" (UNDA Zahn papers (3/04535)).

103 Zahn, "Furfey Lecture," ACUA Furfey papers.

the sociologist as responsible participant in his society" had lost its appeal. And if this "new breed" wanted a model of the possibility and urgency of "wedding sociological scholarship to committed social action," Zahn suggested that they look to Furfey.

Zahn further noted that at a moment when the idea of "Marxist sociology" or "black sociology" or "feminist sociology" had become accepted, perhaps there ought to be a place for a Christian or even "Catholic sociology." Recognizing that a retrieval of such an idea might not be plausible, Zahn argued that it was certainly appropriate to encourage individual Catholic sociologists to address themselves to the "great issues" of the day and to do so in the "special context of the moral and spiritual values to which they presumably are committed." Here Zahn explained that he had dedicated his scholarship to the great issue of war. With this broader focus of resisting war, he then discussed his current research on Camp Simon—a topic which his own values as a Catholic pacifist had enabled him to "recognize and explore dimensions and implications" that other researchers with different values tended to "overlook or ignore."

The fruit of this research eventually became *Another Part of the War: The Camp Simon Story*, which was published three years later in 1979—a book Zahn described as his "somewhat tongue-in-cheek, semi-autobiographical" account of Camp Simon.[104] While there was certainly little danger that the Second World War would fade into the mists of history anytime soon, Zahn wrote that he hoped that his book would help address "another part of that war" often overlooked or ignored—the Civilian Public Service.[105] One of the results of this lacuna, he argued, was that when it was remembered at all, the CPS program had often been held up as evidence of "democracy's tolerance and respect for the rights of individual conscience," while at the same time the COs in the camps had largely been dismissed as "an unpatriotic, self-centered, perhaps even cowardly dissident minority."[106] For Zahn, however, the CPS program was far from an example of state's tolerance of dissenting views or protection of religious freedom. Rather, it was "an experiment in the democratic *suppression* of a dissident religious minority in time of war," very much

104 Gordon Zahn, *Another Part of the War: The Camp Simon Story* (University of Massachusetts Press, 1979).

105 Zahn, *Another Part of the War*, v.

106 Zahn, *Another Part of the War*, vi.

"punitive in practice and intent."[107] He even went so far as to describe the CPS sites as "concentration camps"—at least in intention, if not in fact.[108] Zahn wrote that in the view of the US military, COs were a danger to "the war-supporting consensus." No matter how liberal the regulations or how relaxed the discipline, Zahn argued that the first priority of the CPS was to corral "these potentially troublesome conscientious objectors into isolated work camps, safely out of sight and mind."[109] Clarifying this history was particularly necessary at the moment, Zahn explained, as the CPS was being considered again as a viable model for any future handling of the problem of conscientious objectors if the draft (still dormant in 1979) was ever reignited.[110]

With this in mind, Zahn suggested that the real significance of Camp Simon was the fact that it had existed at all. For all the many theological and ideological differences among the COs, they all seemed to recognize that they were a part of something more than simply an individual witness against the war. Not only did the camp open each CO's eyes to the fact that he was not the only Catholic conscientious objector to World War II, but perhaps even more fundamentally, it provided "irrefutable evidence" that a Catholic *could*, in fact, be a conscientious objector.[111] In this sense, Zahn argued that the very existence of the camp presented a Catholic "corporate witness" against war—a witness both "*for* the Church" and more importantly "*to* the Church."[112] Indeed, Zahn declared that Camp Simon was "the first corporate witness against war and military service in the history of American Catholicism."[113]

107 Zahn, *Another Part of the War*, vi.

108 Zahn, *Another Part of the War*, 81.

109 Zahn, *Another Part of the War*, 81.

110 He also noted that the Ford administration, in considering an amnesty for exiles from Vietnam-era draft, was looking at reestablishing alternative service camps as part of any such deal (Zahn, *Another Part of the War*, vi).

111 Zahn, *Another Part of the War*, 23–24.

112 Zahn, *Another Part of the War*, 23. Indeed, he stated that even the non-Catholic COs at Camp Simon accepted the Catholic identification of the camp and agreed it was important to keep a Catholic camp in existence as "a corporate witness" against war (Zahn, *Another Part of the War*, x).

113 While there had been four recorded US Catholic COs to World War I, Zahn suggested that they could not be viewed as a "true precedent" of such a witness since they each represented a "separate and individual objection" and did not appear to give any indication of wanting to "witness to" the church. Given that fact, he explained it is little wonder that the Catholic COs at Camp Simon were "neither understood nor well received by their fellow communicants" (Zahn, *Another Part of the War*, 247–48). And even after Camp Simon closed in 1942, Zahn argued that Catholic COs continued to preserve that "Catholic witness'" at other CPS units such as the Rosewood site (Zahn, 1994, 28).

Though the lack of support from the church led Catholic COs to feel very much "orphaned by that spiritual mother in whose name they had taken their unpopular stand," Zahn wrote that he and his fellow COs had no doubts about to the Catholicity of their witness:

> This confidence extended further than the ability to defend the legitimacy of their refusal to serve with appropriate theological arguments. Most of them regarded their stand as the correct stand to be taken, a binding moral obligation for them and presumably, for other Catholics as well . . . they would present conscientious objection as the logical and behavioral consequence of the faith they and their detractors alike professed.[114]

And because they viewed their objection as being rooted in the "most authentic expression of the true meaning of Christianity," their marginalization within the church only bolstered their determination to establish and maintain this kind of corporate witness for and to the church.[115]

Furthermore, as "flawed and feeble" as it may have been, Zahn asserted that Camp Simon represented at the time the "only organized peace witness of its kind in the entire Catholic world." Of course, Catholics such as Franz Jägerstätter had also opposed the war, but Zahn saw no indication that such opposition had been anything more than "purely personal acts of individual resistance."[116] And while other displays of pacifism had certainly appeared throughout the long history of the Catholic Church, they tended either to be "shunted aside as the work of a heretical sect," or else incorporated into the "ecclesiastical framework" of individual callings or religious orders.[117] For Zahn, then, Camp Simon presented something unique and an "altogether new phenomenon" in the long history of the church. And perhaps still smarting a bit from Dorothy Day's less than enthusiastic support for the camp, he pointed

114 Zahn, *Another Part of the War*, ix, xi.

115 Zahn, *Another Part of the War*, 23.

116 Zahn, *Another Part of the War*, 248.

117 Zahn noted that this did not mean that the principles on which the act of conscientious objection was based were new or unknown in the church. He highlighted the various Catholic peace movements that emerged in Europe between the two world wars, along with the Catholic Worker, which he described as the only comparable force in US Catholicism.

to the “nice irony” that credit for establishing a Catholic corporate witness against war belonged to this group of much maligned “collaborationists.”[118]

Though the importance of their corporate witness had not been recognized in their day, Zahn saw Catholic COs at Camp Simon as having had a “delayed impact” on the church far in excess of even what they themselves could have reasonably hoped. Indeed, Zahn pointed to the “dramatic changes” that had taken place since the Second World War in the Catholic thinking regarding war and conscientious objection,[119] suggesting that the positions taken by the COs four decades earlier had since been made “eminently respectable” by the Second Vatican Council.[120] Likewise, the interpretations of scripture that rejected even the theoretical possibility of a just war, which Zahn and other COs had used, were now “taken seriously and accepted by highly respected members of the theological community.”[121]

Zahn repeated his earlier claim that these changes had occurred because the very nature of modern war and the modern nation-state had revealed the inadequacy of church teaching. It was this inadequacy that necessitated the bishops at Vatican II to call for an evaluation of war with “an entirely new attitude.”[122] Zahn wrote that the COs at Camp Simon had anticipated all this and should therefore be recognized as having offered a prophetic witness for the church, preparing the way for its “more unambiguous commitment to peace and nonviolence.”[123]

And it was here that Zahn again highlighted what he saw as the continuity between his generation and the next. For if nothing else, thanks to the COs in World War II, it was no longer possible to deny that a Catholic could legitimately claim a conscientious objector classification. The “simple fact

118 Zahn suggested that most historical accounts of the “Catholic peace witness” in World War II misrepresented the Camp Simon experience since their primary source of information on the camp was *The Catholic Worker*'s “overly idealized account,” which presented the image of the COs as “moral heroes eager to bear the hardships and inconveniences of camp life in a perfect spirit of Christian resignation and self-sacrifice.” As Zahn explained, such was “only rarely the case” (Zahn, *Another Part of the War*, 48.

119 Zahn, *Another Part of the War*, 249.

120 Zahn, *Another Part of the War*, 256.

121 Zahn, *Another Part of the War*, 249. For examples, see the two works by John L. McKenzie, SJ:, *The Two-Edged Sword* (Bruce Publishing Co., 1956) and *The Power and the Wisdom* (Bruce Publishing Co., 1965).

122 *Gaudium et Spes*, no. 80.

123 Zahn, *Another Part of the War*, 251.

that there had been a Stoddard, a Warner, and an ACCO," Zahn wrote, "was indisputable proof that they could."[124] He also pointed out that more than a few of those Catholics who opposed the Vietnam war had initially recognized the incompatibility between war and Christian teaching after learning about the World War II-era COs—not to mention that at least a few of those earlier COs (like himself) had participated in protests against the war in Vietnam.

Zahn hoped that recognition of this generational continuity would prevent the kind of "elitism" that still threatened to undermine the effectiveness of what should have been a united Catholic peace movement. Such elitism often downgraded conscientious objection to the status of a "cop-out," Zahn wrote, and dismissed more "restrained forms of dissent against the war" such as petitions, peaceful picketing, and counseling COs as almost equivalent to "open collaboration with the Pentagon"—something that was tolerated, but not enough to earn full admission into the "more activist community of the 'saved.'"[125]

In contrast to the war in Vietnam, which had always been unpopular enough in the United States to at least provide a "cushion of tolerance, if not acceptance" for anyone who opposed it, Zahn highlighted the fact that World War II had always been (and continued to be) a highly popular war. The longer the war and higher its costs, the more complete and intense the national consensus grew in support of it. Under such circumstances, a decision to stand apart and oppose the war required "as much soul-searching and deliberation (perhaps as much courage too)" as was needed to "invade draft board offices and burn their files."[126] Just as the Vietnam-era resisters did not see their witness as any less authentic because they could count on a community to applaud and encourage them, so too, the World War II COs should not feel guilty that their activism was not "radical" enough. Both generations saw it as necessary to refuse to support what each considered to be an unjust war. For both, it came down to "choosing the only thing to be done."[127]

Zahn concluded that the "small and short-lived experiment in the New Hampshire woods" should be viewed as a "forerunner of that 'great Catholic

124 Zahn, *Another Part of the War*, 252.

125 Zahn, *Another Part of the War*, 254.

126 Zahn, *Another Part of the War*, 254.

127 Zahn, *Another Part of the War*, 254.

peace conspiracy' of the Vietnam years."[128] Merely by being there, the Catholic COs of the 1940s helped prepare the way for the Catholic opposition to war that later developed. "It ought to count for something," he hoped, "that, in the face of insistent demands and an almost total consensus in support of that war, there were men who refused to accept or share those justifications."[129] If they accomplished nothing else, Zahn wrote, they at least would prevent any consensus on war and the corruption of the mind that followed from becoming universal.

CONCLUSION

A lot was certainly happening within the Catholic peace movement in the 1970s. As the ideas of pacifism and conscientious objection were becoming more and more accepted within the church, questions about the Catholic identity of the movement and its commitment to nonviolence and an absolute defense of life were also emerging. From his place as an intellectual leader Zahn worked hard to shore up the necessary support for the movement to remain both clearly Catholic and committed to the protection of all human life. Such insistence would continue to put Zahn in conflict with others within the church and the movement.

As the Catholic ultraresistance dissipated for a time by the mid-1970s, Zahn sought to reassert the radicalism of his generation. In doing so, he revealed his own radical critique of US political and military institutions—indeed of the modern nation-state itself. And he made this critique while he was also calling for members of the peace movement to remain loyal Catholics and embrace an "absolutized" reverence for life. In this sense, Gordon Zahn was a true *Catholic* radical.

128 Zahn, *Another Part of the War*, xi.

129 Zahn, *Another Part of the War*, 257.

12

DEAN OF THE CATHOLIC PEACE MOVEMENT

It is strange how radicals gain acceptance as they get older. I remember when Dorothy Day was anathema. It was not respectable to have anything to do with her. Now she is a heroine. Yet neither you nor Dorothy have become less radical. It is not that you or she have mellowed with age. It is just that people think twice. "Now perhaps, after all, Gordon isn't as crazy as I used to think."

—Paul Hanly Furfey to Gordon Zahn[1]

In response to the Soviet invasion of Afghanistan, Jimmy Carter ordered a resumption of draft registration in 1980. Not long after, Zahn became involved with a group of local activists in Boston, including John Leary and Charles McCarthy, who were looking into the idea of starting a counseling center for Catholic COs.[2] Zahn, who had been informally counseling COs since his time at Loyola, brought not only his counseling experience to the effort but also a link

1 Paul Hanly Furfey in letter to Zahn dated March 6, 1976, ACUA Furfey papers.

2 Zahn, 1994, 51. Leary was a Harvard graduate who had joined the Catholic Worker movement. His tragic death in 1982 at the age of twenty-four deeply saddened many in the Catholic peace movement. Zahn wrote a memorial, "John Leary: a different sort of hero," which was published in Gordon Zahn, *Vocation of Peace* (Fortkamp Publishing, 1992).

with Pax Christi-USA and the broader Catholic peace movement. As a result, the Pax Christi Center on Conscience and War was soon established in Boston as an "independent affiliate" to PC-USA in 1981.[3] The center's finances were secured by a $25,000 annual donation from a wealthy Boston book publisher named Robert Bentley, who had read Zahn's book on Camp Simon and was shocked at how little support Catholic COs received during World War II.[4] He hoped the center would address the needs of contemporary COs. Zahn was named president, McCarthy treasurer, and Leary secretary.

After Robert Nee, a priest hired as the director and the only paid staff member, departed to return to parish work, Zahn took on the role of director. While this pleased Bentley, McCarthy and many of the volunteer staff resigned. As Zahn remembered it, this was the result of tension between McCarthy's "style of pacifism" and his own—tension that mirrored the earlier ones between Zahn and the ultraresistance. Many who resigned believed that Zahn's commitment to nonviolence, in contrast to McCarthy's, was "at best half-hearted." In his hand-written resignation letter, Zahn remembered that McCarthy had warned that any effort at peace which was not committed to nonviolence as "the iron law of the Gospel" was doomed to be a wasted effort.[5]

In defense of his pacifist commitment, which Zahn pointed out long predated McCarthy's, Zahn later wrote that "the differences between us are differences in approach to winning the uncommitted over to the 'cause'": McCarthy was seen as "more 'hard-line' in presentation" whereas Zahn (and Pax Christi) "recognize and respect—much as we disagree!—those who are willing to accept the traditional Catholic 'just war' teachings."[6] While acknowledging their longstanding disagreement over openness to advocates of the just-war theory, McCarthy recalled that it was Bentley who had asked him to resign.[7] Despite such criticism, Zahn still had many fans within the Catholic peace movement. Michael Hovey, a CO and former Maryknoll brother who had joined the staff of the center around this time, continued to work closely

3 The center split from PC-USA in 1987 and become the Center on Conscience and War.

4 Zahn to Furfey in letter dated June 14, 1982, ACUA Furfey papers.

5 Zahn, 1994, 53. A longtime peace activist, McCarthy had a law degree from Boston College at the time and was ordained a priest of the Byzantine-Melkite Eastern Catholic Churches on August 9, 1981. He went onto start the Center for Christian Nonviolence, https://www.emmanuelcharlesmccarthy.org/.

6 Zahn, 1994, 54.

7 Interview with Charles McCarthy on October 3, 2024.

with Zahn counseling COs at the center and giving workshops on pacifism and conscientious objection around the country.[8]

THE SECTARIAN CHARGE RETURNS

Around this same time, in recognition of his long career as an activist academic, Thomas Shannon (on whose dissertation committee Zahn had served) put together a *festschrift* of sorts dedicated Zahn titled *War or Peace?: the Search for New Answers*.[9] Shannon opened the volume proclaiming that Gordon Zahn was "almost totally responsible for the new status and respect that pacifism enjoys within American Catholicism."[10] Equally laudatory, Tom Cornell noted in his essay that in its current "era of renewal," the church had begun to take steps toward becoming the "church of Christ's peace" largely due to the fact that Zahn had helped resist "the schismatic impulse that afflicts perfectionists" and had kept the Catholic peace movement rooted in "tradition and the Christian humanist rationalism" that had been "a saving characteristic of Catholicism since the scholastics."[11]

Along similar lines, Bishop Thomas Gumbleton wrote that of the many individuals who had challenged US military escalations, none had done so with more "perseverance, careful analysis, and dedication" than Zahn, whose research challenged the belief that there was some sort of "a divine sanction on all our military preparations." Gumbleton also highlighted Zahn's assertion that at the heart of the moral problem of war was the terrifying increase of the "inhumanity potential" in the modern world. This inhumanity was clearly displayed at both Auschwitz and Hiroshima, not so much in the fact that such holocausts had occurred but that "the human mind was able to develop justification for them."[12]

In his contribution to the volume, David O'Brien pointed out that as US Catholics had become more and more troubled by the horrors of Vietnam and nuclear weapons, they found themselves drawn to the work of "lonely

8 Hovey remembered that McCarthy had insisted on an "iron-law" that COs who came to the center seeking help had to declare that they were absolute pacifists, thereby excluding selective conscientious objectors. Interview with Michael Hovey on June 6, 2022.

9 Thomas Shannon, ed., *War or Peace? the Search for New Answers* (Orbis Books, 1980), v.

10 Shannon, *War or Peace?* v.

11 Thomas Cornell, "The Catholic Church and Witness Against War," in Shannon, *War or Peace?* 212.

12 Thomas Gumbleton, "The Role of the Peacemaker," in Shannon, *War or Peace?* 223.

pacifists" such as Zahn and Dorothy Day. And he noted that for many young Catholics, Zahn's books provided "important landmarks" for coming to terms with their conscientious objections to war.[13] Pointing to many of the same divisions within the US Catholic peace movement already noted, O'Brien described the Catholic ultraresistance as appearing radical on the surface, and yet their willingness to justify the use of force meant that they were in fact much "closer to the liberals and to the bishops."[14] In contrast, O'Brien argued that it was Zahn, Day, and others in the "pacifist wing of the resistance" who were actually much more radical, at least from a religious perspective, for they embodied a "new and profound revelation" of the Gospel's demand for peace as both the means and the end of Catholic social action.

But while O'Brien applauded his long-time friend for having offered an approach that was clearly consistent with Gospel nonviolence, at the same time he also contended that Zahn and other Catholic pacifists threatened to "withdraw" the church from involvement in very real issues of life and death, and in so doing would turn the church in the direction of "sectarian isolation" from history.[15] Echoing Paul Ramsey's "sectarian" charge from decades earlier, O'Brien argued that an "implicit sectarianism" could clearly be found in the writings of Zahn.[16] And while a condemnation of the use of (if not possession of) nuclear weapons had come from the Vatican in recent years, O'Brien reminded readers that no pope, council, nor "responsible" theologian had concurred with Zahn's conclusion that the church needed to become a peace church. Instead, they were repelled by the "sectarian implications" of Zahn's position that O'Brien argued would draw the church away from its traditional reliance upon reason and understanding of Catholic universality.[17]

A similar charge of sectarianism was also leveled by J. Bryan Hehir in his essay, which he began by situating Zahn within contemporary Catholic theology. Hehir pointed out that since the papacy of Pope John XXIII, Catholic teaching on war had been in "a state of movement." And in what would soon become the *de facto* church teaching on war, Hehir asserted that both John and

13 David O'Brien, "American Catholic Opposition to the Vietnam War: A Preliminary Assessment," in Shannon, *War or Peace?* 137.

14 O'Brien, "American Catholic Opposition," 139.

15 O'Brien, "American Catholic Opposition," 140.

16 O'Brien, "American Catholic Opposition," 140.

17 O'Brien, "American Catholic Opposition," 143.

his successor Paul VI had established pacifism as "a new position," thereby giving Catholics two responses to war: the just-war ethic and "Christian pacifism."[18] On this point, Hehir was relying on a notion of "theological pluralism" within Catholicism that was being promoted by Charles Curran and others.[19] Such a pluralism, Hehir wrote, "needs to be acknowledged and legitimized in both personal and social ethics."[20]

In contrast, Hehir argued that implicit in pacifist theology was the conviction that human life had an "absolute value" and an "intrinsic worth," which meant that nothing could justify the taking of it. And he pointed to Zahn's application of such absolutism to the issues of abortion, capital punishment, and euthanasia as examples.[21] In this way, Hehir argued that Zahn and other Catholic pacifists sought to eliminate any exceptions that could be used to legitimize the taking of human life and thus impede theological pluralism—a pluralism that Hehir contended had enabled pacifism to be recognized in the first place.

Hehir then contrasted this with the moral theology held by a growing number of so-called "revisionist" theologians such as Richard McCormick, SJ. Hehir explained that McCormick and other revisionists had rejected the notion of an "intrinsic evil" that would determine the morality of an action apart from its circumstances and consequences. Hehir clearly supported this position and suggested that it sought to move Catholic moral theology more decisively "in the direction of a sophisticated teleological approach."[22] However, this sort of allowance for "doing evil to achieve good," he argued, was in direct contrast to the "style of the pacifist" that was designed "to foreclose the possibilities of exception to the rule of not taking human life."[23] For Hehir, all of this could be

18 J. Bryan Hehir, "The Just-War Ethic and Catholic Theology: Dynamics of Change and Continuity," in Shannon, *War or Peace?* 22.

19 Charles Curran, "Ten Years Later: Reflections on *Humanae Vitae*," *Commonweal*, July 7, 1978, 425–30.

20 Hehir noted that there were "two adversaries" of such pluralism: those who deny the legitimacy of the personal realm and those who "expect the community to be of one mind on social questions." He saw Zahn as falling into the second camp (Hehir, "The Just-War Ethic," 34–35).

21 Hehir, "The Just-War Ethic," 30. Hehir quoted Zahn's "A Religious Pacifist Looks at Abortion."

22 Hehir, "The Just-War Ethic," 31.

23 Hehir quoted Zahn: "All the old calculations aimed at determining 'proportionality,' weighing 'good' effects against 'bad,' making possible the choice of the 'lesser' evil are rendered meaningless by the simple refusal to accept any degree of evil as an appropriate Christian objective." Hehir guessed that the revisionist arguments would only intensify Zahn's critique (Hehir, "The Just-War Ethic," 32).

seen as part of the larger debate going on in moral theology between Catholics such as Zahn, who saw an imperative to "draw distinct lines with little or no qualification on issues of human life," and those like McCormick, who saw life issues as "precisely the kind of 'conflict-case'" that required a "rethinking of key concepts" in Catholic moral theology.[24]

Furthermore, Hehir suggested that Zahn's pacifism also placed him outside of mainstream Catholic ecclesiology. For instance, he wrote that the just-war ethic was theologically and historically tied to a conception of the church—"prominently present in papal social encyclicals"—that assumed a "positive responsibility" (i.e., Weber's "ethics of responsibility") to participate in the process of "building a more just and peaceful human society."[25] In this way, the just-war ethic presupposed an ecclesiological "model of presence" solidly in line with John Courtney Murray's "incarnational humanism." Hehir wrote that this ecclesiology of presence was based on "premises about the relationship of nature and grace, faith and reason, and the proper form and purpose of Christian social ethics."[26] Along very similar lines, in his critique of Furfey written around this same time, Charles Curran explained that Catholic theology traditionally recognized some continuity between grace and nature.[27] "The old maxim" Curran wrote, "maintained that grace does not destroy nature but builds on nature"—though curiously, Curran never points to where this "old maxim" comes from in Catholic theology.[28]

In contrast, Hehir explained that pacifism had historically been related to an ecclesiology that fell into Troeltsch's category of "sect": a "counter-cultural posture" that viewed "the ethics of discipleship" (Weber's "ethic of ultimate ends") and "the obligations of citizenship" as being in tension, if not in opposition.[29] All of this clearly echoed Murray's account of "eschatological humanism."[30]

24 This was the debate which John Paul II looked to address with his 1993 encyclical *Veritatis Splendor*.

25 Hehir, "The Just-War Ethic," 33.

26 Hehir, "The Just-War Ethic," 33.

27 Charles Curran, *American Catholic Social Ethics* (University of Notre Dame Press, 1982).

28 Curran, *American Catholic Social Ethics*, 158. For a discussion of how the unattributed phrase "grace builds on nature" is problematically employed by US Catholic moral theologians, see Benjamin Peters, "Apocalyptic Sectarianism: the Theology at Work in the Critiques of Catholic Radicals," *Horizons* 39 no. 2 (Fall 2012): 208–29.

29 Curran echoed this when he argued, "the Catholic understanding of continuity between nature and grace argues against the radical incompatibility between the present society and the kingdom of God" (Curran, *American Catholic Social Ethics*, 159).

According to Hehir, Zahn's vision of building "a pacifist constituency solidly within the institutional Church" was a call to combine a pacifist ethic with a church-type ecclesiology, which Hehir argued was at least logically, if not theologically, questionable.[30] And while Hehir conceded that pacifism could be compatible with Catholicism, he was nevertheless skeptical that the church should ever fully embrace such a stance.

Hehir concluded that Zahn's vision of the church would not be the "optimal ecclesiological or ethical road for Catholicism to take."[31] It certainly was not open to any sense of theological pluralism. That said, he did acknowledge that the fact that Catholic theology was even engaged in these kinds of debates was in no small part thanks to Zahn, who would undoubtedly continue to be "one of the preeminent voices in the continuing conversation."

As already noted, in making these arguments, Hehir can be read as blurring the "church-sect" categories of Ernst Troeltsch with John Courtney Murray's incarnational-eschatological paradigm. In other words, Murray's "incarnational humanism" (with its more optimistic view of the state) became associated with Troeltsch's notion of a "church," while "eschatological humanism" (and its more critical view) was associated with a "sect." The upshot here—and why all this is important for our discussion—is that Catholics such as Zahn who were critical of US war-making were read by critics through a novel combination of Murray's theological paradigm and Troeltsch's language. This enabled critics to label Zahn and other Catholic pacifists as "sectarian" and thereby largely marginalize (and even silence) them within discussions of Catholic engagement in US society and culture, particularly when it came to war.[32]

THE NIEBUHR DILEMMA

Zahn responded to all this in an afterword to the volume. He began by again noting that very real progress had certainly been made on the issues of war and peace. If nothing else, he noted that there was a willingness in the last

30 Hehir, "The Just-War Ethic," 35.

31 Hehir wrote that it was questionable whether "a sociologically sectarian church could tolerate the kind of pluralism in social ethics advocated by Curran" (Hehir, "The Just-War Ethic," 35).

32 For more on the history of this kind of marginalization, see Benjamin Peters, "'Voices to be Silenced or Ignored': World War II and the Flattening of American Catholicism," in *Weaving the American Catholic Tapestry: Essays in Honors of William L. Portier*, ed. Derek Hatch and Timothy Gabrielli (Pickwick Publications, 2017), 145–62.

two decades to recognize pacifism as a legitimate Catholic option, on par with the just-war ethic. Much was still left to be done, however. For while there certainly had been a shift in the Catholic hierarchy's attitudes and statements on war and conscientious objection, that shift seemed to have had little effect on ordinary Catholics. Zahn pointed to the reality that a US bishop was still more likely to "grace the podium of some 'patriotic function' than support a community-wide peace activity or disarmament rally."[33]

Acknowledging all this, Zahn then turned to his critics and leveled a clear rebuke of their more Weberian tendencies. He asserted that the workings of grace articulated in the Beatitudes and the Sermon on the Mount produced an "otherworldly perspective" from which the practice of statecraft became, at best, "a secondary consideration."[34] From this perspective, the most urgent task of any "Catholic statecraft" would be to oppose the kinds of policies that forced Catholics into situations in which the only way to protect their spiritual and political freedoms was to sin.[35] Instead of spending so much time worrying about "statecraft," Zahn urged church leaders to spend more time working to restore the prominence of the US Catholics' religious identity over their national identity. Rather than leading to some sort of sectarianism or "narrow evangelical fundamentalism," Zahn contended that this would instead produce truly "in-spirited" men and women "governed by a dedication to love and nonviolence even at the cost of humiliation and martyrdom"—the kind of people who could "convert the world" as Christians once did.[36]

Zahn reiterated some of his earlier arguments that the just-war theory was, at best, seen as irrelevant by those in the military and, at worst, used as a means for justifying "what was once 'unthinkable' to become not only 'thinkable' but 'do-able' as well."[37] Zahn further argued that the most telling indictment of the just-war ethic was its "dismal failure" to fulfill even its stated purpose. Indeed, if Catholics were ordered to perform a clearly unjust military

33 Zahn, Afterword, in Shannon, *War or Peace?* 235.

34 Zahn, Afterword, 241.

35 As Zahn lamented, "One cannot but wonder what the effect would be were the American bishops to mount and fund a campaign for nuclear disarmament on a scale comparable to their nationwide campaign against abortion" (Zahn, Afterword, 236).

36 Zahn, Afterword, 244.

37 Zahn pointed to Murray's assertion that "since nuclear war may be a necessity, it must be made a possibility" and called it a "scandalous statement" that stood as a judgement against "the just-war ethic and the claims made for it" (Zahn, Afterword, 239–40). See also Murray, "Remarks," 58.

mission—"Dresden? Hiroshima? My Lai? Doomsday?"—Zahn guessed that most would simply obey. Zahn then made it clear that he opposed the kind of theological pluralism advanced by Hehir and Curran[38] and contended that the church could not hold "two essentially contrary interpretations of Christian belief and mission" when it came to the question of war. For Zahn, the choice was clear: "either it is always wrong to wage war *or* under certain conditions it can be permitted, or even obligatory, to do so."[39]

The embrace of theological pluralism regarding war highlighted the fact, Zahn wrote, that Catholic discussions on just war and pacifism were being conducted "almost entirely within the frame of reference defined by Reinhold Niebuhr and his followers."[40] This "Niebuhr Dilemma," Zahn explained, was based upon the Lutheran theologian's famous "moral man-immoral society" distinction, which implied that human behavior was divided between two separate planes of activity: a "private" sphere subject to moral regulations and a "public" sphere much less regulated.[41] As Zahn read it, this was an arbitrary division that created a kind of "moral schizophrenia" that disassociated (personal) moral responsibility from acts performed in the public sphere—giving such acts priority over those done in the private sphere.[42] While differences certainly existed between "public" and "private" roles, Zahn argued that different moral standards did not.[43]

Zahn did admit that Hehir was correct in observing that his continued absolutized defense of life left Zahn often swimming against the current in the US Catholic theology at the time—which was already becoming polarized along partisan political ideologies. In fact, in a 1981 article, Zahn acknowledged as much when he wrote that as both "a professed pacifist and a dedicated

38 Distancing himself further from Hehir's "revisionists," Zahn argued that it was a "delusion" to think that a military planner would employ the "principle of double-effect" in determining strategy in war and proceed only if the "proportionality" was favorable to the good effect (Zahn, Afterword, 235).

39 Zahn, Afterword, 239.

40 Zahn, Afterword, 242.

41 Reinhold Niebuhr, *Moral Man and Immoral Society: A Study in Ethics and Politics* (Charles Scribner's Sons, 1932).

42 Zahn, Afterword, 243–44. "Those magistrates faced with the choice of surrendering 'national identity' or commanding an act that has been defined as 'an offense against God and man himself," Zahn asserted, "would feel fully justified, even obligated, by their public position to choose the later." (Zahn, Afterword, 244).

43 Zahn, Afterword, 244.

opponent of abortion," he often found himself isolated "on the fringes" of both the peace and prolife movements, even though by every rule of logic his position should attract the same supporters.[44] He suggested that a greater emphasis on a "reverence for life," rather than on the perceived conflict of rights between mother and child, would go a long way to resist proposals for the "socially therapeutic elimination" of human beings—whether through war, euthanasia, genocide, capital punishment, or abortion.[45] Zahn pointed to the German writer Christian Geissler's observation that the twin horrors of Auschwitz and Hiroshima provided striking evidence of the human capacity to accept the "necessity" of mass liquidation of other humans in order to gain some utilitarian objective. The ability to even formulate justifications for such actions, Geissler observed, required a "corruption" of the mind.[46] For Zahn, such corruption was also clearly present in contemporary justifications for nuclear war and abortion.

THE CHALLENGE OF PEACE

Hehir's "pluralistic" suggestion that Catholics had two options for addressing war—just war or pacifism—moved into church teaching with the US Bishops' 1983 peace pastoral, *The Challenge of Peace,* for which Hehir served as the principal author. The immediate lead-up to the pastoral was President Jimmy Carter summoning religious leaders to the White House to seek support for the SALT-II arms control treaty he had just negotiated with the Soviets in the summer of 1979. That September, Cardinal John Krol testified before the Senate during hearings on the ratification of the treaty.[47] The Cardinal Archbishop of Philadelphia explained that the church could accept the possession of nuclear weapons by the United States only for a limited time while the work of disarmament progressed. On Christmas Eve, Soviet tanks began rolling into Afghanistan, throwing these delicate arms control negotiations off balance.

44 Gordon Zahn, "Abortion and the Corruption of the Mind," in *New Perspectives on Human Abortion*, ed. Thomas Hilgers, Dennis Horan, and David Hall (University Press of America, 1981), 332.

45 Zahn, "Abortion and the Corruption of the Mind," 333.

46 Christian Geissler, "Auschwitz, Hiroshima, and the Hopes of Mankind," cited in Gordon Zahn, "The Private Conscience and Legitimate Authority," *New Blackfriars* (January 1966), republished in Zahn, *War, Conscience, and Dissent*, 131.

47 Robert King, "Rhetoric of Morality, Rhetoric of Manipulation: The Catholic Bishops, Peace, and the Reagan Administration," *Cross Currents* 34, no. 4 (1984–85): 456–72.

Carter quickly reinstated the draft and escalated the US military budget. This was in response not only to the Soviet invasion but also to the increasingly bellicose rhetoric of Ronald Reagan, who was campaigning as the Republican nominee for president in the 1980 elections. All of this seemed to call Krol's bluff and demand the church reconsider its position on modern war.

Within this context, calls for a peace pastoral emerged at the bishops' annual meeting in November 1980, when Francis Murphy (an auxiliary bishop from Baltimore) raised the point that the bishops needed for clarify church teaching on war. Murphy was a so-called "Pax Christi bishop" who had been influenced by the stories of both Jägerstätter and George Zabelka.[48] In response to Murphy, a committee of bishops was formed with Bishop Joseph Bernardin (then of Cincinnati) as chair. J. Bryan Hehir, the Director of the Office of International Affairs of the USCCB, and Ed Doherty, a former Foreign Service Officer who had been a staff member of the USCCB, were hired as full-time staff. Bruce M. Russett, a professor of political science at Yale, served as a consultant.[49]

After Bernardin made it clear that the any call for unilateral disarmament was off the table, the committee drafted a letter in July 1981 and sent it out to the bishops for feedback.[50] Seven months later, in February 1982, Russert sent out an outline of a second draft that incorporated that feedback. Gumbleton sent a copy to Zahn, who wrote back that he had sadly read nothing in the draft that could not quickly be "written off" by more hawkish figures such as John O'Connor (the Vicar General of the Military Ordinariate at the time) in much the same way as O'Connor had in his recent book, *In Defense of Life*.[51] Zahn warned that if the pastoral became too abstract or ambiguous, someone like O'Connor would have a field day justifying almost any military action on the

48 Jim Castelli, *The Bishops and the Bomb: Waging Peace in a Nuclear Age* (Image Books, 1983), 14. During World War II, Zabelka had been the Catholic chaplain on the Enola Gay, the plane that dropped the atomic bomb on Hiroshima. Decades later, he met Charles McCarthy and become a dedicated peace activist.

49 The committee also included bishops John O'Connor, Thomas Gumbleton, Daniel Reilly, and George Fulcher. Richard Warner, CSC, and Juliana Casey, IHM (as the heads of the Conference of Major Superiors of Men and the Conference of Major Superiors of Women, respectively) served as nonvoting members.

50 Castelli, *The Bishops and the Bomb*, 79. After the second draft had been released (and Bernardin had been elevated to cardinal), Bernardin and others on the committee traveled to Rome to meet with Vatican officials and bishops from various NATO countries in Europe. At the meeting, Bernardin met privately with John Paul II, who expressed concern that the church not be seen as pacifist and the pastoral not call for unilateral disarmament (Castelli, 130–34).

51 John O'Connor, *In Defense of Life* (Pauline Books, 1981).

grounds that the bishops had a chance to speak out against such actions but did not.[52] To avoid that, Zahn suggested the bishops needed to be clear that their pastoral letter would indicate "a new emphasis" in their thinking and concerns over modern war, rather than any kind of final word on the subject. He argued that the pastoral letter should focus on the moral responsibility of individual Catholics. This would help Catholics recognize that orders from secular authorities may not be unquestionably obeyed, and that they, in fact, did not have the "right" to unquestioningly obey such authorities.

Zahn also told Gumbleton that the bishops must clearly condemn not only any use of nuclear weapons but also the very possession and active preparation for the use of such weapons. The bishops needed to declare that Catholics in the armed forces should "neither seek nor accept" service that was at all related to the preparation to use any weapons of the type condemned by Vatican II, and that, likewise, they were "bound in conscience" to refuse to issue or obey orders to use such weapons. Pointing to Krol's Senate testimony, Zahn recommended that the pastoral add a provision for an annual assessment on the progress being made toward disarmament. A church concerned about "the rights of the unborn," he concluded, should extend that concern to "the rights of whole future generations as well."

THEOLOGICAL PLURALISM ON WAR

That May, as the committee was still putting together its second draft, David O'Brien wrote "An Open Letter to the Bishops" in *Commonweal*. He began by laying out what he saw as the dilemma facing the bishops. If they chose the path of "prophetic witness" and supported the pacifist position, O'Brien argued that the bishops would lose the respect and allegiance of "millions" of Catholics who would disagree with such a position—not all of whom would be "simply selfish or super-patriotic."[53] Likewise, if the bishops supported a more "moderate" stance, "allowing for deterrence and prayerfully awaiting negotiated disarmament," they would lose some of their "most dedicated" and "hard-working" followers. To avoid what he saw as "another *Humanae vitae*,"

52 Zahn guessed that O'Connor would probably also claim "that the failure of the American bishops to use this opportunity to take a stronger anti-war and anti-nuclear position" was further validation of the correctness of his arguments.

53 David O'Brien, "An Open Letter to the Bishops," *Commonweal*, May 12, 1982, 295.

O'Brien suggested that the bishops "refuse to choose as a matter of principle." Like Jesus in the Gospels, they should refuse to either "withdraw or surrender to the world" but instead embrace a "theological pluralism" on the issue of war. Catholics, O'Brien observed, had had their fill of "ecclesiological consensus after Vatican I." Again striking a very Weberian tone, O'Brien then went onto assert that if the bishops wanted to continue to look both "towards the church and toward the public"—to be a church that "included both Phil Berrigan and Alexander Haig"—they needed to be grateful for both the pacifists who reminded the church of the fairly clear demands of Jesus *and* for the "realists" who reminded the church of the fairly harsh "real world."[54] While the continued growth of a strong peace movement "oriented in a pacifist direction" would certainly strengthen the church, O'Brien was clear that the bishops "should avoid the temptation" to adopt such a uniform position.[55]

In response to his fellow peace activist and friend, Zahn sent off a letter to the editor (never published) stating that the church can and should have room for both Berrigan and Haig.[56] That did not mean, however, that its teachings must be "pluralist" enough to permit such contrasting interpretations to stand as equally acceptable answers to the moral crisis of modern war, especially when it came to nuclear war. Zahn again made it clear that he opposed the notion that the church could somehow equally hold both just-war and pacifist ethics. While it was not for the bishops to settle the debate by "proclaiming anathemas or brandishing articles of excommunication," he argued that they did need to "clarify the moral debate" and provide guidance. "If 'violence is not in accord with the Gospels and cannot be Christian,'" Zahn argued (quoting O'Brien), this meant that Catholics must find "other ways to defend the things which are to be defended." He wrote that as long as church leaders continued to find exceptions to what should be "forthright condemnations of these weapons of ultimate violence," they will continue to fail in the church's sacred mission. Zahn concluded by stating that scholars, such as himself and O'Brien, who had long been critical of the failure of German bishops to speak prophetically "in the days of the original Auschwitz," ought to be equally insistent that US bishops do better with respect to "the hundreds or

54 O'Brien, "An Open Letter to the Bishops," 298.

55 O'Brien, "An Open Letter to the Bishops," 300.

56 See Zahn to Editors, letter dated May 19, 1982, UNDA Zahn papers (6/07890).

thousands of Auschwitzes" that their nation possessed and was apparently prepared to use.[57]

A NEW THEOLOGY OF PEACE

In June 1982, in a speech to the United Nations, Pope John Paul II enunciated an "interim ethic" on nuclear deterrence. "In current conditions," he stated, "'deterrence' based on balance, certainly not as an end in itself but as a step on the way toward a progressive disarmament, may still be judged morally acceptable."[58] The following May, the US bishops issued *The Challenge of Peace*, which solidified the pope's interim ethic along with Hehir's theological pluralism on war, while leaving Krol's demand for a timed disarmament without any real deadlines. In a talk he gave later that year, Zahn placed the pastoral within the context of the "new moment" of urgency regarding nuclear war that Jonathan Schell had highlighted in his recently published and widely discussed book *The Fate of the Earth*.[59] Though by no means perfect, Zahn called the bishops' letter a powerful document that could eventually play a significant role in breaking-up what Schell had referred to as humanity's "alliance with death."[60] While part of a steady stream of episcopal statements and papal pronouncements on war and peace, Zahn regarded *The Challenge of Peace* as being particularly useful if Catholics translated its message into effective policy action. It also dramatically highlighted the shift, he noted, that had occurred from the days of "200-per-cent patriotism" that had marked so much of US Catholic history.[61]

Significant as well, Zahn continued, was the fact that rarely (if ever) had there been a process for writing an ecclesiastical document that had been "so open in its conception and execution."[62] For instance, the membership of the

57 Zahn described O'Brien, a history professor at the College of the Holy Cross, as "the moving spirit of Detroit's Call to Action," the 1976 gathering of US Catholics (laity and clergy) that called on the church to resist militarism and other social ills.

58 "Message of His Holiness Pope John Paul II to the General Assembly of the United Nations," June 7, 1982, https://w2.vatican.va/content/john-paul-ii/en/messages/pont_messages/1982/documents/hf_jp-ii_mes_19820607_disarmo-onu.html.

59 Jonathan Schell, *The Fate of the Earth* (Knopf, 1982).

60 Indeed, 1983 marked a moment when humanity came very close to a nuclear war. See Taylor Downing, *1983: Reagan, Andropov, and a World on the Brink* (Da Capo Press, 2018).

61 Cited here as Zahn, "Talk," UNDA Zahn papers (2/02910), 3.

62 Zahn, "Talk," 5.

drafting committee had been carefully balanced to ensure representation of "the major conflicting points of view," and the committee had solicited a wide range of expert opinion and experience. Zahn pointed out that pacifists such as himself and Tom Cornell were called to testify before the committee, alongside military officials, specialists in arms control, and theologians. Zahn also noted that after the committee had circulated a first draft to the bishops for comment, "a remarkable thing happened"—intentionally or not, the draft was made available to an audience far beyond the bishops, and comments inundated the committee. Two more drafts were subsequently released, and the comments were again so overwhelming that the vote on the pastoral, which had been planned for the November 1982 annual meeting, had to be rescheduled to a special May meeting the following year devoted entirely to the pastoral, where it was passed with near unanimity.[63]

For Zahn though, as admirable as the process was, this kind of openness had also contributed to the letter's weakness and inconsistency. In particular, he pointed to the fact that many of the amendments that had been put forth at the May meeting to strengthen the letter were not included in the final draft out of fear that they would disturb the balance of the letter's argument and its broad appeal.[64] While pointing out that the teachings of Jesus were not known for their balance and broad appeal, Zahn acknowledged that the committee did have pragmatic considerations to take into account, the least of which was securing a two-thirds majority of all the bishops. That said, he guessed that a "considerably stronger" version could have been approved, albeit with less unanimity of support.[65]

As a result, Zahn highlighted the pastoral's "strictly conditioned moral acceptance" of the US policy of nuclear deterrence (and therefore of nuclear weapons) as an obvious weakness. While debates on deterrence in the past had usually revolved around the question of possession, Zahn reported that in his testimony before the Bernardin committee, he had focused on the moral issues

63 Zahn, "Talk," 6.

64 Zahn pointed to recommendations such as preparing parents to support their son if he chose to be a conscientious objector and taking pride in knowing that their child was making an unpopular stand because of his faith. Another reminded Catholic military chaplains not only that they might be called upon to support conscientious objectors in the military but also that they should alert all Catholic service members of the immorality of certain actions or orders. There was also a section suggesting that the term "enemy" no longer be used when referring to the Soviet Union (Zahn, "Talk," 9).

65 Only nine bishops voted against the final draft (Zahn, "Talk," 6).

involved when Catholics are trained and prepared to use nuclear weapons. Such weapons were not stacked away in armories, he explained, but rather they were sited, targeted, and ready to launch. Perhaps most concerning, though, was the fact that members of the armed forces (many of them Catholics) were "already being trained under orders to press the button or turn the key" and thereby commit the kind of "crime against God and man himself" that Vatican II had squarely condemned.[66] By not providing any standards or mechanisms for monitoring the progress of disarming these weapons—something the bishops' "strictly conditioned moral acceptance" required and Krol had earlier demanded—Zahn lamented that *The Challenge of Peace* would be too easily dismissed as "little more than a pious resolution."[67]

Zahn then pointed to what he saw as an even more fundamental theological weakness in the bishops' unwillingness to recognize the irrelevance of the just-war theory for contemporary war.[68] Acknowledging that this unwillingness may have been based on concerns over changing church teaching too suddenly (and thus endangering the document's acceptance), nevertheless Zahn argued that such a public recognition was "long overdue."[69] The grim realities of modern war had made "a pious fiction" out of all the "elaborately contrived theses" in Catholic just-war teaching. Zahn suggested that the very nature of modern war had made it increasingly self-evident that the only appropriate Catholic response was a return to "the absolute pacifism and total commitment to non-violence of the pre-Constantinian church."[70]

Indeed, the bishops' acknowledgment of the legitimacy of pacifism had only served to highlight its stark contrast to the just-war theory. For instance, Zahn noted that the section on pacifism in their letter placed its roots firmly in the New Testament and the Early Church, while the section on just-war rooted it in the natural law and Aristotelian ethics. For Zahn, this difference was revealing, as Aristotle had provided standards for the life of a "good pagan," while the Christian life aspired to something far greater. A total commitment to nonviolence may not always end in victory as the world knows it, Zahn

66 Zahn, "Talk," 7.

67 Zahn, "Talk," 7.

68 "However laudable its original intent to limit the occasions of war and restrain its horrors," Zahn stated that the just-war theory actually "legitimated the centuries of scandal which have found Christian killing Christian, literally tearing asunder the Mystical Body of Christ" (Zahn, "Talk," 7).

69 Zahn, "Talk," 8.

70 Zahn, "Talk," 12.

explained, once again revealing his eschatological emphasis. Indeed, for Catholic pacifists, the refusal to return evil for evil in complete abandonment and hope is the true way to ensure the only victory that counted, he declared, "In God's way. In God's own time."[71]

The appeals for theological pluralism aside, Zahn argued that the idea that the church, the "ultimate repository of Christian truth," could ever comfortably hold two "contradictory patterns of thought and behavior," particularly in a matter as crucial as war, was problematic. That said, he did acknowledge that there were some possible points where the pacifist and just-war positions could converge.[72] For instance, there was the shared awareness that the prevention of nuclear war was a moral imperative. There also seemed to be agreement that the elimination of international conflict required a more intense dedication to building a more just world order. In fact, if the just-war theory were ever taken seriously and applied conscientiously, Zahn guessed that it would ultimately arrive at the conclusion that no modern war could ever meet its criteria. In light of this, he commended the bishops for spelling out the conditions of the just-war theory in their pastoral in greater detail than had previously been available and thereby making it much more accessible to Catholics.[73] Zahn even went so far as to suggest that by doing so, the letter would actually hasten the eventual end of the church's just-war tradition.

Likewise, Zahn applauded the bishops for explicitly condemning any use of nuclear weapons or other instruments of mass slaughter for the purpose of destroying civilian targets, even in retaliation—a point implied in the just-war theory but never so clearly stated. The letter also condemned any deliberate initiation of nuclear warfare as morally unjustifiable, thereby placing the bishops, Zahn noted, in direct contrast with the US military's stated policy of not giving up any "first strike" option.[74] And in what Zahn saw as an important advance from the stance taken by the majority of the US bishops at Vatican II, in *The Challenge of Peace*, the bishops showed a profound skepticism that a nuclear war could ever be "limited." They also repeated their assurances

71 Zahn, "Talk," 11.

72 Zahn, "Talk," 11–12.

73 Prior to this, he noted, just-war teachings were largely restricted to "specialists in theology" (Zahn, "Talk," 8).

74 Zahn, "Talk," 4.

that conscientious objection and selective conscientious objection were both legitimate options for Catholics, and deserved respect and legal recognition.

For Zahn, though, the most significant contribution of the pastoral was its urgent call for the development of a "theology of peace." Taken in conjunction with their recognition of pacifism, Zahn read the bishops as having opened a debate within the church that could finally lead to the "entirely new attitude" toward war called for at the Second Vatican Council. He was confident that this new attitude would, in fact, return to the "old attitude" that held sway in the earliest centuries of the church's history, "long before there was any thought that war and violence could ever be compatible with the Christian witness."[75] Assuming that their plans (as articulated in the pastoral) for a large-scale educational program succeeded, Zahn was hopeful that US Catholics, "once awakened to the nature of modern war and their responsibilities as Christians," would soon become a major force for peace.[76]

"ON NOT WRITING A DEAD LETTER"

In the wake of the bishops' peace pastoral, Zahn's status as a spokesman for Catholic pacifism only increased. In a volume of commentaries on *The Challenge of Peace*, Zahn was asked to contribute. Noting that much had already been written about the topic of peace (including by him), Zahn suggested that more could still be said about a "spirituality of pacifism"—the "core perceptions" from which the Catholic pacifist commitment drew.[77] One such perception was a view of God that emphasized God's loving concern for creation and infinite willingness to forgive.[78] Any spirituality of peace would therefore center on an understanding of humanity's relationship with such a loving and forgiving God. Zahn described this as a relationship of complete abandonment, along the lines of what he had read in the writings of mystical writers such as (now Saint) Charles de Foucauld.

Zahn explained that this kind of abandonment was always tempered by the equally thorough confidence that good would ultimately prevail "in God's

75 Zahn, "Talk," 5.

76 Zahn, "Talk," 13.

77 Gordon Zahn, "Pacifism and Just War," in *Catholics and Nuclear War: A Commentary on* The Challenge of Peace, *The US Catholic Bishops' Pastoral Letter on War and Peace*, ed. Philip Murnion (Crossroad, 1983), 120–21.

78 Zahn, "Pacifism and Just War," 122.

time and in God's way"—a confidence that pacifists insisted offered greater security than any reliance (permanent or temporary) on nuclear deterrence.[79] This, in turn, once again pointed to a clear pacifist eschatology. These are "the last days," Zahn wrote, but for pacifists, they are "days of hope, of confident expectation, of anticipation here and now of the promised eternal rewards."[80] Through the lens of such hope in the Resurrection, the "insane rush for security" through new and more destructive weapons looked like the real threat to true security and a denial of hope that may ultimately "put salvation itself in serious jeopardy."

For Zahn, the horrors of modern weapons, which he argued had already "broken through" any moral limits set forth under traditional just-war teachings, left Catholics with no choice but to return to the weapons in their "spiritual armory." While this did not imply any sort of "angelistic detachment" from worldly concerns, such a "risk for peace" did require that Catholics be prepared for a possible military defeat, a loss of freedom, and a host of other sacrifices and hardships. And should the risk be taken and the gamble lost, Zahn wrote that Christians might very well be faced with persecution and even martyrdom—"a return to the catacombs" that even the bishops themselves had warned of in their letter. Throughout its long history, however, the church, as Zahn pointed out, had often faced persecutions of this sort and had endured, "its witness outlasting the tyrannies which have repeatedly sought to eradicate Christ and his message."[81]

While such a stance could be criticized as utopian or unrealistic, Zahn argued that within the kind of spirituality of peace he was advocating, it was much more realistic than any other just-war theory's attempt to defend the slaughter of millions of people through a tortured reasoning that weaved a "cloak of plausibility" over such justifications. For all the claims to realism and expertise made by its proponents, the just-war theory, Zahn concluded, was "the theologian's equivalent of the Rubik's cube, a dazzling display of intellectual dexterity with nothing to show for it when it is done."[82] And by

79 Zahn explained that this was not an indifference to evil but rather the refusal to succumb to the delusion that it is somehow possible to overcome evil by adding to it (Zahn, "Pacifism and Just War," 123).

80 Zahn, "Pacifism and Just War," 124.

81 Zahn, "Pacifism and Just War," 127.

82 Zahn, "Pacifism and Just War," 129.

maintaining the possibility of a just war in their letter, the bishops had fallen short of the kind of prophetic leadership that the church and world needed at that critical moment. Nevertheless, while the bishops' pastoral "may not be enough to put us back on the right path," Zahn acknowledged that it at least did "represent a slight turn in the right direction."[83]

Two years later, in 1985, Zahn feared that that moment might have already passed, however. In a piece for *Commonweal,* he began by declaring that *The Challenge of Peace* was one of the "most significant achievements" of the US hierarchy or any nation's Catholic hierarchy and recalled the optimism with which Catholic pacifists had read the pastoral as a starting point to "a more consistent, less ambiguous official Church posture in the future." In particular, by clearly setting forth the just-war criteria, the bishops had "freed the issue of the morality of modern war from the more limited realm of specialized theological disputation and opened it to the judgment of the individual conscience."[84] Two years on, though, Zahn noted that such optimism had largely faded, and fears had already arisen that the pastoral would soon become a "dead letter" and "go the way of so many others" ending up as little more than "an occasional footnote in some theological treatise."

For Zahn, this pessimism was rooted in what he saw as the three essential flaws of the pastoral, the first being the bishops' excessive reticence to "tell it like it is," particularly with regard to educating Catholics on the morality of war, for instance by instructing Catholics in the military to reject assignments in which they would be trained to carry out "on command" any actions that the church had declared immoral. Catholic lawmakers could also have been exhorted to consider the moral implications of approving the use of tax dollars to support building and maintaining nuclear arsenals. Similarly, the bishops' "strictly conditioned moral acceptance" of nuclear deterrence had refused to establish any kind of mechanism to monitor the progress of arms reduction that was stipulated in the pastoral. He suggested that the bishops call together a select "blue ribbon" panel of experts to produce annual assessment reports on disarmament.[85]

83 Zahn, "Pacifism and Just War," 131.

84 Gordon Zahn, "On Not Writing a Dead Letter," *Commonweal*, March 8, 1985,: 141.

85 Pax Christi-USA had released its own detailed assessment, but Zahn wrote that it had been largely ignored by the bishops.

The bishops had also failed to follow through on their recommendations to provide support services for Catholics COs and peace education programs in every diocese. He suggested that this, too, could be addressed if each bishop only devoted the same money and resources to peace education as they do to other "pro-life" organizations and activities in their dioceses. Zahn feared that the failure to follow through on their own recommendations would only undermine the credibility of the bishops. This was especially pertinent as the bishops looked ahead to their forthcoming economic pastoral.[86] For if the bishops abandoned their "challenge of peace," Zahn lamented, how could they expect any better from those to whom the letter had been addressed.[87]

A NEW PROGRESS REPORT

All that said, the aftermath of the peace pastoral did offer Zahn an occasion to once again assess the state of the US Catholic peace movement in an article for the *New Oxford Review*.[88] Noting that the last time he had done so, back in 1973, the idea of Catholic pacifism was still largely dismissed as "dangerously extreme"—the mark of the "lunatic fringe" or even "dangerous heretics." In 1987, however, Zahn could report that pacifism was on the verge of becoming almost "mainstream" in the church, and he saw even further signs of hope. Groups such as the Catholic Peace Fellowship and Pax Christi-USA were strong and, in the case of the latter, had substantially grown. During the then-ongoing Cold War, many young Catholics were working for peace and justice. Even the church hierarchy's attitudes on war had shifted—though he pointed out that any shift must be recognized as the result of "agitation" by the laity. And for all his criticism, Zahn described *The Challenge of Peace* as a document of "'breakthrough' significance" that provided the "foundation upon which a more promising future for the Catholic peace movement" could be built. In short, as Zahn saw it, the future of the Catholic peace movement

86 *Economic Justice for All* was issued by the bishops in 1986.

87 It is important to remember that the US bishops did issue another peace pastoral in 1993 titled *The Harvest of Justice is Sown in Peace*, which sought to address some of the criticism of *The Challenge of Peace*.

88 Gordon Zahn, "American Catholics and Peace: A Progress Report," *New Oxford Review* (June 1987): 14–17.

looked "more promising than it did in 1973—and certainly much more promising than it did in 1945."[89]

Nevertheless, weaknesses remained.[90] Hinting at what Pope John Paul II would a decade later describe as a "culture of death," Zahn called out the "culture of violence" that prevailed in the United States.[91] He repeated his earlier warnings that the Catholic peace movement needed to resist the temptation to get involved with too many outside causes—a problem made worse when those other causes detracted from or even contradicted the values of the movement.[92] Consequently, the movement needed to clearly reject any attempts, however well-intentioned, to justify the instrumental destruction of human life. Acknowledging that this was certainly a difficult position to hold and "one which sometimes separates us from many of our friends," Zahn insisted that it had to be maintained—whether the issue was "violent revolution in the Third World or the violence of abortion."

Zahn also repeated his strong belief that identification with the *Catholic* peace movement should mean that its members, at the very least, presented themselves as "loyal and committed" members of the church. Rebuffing earlier charges that he was attempting to "excommunicate" anyone, Zahn argued that the failure to respect and abide by the "the rules" of the church would lessen the effectiveness of one's contribution to the movement. If, as some of his critics charged, such a suggestion was too "old Church," Zahn countered that it was the position that had also been held by Dorothy Day—a "holy old woman" who had always insisted that the Catholic Worker would be nothing if it was not recognizably Catholic.

Standing on his long record of criticizing the hierarchy, Zahn made it clear that the kind of loyalty he was talking about did not imply "sheep-like subservience." He reminded his readers that criticism of the church, to be most effective, must come "from within" the church itself.[93] This had certainly always been the case with Zahn. While the Catholic peace movement must

89 Zahn, "American Catholics and Peace," 15.

90 Zahn again noted that no "objective after-the-fact application of 'just war' criteria" had ever been made on the US war in Vietnam, though few would argue that the US war effort (led by many "professedly sincere Catholics") had followed any of the church's just-war criteria (Zahn, "American Catholics and Peace," 14.

91 John Paul II, *Evangelium Vitae* (March 25, 1995).

92 Zahn, "American Catholics and Peace," 16.

93 Zahn, "American Catholics and Peace," 17.

always challenge church leaders to "keep them honest," Zahn distinguished that from flaunting one's disregard for the institution and its rules.

Working from within a not-always-responsive religious institution could certainly be frustrating and, at times, a seemingly hopeless experience, Zahn acknowledged, but he pointed to Day and Merton as models of perseverance in this regard. As always, he concluded, the Catholic peace movement's first responsibility must be to the church itself, as every diocese, parish, high school, or college that presumes to call itself "Catholic" has its part to play in the promotion of peace.[94] This hope of keeping the peace movement within the church, while still maintaining a necessary critical distance from the hierarchy, in many ways succinctly captures Zahn's vision for the movement and his contributions to it.

CONCLUSION

By the end of the 1980s, Zahn was facing criticism on many fronts. His insistence that the peace movement remain Catholic was regarded with suspicion by many younger activists. His continued engagement with nonpacifist Catholics was seen as being too lukewarm by many pacifists. For many Catholic moral theologians, Zahn's absolutist defense of human life was not pluralist enough, and for US Catholics in general, Zahn's Catholic pacifism largely remained, of course, irresponsible and sectarian.

The lonely position Zahn found himself in was captured by the fact that the hawkish Catholic neoconservative George Weigel included him on a list of US Catholics who he said had abandoned the church's heritage on war—a list that also included Day, Merton, the Berrigans, and Jim Douglass. While Weigel was certainly critical of Zahn, his portrayal of Zahn's "traditionalist Catholic pacifism" was also clearly much more sympathetic (if not laudatory) than what he wrote about the others.[95] This was but one indication of how Zahn did not fall easily into theological or ideological categories—even among the tiny collection of Catholic pacifists in the United States. It also meant that

94 Zahn, "American Catholics and Peace," 17.

95 Weigel highlighted as praiseworthy Zahn's work to remain "in the Church," his opposition to abortion and embrace of the "seamless garment of life," and his resistance to aspects of the Catholic Left beyond the issue of pacifism. See George Weigel, *Tranquillitas Ordinis: The Present Failure and Future Promise of American Catholic Thought on War and Peace* (Oxford University Press, 1987).

Zahn had to constantly explain himself and his position, a defense would continue almost to the end of his life.

13

LEGACIES

Your blessing on my efforts for peace give me much pleasure and pride. In a very real sense, as I see it, what you call my "great work" is really a continuation of yours. Now at 72 I look to others to continue the struggle.

—Gordon Zahn to Paul Hanly Furfey in 1991[1]

Since retiring from UMass-Boston to professor emeritus status in 1980, Zahn's work had largely focused on the Center for Conscience and War. He and Michael Hovey were regularly counseling conscientious objectors through the discharge process, work that also included writing numerous bishops around the United States asking them to support young members of their diocese applying to be COs.[2] They also wrote to presidents of Catholic universities with ROTC students seeking assistance in getting out of their commitment to military service, and even proposed that Catholic colleges begin to give ROTC programs on their campuses "strictly limited moral acceptance."[3] Zahn and Hovey also gave workshops on pacifism and conscientious objection to various dioceses, parishes, and schools as part of what they understood to be one of the pastoral directives in *The Challenge of Peace*. And when Hovey

1 Zahn to Furfey in letter dated January 12, 1991, ACUA Furfey papers.

2 Zahn's papers in the archives at Notre Dame are full of these letters.

3 Zahn made this proposal to Edward Malloy, newly installed president of the University of Notre Dame, when he wrote to Malloy about an ND student seeking help from the center. See Zahn to Malloy in letter dated 1988, UNDA Zahn papers (10/13638).

left to begin graduate studies in 1990, Zahn carried on the work largely by himself until the center closed in July 1991, though Zahn continued to work out of his Boylston Street apartment.[4]

Perhaps most notably, in the fall of 1987, Zahn was invited by Archbishop John Ryan of the Military Archdiocese to be one of four panelists at a symposium on "The Just-War and Pacifism" at Georgetown University.[5] In a letter to Furfey, Zahn reported that since this would probably be his only opportunity to speak to over 300 active military chaplains, he "gave a 'hard-line' talk."[6] To Zahn's surprise, however, his talk was well received, and he and Ryan continued to meet regularly. "Neither side is likely to be 'converted,' but I think both can derive benefit from it," Zahn wrote hopefully about his conversations with nonpacifists, a stance that continued to distinguish him from others in the Catholic peace movement.

Zahn also continued to write and speak about Franz Jägerstätter. Since the publication of *In Solitary Witness* in 1964, Jägerstätter's story had certainly become well-established. The Austrian Catholic martyr, whose life was unknown outside of his remote village in the early 1960s, was by the late 1980s recognized and honored as a hero of the church. Zahn's book had been translated into German, French, Italian, and Greek,[7] and in 1971, a made-for-television movie about Jägerstätter, called *Der Fall Jägerstätter*, was broadcast in West Germany and Austria. Zahn worked to have the film dubbed into English, and it was eventually released as *The Refusal*.[8] In 1986, Templegate Publishers released a fourth edition of *In Solitary Witness*.[9] And by the late 1980s, as Zahn had first predicted back in 1958, St. Radegund had become a site of pilgrimage for many Catholics and others.

4 Zahn to Furfey in letter dated January 16, 1992, ACUA Furfey papers.

5 On the panel, the just-war position was defended by Bishop Angelo Acerra of the Military Archdiocese and James Dougherty, a political science professor at St. Joseph's University in Philadelphia and long-time member of the CAIP. The other panelist on the "pacifist" side was Bishop Leroy Matthiesen of Amarillo, who was most known for calling on workers assembling neutron bombs at a Pantex facility in his diocese to quit their jobs in September 1981. See A. G. Mojtabai, *Blessed Assurance: At Home with the Bomb in Amarillo, Texas* (Houghton Mifflin Co. 1986).

6 Zahn to Furfey in letter dated December 14, 1987, ACUA Furfey papers.

7 Zahn, Preface to 1986 revised edition of *In Solitary Witness* (Templegate Publishers, 1986).

8 Zahn to Furfey in letter dated November 1, 1980, ACUA Furfey papers.

9 Beacon Press published a second edition in 1968, and Liturgical Press released a third edition in 1977.

With this increased recognition, however, came increased scrutiny. In the summer of 1988, the legacy of Franz Jägerstätter (and that of Zahn) came into question. In June, the *London Times* included a brief article by Roger Boyes on Pope John Paul II's visit to Austria the day before under the headline, "Pope Left Without Austrian War Hero."[10] Boyes wrote that while it was customary for the pope to beatify or even canonize someone from the country during a papal visit, no suitable Austrian candidate could be found for such an honor. The original plan, even as late as February, Boyes reported, had been to honor Jägerstätter, whose story could have served as a "useful counterpoint" to Kurt Waldheim, the Catholic president of Austria and former UN general secretary who had stirred international controversy a few years earlier when it was revealed that he had served as a German intelligence officer during World War II. According to Boyes, however, "worried messages came from Rome" concerning allegations that some of Jägerstätter's words had been "manufactured" after his death (the "historical records," Boyes reported, indicated that he had been "poorly educated" and "inarticulate") and that Jägerstätter's objection to the Nazis had been "politically-motivated."[11] As a result of all of this, the pope left Austria without ever mentioning Franz Jägerstätter.

After reading this article, Zahn immediately wrote to several members of the Catholic hierarchy, including to the pope.[12] He indicated his disappointment that the pope had not mentioned Jägerstätter even during his visit to Enns and asked the pope to initiate a thorough investigation into the facts surrounding Jägerstätter's martyrdom, as well as "the messages from Rome" mentioned in the article, in order to ascertain the truth and thereby correct the injustice that appeared to have been done to the Austrian Catholic martyr's memory.

Zahn went onto to explain to the pope that it had been his "privilege to 'discover' this authentic Austrian hero." He described how he came across Jägerstätter's writings and translated handwritten documents carefully to reproduce Jägerstätter's thoughts "just as they had been written and as accurately as possible." Zahn wrote that while Jägerstätter might not have had much in the way of a formal education, he was remembered for regularly reading the Bible along with any other religious texts he could get his hands

10 Roger Boyes, "Pope Left Without Austrian War Hero," *London Times* (June 25, 1988).

11 Boyes noted that the pope did honor Marcel Callo, a French Catholic who died in an Austrian concentration camp in 1945.

12 Zahn to Pope John Paul II in letter dated July 11, 1988, CPF Zahn papers.

on—particularly books on saints and martyrs. Though many remembered him as a "stubborn *Dickschaedel*," and even a "religious extremist," Zahn explained that Jägerstätter was not in any way "inarticulate." Regarding the charge that Jägerstätter's objection to the Nazis was political and not religious, Zahn pointed out that when one lived under "un-Christian" totalitarian rule, as the pope surely understood from his experience in Communist Poland, a Christian's political views and religious commitments became "almost inseparable." Repeating the claim he first made in *In Solitary Witness*, Zahn asserted that there could be no doubt that Jägerstätter's intense opposition to Hitler and the Nazis was based on "his religious conviction that they were enemies of the Church and, in time, intended to destroy her."

Less than a month after writing the Pope, Zahn published an article for *Commonweal* titled, "The Pope in Austria: two swings and two misses."[13] As Zahn saw it, John Paul II's avoidance of any mention of Jägerstätter was part of a broader "Waldheim problem" that hung over the entire trip to Austria and went far past any of the particular concerns about Jägerstätter raised in the *London Times* article. Zahn suggested that the papal snub had more to do with concerns over honoring a Catholic conscientious objector and thereby risking too direct a critique of Waldheim, who had insisted that he had done nothing more than his "duty" during the war and that he had "no alternative" but to join Hitler's military. Obviously, Jägerstätter found himself in a very similar situation but had understood his "duty" very differently.[14] Unlike Waldheim, Zahn pointed out, Jägerstätter understood that "there was 'no alternative' but to be true to the commands of conscience."

Zahn further suggested that Jägerstätter's story had focused a critical light beyond the Austrian president's war record. When the Bishop of Linz, for instance, had organized a three-day commemoration for Jägerstätter's eightieth birthday the previous year, he was roundly criticized by Austrian veterans and their families for honoring a man who they said had betrayed and abandoned his countrymen and demeaned those who had done their "duty" for the Fatherland. For Zahn, this highlighted the fact that the pope had missed an opportunity to teach a much-needed lesson: "the choice that

13 Gordon Zahn, "The Pope in Austria: Two Swings and Two Misses," *Commonweal*, August 12, 1988, 421.

14 Zahn, "The Pope in Austria," 423.

must sometimes be made between the demands of nation and the obligation to follow Christ's teachings and example."[15]

JÄGERSTÄTTER'S DISPUTED WITNESS

With the fall of the Berlin Wall in 1989, Jägerstätter's legacy and Zahn's role in it took an even more dramatic twist as news broke in January 1990 that the military historical archives in Prague had made available previously sealed Nazi records, including those from Jägerstätter's 1943 court martial—documents that Jägerstätter's attorney Leo Feldmann had told Zahn no longer existed. On August 9, 1990, the forty-seventh anniversary of Jägerstätter's death, Zahn sent out a news release from the Center on Conscience and War announcing the news that the long-assumed lost court records had been found[16] and described the documents as crucial to the emerging cause for Jägerstätter's canonization that had been building in Austria because they provided "irrefutable evidence" that his refusal was for religious, not just political, reasons.

Zahn pointed out "that as a believing Catholic," Jägerstätter was not permitted to perform any military service because "it was impossible for him to be a Nazi and a Catholic at one and the same time." He noted that the court records reported that Jägerstätter had acknowledged taking the military oath at his initial military induction in 1940 because he believed at the time that it would have been a sin not to obey the legitimate authority of the German state. After his initial training, however, God had shown him that it was not sinful to refuse armed service and that there were times in which "one must obey God rather than man."

Zahn further mentioned, almost in passing, that these documents also included a single sentence that noted that Jägerstätter had expressed a readiness to serve in the German medical corps "as an act of Christian charity." As he had in *In Solitary Witness*, Zahn dismissed this as simply a "change of heart" that Jägerstätter had undergone early in his imprisonment, one that he had "regretted immediately as a shameful compromise and never repeated." In the end, Zahn saw these newly-discovered records as offering "definitive evidence of authentic martyrdom" that would greatly help Jägerstätter's cause for canonization.

15 Zahn, "The Pope in Austria," 423.

16 Zahn, News Release, August 9, 1990 (CPF Zahn papers).

Obstacles to such a goal still remained, however. Foremost, as Zahn noted, was the concern voiced by many in Austria—including many prominent church leaders—that canonizing a conscientious objector would alienate many of the Catholics who had fought in Hitler's military. In light of this, Zahn pointed to a commission that had been established in Austria to promote Jägerstätter's cause and was gathering testimony from individuals who had found "inspiration in or gained other spiritual benefit" from knowing of Jägerstätter's heroic witness. Zahn asked that anyone who would like to add their testimony to send in statements.

Despite Zahn's confidence that the Prague records did not change the fundamentals of Jägerstätter's story, some German and Austrian scholars were not as dismissive. Earlier that year in May, Pax Christi International had held a symposium on Jägerstätter in Vienna, during which the newly unearthed records were discussed. Zahn attended, as did Erna Putz, an Austrian journalist and historian who for years had been investigating both Franz and Franziska Jägerstätter. The proceedings from the meeting contain a statement from Putz in which she pointed to the letter that Franz wrote to Franziska in which he again had expressed his willingness to serve in the German military's medical corps.[17] Putz did acknowledge (as had Zahn) that this letter was written during the dark early days of Jägerstätter's imprisonment—a time, she noted, during which he had been haunted by depression and possibly even thoughts of suicide. Nevertheless, she asserted that this letter, combined with the newly released court records, "made it explicitly clear: Franz was willing to serve in a medical unit, but not to fight with weapons in his hands."

Putz also argued that Feldmann had never been all that supportive of Jägerstätter, and she suggested that his lawyer's statements to Zahn should be regarded as part of Feldmann's efforts to place himself in a better light after the war. And no doubt in response to Zahn's depiction of Jägerstätter as a "solitary witness" in the Austrian Church, Putz pointed out that the "worst persecution" of the church in Austria and Germany during the war had taken place in Jägerstätter's home diocese of Linz.[18] The Catholic Church in Linz had been under "heavy pressure," which had led to its official strategy to remain as

17 Erna Putz, "Not with Weapons in the Hands," *Proceedings of Franz Jägerstätter: An International Symbol of Conscience* (Pax Christi International, 1992). I am grateful to Andreas Schmoller at the Franz and Franziska Jägerstätter Institute (Diocese of Linz, Austria) for sharing this document with me.

18 She noted that forty diocesan priests were sent to concentration camps.

silent as possible vis-à-vis politics. Putz wrote that Jägerstätter fundamentally "questioned this policy."[19]

That fall, Norbert Haase, the German historian who had first unearthed Jägerstätter's court records in Prague, published an article stating that Zahn's account in *In Solitary Witness* was incorrect on the question of Jägerstätter's willingness to serve as a medical orderly in the military, which was largely due to the fact that Zahn did not have access to these records.[20] Haase noted, however, that even after the discovery of the records, Zahn continued to be unwilling to change his view of Jägerstätter in light of this new evidence.

Around this same time, *Making Saints*, Kenneth Woodward's book on the church's process for canonizing saints, was published.[21] In his chapter on martyrs, Woodward noted that no Catholic had yet to be declared a martyr solely for resisting the Nazis or for protecting Jews, though many Catholics had done both. In particular, Woodward held up Jägerstätter and noted that it was significant that after decades of discussion, no process for canonization had been initiated on the Austrian martyr's behalf.[22] Woodward suggested that this may have been due to the fact that "some Austrian bishops, and not a few disinterested parties in Rome," felt that Jägerstätter's canonization would be interpreted as an official endorsement of pacifism—"a position which conflicts with the church's 'just-war' theory and an attitude with which John Paul II has shown little sympathy."[23]

SAINT FRANZ

Zahn read all of this as further attempts to delegitimize Jägerstätter's witness along with his portrayal of him. In an article in *Commonweal* in October 1990, Zahn described the church's canonization process as one that traditionally had looked to elevate saints to the "status of models suited to the particular urgencies of a specific time and situation," and he pointed to the cause for

19 Putz explained that Bishop Fliesser of Linz wanted to avoid postwar discussion of the war so as to avoid any Catholic veterans asking, "Why didn't you tell us it would have been better not to fight?"

20 Norbert Haase, "Gott mehr gehorcht als dem Staat," *Tribüne, Zeitschrift zum Verständnis des Judentums*, 29/114 (1990), 198–205.

21 Kenneth Woodward, *Making Saints: How the Catholic Church Determines Who Becomes a Saint, Who Doesn't, and Why* (Simon and Schuster, 1990).

22 Woodward, *Making Saints*, 150.

23 Woodward, *Making Saints*, 377.

Dorothy Day as one such an example.[24] It would be a grave problem, he argued, if this process were to be "reversed" and formal recognition of an otherwise qualified candidate was denied because of fears that honoring such a Catholic might "send the wrong message." This, for Zahn, was what seemed to be happening with Jägerstätter. While acknowledging his personal investment in Jägerstätter's legacy, Zahn explained that he had always thought it best to remain distant from the campaign on the Austrian's behalf that was being led by the Diocese of Linz. Recent developments and controversies, however, had forced him to address some of the serious challenges that were casting doubt on the "validity of Jägerstätter's claim to recognition" as well as on Zahn's own professional integrity.

Zahn repeated the charges that had been reported in the *London Times* back in 1988—that Jägerstätter was poorly-educated, inarticulate, and that his refusal was more political than religious—as well as his responses to them. He also noted the supposed concerns by those in "higher ecclesiastical circles" that honoring Jägerstätter would alienate Austria's Catholic World War II veterans. "It is troubling to consider that 'following orders' in such a war can serve as a political asset (consider Waldheim's election as president)," Zahn wrote, "while refusing to do so on moral grounds becomes an embarrassment to responsible leaders of the church."[25]

Zahn then pointed to an "even more threatening objection" that had been raised, one that ignored Jägerstätter's spiritual commitment and heroic virtue altogether—an objection that appeared to be very influential in the Vatican. Here Zahn turned to the work of Robert Sarno, a priest from Brooklyn and member of the Vatican's Congregation for the Cause of Saints whose 1988 dissertation from the Pontifical Gregorian University in Rome had suggested that canonizing Jägerstätter "could go beyond a declaration of sanctity of one individual to imply a preference for pacifism, which would have serious implications for the just-war theory."[26] Sarno, who cited Erna Putz (but not Zahn) had described Jägerstätter as a "total pacifist."[27] Zahn reiterated that such was

24 Gordon Zahn, "How Narrow the Gate?" *Commonweal*, October 26, 1990, 607–9.

25 Zahn, "How Narrow the Gate?" 608.

26 Robert Sarno, *Diocesan Inquiries Required by the Legislator in the New Legislation for the Causes of Saints* (JCD diss., Pontifical Gregorian University, 1988), 35.

27 Erna Putz, *Franz Jägerstätter . . . besser die Hände als der Wille gefesselt* (Veritas-Verlag, 1985), 176ff.

not the case, as the Austrian martyr had twice reported for military training before his final refusal at Enns. "What he proclaimed at the induction center and, later, at his trial before the Supreme Military Tribunal," Zahn wrote, "was the unshakeable moral conviction that as a Catholic he was forbidden to take part in an unjust war and serve an immoral regime that was persecuting his church." In a noteworthy shift in his view, Zahn suggested that Jägerstätter's refusal might actually be regarded as "a model of how the 'just war' theory could work if it were taken seriously."[28] For although Jägerstätter might not have been able to explain his actions in terms of just-war conditions and principles, Zahn argued, he clearly saw the situation he was in: "the war was wrong and Hitler and his regime were evil" and therefore to participate in their military would be immoral.

Setting aside the question of whether being a total or absolute pacifist should be a disqualification for sainthood, Zahn argued that Sarno had raised the issue of the implications of Jägerstätter's sainthood—specifically, a concern that canonizing Jägerstätter "would imply honoring him as a *conscientious objector*." According to Zahn, this was *the* central issue. For despite official statements over the years from popes, the Second Vatican Council, and even the US bishops in their 1983 peace pastoral; the majority of Catholics (both laity and clergy) still did not recognize the legitimacy of Catholic conscientious objectors. Even the "simple logic" of the just-war theory, that Catholics should not support or participate in wars that violated the just-war criteria, was rarely promoted by those responsible for the formation of Catholics and so was rarely followed.[29] Zahn asserted that while recognition of Jägerstätter's martyrdom would not pose any real threat to the Church's just-war teaching, it might very well cause some Catholics to begin to take the teaching seriously and thereby threaten the "easy acceptance of every nation's expectation of automatic obedience on the part of Catholics called to arms."[30] This, Zahn declared, was the real threat posed by Jägerstätter.

28 Zahn, "How Narrow the Gate?" 608.

29 He pointed out that even John Paul II, while praising conscientious objection as "a sign of maturity," had ultimately described it as a "problem" (Zahn, "How Narrow the Gate?" 609.

30 "It is true, of course," Zahn wrote, "that if (as I believe) no modern war can meet the theological conditions for a 'just war,' Jägerstätter's canonization could create a troublesome model for young people called to service in any future war"
(Zahn, "How Narrow the Gate?" 609.

PATRON SAINT OF THE JUST-WAR THEORY?

The following year, Zahn further attempted to "clarify" Jägerstätter's witness and his account of it.[31] While the court records had provided helpful "official clarification" on the religious motivations behind Jägerstätter's refusal, he noted that they also introduced a "note of confusion" as to whether Jägerstätter had expressed a willingness to serve in the medical corps—a crucial point, Zahn wrote, that threatened to "lessen the meaning and impact" of Jägerstätter's witness.[32] Zahn again admitted to his own strong bias in seeing Jägerstätter as a "model and future 'patron'" of conscientious objectors, but he contended that it was this very bias that had enabled him four decades earlier to recognize the importance and uniqueness of Jägerstätter when he first read "Franz II" in Kreuzberg's book. Indeed, he asserted that to put Jägerstätter's story in its "proper context" required the perspective of someone who had also refused military service ("but with none of the risk!") in order to recognize what it meant for one Catholic—"among the millions of Catholics in Hitler's *Grossdeutschland*"—to have the clarity and courage to refuse to participate in one of the most clearly unjust military campaigns in recent history.[33]

The extent to which Jägerstätter's witness was being disputed, Zahn wrote, had little bearing on its essential validity. It was largely a dispute among "scholars who remain good friends" and were united in their shared belief that Franz Jägerstätter was both a martyr and saint. For Zahn, any dispute revolved around "more peripheral" questions of research methods and approach. He explained that sociologists and historians sometimes disagreed on the absolute priority of documentary evidence even when it appeared to contradict situational evidence or personal testimony. Implying that this was the case with the Prague records, Zahn suggested that they could have been written in error, or as intentionally misleading, or even as false.

31 Gordon Zahn, "Clarifying the Disputed Witness of Franz Jägerstätter," *New Oxford Review* (September 1991): 14–19. Zahn had responded previously to the "dispute" caused by the court records in "Franz Jägerstätter's Disputed Witness: A Personal Re-Affirmation," which he wrote in October 1990 and was published in *Proceedings of Franz Jägerstätter: An International Symbol of Conscience* (Pax Christi International, 1992).

32 Zahn, "Clarifying the Disputed Witness," 18.

33 Zahn, "Clarifying the Disputed Witness," 18.

Regarding the question of Jägerstätter and whether or not he had requested to serve in the German medical corps, Zahn reaffirmed his conclusions from *In Solitary Witness* and maintained that Jägerstätter's refusal to serve was a total rejection of any form of military service. He repeated his argument that the vast majority of Jägerstätter's writing, as well as the personal recollections of those who met with Jägerstätter in prison—including his declaration upon returning from his second stint of military training that he would never go back because even putting on a uniform made him "feel dirty"—all contradicted this one short statement to the contrary found in the military records.[34] For Zahn, there was simply too much to the contrary to accept this new and otherwise welcome evidence at its face value on this crucial point.[35]

But Zahn did worry about the "enthusiasm" with which this new evidence had been received, and he suggested that it might reflect some deeper and "more hidden" objections to Jägerstätter from both Austrian Catholic veterans and the clergy who had encouraged them to "do their duty." In an earlier article, Zahn had been less diplomatic and had pointed to some "troubling questions" that still remained as to why it took so long (twenty years) for Jägerstätter's story to be recognized at all—and then only by a foreigner.[36] Troubling, too, was the fact that even as his story had become known, it had been a British cleric, not one from Germany or Austria, who praised Jägerstätter at Vatican II.

While Jägerstätter's bravery and commitment had certainly been honored, Zahn feared that the "essence of his witness"—his refusal to serve in the armed forces of "an immoral regime waging an unjust war"—was being "played down if not avoided altogether," particularly in Austria. Zahn again pointed

34 Zahn mentioned some scholars had suggested that he had been duped by Feldmann because the attorney wanted to look good to a visiting US scholar and that, in fact, it was Jägerstätter who had requested to serve in the medical corps, not the military officers, as Feldmann had contended. Zahn reaffirmed his belief in the lawyer's account, suggesting that he had no reason to make up such a story (Zahn, "Clarifying the Disputed Witness," 17). In her account, Erna Putz wrote: "After the end of the war, the case of Franz Jägerstätter was to become important again, with respect to whether or not the same lawyer would be allowed to continue practicing his profession: the chaplain at Berlin prison, Kreutzberg, testified that Feldmann had spoken up in defense of an Austrian farmer who was accused of undermining military morale, and this was decisive in the proceedings to denazify the lawyer. In 1961, Feldmann incorrectly described the case of Franz Jägerstätter to the American sociologist Gordon C. Zahn" (Putz, *Franz*, 107).

35 As to why the records even included the statement about the medical corps, Zahn guessed that it could have been added as a "loophole" by the military tribunal to allow for a last-minute change of heart on Jägerstätter's part or it was a simple misunderstanding by the court reporter (Zahn, "Clarifying the Disputed Witness," 17).

36 Zahn, "Clarifying the Disputed Witness," 19.

out that when the bishop of Linz had commemorated Jägerstätter's eightieth birthday, he was met with protest from those Austrians who insisted that Jägerstätter had "abandoned, or even betrayed his fellow Austrians." Zahn also noted that the war memorial in St. Radegund had been vandalized in an attempt to remove Jägerstätter's name. While such actions could certainly be seen as extreme, Zahn wrote that he sensed that a "lingering unwillingness to honor Franz for his full witness" had found expression in the enthusiasm that welcomed the Prague record's implication that Jägerstätter had been ready to serve in the military as a medic. Zahn guessed that it would be much more palatable to those Austrian Catholics to think that Jägerstätter was executed simply because he had not been permitted to serve as a medic rather than having been martyred for refusing to serve Hitler in any way.

This issue certainly had significant implications for more than just Jägerstätter or Zahn. Since the time Zahn first began to publish his research on Jägerstätter in the late 1950s, it had come to light that Jägerstätter may not have been the "solitary witness" he had originally appeared to be. Other Austrian Catholics had taken similar stands during the war. Zahn recognized this and suggested that it was because Jägerstätter's story had already become widely known that these other Austrian Catholics could be better recognized—as scholars were now searching for more parallels to Jägerstätter. In this sense, the claim that Jägerstätter was willing to compromise his opposition to the Nazi war effort would not only weaken his sacrifice but also the sacrifices of these other Catholic resisters. For it would reduce Jägerstätter's outright refusal to cooperate with evil to merely an unwillingness on the part of the Nazis to grant Jägerstätter his preferred assignment. For Zahn, this would threaten to "violate the clarity of Jägerstätter's commitment and purity of his witness."[37] That is why this was such an important point for Zahn.

But if he were incorrect, and Jägerstätter had indeed been willing to serve in the medical corps, Zahn pointed out that that would mean that he was not the "total pacifist" Sarno and others feared. In this sense, the newly unearthed court records could actually smooth the path toward Jägerstätter's canonization by removing the "stigma of pacifism."[38] And in another revision of his earlier account, Zahn wrote that he had always made it clear that it was only after months in prison that "hints" appeared that implied that Jägerstätter

37 Zahn, "Clarifying the Disputed Witness," 17.

38 Zahn, "Clarifying the Disputed Witness," 17–18.

may have become inclined to "the nonviolence and pacifism of the Early Church," though this was certainly not the case when he had first made his refusal. If anything, Zahn suggested, advocates of the just-war theory should embrace Jägerstätter as their patron saint, a rare example of how such teachings could work "if believers (including, one must add, the just-war theologians themselves) took them seriously."[39]

In the end, Zahn seemed to recognize that his defense of the essential integrity of Jägerstätter's witness was rooted in his own story. Almost fifty years earlier, he had been told by a priest that a Catholic could not be a conscientious objector. And despite the significant shift in the church's thinking since then, Zahn reported that a young AWOL soldier had recently come to the Center on Conscience and War and reported that when he had asked his unit's Catholic chaplain for help in applying of a CO discharge, he, too, had been told that a Catholic could not be a conscientious objector. For Zahn, the canonization of Jägerstätter would go a long way in helping to counter these false but still widely held beliefs. And so he explained that this dispute over the court records was, in fact, maybe more than just a difference in scholarly interpretation after all. "For my part, I prefer to remember the Jägerstätter of his writings, as a simple but almost unbelievably heroic man, a martyr who insisted that the Christian in the Third Reich was faced with nothing less than a choice between the Nazi's 'folk community' and the community of saints to which he aspired," Zahn wrote.[40] Jägerstätter made his choice and died for it. Zahn credited Austria with giving formal and official recognition to the heroism of that choice, and many Catholics now hoped that the church would do the same—granting Jägerstätter the "full respect of the Church to which he devoted his life and dedicated his death."

That October, in a letter to Franz König, the Cardinal-Archbishop of Vienna, who Zahn had meet at the Pax Christi conference in Brussels, Zahn addressed the issues that the Prague records raised for Jägerstätter's cause. "Martyrdom for the faith, I have been told, requires that the martyr refuse to retreat from the stand he has taken in defense of that faith," he wrote, with regard to any implied compromise on the part of Jägerstätter.[41] And in what

39 Zahn, "Clarifying the Disputed Witness," 18.

40 Zahn, "Clarifying the Disputed Witness," 19.

41 Zahn to König in letter dated October 9, 1991, CPF Zahn papers.

can be read as an attempt at some kind of resolution of the dispute, Zahn recommended to the Cardinal that it

> would be far better not to impose an "official" judgement but to admit instead that, while there is "documentary" evidence that seems to support the "compromise," there is "other" strong evidence that contradicts it. (It might also be well to note in this connection that the documentary evidence came from a military source, and this could render it at least partly suspect.)

In the end, Zahn suggested that König "stay as far away from the issue as possible, leaving it to the Austrians to promote the cause."[42]

THE GULF WAR

Of course, swirling around this dispute over Jägerstätter was Iraq's invasion of Kuwait in August 1990 and the US-led "Operation Desert Storm" that followed in January 1991. This was a very busy time for the seventy-two-year-old Zahn. In addition to responding to Jägerstätter's newly found court records, the Center for Conscience and War saw an uptick in requests to assist conscientious objectors. Zahn reported that between fifteen to twenty calls a day came in with requests for advice and information.[43] This, along with his sensitivity to the ignored struggles of COs, particularly during a very popular war, led Zahn to write an essay for *America* that he titled "Prisoners of Conscience, U.S. Style." Written in November 1991, months after the United States had ended its bloody military campaign, Zahn raised awareness of the COs still being held in US military prisons, which he claimed numbered between one and three hundred. He wrote that this "vindictive, even vicious" treatment of these "prisoners of conscience" was "one more reason for serious second thoughts as to the morality of the Gulf War."[44]

Zahn described his own work with service members whose "crystallization of conscience" had led to their objections and the struggles they faced

42 It is worth noting that in a 2008 article, Putz insisted that Jägerstätter had "asked several times" to be transferred to the military ambulance service. See Erna Putz, "Franz Jägerstätter: Better the Hands in Chains, Than the Will," in *Christianity and Resistance in the 20th Century*, ed. Søren Dosenrode (Brill, 2008), 57.

43 Zahn to Furfey in letter dated January 16, 1992, ACUA Furfey papers.

44 Gordon Zahn, "Prisoners of Conscience, U.S. Style," *America*, November 16, 1991, 360.

applying for CO status while having to remain in a military at war. With the debate over Jägerstätter's pacifism still very much in mind, Zahn highlighted the particular difficulties of those service members who were not pacifists but who based their objection instead on "the traditional distinction between 'just' and 'unjust' wars" and so had their claims rejected as selective conscientious objection (SCO). He declared that the continued refusal of the US military to recognize SCOs constituted "a violation of the spirit if not the letter of the First Amendment." And in yet another sign of the shift in attitudes since his days at Camp Simon, Zahn pointed out that over thirty Catholic bishops had petitioned President Bush for amnesty for these prisoners of conscience, who, Zahn wrote, languished in US military prisons "because, put to the test, they chose to serve a higher authority."

As had been the case during other US military campaigns, Zahn was also invited to once again weigh-in on the US war effort. And once again, he was generally the only pacifist invited to do so. For instance, in June 1991, Zahn joined two Georgetown moral theologians in an "Exchange of Views" on the war in the pages of *Commonweal.*[45] Zahn was included to represent the pacifist position, but he spent the bulk of his contribution employing the criteria of the just-war theory to critique the Gulf War as unjust—a conclusion neither of his interlocutors shared. While noting that in *The Challenge of Peace* the bishops had called for a "theology of peace," Zahn argued that what was even more urgently needed was "a new (perhaps a resurrected?) theology of war."

Zahn further developed this argument in a symposium on the war for *St. John's Law Review* in the fall of 1992. William O'Brien, chief architect of CAIP's "secret memorandum" on nuclear weapons during Vatican II, also contributed—and not surprisingly declared that in Operation Desert Storm "all of the just-war requirements were clearly met."[46] Coming to a very different conclusion, Zahn distinguished between what he called "moral ethics" and "secular ethics," the former of which rest upon "supernatural values made known through some form of revelation," while the latter have "no outside superior power or universal source by which they can be judged."[47] Zahn

45 John Langan, SJ, "An Imperfectly Just War," *Commonweal*, June 1, 1991, 361–65; Gordon Zahn, "An Infamous Victory," *Commonweal*, June 1, 1991, 366–67; Francis X. Winters, "Freed to Resist Coercion," *Commonweal*, June 1, 1991, 369–72.

46 William V. O'Brien, "Desert Storm" *St. John's Law Review* 66, no.3 (1992): 822.

47 Gordon Zahn, "Morality and War: Ethics, Morality, and the Gulf War," *St. John's Law Review* 66, no. 3 (1992): 779.

noted that his earlier analysis of the war in *Commonweal* had been from a moral ethics approach, but he was now going to shift to a more secular ethics approach. That said, Zahn reached a similar conclusion that Saddam Hussein and the Bush administration had both waged unjust wars. And as the devasting aftermath of US campaign in Iraq continued to evolve, Zahn concluded that the "horrors Hussein undoubtedly would have committed had it been within his power to do so may have been equaled by the United States. . . .. Indeed, when the final accounting is made, they may have been surpassed."[48]

His use of the just-war tenets, however, was in no way a wavering of Zahn's longstanding criticism of the church's just-war tradition. Indeed, in the St. John's symposium, he clearly stated that the just-war theory is "more secular than moral in its origin and application and, therefore, has little or no intrinsic relevance to the specifically Christian belief systems upon which most such analyses are purportedly based."[49] He also called attention to a widely discussed July 1991 editorial that appeared in *La Civilta Cattolica*, an influential Jesuit periodical published in Rome. The editorial described the just-war theory as a formulation by theologians that "never became 'official,' [and was] never, therefore, sanctioned by the church's teaching authority."[50]

Zahn's employment of the just-war criteria to denounce the US actions in the Gulf War more likely stemmed from his recent experience both revisiting Jägerstätter's objections and whether they were pacifist or based more on just-war thinking, as well as Zahn's own counseling of service members, many of whom were not pacifist. As we have seen, Zahn had long recognized the place of advocates of the just-war tradition within the church, as well as the necessity to engage with them. Zahn's thinking—emerging from both his academic and activist work—clearly evolved along these lines. The just-war theory, despite being rooted in natural law thinking (what Zahn termed "the ethics of 'the good pagan'") as well as its long history of being employed to simply justify a nation's war effort, could still be used as a tool to critique war, particularly modern war.[51] Indeed, the just-war theory's origins in the

48 Zahn, "Morality and War," 793.

49 Zahn, "Morality and War," 781.

50 *La Civilta Cattolica*, July 6, 1991. The editorial was published in English in *Origins*, December 9, 1991, and then republished in an appendix in David DeCosse, ed., *But Was It Just? Reflections on the Morality of the Persian Gulf War* (Doubleday, 1992).

51 See Frederick Russell, *The Just War in the Middle Ages* (Cambridge University Press, 1975).

sacrament of confession make it fundamentally pastoral, something Zahn appeared to recognize in his counseling of morally conflicted members of the military.[52] And this certainly seemed to be what Zahn was doing by employing the just-war tenants to denounce the Gulf War.

VOCATION OF PEACE

On June 8, 1992, Paul Hanly Furfey died in Washington, DC. In a tribute to his old teacher and friend, Zahn lamented that few publications, Catholic or otherwise, had noted Furfey's passing, despite the fact that Furfey had established himself as "one of Catholicism's greatest champions of peace and social justice."[53] Zahn wrote that Furfey led many US Catholics, "including this high school accounting major newly discharged from alternate service as a conscientious objector to World War II," to choose an academic career as a sociologist, not only for the honor and status but more importantly for "the opportunity to serve others and contribute to the betterment of society." Likewise, Zahn pointed out that many of the priests involved in efforts to eliminate the multitude of "social problems which still shame American society" could trace their "awakening" to reading *Fire on the Earth* while in the seminary. When the final history of Catholic social thought is eventually compiled, Zahn declared, "there will be very few deserving to be ranked with Paul Hanly Furfey."

That year Zahn also published *Vocation of Peace*, another collection of earlier essays. He introduced the volume by noting that October 1992 marked the fiftieth anniversary of his arrival at Camp Simon and thus his "official entry" into the Catholic peace movement.[54] While the past five decades had witnessed many changes in the church, he wrote, few had been greater than its awakening to the "pacifist implications" of Catholicism, especially on the part of the "institutional Church." That said, Zahn reminded readers that the struggle was "far from over." All Christians, he noted, whether they realized it or not, had a "vocation of peace"—a sociotheological task to eliminate war by combining the "moral insights and objectives" of theology with the "behavioral

52 See Paul Ramsey, *War and the Christian Conscience: How Shall Modern War Be Conducted Justly?* (Duke University Press, 1961).

53 Gordon Zahn, "Tribute to a Mentor: Paul Hanly Furfey (1896–1992)," *New Oxford Review* (September 1992): 8–10.

54 Gordon Zahn, *Vocation of Peace* (Fortkamp Publishing Co., 1992), vii.

insights and potential" provided by sociology.[55] "To divorce either from the other," Zahn asserted, invited "the kind of behavioral compartmentalization that accounts for the scandal of Christians fighting and killing other Christians in almost every major war in history."

Zahn explained that his primary scholarly focus had always been on the Catholic Church. This was rooted in his conviction that as a Catholic he had an obligation to do everything he could to make the church "the most effective vehicle for promoting the vocation of peace"—an obligation that also included criticism of the church and "even a kind of 'conversion' effort." And while his attempts to "convert" the church (or "keep her honest") on questions relating to war had not always been welcomed, Zahn noted that such "unpleasantness" was simply another aspect of the vocation of peace.

Looking back on the shifts in the church's thinking on war over the past half-century, Zahn argued that credit was due to a relative few: "maverick" bishops like Thomas Roberts, "way-out" radical priests such as Philip and Daniel Berrigan, and "rebellious" laity like Franz Jägerstätter. These were Catholics who had been "ignored or even ridiculed (if not disciplined and condemned)" for keeping the issues of pacifism and conscientious objection alive when "considerations of 'prudence' or 'orthodoxy' advised silence." While humbly acknowledging that his own work did not play a major role in demonstrating the need for an "entirely new attitude" on war within Catholicism, Zahn wrote that as part of the still-growing Catholic peace movement, he hoped that he had contributed at least something to what George Weigel had derided as the "abandonment of the heritage" of the just-war tradition. "If he is right," Zahn sarcastically concluded, "I take some gratification from knowing my fifty years have not been wasted."

In November 1994, the annual meeting of the Society for the Scientific Study of Religion hosted a panel on Zahn's life and work titled "Gordon Zahn: A Challenge For and To Public Intellectuals"—and Zahn responded to the papers with one of his own.[56] That same year, Zahn drafted a hundred-page memoir, building upon a shorter version he had written back in 1988. Helpfully filling in some biographical gaps, the memoir ended with Zahn taking a "grandfatherly" view of the Catholic peace movement to which he had

55 Zahn, *Vocation of Peace*, viii.

56 Richard Robbins, Michael Hovey, Loretta Morris, and James Kelly presented papers (CPF Zahn papers).

dedicated his life. Despite the changes that occurred during his lifetime in the church's attitudes on war, Zahn again acknowledged that there was yet much to be done, for he still hoped to establish within the church a truly "Catholic pacifist commitment and movement."[57] Recognizing that others would now have to take the lead in this effort, Zahn concluded, "I am more than ready to turn the task over to them knowing that I and others of my generation have presented them with a starting point more promising than the one we faced when it all began." It was in helping to build the Catholic peace movement, particularly in the United States, that Zahn saw himself as having made his most significant and lasting contribution. Indeed, as we have seen, such a movement barely existed when he was born.

The final decade of his life saw Zahn gradually slow down in his writing and activism. As his struggles with dementia increased, he eventually moved into St. Camillus nursing home in Wauwatsoa, Wisconsin, outside of Milwaukee. On December 9, 2007, Zahn passed away at the age of eighty-nine.[58]

WHY ZAHN MATTERS

Gordon Zahn was a consistent voice describing, promoting, defending, justifying, and practicing Catholic pacifism. David O'Brien put it well when he depicted this as "lonely" work. And in what may be the best description of such work, in his book on Catholic activists, Michael Gallagher titled his chapter on Zahn "Laboring Through the Heat of the Day."[59] Many thought—and still think today—that Zahn was trying to hold together two contradictory positions. As we noted, Zahn often described his pacifist position as being on the "fringe" of US Catholicism, yet as O'Brien pointed out, eventually that all began to change, and nonviolence is now at "the center" of Catholic teaching on war while the just war is the exception.[60]

And while he was clearly opposed to the church's promotion of the just-war theory, and even called for the church to cease teaching it on more than one occasion, Zahn also seemed to recognize that the Catholic Church

57 Zahn lamented that Pax Christi-USA's various concerns included "too heavy an emphasis upon spirituality and liturgical display, exaggerated feminism, environmentalism, etc."

58 Michael Hovey, "A Man of Peace: Gordon C. Zahn, 1918–2007," *Commonweal*, February 15, 2008, 6.

59 Gallagher, *Laws of Heaven*, 244.

60 David O'Brien, "Gordon C. Zahn," *American Catholic Studies* 126, no. 3 (2015): 111.

could never truly jettison the just war any more than it could ever jettison natural law tradition—in other words (to borrow from the late Tom Cornell), if the church gets rid of the just-war theory today, it would be back tomorrow. Certainly, in his later writings, Zahn seemed to acknowledge this reality and called upon its proponents to take the just-war criteria seriously and employ them as a critique of modern war rather than an accommodation to it.[61] This point was clearly seen in his suggestion that Jägerstätter was something of a patron saint of the just-war tradition.

Zahn's openness to the possibilities of the just-war theory, or at least his openness to talking to its advocates, did lead some of his fellow pacifists to regard him as less than committed in his stance. Zahn clearly resisted this sort of elitism within the Catholic peace movement, recognizing it as contributing to the break-up of the Mystical Body. Indeed, as one scholar has recently noted, reflection on the church's teaching on peace often gets mired in debates between just warriors and pacifists, "which all too readily take on the tone of the 'culture wars' between Catholic liberals and conservatives, with each insisting that its viewpoint is the most—or only—faithful way to read the tradition."[62] I would argue that Zahn can here offer a model of the (perhaps sometimes overused) notion of "dialogue" within the context of an ideologically polarized US Catholic Church. Zahn's goal was to transform the church into a vehicle to bring about the end of war, and such a transformation meant taking the church, its tradition, and *all* its members seriously.

This commitment to the church was certainly at the heart of Zahn's repeated insistence that the Catholic peace movement remain Catholic and its leaders take church teaching seriously. For Zahn, this was not only a theological imperative but also a sociological one, as he saw the church as the only institution left capable of resisting the modern nation-state. The church as a "source of dissent" could offer an alternative value-system that countered the one promoted by the state. It was also the only institution able to provide support for COs and others who resisted the power of the state in war time. It was, in short, a "church" that could act like a "sect." None of which meant that criticism of the church (and its leaders) was off the table, of course, but as

61 The 1944 critique of Allied obliteration bombing by John C. Ford, SJ, is an excellent example of such a use of the just-war theory.

62 Theodora Hawksley, *Peacebuilding and Catholic Social Teaching* (University of Notre Dame Press, 2020), 6.

Zahn made it clear, such criticism was stronger when it came from within the church—something Zahn always saw himself as doing. In the end, he argued, the mission and purpose of the Catholic peace movement was as "a witness *to* the Church"—transforming it into a vehicle for bringing about true peace. And it was this kind of church-centered politics that Zahn's many critics regarded as sectarian, irresponsible—too focused on ultimate ends.

It was a clear rejection of the two-tiered, neoscholastic social theory and the Weberian version it mirrored that was at the heart of the sociotheological approach that Zahn learned from Furfey and developed throughout his career, an approach clearly seen in Zahn's rejection of the separation of sociology from theology, the political from the religious, or even his activism from his academic life. As we have seen, by rejecting these kinds of separations, Zahn's sociotheological method, like Furfey's supernatural sociology, was in concert with the many other moves against neoscholasticism happening in twentieth-century Catholicism—from Blondel and Sturzo to de Lubac. Likewise, his strong emphasis on Catholic pacifism's eschatological "witnessing" echoed the eschatological tendencies in the *nouvelle théologie*. Recognizing Zahn (and Furfey) as kindred spirits within these theological currents is certainly important for recognizing the vitality of twentieth-century US Catholicism, which has often been portrayed as bland and uniform. And as I have argued elsewhere, two-tiered neoscholasticism can often look a lot like the so-called "public theology" that has replaced it today, with its notion of an "always/already" graced nature appearing strikingly similar to the neoscholastic conception of a self-sufficient nature.[63] Here too, Zahn's work can serve as a helpful corrective.

CATHOLIC RADICALIST TRADITION

All of which points to the fact that Gordon Zahn was clearly part of a "counter-tradition"—very much in contrast to the prevailing Catholic Americanist tradition—which Michael Baxter called the "Catholic radicalist tradition."[64] This is a tradition that rejects the strict neoscholastic separation of nature and the supernatural, and instead regards the relationship as being distinct but

63 See Benjamin Peters, "Apocalyptic Sectarianism: The Theology at Work in Critiques of Catholic Radicals," *Horizons* 39, no. 2 (2012): 208–29.

64 Baxter, "Notes on Catholic Americanism," 60.

not separate. This has allowed those within the radicalist tradition to critically engage with political and economic institutions in the United States though the lens of the Gospels. The "political" is distinct but not separate from the "religious"—nor, for that matter, is sociology separate from theology.

It is through this lens that Catholics such as Zahn have been able to judge that America, or any modern nation-state for that matter, has never been "good" for Catholics, and that, in fact, Catholics need to be wary and skeptical when engaging with America. Rather than a marriage that needs to either be saved or ended (as one US Catholic commentator recently analogized), for Catholic radicals, the marriage between Catholics and the United States never actually existed in the first place.[65] What is needed, therefore, is something more akin to an annulment. When Zahn argued that Catholics must begin with a presumption of injustice when looking at US war-making, he was clearly arguing from such a perspective. In this way, Zahn's work offers a form of "selective engagement" compatible with a Gospel nonviolence, in which the works of mercy have primacy and Catholics engage selectively with public policy—on nuclear weapons or war, for example. Such an approach is not sectarian or "prophetic," in the sense it is often marginalized by critics, but rather provides a public alternative to Americanism.[66]

In presenting this radicalist countertradition within US Catholicism, Baxter included Dorothy Day and Peter Maurin, of course, as well as clerics such as Virgil Michel, John Hugo, and Furfey. Beyond such usual suspects, though, examples of this Catholic radicalist tradition become harder to find. More than anything, this is because they have often been overlooked or ignored in US Catholic studies as marginalized figures on the fringes of the (Americanist) Catholic mainstream.[67]

In his groundbreaking book, *Black Marxism: the Making of the Black Radical Tradition*, Cedric Robinson acknowledged that his account of the Black radical tradition was far from complete, but that "as a scholar it was

65 For an example of this marriage analogy, see Patrick Deneen, "A Catholic Showdown Worth Watching," *The American Conservative*, February 6, 2014, https://www.theamericanconservative.com/a-catholic-showdown-worth-watching/.

66 For an example of this well-worn use of "public" and "prophetic," see Kristin Heyer, *Prophetic and Public: the Social Witness of U.S. Catholicism* (Georgetown University Press, 2006).

67 Michael Baxter makes this argument in "Writing History Without Ends: An Evangelical Catholic Critique of United States Catholic History," *Pro Ecclesia* 5, no. 4 (1996):440–69.

never my purpose to exhaust the subject, only to suggest that it was there."[68] Along these same lines, my goal has been to help readers recognize that there is a Catholic radicalist tradition and that Gordon Zahn is a key figure in it. Throughout his life, Zahn clearly rejected the Catholic version of the Weberian "ethic of responsibility" and instead judged the United States and its war-making through the lens of the Sermon on the Mount. His consistent and long-standing opposition to US militarism, as well as his ever-increasing suspicion of US political institutions, meant that he was in direct contrast with the Americanist tradition embodied by so many of his critics over the years. And his conscientious objection and activism placed him in relationship with other US Catholic radicals—from Day and Furfey to the Berrigans and the Catholic Peace Fellowship. Recognizing Zahn in this way, I would argue, is an important and necessary step in further acknowledging the existence of this Catholic radicalist countertradition.

In his foreword to Torin Finney's 1989 biography of Ben Salmon, *Unsung Hero of the Great War*, Zahn recounted the story of his initial meeting with Finney,

> During one of my unscheduled appearances at my university office, a newly enrolled graduate student happened by and stopped to talk. In the course of that friendly visit he asked for suggestions of a possible topic of study, one that was related to Catholicism and peace. Despite the fact that I had not thought of Ben Salmon for years—more likely decades—his name popped into my mind.[69]

While he hesitated to speak too freely of "mystical forces or purposes" in connection with scholarly work, Zahn wrote that he was pleased to have played some role in bringing Salmon's story the attention and respect it deserved—noting that he had first learned of Salmon in 1942 while reading *The Catholic Worker* at Camp Simon. Zahn concluded by stating that Finney's book was "a valuable addition to the slowly burgeoning efforts to make that largely unknown past (and its 'unsung heroes') more accessible to this and future generations." Such is my hope for this book as well.

68 Cedric Robinson, *Black Marxism: The Making of the Black Radical Tradition* (UNC Press, 1983), iii.

69 Torin R. T. Finney, *Unsung Hero of the Great War: The Life and Witness of Ben Salmon* (Paulist Press, 1989), xi.

Appendix I

ARCHBISHOP THOMAS ROBERTS, SJ,'S INTERVENTION AT FOURTH SESSION OF SECOND VATICAN COUNCIL

Venerable Fathers

Rather than support my comments with arguments from abstract principles, I prefer to set the case in terms of a specific example which illustrates the task before this Council. The case concerns a young Christian layman, an Austrian peasant named Franz Jägerstätter, who was executed in Berlin on August 9, 1943 for his conscientious objection to a war effort which was later condemned at Nuremberg as a "a crime against humanity." He was a poor and simple man, but we all know how often the simple and uneducated have been chosen by the Holy Spirit to bear witness to truths that were not recognized or accepted by mightier or (as the world sees it) wiser men.

This young man, a husband and father, was called upon to make such a witness; to declare that the Christian may never serve in a war he believes unjust and to lay down his life, if need be, whenever the law written in his heart by God comes in conflict with the orders issued by a secular ruler.

This man's witness was a solitary witness. All of his fellow Catholics in his little village, the priests to whom he turned for spiritual guidance, even his bishop told him it was his duty to serve as ordered, since it was not for him to say whether his nation's war was just or unjust. Nevertheless, his conscience insisted that he could not let the civil authority define for him his moral obligation; he was convinced that the war was unjust and that it would be a sin for him to serve in it. To those who reminded him of the hardships his refusal would bring down upon his wife and children, he could only reply that God would surely provide for them if he obeyed the dictates of his conscience. And when the time came, he offered his life willingly in reparation for the sins of the world and went to his death thanking God for the privilege of witnessing to the Faith in this manner.

I offer this case for the guidance and inspiration of us all. This is what we are talking about when we speak of conscientious objection; and it is by this standard we must measure what we finally proclaim. I gravely fear that the present Schema fails in at least two very important ways:

FIRST: It provides that the Christian is to give the presumption of justice to lawful secular authority when the injustice is not manifestly clear. The tragic fact is that the injustice of the Nazi cause apparently was not manifestly clear to the millions of Jägerstätter's fellow Catholics who did accept military service. Nor was it manifest to their spiritual leaders, even to those of highest rank, who encouraged and praised their military service.

Since, therefore, the war's injustice did not become sufficiently manifest until large areas of the world had been laid waste and until the criminals were brought to judgment at Nuremberg, are we to declare now that Jägerstätter and the unknown others who made a similar witness were wrong, that they should have given the presumption of the justice to Hitler and his allies? I think not; certainly I hope not.

SECOND: There is a recommendation in the Schema that governments should positively favor the rights of conscience in making their laws. This is lamentably weak and insufficient. Jägerstätter always knew that his conscientious objection would mean death, and he was prepared for that. But during his last few weeks in prison he continued to be troubled by his fear that he might be committing a sin by not following the advice offered by the spiritual leaders of his Church.

What we must do here is to give clear testimony that the Church affirms the right of the individual conscience to refuse unjust military service, and assure those of the Faithful who bear such witness that they will always have her fullest support. Once this has been done, martyrs like Jägerstätter will never again have to feel they take their stand alone.

I plead with the Fathers to consider this man and his sacrifice in a spirit of gratitude. May his example inspire our deliberations. This does not mean that we should limit our thoughts to this one war or to any one nation's part in that war. Perhaps the major scandal of Christianity for too many centuries now has been precisely that almost every national hierarchy in almost every war has allowed itself to become the moral arm of its own government, even in wars later recognized as palpably unjust. Let us break with this tragic past by making a clear and unambiguous affirmation of the right and obligation of each Christian to obey the voice of his informed conscience before and during a time of war.

I propose, therefore, the following:

1) Let the paragraph on Page 80, Section 101 of the Schema relating to the presumption of justice be omitted

2) For the words, "it would seem fitting for legislation to reflect a positive attitude towards those people who, in conscience, refuse to do military service," let the following be substituted: "the Council commends the example of those nations which for more than half a century have successfully provided for the informed conscientious objection of their subjects, even in the hour of utmost peril."

3) The Council support <u>all</u> efforts, as by the United Nations and the World Court of Justice, giving the full force of law to individuals refusing blind obedience.

I am sending a copy of this intervention to the widow of Franz Jägerstätter presently residing in St. Radegund, Austria.

Thomas D. Roberts, S.J.
Titular Archbishop of Sygdea

Appendix II

COURT RECORDS FROM MILITARY TRIBUNAL OF FRANZ JÄGERSTÄTTER ON JULY 6, 1943

(translated by Gordon Zahn)

In the name of
The German Volk

In the Criminal case against:
Franz Jägerstätter
for undermining the military forces.

Participants:
As Judges:
Reich's Military Tribune Counselor Lueben, Session Leader
General of the Air Force Musshoff
Vice-Admiral Arps
Major General Schreiber
Superior Reich's Military Tribunal Counselor Ranft

As Prosecutor:
Superior Reich's Military Tribunal Counselor Dr. Kleint

As Recording Officer:
Reich's Military Tribunal Superior Inspector

Disposition:

The Accused is sentenced to death for undermining the military forces and is deprived of all military benefits and civil rights.

GROUNDS

I

The Accused, Franz Jägerstätter, was born on May 20, 1907 in Radegund (Upper Danube) the son of a farmer. After attending Volkschule for eight years he was occupied in farming and mining. He is the owner of a farm of 18-Joch. He is married and the father of three children ranging in age from 3 to 6.

On June 17, 1940 he was called to active military service at Braunau, sworn in in the name of the Führer and Supreme Commander of the armed forces, but was deferred released for essential agricultural labor. On October 5, 1940, he was recalled to service in the 4th Transport Reserve 17 at Enns and after completing basic training, dismissed on December 6, 1940, according to [military regulation cited]. On April 9, 1941, at the request of local authorities, he was again classified as indispensable and released for agricultural service on his farm.

The Accused is a German citizen, Roman Catholic by religious affiliation, and resides in Radegund (Upper Danube); he had a previous record of three days arrest for fighting. There is no record of military offenses charged against him. He is neither a member of the Party nor any of its organizations.

On March 2, 1943, he was arrested and held in custody since March 10, 1943, upon the orders of the Divisional Court 487 for investigation.

II

In February 1943 the Accused was ordered in writing to report for renewed active military service in the Transport Reserve, Section 17, at Enns on February 25, 1943. At first he did not report because he rejected National Socialism and for that reason was not willing to perform military service. Upon the urging of family members and the advice of his local pastor he finally reported at the unit headquarters in Enns on March 1, 1943, but immediately declared his refusal to bear arms in military service because of his religious convictions. Under interrogation by the court officer he held to that position despite advice and warnings as to the consequences of such refusal. He declared it would be violating his religious conscience if he were to fight for the National Socialist state. He reiterated his refusal in his hearing before the investigator for the Division 487 Court in Linz as well as to the representative of the Military Tribunal's legal staff. He declared himself ready, however, to serve as a medical orderly as an exercise of Christian charity. In the final formal proceeding he repeated his refusal and explained that he had arrived at his conviction that as a believing Catholic he was not permitted to perform any military service, that it was impossible for him to be a Nazi and a Catholic at one and the same time. He explained that he had taken the military oath earlier because he believed then it would be a sin not to obey the command of the State, but that God has shown him it is not sinful to refuse armed service, that there are things in which one must obey God rather than man. He may not fight with weapons because of the Commandment "you should love your neighbor as yourself." He is, however, ready to serve as a medical orderly.

These findings are based upon the personal and authentic statements of the Accused, who acknowledged them in their entirety, as well as on the basis of the confirmed results of the preliminary proceedings under [specific military regulation cited].

III

As a German citizen, the Accused who is in the militarily eligible age range, is subject to call for military service. On the day he received his order to report he became a soldier. By not reporting immediately, instead delaying his appearance for a week and then refusing to perform the required service, he undertook to withdraw from military service. In that action he made himself guilty of undermining the military forces and is, accordingly, to be punished under [specific military regulations cited]. The culpability of his action is not excused because in his opinion his action was demanded by his conscience and religious conviction [specific legal code cited]. There is no basis for holding that he is not responsible for his action. According to the expert opinion of Dr. Nitze, chief staff physician of the Military Investigatory Prison, Berlin-Tegel, the accused is completely normal. No record of cases of psychological or hereditary disease has been established for his family.

The crime of undermining the military forces makes one subject to the death penalty. Only in minor offenses can penitentiary or prison be substituted. No such mitigating circumstance is present here. The Accused had already served six months as a soldier; he had sworn the oath to the Führer and Supreme Commander; and in his period of service he had been fully instructed in the duties of German soldiers. Nevertheless, he has stubbornly refused to fulfill his patriotic duty as a soldier in Germany's critical war for survival in spite of reminders of the consequences of his decision on grounds of personal reasons. The sentence of death is, therefore, affirmed.

According to [explicit military regulation cited] the death sentence carries with it the loss of all military benefits. Since the Accused has proven himself without honor by his actions, he is also to be deprived of all civil rights under [specific legal code citation].

July 14, 1943
I confirm the verdict. The verdict is to be carried out.
[signed] Bastian, Admiral

Bibliography

Anderson, Floyd, ed. *Council Daybook: Vatican II, Session 3*. National Catholic Welfare Conference, 1965.

Amery, Carl. *Capitulation: The Lesson of German Catholicism*. Translated by Edward Quinn. Herder and Herder, 1967.

Au, William. *The Cross, the Flag, and The Bomb: American Catholics Debate War and Peace, 1960–1983*. Greenwood Press, 1985.

Baxter, Michael, CSC. "In Service to the Nation." PhD Diss., Duke University, 1996.

Baxter, Michael. "Notes on Catholic Americanism and Catholic Radicalism: Toward a Counter-Tradition of Catholic Social Ethics." In *American Catholic Traditions: Resources for Renewal*, edited by Sandra Yocum-Mize and William Portier. Orbis Books, 1996.

Baxter, Michael. "Writing History Without Ends: An Evangelical Catholic Critique of United States Catholic History." *Pro Ecclesia* 5/4 (1996): 440–69.

Baxter, Michael. "The Unsettling of Americanism: A Response to William Portier." *Communio* 27 (Spring 2000): 161–70.

Bell, Daniel. *The End of Ideology: on the Exhaustion of Political ideas in the Fifties*. Harvard University Press, 1960.

Bergman, Roger, "Toward A Sociology of Conscience: The Example of Franz Jagerstatter and the Legacy of Gordon Zahn." *Journal for Peace and Justice Studies* 23, no.2 (2013): 73–97.

Bergman, Roger, *Preventing Unjust War: A Catholic Argument for Selective Conscientious Objection*. Cascade Books, 2020.

Browne, Harry J. "Catholicism in the United States." In *The Shaping of American Religion*, edited by James Ward Smith and A. Leland Jamison. Princeton University Press, 1961.

Cajka, Peter. *Follow Your Conscience: The Catholic Church and the Spirit of the Sixties*. University of Chicago Press, 2021.

Cameron, J. M. "A Martyr of Conscience." *The New York Review of Books*, December 5, 1965.

Catholic Peace Fellowship. "Selective Conscientious Objection." *The Sign of Peace* 4, no.2 (2005): 16–21.

Castelli, Jim. *The Bishops and the Bomb: Waging Peace in a Nuclear Age*. Image Books, 1983.

Cavanaugh, William. *The Myth of Religious Violence*. Oxford University Press, 2009.

Chappel, James. *Catholic Modern: The Challenge of Totalitarianism and the Remaking of the Church*. Harvard University Press, 2018.

Collinge, William. "'You Say You Want a Green Revolution?' Eugene and Abigail McCarthy and Catholic Agrarianism." In *You Say You Want a Revolution? 1968–2018 in Theological Perspective*, edited by Susie Babka, Elena Procario-Foley, and Sandra Yocum. Orbis Books, 2019.

Cook, Bruce. "It Takes a Worried Man." *U.S. Catholic* 22, no. 7 (1966): 8–13.

Cooper, Sandi E. *Patriotic Pacifism: Waging War on War in Europe, 1815–1914*. Oxford University Press, 1991.

Connor, John, SJ. "Can a Catholic be a Conscientious Objector?" *The Ecclesiastical Review* 58 (1943): 125–38.

Cornell, Thomas. "The Catholic Church and Witness Against War." In *War or Peace? The Search for New Answers*, edited by Thomas Shannon. Orbis Books, 1980.

Cosacchi, Daniel, and Eric Martin, eds. *The Berrigan Letters*. Orbis Books, 2016.

Curran, Charles. "Ten Years Later: Reflections on *Humanae Vitae*." *Commonweal*, July 7, 1978, 425–30.

Curran, Charles. *American Catholic Social Ethics*. The University of Notre Dame Press, 1982.

Daly, Gabriel, OSB. *Transcendence and Immanence: A Study in Catholic Modernism and Integralism*. Clarendon Press, 1980.

Day, Dorothy. *The Long Loneliness*. Sheed & Ward, 1952.

Day, Dorothy. *Loaves and Fishes*. Harper & Row, 1963.

Day, Dorothy. "Review of *In Solitary Witness*." *The Catholic Worker*, June 1965, 4.

Day, Dorothy. "Review of *In Solitary Witness*." *The Catholic Worker*, July-August 1965, 5, 7.

Day, Dorothy. "Saint or Sacrifice." *The Catholic Worker,* November 1965, 1.

DeCosse, David, ed. *But Was It Just? Reflections on the Morality of the Persian Gulf War*. Doubleday, 1992.

Douglass, James. *The Non-Violent Cross: A Theology of Revolution and Peace*. Macmillan, 1966.

Downing, Taylor. *1983: Reagan, Andropov, and the World on the Brink*. Da Capo Press, 2018.

Danielson, Leilah. *American Gandhi: A. J. Muste and the History of Radicalism in the Twentieth Century*. University of Pennsylvania Press, 2014.

Dohen, Dorothy. *Nationalism and American Catholicism*. Sheed & Ward, 1967.

Egan, Eileen. "The Struggle of the Small Vehicle, Pax." In *American Catholic Pacifism: The Influence of Dorothy Day and the Catholic Worker Movement*, edited by Anne Klejment and Nancy Roberts. Praeger Publishers, 1996.

Ellsberg, Robert, ed. *The Duty of Delight: The Diaries of Dorothy Day*. Marquette University Press, 2008.

Ellsberg, Robert, ed. *All the Way to Heaven: The Selected Letters of Dorothy Day.* Marquette University Press, 2010.

Emmanuel, Cyprian, OFM. *Ethics of War*. The Catholic Association for International Peace, 1932.

Emmanuel, Cyprian, OFM. *The Morality of Conscientious Objection to War*. The Catholic Association for International Peace, 1941.

Finn, James. *Protest: Pacifism and Politics: Some Passionate Views on War and Nonviolence*. Vintage Books, 1968.

Finnis, John., Joseph Boyle Jr., and Germain Grisez. *Nuclear Deterrence, Morality and Realism*. Clarendon Press, 1988.

Finney, Torin R.T. *Unsung Hero of the Great War: The Life and Witness of Ben Salmon*. Paulist Press, 1989.

Fitzgerald, Timothy. *The Ideology of Religious Studies*. Oxford University Press, 2000.

Ford, John C. "The Morality of Obliteration Bombing." *Theological Studies* 5, no. 3 (1944): 261–309.

Forest, James H. "No Longer Alone: The Catholic Peace Movement." In *American Catholics and Vietnam*, edited by Thomas Quigley. Eerdmans, 1968.

Forest, Jim. *At Play in the Lions' Den: A Biography and Memoir of Daniel Berrigan*. Orbis Books, 2017.

Fried, Jakob. *Nationalsozialismus und katholische Kirche in Österreich*. Wiener Dom-Verlag, 1947.

Furfey, Paul Hanly. *Fire on the Earth*. Macmillan, 1936.

Furfey, Paul Hanly. "Why a Supernatural Sociology?" *American Catholic Sociological Review* 1 (1940): 167–71.

Furfey, Paul Hanly. *The Mystery of Iniquity*. Bruce Publishing, 1944.

Gabrielli, Timothy R. *One in Christ: Virgil Michel, Louis-Marie Chauvet, and Mystical Body Theology*. Liturgical Press, 2017.

Gallagher, Michael. *Laws of Heaven: Catholic Activists Today*. Ticknor & Fields, 1992.

Gallup, Jr., George, and Jim Castelli, *The American Catholic People: Their Beliefs, Practices, and Values*. Doubleday, 1987.

Gleason, Philip. *Contending with Modernity: Catholic Higher Education in the Twentieth Century*. Oxford University Press, 1995.

Gouldner, Alvin. "Anti-Minotaur." *Social Problems* 9, no. 3 (1962): 194–213.

Gumbleton, Thomas. "The Role of the Peacemaker." In *War or Peace? The Search for New Answers*, edited by Thomas Shannon. Orbis Books, 1980.

Halsey, William. *The Survival of American Innocence: Catholicism in the Era of Disillusionment: 1920–1940*. University of Notre Dame Press, 1980.

Haase, Norbert. "Gott mehr gehorcht als dem Staat: Franz Jägerstätter vor dem Reichskriegsgericht." *Tribüne, Zeitschrift zum Verständnis des Judentums* 29, no. 114 (1990): 198–206.

Hawksley, Theodora. *Peacebuilding and Catholic Social Teaching*. The University of Notre Dame Press, 2020.

Hayes, Carlton J. H. *Nationalism: A Religion*. Macmillan, 1960.

Hehir, J. Bryan. "The Just-War Ethic and Catholic Theology: Dynamics of Change and Continuity." In *War or Peace? The Search for New Answers*, edited by Thomas Shannon. Orbis Books, 1980.

Heineman, Kenneth J. *Catholic New Deal: Religion and Reform in Depression Pittsburgh*. Penn State University Press, 1999.

Heyer, Kristen. *Prophetic and Public: The Social Witness of U.S. Catholicism.* Georgetown University Press, 2006.

Higgins, George. "Pacifist Attack." National Catholic Welfare Conference News Release (February 22, 1965): 9–10.

Isserman, Maurice. *If I Had a Hammer: The Death of the Old Left and the Birth of the New Left*. Basic Books, 1987.

Judt, Tony. *Postwar: A History of Europe Since 1945*. Penguin Press, 2005.

Kelly, James, SJ. "Review of *In Solitary Witness*." *Sociological Analysis* 26, no. 1 (1965): 55–56.

Kenneson, Philip. *Beyond Sectarianism: Re-imagining Church and World*. Trinity Press International, 1999.

Kerby, William J. "Sociology." In *The Catholic Encyclopedia*. Vol. XIII 117. Robert Appleton Co., 1912.

Kiem, Albert. *The CPS Story: An Illustrated History of Civilian Public Service.* Good Books, 1990.

King, Robert. "Rhetoric of Morality, Rhetoric of Manipulation: The Catholic Bishops, Peace, and the Reagan Administration." *Cross Currents* 34, no. 4 (1984–85): 456–72.

Komonchak, Joseph. "Theology and Culture at Mid-Century: The Example of Henri de Lubac." *Theological Studies* 51 (1990): 579–602.

Komonchak, Joseph. "John Courtney Murray and the Redemption of History: Natural Law and Theology." In *John Courtney Murray & the Growth of Tradition*, edited by J. Leon Hooper, SJ, and Todd Whitmore. Sheed & Ward, 1996.

Komonchak, Joseph, ed. *The History of Vatican II, Vol. 4: Church as Communion: Third Period and Intersession, September 1964--September 1965*. Orbis Books, 2004.

Kreuzberg, Heinrich. *Franz Reinisch. Ein Märtyrer unserer Zeit*. Lahn-Verlag, 1953.

Langan, John, SJ. "An Imperfectly Just War." *America*, June 1, 1991, 361–65.

Lescher, Bruce. "The Spiritual Life and Social Action in American Catholic Spirituality: William J. Kerby and Paul Hanly Furfey." PhD diss., Graduate Theological Union, 1991.

Lifton, Robert Jay, and Greg Mitchell. *Hiroshima in America: Fifty Years of Denial.* Putnam's Sons, 1995.

Maislinger, Andreas. "Franz Jägerstätter." In *Conquering the Past: Austrian Nazism Yesterday & Today*, edited by F. Parkinson. Wayne State University Press, 1989.

Marling, William. *Christian Anarchist: Ammon Hennacy: A Life on the Catholic Left*. NYU Press, 2022.

McBrien, Richard, ed. *Encyclopedia of Catholicism*. Harper Collins, 1995.

McCarraher, Eugene. *Christian Critics: Religion and the Impasse in Modern American Social Thought*. Cornell University Press, 2000.

McGovern, William Montgomery. *From Luther to Hitler: The History of Nazi-Fascist Philosophy*. Houghton Mifflin Co., 1941.

McKenzie, John, SJ. *The Two-Edged Sword: An Interpretation of the Old Testament*. The Bruce Publishing Co., 1956.

McKenzie, John, SJ. *The Power and the Wisdom: An Interpretation of the New Testament*. The Bruce Publishing Co., 1965.

McNeal, Patricia. *Harder than War: Catholic Peacemaking in Twentieth-Century America*. Rutgers University Press, 1992.

Meconis, Charles, *With Clumsy Grace: The American Catholic Left 1961–1975*. Seabury Press, 1979.

Menno, Justin. "Sociology and Sanctity: Paul Hanly Furfey, Franz Mueller, and Luigi Sturzo on 'Supernatural Sociology,' a Trans-Atlantic Debate, 1928–1946." PhD diss., University of Dayton, 2017.

Merton, Robert K. *Theory and Social Structure*. The Free Press, 1957.

Milbank, John. *Theology and Social Theory: Beyond Secular Reason*. Blackwell, 1990.

Mill, C. Wright. *The Power Elite*. New York: Oxford University Press, 1956.

Mojtabai, AG. *Blessed Assurance: At Home with the Bomb in Amarillo, Texas*. Houghton Mifflin Co., 1986.

Moon, Penelope. "'We Have Got to Lead Them in the Ways of Peace': The Catholic Peace Fellowship in the Vietnam Era." PhD diss., Arizona State University, 2001.

Murray, John Courtney, SJ. "Remarks on the Moral Problem of War." *Theological Studies* 20, no. 1 (1959): 40–61.

Murray, John Courtney, SJ. *We Hold These Truths: Catholic Reflections on the American Proposition*. Sheed & Ward, 1960.

Myrdal, Gunnar. *The American Dilemma: The Negro Problem and Modern Democracy*. Harper & Row, 1944.

Nagle, William. *Morality and Modern War*. Helicon Press, 1960.

National Conference of Catholic Bishops. *The Challenge of Peace: God's Promise and Our Response*. United States Catholic Conference, 1983.

Niebuhr, Reinhold. *Moral Man Immoral Society: A Study in Ethics and Politics*. Charles Scribner's Sons, 1932.

Niebuhr, H. Richard. *Christ and Culture*. Harper Brothers, 1951.

Neuhäusler, Johannes. *Kreuz und Hakenkreuz*. Verlag Katholische Kirche Bayerns, 1946.

Nuesse, C. Joseph. "'Catholic Sociology': Memoir of a Mid-Century Controversy." *US Catholic Historian* 16, no. 3 (1998): 94–110.

Nuesse, C. Joseph. "William Joseph Kerby (1870–1936): The Approach to His Field of the First American Catholic Sociologist." *American Catholic Studies* 111 (2002): 77–96.

O'Brien, David. "American Catholic Opposition to the Vietnam War: A Preliminary Assessment." In *War or Peace? The Search for New Answers*, edited by Thomas Shannon. Orbis Books, 1980.

O'Brien, David. "An Open Letter to the Bishops." *Commonweal*, May 12, 1982, 295–301.

O'Brien, David. "Gordon C. Zahn." *American Catholic Studies* 126, no. 3 (2015): 107–11.

O'Brien, William. "Desert Storm." *St. John's Law Review* 66, no. 3 (1992): 797–823.

O'Connor, John. *In Defense of Life*. Pauline Books, 1981.

O'Rourke, William. *The Harrisburg 7 and the New Catholic Left*. Thomas Y. Crowell, Co., 1973.

Oyer, Gordon. *Pursuing the Spiritual Roots of Protest: Merton, Berrigan, Yoder, and Muste at the Gethsemani Abbey Peacemakers Retreat*. Cascade Books, 2014.

Peters, Benjamin. "Apocalyptic Sectarianism: The Theology at Work in Critiques of Catholic Radicals." *Horizons* 39, no. 2 (2012): 208–29.

Peters, Benjamin T. *Called to be Saints: John Hugo, the Catholic Worker, and a Theology of Radical Christianity*. Marquette University Press, 2016.

Peters, Benjamin T. "'Voices to be Silenced or Ignored': World War II and the Flattening of American Catholicism." In *Weaving the American Catholic Tapestry*, edited by Derek Hatch and Timothy Gabrielli. Pickwick Publications, 2017.

Peters, Benjamin T. "Is the Catholic Worker Racist?" *Church Life Journal*, July 17, 2023. https://churchlifejournal.nd.edu/articles/is-the-catholic-worker-racist/.

Peters, Shawn. *The Catonsville Nine: A Story of Faith and Resistance in the Vietnam Era*. Oxford University Press, 2012.

Portier, William. "Theology of Manners as Theology of Containment: John Courtney Murray and *Dignitatis Humanae* Forty Years After." *U.S. Catholic Historian* 24, no. 1 (2006): 83–105.

Putz, Erna. *Franz Jägerstätter: A Shining Example in Dark Times*. Translated by Catherine Laura Danner. Buchverlag Franz Steinmassl, 2007.

Putz, Erna. "Franz Jägerstätter: Better the Hands in Chains, than the Will." In *Christianity and Resistance in the 20th Century*, edited by Søren Dosenrode. Brill, 2008.

Potvin, Raymond. "Sociology." In *New Catholic Encyclopedia* 13. McGraw-Hill, 1967.

Rademacher, Nicholas. *Paul Hanly Furfey: Priest, Scientist, Social Reformer*. Fordham University Press, 2017.

Ramsey, Paul. "The Just War Theory on Trial." *Cross Currents* (Fall 1963): 477–90.

Rhodes, Richard. *Dark Sun: The Making of the Hydrogen Bomb*. Simon and Shuster, 1995.

Riesman, David. *The Lonely Crowd: A Study of the Changing American Character*. Yale University Press, 1961.

Robinson, Cedric. *Black Marxism: The Making of the Black Radical Tradition*. UNC Press, 1983.

Ruff, Mark. *The Battle for the Catholic Past in Germany: 1945–1980*. Cambridge University Press, 2017.

Russell, Frederick. *The Just War in the Middle Ages*. Cambridge University Press, 1975.

Samet, Elizabeth. *Looking of a Good War: American Amnesia and the Violent Pursuit of Happiness*. Farrer, Straus & Giroux, 2021.

Sarno, Robert. *Diocesan Inquiries Required by the Legislator in the New Legislation for the Causes of Saints.* JCD diss., Pontifical Gregorian University, 1988.

Schell, Jonathan. *The Fate of the Earth.* Knopf, 1982.

Schwartz, Robert. "Burckel and Innitzer." In *Conquering the Past: Austrian Nazism Yesterday and Today*, edited by F. Parkinson. Wayne St. University Press, 1989.

Sheehan, Arthur. "CPS 'Collaboration' Repudiated by ACCO." *The Catholic C.O.* (January-March 1946): 1–2.

Shirer, William. *The Rise and Fall of the Third Reich: A History of Nazi Germany.* Simon and Schuster, 1960.

Shortall, Sarah. *Soldiers of God in a Secular World: Catholic Theology and Twentieth-Century French Politics.* Harvard University Press, 2021.

Stein, Walter, ed. *Nuclear Weapons and the Christian Conscience.* Merlin Press, 1961.

Stratmann, Franziskus, OP. *The Church and War: A Catholic Study.* PJ Kennedy and Sons, 1928.

Sturzo, Luigi. *The True Life: Sociology of the Supernatural.* St. Anthony's Guild Press, 1943.

Taylor, John. "Whether the Human Family Will Live or Die." *The Catholic Worker*, July-August 1965, 3.

Thompson, Charles S., ed. *Moral and Missiles: Catholic Essays on the Problem of War Today.* James Clarke & Co., 1959.

Tobey, Kristen. *Plowshares: Protest, Performance, and Religious Identity in the Nuclear Age.* Penn State University Press, 2016.

Troeltsch, Ernst. *The Social Teaching of the Christian Churches.* 2 vols. Translated by Olive Wyon. Harper Torchbooks, 1960.

Vanderhaar, Gerard. "Pax Christi USA: The Early Years 1972–78." Unpublished manuscript, 1989.

Vann, Gerald, OP. *Morality and War.* Burns, Oates, and Washbourne, 1939.

Viereck, Peter. *The Unadjusted Man: A New Hero for Americans.* Beacon Press, 1956.

Weber, Max. "Religious Rejection of the World and Their Directions." In *From Max Weber: Essays in Sociology*, edited and translated by H. H. Gerth and C. Wright Mills. Oxford University Press, 1946.

Weber, Max. "Politics as a Vocation." In *From Max Weber: Essays in Sociology*, edited and translated by H. H. Gerth and C. Wright Mills. Oxford University Press, 1946.

Weigel, George. *Tranquillitas Ordinis: The Present Failure and Future Promise of American Catholic Thought on War and Peace*. Oxford University Press, 1989.

Wills, Garry. "Relicts of a Catholic Renaissance." *New York Review of Books*, October 10, 2013, 37–38.

Winters, Francis X. "Freed to Resist Coercion." *America*, June 1, 1991, 369–72.

Woodward, Kenneth. *Making Saints: How the Catholic Church Determines Who Becomes a Saint, Who Doesn't, and Why*. Simon and Schuster, 1990.

Zahn, Gordon. "An Open Challenge." *The Catholic C.O.* (January-March 1946): 3.

Zahn, Gordon. "Catholic Pacifism." *St. John's Quarterly* (February 1947).

Zahn, Gordon. "A Study of the Social Backgrounds of Catholic Conscientious Objectors in Civilian Public Service During World War II." MA thesis, The Catholic University of America, 1950.

Zahn, Gordon. "*A Descriptive Study of the Social Backgrounds of Conscientious Objectors in Civilian Public Service During World War II.*" PhD diss., The Catholic University of America, 1953.

Zahn, Gordon. "Vision of the Future: An Island Disappears." *The Catholic World* (May 1953). Republished in Zahn, *War, Conscience and Dissent*, 66–74.

Zahn, Gordon. "The Content of Protestant Tensions: Personal Experiences and 'Known Facts.'" *American Catholic Sociological Review* 16, no. 1 (1955): 12–22.

Zahn, Gordon. "Racism: A Christian Dilemma." *Apostolate* 3, no. 4 (1956): 30–39.

Zahn, Gordon. "The Content of Protestant Tensions: Fears of Catholic Aims and Methods." *American Catholic Sociological Review* 18, no. 3 (1957): 205–12.

Zahn, Gordon. "He Would Not Serve." *America*, July 5, 1958, 388–90.

Zahn, Gordon, ed. *Readings in Sociology*. Newman Press, 1958.

Zahn, Gordon. "Catholics and Organized Action for Peace." *The Catholic World* (August 1958). Republished in Zahn, *War, Conscience and Dissent*, 87–97.

Zahn, Gordon. "The German Press and Hitler's Wars." *Cross Currents* 10, no. 4 (1960): 337–52.

Zahn, Gordon. "Social Science and the Theology of War." In *Morality and Modern War*, edited by William J. Nagle. Helicon Press, 1960.

Zahn, Gordon. *German Catholics and Hitler's War: A Study in Social Control.* Sheed & Ward, 1962.

Zahn, Gordon. "The Case for Christian Dissent." In *Breakthrough to Peace*, introduced by Thomas Merton. New Directions Books, 1962.

Zahn, Gordon. "The Church as a Source of Dissent." *Continuum* 1, no. 2 (1963): 154–65.

Zahn, Gordon. "'The Vicar': A Controversy and a Lesson." *The Critic* (October-November, 1963).

Zahn, Gordon. *An Alternative to War.* The Council on Religion and International Affairs, 1963.

Zahn, Gordon. *What Is Society?* Hawthorn Books, 1964.

Zahn, Gordon. "Forward: The Church and Totalitarianism." *Continuum* 2, no. 2 (1964): 153–57.

Zahn, Gordon. "American Experts and Schema XIII." *The Catholic Worker*, July-August 1965, 6.

Zahn, Gordon. "Davy Crockett and the Bishops." *Ramparts*, March 1965, 62–65.

Zahn, Gordon. *In Solitary Witness: The Life and Death of Franz Jägerstätter.* Holt, Rinehart and Winston, 1964.

Zahn, Gordon. "The Test of the 'Just War.'" *Worldview* (December 1965): 10–13.

Zahn, Gordon. "Crime of Silence." *Commonweal* 84, June 17, 1966, 354–56.

Zahn, Gordon. "Saint or Suicide." *Pax Bulletin* (September 1966): 6–7.

Zahn, Gordon. *War, Conscience, and Dissent*. Hawthorn Books, 1967.

Zahn, Gordon. "A Man Ahead of His Times." *Ave Maria* (May 1968): 11–15.

Zahn, Gordon. Forward. In *American Catholics and Vietnam*, edited by Thomas Quigley. Eerdmans, 1968.

Zahn, Gordon. "Religion, Sociology and the Milieu: Formula for Activism?" *Sociological Analysis* 29, no. 3 (1968): 115–21.

Zahn, Gordon. *Military Chaplaincy: A Study of Role Tension on the Royal Air Force*. University of Manchester Press, 1969.

Zahn, Gordon. "The Great Catholic Upheaval." *Saturday Review,* September 11, 1971, 24–27, 54–56.

Zahn, Gordon. "Original Child Monk: An Appreciation." In *Thomas Merton on Peace*, edited by Gordon Zahn. McCall Publishing, 1971.

Zahn, Gordon. "The Berrigans: Radical Activism Personified." In *The Berrigans*, edited by William Van Etten Casey, SJ, and Philip Nobile. Praeger Publishers, 1971.

Zahn, Gordon. "A Religious Pacifist Looks at Abortion." *Commonweal*, May 28, 1971.

Zahn, Gordon. "The Future of the Catholic Peace Movement." *Commonweal*, December 28, 1973, 337–42.

Zahn, Gordon. "Carrying Our Weight in the Catholic Peace Movement." *America*, September, 20, 1975, 143–46.

Zahn, Gordon. "The Bondage of Liberation: A Pacifist Reflection." *Worldview* (March 1977): 20–24.

Zahn, Gordon. *Another Part of the War: The Camp Simon Story.* University of Massachusetts Press, 1979.

Zahn, Gordon. "Afterward." In *War or Peace? The Search for New Answers*, edited by Thomas Shannon. Orbis Books, 1980.

Zahn, Gordon. "Abortion and the Corruption of the Mind." In *New Perspectives on Human Abortion*, edited by Thomas Hilgers, Dennis Horan, and David Hall. University Press of America, 1981.

Zahn, Gordon. "Pacifism and Just War." In *Catholic and Nuclear War: A Commentary on* The Challenge of Peace, *the US Catholic Bishops' Pastoral Letter on War and Peace*, edited by Philp Murnion. Crossroads, 1983.

Zahn, Gordon. "On not writing a dead letter." *Commonweal*, March 8, 1985, 141–43.

Zahn, Gordon. "American Catholics and Peace: A Progress Report." *New Oxford Review* (June 1987): 14–17.

Zahn, Gordon. "The Pope in Austria: Two Swings and Two Misses." *Commonweal*, August 12, 1988, 421–23.

Zahn, Gordon. "How Narrow the Gate?" *Commonweal*, October 26, 1990, 607–9.

Zahn, Gordon. "Clarifying the Disputed Witness of Franz Jägerstätter." *New Oxford Review* (September 1991): 14–19

Zahn, Gordon. "Franz Jagerstatter's Disputed Witness: A Personal Re-Affirmation." *Proceedings of the Pax Christi International* (1991).

Zahn, Gordon, "An Infamous Victory." *America*, June 1, 1991, 366–67.

Zahn, Gordon. "Tribute to a Mentor: Paul Hanly Furfey (1896–1992)." *New Oxford Review* LIX, no. 7 (September 1992): 8–10.

Zahn, Gordon. *Vocation of Peace*. Fortkamp Publishing Co., 1992.

Zahn, Gordon. "Morality and War: Ethics, Morality, and the Gulf War." *St. John's Law Review* 66, no. 3 (1992): 777–95.

Zwick, Mark and Louise. *The Catholic Worker Movement: Intellectual and Spiritual Origins*. Paulist Press, 2005.

Index

H

I

J

K

L

M

N

O

P

R

S

T

U

W

Y

Z